BEGINNING

MOBILE
PHONE

GAME PROGRAMMING

Michael Morrison

SAMS 800 East 96th St., Indianapolis, Indiana, 46240 USA

Beginning Mobile Phone Game Programming

International Standard Book Number: 0-672-32665-5

Library of Congress Catalog Card Number: 2004095066

Printed in the United States of America

First Printing: October 2004

07   06   05   04   4   3   2   1

Trademarks

Warning and Disclaimer

Associate Publisher
Michael Stephens

Acquisitions Editor
Loretta Yates

Development Editor
Mark Renfrow

Managing Editor
Charlotte Clapp

Project Editor
George Nedeff

Copy Editor
Margo Catts

Indexer
Chris Barrick

Proofreader
Jessica McCarty

Technical Editor
David Franson

Team Coordinator
Cindy Teeters

Designer
Gary Adair

Page Layout
Cheryl Lynch

Contents at a Glance

Table of Contents

Part VI: Appendixes

About the Author

Michael Morrison is a writer, developer, toy inventor, and author of a variety of computer technology books and interactive web-based courses. In addition to his primary profession as a writer and freelance nerd for hire, Michael is the creative lead at Stalefish Labs, an entertainment company he cofounded with his wife, Masheed. The first commercial debut for Stalefish Labs is a traditional social/trivia game called *Tall Tales: The Game of Legends and Creative One-Upmanship* (http://www. talltalesgame.com/). When not glued to his computer, playing hockey, skateboarding, or watching movies with his wife, Michael enjoys hanging out by his koi pond. You can visit Michael on the web at http://www.michaelmorrison.com/.

Dedication

*To my late friend Randy Weems, who taught me practically everything
I know about game programming, and who helped me develop my first mobile
game in a single night almost 15 years ago.*

Acknowledgments

Thanks to Mike Stephens, Loretta Yates, Mark Renfrow, and the rest of the wonderful people at Sams Publishing for making the development of this book such an enjoyable experience. I also owe enormous thanks to my wife, Masheed, for being my best friend and biggest supporter.

We Want to Hear from You!

As the reader of this book, *you* are our most important critic and commentator. We value your opinion and want to know what we're doing right, what we could do better, what areas you'd like to see us publish in, and any other words of wisdom you're willing to pass our way.

As an associate publisher for Sams, I welcome your comments. You can email or write me directly to let me know what you did or didn't like about this book—as well as what we can do to make our books better.

Please note that I cannot help you with technical problems related to the *topic* of this book. We do have a User Services group, however, where I will forward specific technical questions related to the book.

When you write, please be sure to include this book's title and author as well as your name, email address, and phone number. I will carefully review your comments and share them with the author and editors who worked on the book.

Email: feedback@samspublishing.com

Mail: Michael Stephens
            Associate Publisher
            Sams Publishing
            800 East 96th Street
            Indianapolis, IN 46240 USA

Reader Services

For more information about this book or others from Sams Publishing, visit our website at www.samspublishing.com. Type the ISBN (0672326655) or the title of the book in the Search box to find the book you're looking for.

Introduction

So I'm sitting in the dentist's chair waiting for the Novocain to set in and allow me to numbly enjoy my root canal when it occurs to me that I could be spending my time so much better than this. Although the confines of a dentist's chair and the goofy drool bib certainly limit my activities to some degree, they don't stop me from playing a wireless, online, multiplayer adventure game with a few hundred of my closest friends and enemies. Quickly I slip my Java-powered mobile phone out of my pocket and fire up a quick game so that I can momentarily divert my uneasy mind from the inevitable onslaught of medieval dental tools. And this, my friends, is what mobile gaming is all about!

I know, you've been hearing talk about the "wireless revolution" for several years now, and you've chalked it up to techno hype. I don't blame you. Up until recently I was skeptical myself of what could realistically be done on a device that I frequently pick up off the ground and pray that it still works. Let's face it: Mobile phones are not what most of us think of when we contemplate the future of digital interactive entertainment. But we can't afford to maintain this attitude much longer. The reality is that mobile phones have arrived as game machines, and if you're reading this book you are obviously interested in "getting in the game."

Although it's perfectly legitimate to group together mobile phones with other kinds of handheld entertainment devices such as Palm Pilots, Pocket PCs, and Game Boys (to name a few) this book takes a narrower look at mobile game programming by focusing solely on games as they apply to mobile phones. It's not that I'm against any of the other devices, but none of those devices have anywhere near the same reach as mobile phones in terms of users. Think of five of the least technical people you know, and count how many own a mobile phone. If the answer is less than four or five, just give them a couple of years. Whether or not my informal poll convinces you, mobile phones represent the broadest installation of computers the world has ever seen, and it's growing at a staggering rate.

So you have all these people toting personal communicators (mobile phones), and primarily using them to talk to each other. And then technologies arrive that make it possible to extend those communicators beyond simple voice communications. Technologies such as Java empower mobile phones with roughly the same capabilities as desktop computers. Couple this with the wireless networking support common to all mobile phones and you have quite a unique device on your hands: rugged, compact, portable, networked, programmable…a game programmer's dream.

FIGURE 1
The Henway game is somewhat of a take-off on the classic Frogger arcade game.

FIGURE 2
The High Seas game takes advantage of a scrolling background and "intelligent" computer enemies.

I'd be lying if I said that mobile game programming wasn't still in its infancy. The technologies are new and the phones that support them are even newer. But as you may know about technology, the only way to keep up with it is to stay as far ahead of the curve as possible. By learning how to design and build mobile games as the industry unfolds, you'll be better prepared to take advantage of opportunities as they arise. Whether it's a mobile game just to share with family and friends, or a full-blown commercial endeavor to fund your early retirement and cement your place in the mobile game hall of fame, this book will provide you with everything you need to get started with game programming for mobile phones. Check out Figure 1 for an example of one of the games you design and build in this book.

The Henway game shown in Figure 1 is loosely based on the classic Frogger arcade game. If getting a chicken across the road isn't to your liking, then maybe the High Seas game in Figure 2 will get your attention.

The High Seas game is a pirate game where you cruise around a nautical map rescuing lost pirates while avoiding roaming squids, floating mines, and a large enemy pirate ship. These are just two of the five complete mobile games you build throughout the book. I'll let the others remain a surprise!

Java is the programming language of choice used throughout this book to develop mobile games, and there is a good reason for it. I go into more details on this choice in Chapter 1, "Games on the Go," but the quick reason is simply that Java is the dominant game development technology for mobile phones now and into the foreseeable future. A bonus Java tutorial, "Java Programming Primer," is included on the CD-ROM, just in case you aren't a Java whiz. Regardless of your views on Java as you go into this book, I think you'll agree by the end that Java is an ideal technology for mobile game development.

People often ask me what kind of phone I use to tinker with mobile game programming, and I always tell them the huge one sitting on my desk. I'm talking about my desktop PC, which I use the vast majority of the time during mobile game development as a mobile phone emulator. There are so many phones on the market and new models are released so frequently, it would be impossible for me to endorse a particular phone without outdating this book instantly. So I recommend using the Java emulator built into the J2ME Wireless Toolkit, which is included on the accompanying CD-ROM. Of course, you'll certainly want to test your games on a real phone throughout the development process, but you'd be surprised how handy an emulator can be.

Like game programming for desktop computers and console systems, mobile game programming isn't easy. You'll be called upon to master and combine a wide range of software development skills, not to mention a good dose of creative and artistic sensibilities. This unique blend of art and technical skill is likely what makes game programming so alluring. Add the sizzle of doing all of this on a tiny device with a wireless network connection, and you have the recipe for some serious techie fun.

How This Book Is Structured

This book is organized into five parts, each of which tackles a different facet of game programming:

▶ **Part I, "Getting Started with Mobile Game Programming"**—In this part, you learn the basics of mobile game development and what goes into creating a mobile game with Java and the J2ME Wireless Toolkit. You construct a mobile game skeleton that serves as a template for future games throughout the book, and test the game with a Java mobile phone emulator.

▶ **Part II, "Mobile Game Programming Essentials"**—In this part, you learn how to draw graphics for mobile games, including images. You also learn the ropes of sprite animation, which is the cornerstone of two-dimensional game programming. You also develop a couple of complete games, including Henway and Cat Catcher. There's admittedly a bit of an animal theme going on here, but don't worry; you get into pirates and aliens later in the book.

▶ **Part III, "Virtual Worlds and Mobile Game Intelligence"**—In this part, you learn about game layers and how they are used to construct games as overlapping visual pieces. You also explore the fundamentals of artificial intelligence (AI), and why it is important to games. AI can be a daunting topic, so I focus on some basic AI techniques that are easy to understand and apply in your own games. This part of the book also includes the development of another complete game, High Seas, which is a pirate game where you sail around a large sea map battling other pirates and sea monsters.

▶ **Part IV, "Taking Advantage of the Wireless Network"**—In this part, you find out how to make the most of the killer feature of mobile phones: the wireless network. After learning the basics of network programming for mobile games, you develop a game called NetConnect4, which is a mobile networked version of the classic Connect4 game. You then design and build a networked action game called Mad Plumber, where you race against another player to lay plumbing pipes.

▶ **Part V, "Sprucing Up Your Games"**—In this part, you explore some interesting game programming techniques that enable you to get the most performance out of your mobile games. You also learn how to create and manage a high score list that is stored on the phone. This part of the book guides you through the design and development of another complete game, Space Out, which is a space shoot-em-up that incorporates much of what you've learned throughout the book.

What You'll Need

This book assumes that you have a knowledge and understanding of the Java programming language. I really don't rely on any complex Java programming constructs, so a basic understanding of Java is all you need. If your Java skills are a bit rusty, you can get a refresher by reading the Java tutorial included on the CD-ROM. The book doesn't assume any knowledge of mobile Java programming, so don't worry if you've never tinkered with a Java-powered phone.

All the examples in the book are available on the accompanying CD-ROM, including batch files for using the command-line J2ME Wireless Toolkit tools to build and run them from a command prompt; the J2ME Wireless Toolkit is also included on the CD-ROM. As I mention several times throughout the book, you'll likely find the KToolbar visual tool that comes with the J2ME Wireless Toolkit to be extremely useful for building and testing the examples. All the examples are designed to be easily opened, compiled, and emulated with KToolbar.

Beyond some Java knowledge, all you really need is an open mind and a little creativity to get the most out of this book. They will serve you well as you embark on this journey into the world of mobile game creation. And if you happen to get lost along the way, drop by my website at http://www.michaelmorrison.com/ and you may be able to find some help in the forum for this book. Have fun!

PART I

Getting Started with Mobile Game Programming

CHAPTER 1

Games on the Go

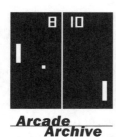

Arcade Archive

Released in 1971 by Nutting Associates, Computer Space holds the distin-guished honor of being the first ever arcade video game. The game was created by Nolan Bushnell, who a year later founded Atari and went on to spark the video game revolution with Pong. Computer Space is a very sim-ple space game, but its physical and electrical design laid the groundwork for all future arcade games. The original coin box in Computer Space was a paint thinner can; that part of the design was not duplicated in future games! A Computer Space game can be spotted in the classic 1975 movie, "Jaws," in the scene where an arcade is shown near the beach.

Dating back at least as far as the popular handheld electronic sports games of the early 1980s, mobile gaming is really nothing new. The most successful modern mobile electronic game system is undoubtedly the Nintendo Game Boy, which has gone through several revisions and is still popular to this day. Mobile games have always lagged behind their full-size counterparts, primarily because of the difficulty in packing processing power into small devices. But this is rapidly changing as the latest crop of handheld computers and mobile phones prove that real computing power can now fit into your pocket. With increased pocket computing power comes increased opportunities for mobile game developers. As a mobile game developer, it's important for you to have an understanding of the tools and technologies surrounding mobile gaming.

In this chapter, you'll learn

- ▶ About the massive market for mobile games
- ▶ What's on the horizon for mobile gaming
- ▶ Why Java is the ideal platform for developing mobile games
- ▶ What J2ME is and how it fits into the mobile Java equation

Essentials of Mobile Gaming

By definition, a mobile game is a game you can play while on the move. Although you could argue that a game on a notebook computer is technically a mobile game by this definition, we're going to limit the definition to games you can play on compact mobile devices that fit into the palm of your hand. This includes mobile phones, pagers, handheld computers, personal digital assistants, and handheld game systems. For the purposes of this book, we're going to further limit the discussion of mobile games only to games that are capable of being run on a mobile phone. Although this may seem like an arbitrary distinction to make, you'll find that mobile phones represent a unique and extremely important type of device for mobile game development.

Why focus just on mobile phones in this book, and not tackle handheld computers and PDAs as well? Because unlike desktop computers, notebook computers, handheld computers, PDAs, and even handheld game systems to some degree, mobile phones reach across an incredibly wide range of social and economic boundaries. Because all people like the idea of being able to communicate with the utmost in flexibility, mobile phones don't cater solely to computer enthusiasts, gadget lovers, or gamers; if you like to talk, you're apt to have a mobile phone. Yet mobile phones are some of the most powerful compact devices available for mobile computing purposes. This combination of an enormous audience and rapidly increasing technical capability make mobile phones an incredibly enticing new frontier for game development.

Gamer's Garage

Wireless carriers have already established an infrastructure for selling and delivering wireless mobile games to users. Unlike traditional PC and console games, which require printed boxes, CD-ROMs, and physical shelf space in a retailer, mobile games can be delivered to market entirely over the air. This is an enormously compelling advantage for upstarts in breaking into the mobile game business.

So a good argument can be made that mobile phones represent a significant opportunity for game developers. That leaves us with figuring out what is required to develop games for mobile phones, which leads to the technological reason why this book focuses solely on mobile phone game programming. Given the limited hardware and unique operating system requirements of mobile phones, games on them are unlike games on most other devices. The development of such games therefore has to be finely tuned to the specific needs of mobile phones.

So although you can certainly port a game from a desktop or handheld computer platform, the reality is that mobile phone games require a unique development approach to address the specific limitations imposed by their size and technological constraints. Additionally, mobile phones have built-in wireless networking support, so many mobile phone games are designed to take into consideration wireless multiplayer networking.

The First Mobile Phone Game

To help put mobile phone games into context, it's worth a brief history lesson; I'm only going back to 1997, so we're still talking recent history. In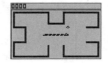

FIGURE 1.1
The classic Snake game represents one of the first games to appear on mobile phones.

1997 the first mobile phone game was created and offered on Nokia phones. The game was called Snake, and was extremely simple in both graphics and game play; you guide a snake around the screen eating pills to score points and grow the snake (see Figure 1.1).

Although Snake is a very simplistic game, it forever changed the perception of mobile phones—they weren't just communication devices anymore. Many other games followed soon after Snake, and people began to think more about the entertainment capabilities of their phones.

The Snake game is actually a classic computer game that has been around for quite some time. Some of the earliest published versions of Snake appeared on Commodore VIC-20 and Commodore 64 personal computers, although I wouldn't be surprised if Snake existed long before then.

Gamer's Garage

One important thing to keep in mind in regard to Snake is that it was designed as a quick little distraction to be played in a matter of minutes, or even seconds. Even with no instructions, you can figure out the game very quickly and begin playing and having fun. And if you get interrupted with a phone call, it's no big deal because you don't have a lot of effort invested in the game anyway. In this way, Snake represents in my opinion the true spirit of mobile gaming: simple, intuitive, and fun. You will no doubt see complex games ported to and developed for mobile phones, but I see the majority of mobile phone users gravitating toward the quick diversionary games such as Snake.

The Market for Mobile Games

If the situational logic of people playing mobile games while waiting in airplane terminals and doctors' offices hasn't convinced you of the bright future for mobile games, then maybe some hard numbers will. Datamonitor, a New York research firm, has estimated that 200 million people will be playing games on their mobile phones in 2005, thereby creating a market for mobile games in the neighborhood of $6 billion. This isn't some far-off prediction; this is the present! The key to understanding the numbers behind the mobile gaming phenomenon is to realize that although the increase in actual mobile users will certainly level off, the increase in mobile game players over the next few years will increase dramatically. It's simply a matter of more powerful phones entering the marketplace that are capable of supporting games.

By some estimates, the 200 million user number for 2005 is low. Other wireless industry experts have projected the number of mobile game players as high as 850 million by 2006. That's a lot of people! When you compare these projected statistics to the number of owners of traditional console video games—and even personal computers for that matter—the commercial potential for mobile gaming is staggering.

But maybe I'm getting ahead of myself. Maybe you just like the idea of creating mobile games for fun, and you really don't care about trying to become a mobile game mogul. Maybe you see mobile games as a cool new way to connect with people in other places and enjoy friendly competition. So let's set capitalism aside and look at mobile games from a purely social perspective.

The Culture of Mobile Games

Just as instant messaging has put us in touch with each other globally with much more immediacy than we perhaps ever thought was possible, mobile games are setting the stage to turn the whole concept of video game playing on its ear. Am I being overly dramatic with that statement? Possibly, but consider a scenario where you're able to participate in a massively networked multiplayer game with people from all over the world, and you're doing this while taking a break during a nature hike. Certainly, it's worth asking why you're playing a game instead of taking in the view, but the point is that mobile games are making it possible to connect and engage with people anywhere and at any time via an entertainment medium. This is not a pie-in-the-sky dream; there are games such as I described already available now.

I know: The idea of a global multiplayer network game is nothing new; people have been doing it on their desktop computers for years. But that requires a network connection and a computer that is often too bulky to lug around. Even the slimmest notebook computers still require a flat surface to be laid on, as well as some kind of wireless network to tap into. Mobile phones can fit in your pocket and are wirelessly connected by default. They make it possible to pop in and out of multiplayer network games with ease.

By fostering an environment where game players can come and go with much more flexibility, the communal facet of mobile gaming will likely be one of its biggest draws as games and related technologies mature. Mobile communications has already made the world quite smaller, and mobile games are taking things to a new level by allowing people to play games together with no regard for physical location. There is the potential to not only overcome geographic barriers with mobile games, but also language and cultural barriers. You don't need to speak the same language to enjoy a quick game of Pong or Snake. And even more inventive games will likely be designed so that cultural differences are minimized between game players.

You might not immediately think of games as a cultural vehicle for learning about other people, but consider the fact that most traditional (noncomputer) children's games have been passed on for countless generations, often across different cultures. Just like stories and legends, the games people play say a lot about their culture. Sharing games with people all around the world is indeed a potential way to learn about other people and teach them about you.

Gamer's Garage

The Bleeding Edge of Mobile Gaming

Perhaps the most interesting thing about mobile gaming right now is the territory that still remains uncharted. New genres of games haven't even been created yet. Consider, for example, how GPS (Global Positioning System) features built into mobile phones could potentially be combined into games. It could be technically feasible to play out a game in terms of real world geography. In other words, you have to move in the real world to move your character in a game; real-time GPS data in mobile phones can make this possible.

If you think the idea of a GPS-driven mobile game played out in real time and space is a bit of a stretch, then please allow me to introduce Pac-Manhattan. Pac-Manhattan is an ingenious "largescale urban game" that uses New York City as a grid to re-create the arcade classic Pac-Man. The idea behind Pac-Manhattan is to shift a classic game from the realm of digital (computers) to the real world of analog.

More specifically, the characters in the game are played by real people who run around in the real streets of Manhattan while playing the game. A player dressed as Pac-Man navigates his way through Washington Square Park while being pursued by players dressed as the familiar ghosts Inky, Blinky, Pinky, and Clyde. Figure 1.2 shows the game map for Pac-Manhattan, which maps New York streets to a Pac-Man maze.

FIGURE 1.2
The game map for Pac-Manhattan translates a video game maze into streets in New York.

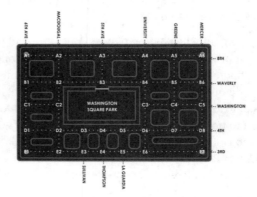

Using mobile phones and WiFi network connections to relay game data, a control center keeps track of the action and updates a game screen that can be viewed on the Pac-Manhattan website (http://www.pacmanhattan.com/). Figure 1.3 shows an example game screen from Pac-Manhattan with a game in full swing. Keep in mind that this screen is reflecting a game that is being played in real life on the streets of New York.

FIGURE 1.3
Pac-Manhattan looks a lot like the original Pac-Man game, but it reflects real people chasing each other around Manhattan.

Although there is definitely some creative communication going on to make Pac-Manhattan possible, it doesn't truly qualify as a mobile game according to our definition because mobile phones are used in it solely as voice communicators. In other words, no game is being played on the phones—you could just as easily use a walky-talky. A more technologically interesting Pac-Manhattan would rely on mobile game clients that utilize GPS to relay the position of each character back to a central game server automatically. Rumor is the Pac-Manhattan folks are working on this, so stay tuned to their website if you're interested in how it unfolds.

> If you'd like to stage your own game of Pac-Manhattan, the Pac-Manhattan website offers a free downloadable "In Your City Kit," which contains all the information you need to stage a Pac-Manhattan game in your own town. Just be forewarned that this game is more dangerous than the arcade version, so you're playing at your own risk.

Gamer's Garage

GPS with Pac-Manhattan is just one example of how mobile phones are capable of merging previously unrelated technologies to make entirely new things possible in the way of mobile gaming. We are living in an extremely exciting and dynamic time for mobile gaming!

Getting to Know Mobile Platforms

Before I get into any specifics regarding mobile game platforms, it's important to point out that wireless mobile gaming is still in its infancy. This is significant because it means that the tools and technologies change rapidly. It's very important for you to be vigilant in keeping up with current trends and technologies, including what phones wireless providers are carrying and what technologies they support.

Although the mobile game landscape is certainly changing fast, the writing is on the wall to some degree when it comes to dominant platforms. It's fairly safe to narrow down the mobile phone platforms suitable for game development to the following:

- Java 2 Micro Edition (J2ME)
- Binary Runtime Environment for Wireless (BREW)
- Symbian
- Windows Mobile Smartphone

Another mobile platform that I didn't mention is SMS, or Short Message Service. SMS is a technology that allows you to send short little text messages back and forth between your phone and a game server. SMS is a decent option for text-based "choose your own adventure" type games and possibly a chat-based game, but it is cumbersome for much else. Additionally, you are typically charged for each SMS message, which means an SMS game can get expensive if there is a lot of back and forth communication going on.

All four of these platforms are supported in current phones, and they all include rich support for developers in the way of free tools and documentation. The next few sections explore each platform in more detail, and help you to understand how they differ from one another.

One of the most difficult decisions during the planning of this book was whether to commit to a mobile game platform or not. It was eventually decided that there was no way to present the basics of mobile game programming and also cover two or three different platforms. So we chose the platform with the most industry support and the brightest future, which is J2ME. Fortunately, a lot of the mobile game programming techniques you learn throughout the book can be applied to other mobile platforms.

Java 2 Micro Edition (J2ME)

J2ME is the compact version of Sun Microsystems' popular Java programming language. A lot of people don't realize that Java originated as a language for use in programming mobile devices, so it has finally come full circle in the form of J2ME. J2ME consists of a suite of development tools and a rich application programming interface (API) for developing mobile phone applications known as MIDlets (more on the meaning of this term later).

J2ME also includes the K virtual machine, which is responsible for assisting in the execution of Java bytecode on each specific phone. By relying on generic bytecode instead of native application code, J2ME makes it possible to develop a code base for your games that can be ported to a variety of different mobile phones with very little effort. In fact, if it wasn't for variations in screen size and graphics capabilities, the effort required to port a game between J2ME phones would be zero.

J2ME enjoys the broadest industry support in the U.S. among mobile phone manufacturers. Heavy hitters such as Motorola, Nokia, Research In Motion (RIM), and Samsung all have J2ME-powered phones on the market.

Binary Runtime Environment for Wireless (BREW)

Unlike J2ME, which is supported across a wide range of mobile phones, BREW is a platform specifically targeted at phones based on Qualcomm's Code Division Multiple Access (CDMA) technology. This isn't to say that BREW doesn't have a relatively large support base of phones. BREW developers typically use the C or C++ programming language in combination with the BREW API to develop mobile games for BREW devices. BREW also supports other software development technologies such as XML and even Java.

Similar to J2ME, BREW can run as an intermediary between a game and the underlying phone's operating system. Unlike J2ME, BREW also supports native code, which means a game can be compiled specifically for a certain phone's processor. Native code games are usually much faster than their interpreted counterparts, but they can be trickier to port between devices.

BREW has caught on and has a surprisingly large user base in parts of Asia, including Japan and South Korea. In the U.S., Alltel and Verizon Wireless are currently the leading wireless providers offering phones that support BREW.

Symbian

Symbian is a mobile operating system that takes a very different approach than BREW in that it is an open operating system, available for license by any device manufacturer. Symbian was developed by Symbian Ltd., which is a consortium of mobile phone manufacturers including Motorola, Nokia, Panasonic, and Sony/ Ericsson. Symbian is currently supported on a wide range of mobile phones, thanks to its relative ease in licensing.

There are plenty of options for developing mobile games for Symbian devices because Symbian supports the C++, Java, and Visual Basic programming languages. Most commercial Symbian games to date have been developed in C++ as native Symbian applications, which makes them a bit faster and more integrated into the Symbian OS than their Java counterparts. Granted, Java has begun closing the performance gap between Java programs and native programs, but a pure native application is almost always more efficient than a Java program. This can be especially important when it comes to games, which typically require every ounce of spare processing power.

So why not focus on Symbian in this book, as opposed to Java? The simple answer is that Java is ubiquitous, whereas Symbian is still but one mobile operating system.

Mobile phones are much different than PCs in terms of having both widely varying hardware and software. Java is the unifying development technology that allows you to build a game once, and deploy it on a wide range of phones with minimal effort.

Windows Mobile Smartphone

You didn't honestly think Microsoft would sit on the sidelines and watch mobile gaming take off without their involvement, did you? Of course not! Microsoft has seen some success with their Windows Mobile operating system, which is deployed on handheld computers known as Pocket PCs and advanced mobile phone devices known as Smartphones. Although some Pocket PCs double as mobile phones, they are more akin to PDAs than they are mobile phones, at least in terms of their physical dimensions; Pocket PCs have fairly large screens (240×320) and rely on a stylus for most user input.

Although Pocket PCs as devices aren't really a fair comparison to mobile phones, the Windows Mobile operating system is a different story. Microsoft was apparently just biding their time until mobile phone technology caught up to them because they recently released Smartphone, which is the Windows Mobile operating system reformulated for mobile phones. What makes the operating system so interesting is that it isn't really scaled down from the Pocket PC version; the only significant differences are user interface changes to account for smaller screens and the lack of styli in mobile phones. Otherwise, you get the full-blown Windows Mobile operating system on a mobile phone with the Smartphone logo.

What this means from a mobile game development perspective is that you can use the same tools and APIs that are already being used to build Pocket PC games. This typically means using C, C++, or Microsoft's C# programming language in combination with the Windows Mobile APIs. Pocket PC game development has been going on for several years now, so in some ways Smartphone has a significant jumpstart, even though it is relatively new to the marketplace.

Motorola and Samsung are both manufacturing Smartphone mobile phones in the U.S., and they are currently being offered through AT&T Wireless and Verizon Wireless. With Microsoft's marketing muscle and industry presence, I expect to see Smartphone technology grow rapidly in the way of additional devices and wireless providers in the very near future.

Java As a Mobile Game Platform

If you've been astute enough to read all the Gamer's Garage notes, you already know that J2ME is the platform of choice for this book. I'll get to the reason for this in just a moment, but first let's take a quick look at the Java technology and what it has to offer in the way of mobile game development.

What Is Java?

Earlier I mentioned that Java began as a programming language that enabled networked devices to communicate with each other. More specifically, Java started out as a project at Sun with engineers studying how to put computers into every-day household items. One primary focus of the project was to have these comput-erized devices communicate with each other. As it played out, Sun was a little ahead of its time in applying Java to network everyday devices. However, the company was quick to react and ended up making Java a huge success by target-ing it for the web.

As soon as technology and public perception caught up with Java's earlier aspira-tions, Sun went back to the drawing board and retooled Java for the mobile com-puting domain. Not only was J2ME designed for the constraints of mobile devices, but it is also well suited for wireless networking. J2ME is actually a subset of the larger Java technology, which consists of a programming language, an API, and a runtime environment.

Why Java?

Even with Java being ideally suited for mobile phone development, it wouldn't be of much use if it didn't have broad industry support. Java is currently the pre-dominant software development technology for mobile phones, and all signs point to it maintaining and possibly even expanding its market share. Some analysts estimate that by 2007 some 450 million mobile phones will be sold with Java support, representing 75% of the entire mobile phone market.

Developers have flocked to Java largely because it is considered an open platform, which means that you can develop one set of code and have it run across a wide range of mobile devices. Unfortunately, the "openness" of Java has been compli-cated a bit because of third party APIs and hardware variations among different devices, but generally speaking, you can write a game once and use the majority of the code unmodified on a variety of mobile phones. Contrast this with BREW, which is geared solely for phones operating on Qualcomm CDMA networks.

Gamer's Garage

Technically speaking, even though Java and J2ME are more "open" than BREW, they still are not "open source." All facets of the Java technology, including J2ME, are owned by Sun Microsystems. Fortunately, Sun has been very forthcoming with outside input on the Java standards, but many developers are still lobbying them to turn Java over to the Open Source community.

An interesting twist on the relationship between Java and BREW came about in late 2002 with the introduction of a Java virtual machine for BREW devices. This means that BREW devices can effectively support J2ME just as if they were factory Java-powered devices. In this way, Java doesn't really compete with BREW as a platform for game development. However, because "pure" Java phones don't support BREW, it does mean that you reach the largest market by going with Java.

Gamer's Garage

Incidentally, you may have noticed that I use the terms Java and J2ME interchangeably. Although J2ME is technically a subset of the larger Java technology, within the confines of this book the two terms mean the same thing because I'm usually discussing Java within the context of mobile phones.

Java and Mobile Game Programming

You know the "what" and the "why," and now it's important to get into some of the details of the "how." In other words, how does Java make mobile programming possible? The primary areas of importance for any game programming technology include the following:

- Graphics and animation
- User input
- Sound
- Networking

The next few sections explore these game programming topics in the context of J2ME.

Graphics and Animation

The standard J2ME API includes support for all kinds of neat graphics features such as images, 2D graphics primitives, and animation. 2D graphics primitives include lines, rectangles, ellipses, and so on. In terms of animation, J2ME supports sprites, which are images that are capable of being independently moved and animated. The J2ME API also supports sprite collision detection, which allows you to determine whether two sprites have collided with each other; this is a critical requirement of virtually every action game. You are introduced to sprites in Chapter 5, "Using Sprite Animation."

Another very interesting feature specific to games in the J2ME API is tiled layers, which enable you to arrange small rectangular image tiles to create much larger backgrounds. Tiled layers make it possible to create large maps that can be reconfigured in games while also conserving memory because the individual image tiles are being reused whenever possible. It is also possible to manage multiple layers with ease, thanks to a handy layer manager provided by J2ME. This makes it possible to create one background layer that serves purely as decoration, and another layer that provides barriers to prevent a character from moving around freely in a game. Chapter 10, "Creating Tiled Game Layers," explores tiled layers, whereas Chapter 11, "Managing Multiple Game Layers," shows how to manage them with the layer manager.

Responding to Mobile User Input

User input is a very critical area of game development because it dictates how a game "feels" to the game player. User input is also important because it establishes the primary interface between the player and the game. J2ME provides support for key input, which is currently the only mode of input for mobile phones. There is specific support for directly reading the state of the keys on a phone, which is very important for games because you want the keys to be highly responsive. The specifics of handling user input for games via the J2ME API are covered in Chapter 6, "Handling Mobile User Input."

Keep in mind that the key configurations for mobile phones vary considerably, but they all have common keys for performing certain tasks. More specifically, every Java-powered mobile phone has keys that correspond to Up, Down, Left, Right, and Fire, along with several other "utility buttons." For phones that actually have game pads, each side of the game pad maps to a directional key such as Up, Down, and so on.

Playing Sound in Mobile Games

Rounding out the "big three" areas of game development is sound. J2ME supports the playback of digital sounds that are in either the PCM or WAV formats, as well as MIDI music. The sound support in the J2ME API is based on Java's Mobile Media API, which is an API for allowing the playback and recording of audio and video on mobile devices. For the purposes of game development, all you're really concerned with is the efficient playback of audio and possibly video at some point.

To keep from straying too far away from core game programming topics, this book focuses solely on playing sounds with J2ME, and doesn't tackle video.

You learn all about sound programming in J2ME, as well as the WAV sound format and MIDI music format, in Chapter 8, "Making Noise with Tones."

Mobile Networking

The true killer application of mobile phone games will likely be the built-in network available to all mobile phones. With this in mind, it only stands to reason that the network features of Java play heavily into its usefulness as a mobile game platform. Fortunately, networking is one area where Java really shines because it is such an integral part of the Java runtime system. Unlike other popular game programming languages such as C and C++, Java was designed from the ground up to support networking.

Combine Java's extensive network support with its platform independence and you have a gaming platform that crosses all boundaries for availability to users. This is very important when you consider that mobile game players will want to play games across a variety of different devices and wireless carriers. Game players shouldn't have to concern themselves with the technical distinctions between their mobile phone and a phone made by a different manufacturer. Thanks to the networking features built into Java, developers don't have to worry about these distinctions, either.

Networked mobile games are first introduced in Chapter 14, "Mobile Game Networking Essentials," with example network games appearing in Chapter 15, "Connect 4: A Classic Game Goes Wireless."

A Quick J2ME Primer

The core set of tools and APIs used to construct normal Java applications is known as J2SE, which stands for Java 2 Standard Edition. J2SE is used to construct both web-based applets and standalone applications. J2EE (Java 2 Enterprise Edition) is another version of Java designed solely for building enterprise applications. J2EE is different from J2SE because it adds significant functionality to support enterprise applications. Think about big networked applications such as the engine that runs eBay or Amazon.com, and you'll have an idea of what J2EE is designed for.

Given that wireless mobile devices have less computing power and smaller screens than their desktop counterparts, it stands to reason that J2ME represents a simplified version of J2SE with a reduced feature set. J2ME is in fact a subset of J2SE that supports a minimal set of features that are applicable to mobile devices, both wireless and wired.

J2ME also throws in some features that are entirely unique to mobile devices. Together, these three Java development suites (J2ME, J2SE, and J2EE) compose the Java 2 technology.

If you're concerned about why I'm going into so much detail about J2ME when this is a game programming book, it's because there are some bare minimums you need to understand in regard to J2ME. Don't worry—after you get a little more J2ME knowledge under your belt, we'll take off with the mobile game stuff!

Configurations and the Connected Limited Device Configuration (CLDC)

If you use J2ME, you will encounter some new terms and acronyms that you might as well go ahead and get behind you. The first one is a *configuration*, which is a minimum set of APIs used for developing applications to run on a certain range of devices. A standard configuration for wireless devices is known as the Connected Limited Device Configuration, or CLDC. The CLDC describes a minimum level of functionality required for all wireless mobile devices. The CLDC takes into consideration factors such as the amount of memory available to such devices, along with their processing power.

To be a little more specific, the CLDC clearly outlines the following pieces of information with respect to wireless mobile devices:

▶ The subset of Java programming language features

▶ The subset of functionality of the Java virtual machine

▶ The core APIs required for wireless mobile application development

▶ The hardware requirements of the wireless mobile devices targeted by the CLDC

You might assume that the entire Java programming language is available for use in mobile devices, but in fact some features are disabled under the CLDC because of the limited processing power of mobile devices. In addition to spelling out API details, the CLDC also specifies minimum hardware requirements for Java-powered devices:

▶ 160KB of total memory available for Java

▶ 16-bit processor

▶ Low power consumption (often battery power)

▶ Network connectivity (often wireless with a 9,600bps or less bandwidth)

As this list reveals, CLDC devices include, but are not limited to, mobile phones, pagers, PDAs, pocket computers, and home appliances. Of course, our interest is in the CLDC as it applies to mobile phones.

Gamer's Garage

In addition to the CLDC, J2ME defines another configuration known as the CDC (Connected Device Configuration), which is geared toward devices that are larger and more powerful than CLDC devices. Consequently, the CDC has more features than the CLDC.

Profiles and the MIDP

On top of a configuration sits a *profile*, which is a more specific set of APIs that further targets a particular type of device. A configuration describes in general terms a family of devices, whereas a profile gets more specific and isolates a particular type of device within that family. The Mobile Information Device Profile, or MIDP, is a profile built on top of the CLDC that describes a wireless mobile device such as a mobile phone or pager.

In addition to specifying APIs for use in MIDP application development, the MIDP also describes minimum hardware and software requirements for an MIDP device. The next two sections outline these hardware and software requirements, which are very important because they let you know the worst case scenario your games will face when it comes to mobile phone hardware and software.

Gamer's Garage

There are actually two versions of the MIDP profile: 1.0 and 2.0. Although MIDP 1.0 phones have a wide installed base, MIDP 2.0 is where J2ME offers serious features for mobile game developers. This book focuses solely on the newer MIDP 2.0 standard. MIDP 2.0 phones are rapidly replacing the first generation 1.0 phones, if they haven't already as you read this.

Assessing the MIDP Hardware Requirements

The hardware requirements for MIDP 2.0 devices are an important part of the MIDP standard. These requirements are broken down into the following device properties:

- Memory
- Input
- Display
- Networking

The memory requirements for MIDP devices are as follows:

- ▶ 256KB of nonvolatile memory for the MIDP API libraries
- ▶ 128KB of volatile memory for the Java runtime system
- ▶ 8KB of nonvolatile memory for persistent application data

The input requirements of MIDP devices stipulate that an MIDP device must have a keyboard or touch screen. The keyboard can be either one-handed or two-handed, and it is possible that a device might have both a keyboard and a touch screen. Notice that a mouse isn't an input requirement because it is unlikely that a mobile device would be capable of using a mouse. However, it is quite possible for a device to use a stylus with a touch screen.

Gamer's Garage

In case you're wondering, joysticks are starting to enter the MIDP equation. Sony/ Ericsson and Samsung offer mobile phones with a tiny little joystick embedded in the keypad. Because the MIDP doesn't specifically support joysticks, the four basic directions (up, down, left, and right) allow a joystick to be supported if joystick directions were mapped to keys.

The display requirements for MIDP devices are a little more interesting because the screens for mobile devices represent one of the most constrained hardware properties. MIDP device displays must have a screen size of 96 pixels by 54 pixels with a 1-bit color depth. This means that the screen must be at least 96 pixels wide and 54 pixels high, and must be at least black and white. Furthermore, the aspect ratio of the display must be 1:1, which simply means that pixels must be square. Believe it or not, many computer monitors don't have a 1:1 aspect ratio, which means that pixels are actually rectangular in shape. Not so with MIDP device screens!

Gamer's Garage

In reality, the vast majority of mobile phones blow out the MIDP 2.0 screen minimum by supporting color, and in most cases also have screens larger than the 96×54 minimum.

The last hardware area targeted by the MIDP specification is *networking*, which dictates the minimum networking support required of an MIDP device. An MIDP device must have a two-way, wireless network connection of some sort. It is expected that such a connection may be intermittent, such as a dial-up connection, and that it also may have limited bandwidth (9,600bps). This is important because it informs you that you must be very conscious of bandwidth issues when designing network games, especially games that rely on lots of time-critical updating such as action games.

Examining the MIDP Software Requirements

The cross-platform nature of Java helps alleviate concerns over the wide range of mobile device operating systems. Even so, the MIDP specification lays some ground rules about what is expected of the operating system in an MIDP device. Following are the major software requirements for MIDP devices:

- ▶ A minimal kernel to manage low-level hardware features such as interrupts, exceptions, and scheduling
- ▶ A mechanism to read from and write to nonvolatile (persistent) memory
- ▶ A timing mechanism for establishing timers and adding time stamps to persistent data
- ▶ Read/write access to the device's wireless network connection
- ▶ A mechanism to capture user input from a keyboard or touch screen
- ▶ Minimal support for bitmapped graphics
- ▶ A mechanism for managing the life cycle of an application

These requirements, although somewhat minimal, still provide a reasonably rich set of features that are available for use by an MIDP game.

Summary

I know, you were probably itching to try out some code and get your feet wet programming a mobile game right out of the gate, but some ground work was in order in this chapter. Not only did you learn a great deal about mobile gaming in general, but you found out about the different development options for creating mobile games. More specifically, you found out why Java is leading the pack, and why it will likely be the dominant mobile game platform well into the future. Toward the end of the chapter you got up close and personal with J2ME, the version of Java that targets mobile phones. I hated to throw so much "background information" at you all at once, but it will be valuable as you quickly move into the details of building games for Java-powered mobile phones.

Field Trip

I'd hate for you to finish up this chapter without having some real fun. Assuming you have a Java-powered phone at your disposal, take a visit to Handango at http://www.handango.com/ and find a game to download for your phone. Yes, it's Handango the mobile software site, not Fandango the movie ticket site! Most of the games on Handango include evaluation versions that you can try before you buy, so this field trip doesn't necessarily have to cost you anything. As you browse through the games, look around to see what might be missing so you can get some ideas for mobile games of your own.

CHAPTER 2

Mobile Java Game Development Basics

Arcade Archive

Released in 1976 by Midway, Sea Wolf is a submarine game where you look through a periscope and fire torpedoes at ships cruising across the top of the screen. Sea Wolf had a very discernable "ping" sound that simulated the sound of a submarine. Sea Wolf was based on a large mechanical submarine game by Sega called Periscope, which dates back to the mid 1960s. Interestingly enough, Periscope was the first game (mechanical, not video) to charge a quarter for each play; this pricing standard eventually carried over into arcade video games.

With an understanding of why Java is the mobile game development platform of choice for the foreseeable future, you're ready to find out more about how to use J2ME to build and play games. Fortunately, Sun Microsystems offers the J2ME Wireless Toolkit free of charge for developing game MIDlets with J2ME. This chapter introduces you to the J2ME Wireless Toolkit and how it is used to build mobile games for Java-powered devices. You also learn how to use the J2ME emulator to explore and play mobile games on your desktop computer without even using a physical J2ME device. You find out that emulating games is an extremely important part of the mobile game development process.

In this chapter, you'll learn

- ▶ The basics of game design
- ▶ How J2ME is used to construct mobile games
- ▶ How to use the KToolbar application to build and test mobile games
- ▶ How the J2ME emulator allows you to emulate physical mobile phone devices

Game Design Basics

Before we dig into the J2ME Wireless Toolkit and how it is used to build and test mobile Java games, it's worth taking a moment to cover some basics of game design. Do you have some ideas of games you would like to write? If so, you probably already realize that coming up with a good game idea is often the easy part. Taking a game concept and making it reality is where most of us fall short. That's okay; you just have to take it a step at a time and think through the development process.

The first step in taking a game from concept to reality is to get a solid idea of what you want the game to be. This doesn't need to be an itemized list of every scene and every little creature and interaction. It simply needs to state some minimal ground rules about what your goal is for the final game. Here are the key items you should address when beginning the game development process:

- Basic idea
- Storyline
- Play modes

Coming Up with the Basic Idea

The first thing you should do is determine the basic idea behind your game. Is it a shoot-em-up, a maze game, a role-playing adventure game, or some mixed combination? Or do you have an idea of a game that doesn't really fit into an existing category? Is the object to rescue good guys, kill bad guys, or just explore a strange environment? What time frame is your game set in, or does it even have a time frame? Write all this stuff down. Whatever comes to mind, write it down, because brainstorms come and go and you don't want to forget anything. Forcing yourself to formalize your ideas causes you to think more about the game and clears up a lot of things.

If you are having trouble coming up with a basic game idea, think about the influences of a lot of the popular computer games. Many games are based on movies, some on historical events, and others on sports. Ultimately, computer games are models of the world around us, whether fantasy or real, so look no further when dreaming up your game. Movies in particular can provide a lot of good creative settings and storylines for games. Just keep in mind that many movies are already being turned into commercial video games. For this reason, you should think of movies in terms of broad ideas and concepts, as opposed to modeling your own game exactly after a movie premise.

Currently, there are a few cases in which a game idea has served as the basis for a movie. Examples include Mortal Kombat, Final Fantasy, and Resident Evil, to name a few games that have been turned into movies.

Regardless of your inspiration, just remember that your game has to be fun. Actually, that's why I think computer games are so alluring to programmers. The overriding design goal is always to maximize fun! Who wouldn't want to spend all day trying to figure out the best way to have fun? If your game isn't fun to play, the most dazzling graphics and sound won't be able to save it. The point I'm trying to make is that you must make fun the priority when designing your game. After you have a basic idea of what your game will be and you've decided that you're going to make it fun at all costs, you can develop a storyline.

Developing the Storyline

Even if your game is a simple action game, developing a storyline helps you to establish the landscape and think up creatures to populate your game world. Putting your game in the context of a story also brings the game player closer to your world. For games in which the story is a more integral part, it is often useful to develop a storyboard along with the storyline. A storyboard tells the story scene by scene by using rough sketches of each scene. A storyboard basically enables you to create a visual layout of the entire game, based on the story. Having a storyboard to reference helps ensure that you don't lose sight of the story when you get into heavy development.

Establishing the Play Modes

The final thing to consider when laying out your initial game design is what play modes you will support. Will it be single player, two player, networked, or some combination? This might sound like a fairly simple decision, but it can have huge repercussions on the game logic later. Even though Java provides a lot of support for networking, network games typically incur a significantly more complex design.

On the other hand, many single-player games require some degree of artificial intelligence to make the computer opponent challenging to play against. Artificial intelligence can get complicated and difficult to implement, so you need to weigh your resources heavily into your game design when deciding on play modes. Speaking of artificial intelligence, you learn all about it in Chapter 13, "Teaching Games to Think."

A J2ME Game Development Primer

As with just about any game, mobile Java games developed with J2ME require various development tools for compilation and testing. The compiled Java classes that make up a game must go through a preverification process that verifies that the code doesn't violate J2ME security constraints. J2ME games also require a special emulator for testing in an environment similar to a real mobile phone. Of course, you should always test a game directly on a real phone, but it is much more efficient to do the majority of testing with an emulator and then save later testing for the actual phone. The standard Java compiler is used to build J2ME games, after which the additional tools enter the picture.

Gamer's Garage

The standard Java compiler is part of the Java Software Development Kit (SDK), which is available for free download from Sun Microsystems' Java website at http://java.sun.com/. There you will also find the J2ME Wireless Toolkit, which is also required for mobile game development in Java.

J2ME applications developed to the MIDP specification are referred to as *MIDlets*. So any games you create with J2ME MIDP are actually MIDlets. MIDlet classes are stored in Java bytecode files with a `.class` file extension. However, MIDlet classes must be verified prior to distribution to guarantee that they don't perform any illegal operations. The reason for this preverification step has to do with the limitations of the virtual machine used in mobile devices. This virtual machine is referred to as the *K Virtual Machine*, or KVM for short. To keep the KVM as small and efficient as possible, the amount of verification performed on a MIDlet class at runtime is minimized. So, some of this verification is handled at design-time during the preverification process.

Gamer's Garage

The naming of the KVM has to do with the resource requirements of the virtual machine; the KVM requires Ks of memory, as opposed to MBs. In other words, the KVM is designed to fit within several kilobytes (K) of memory, as opposed to a full-blown J2SE virtual machine that might take up several megabytes of memory (MB).

Preverification takes place just after compilation, and results in a new class file being generated that is verified and ready for testing or distribution. MIDlets must be specially packaged in JAR (Java ARchive) files for distribution, which are very similar to ZIP files that you've probably used before to compress large files. MIDlets also require some additional descriptive information to be included in the JAR file. Following are the pieces of information typically included in a MIDlet JAR file:

▶ MIDlet classes

▶ Support classes

▶ Resources (images, sounds, and so on)

▶ Manifest file (`.mf` file)

▶ Application descriptor (`.jad` file)

JAR files are used to package Java classes into compressed archives for more efficient distribution. A manifest file is a special text file included in a JAR file that describes the classes contained within the archive.

Gamer's Garage

The application descriptor, or JAD file, is a file that provides descriptive information about the MIDlets contained within a JAR file. Notice that I said "MIDlets," plural. Yes, multiple MIDlets are often contained within a single JAR file. Such a collection of MIDlets is referred to as a *MIDlet suite*. In the case of mobile games, you might want to offer a collection of games together as a single product, such as a suite of related trivia games, in which case you would bundle all the games into a single JAR file.

The idea behind a MIDlet suite is that it enables multiple MIDlets to share the limited resources available in a mobile device. The KVM for the device is required to provide a means of navigating and selecting a particular MIDlet to run from the MIDlet suite. The JAD file included in the JAR file for a MIDlet suite is instrumental in providing information relevant to installing and accessing the individual MIDlets.

I know—you probably thought this section was about J2ME game development, not the inner workings of JAR files and MIDlet suites. The reality is that you need to know some basics about assembling MIDlets for distribution to understand the process of developing them. The MIDlet development process is summarized in the following steps:

1. Edit
2. Compile
3. Preverify
4. Emulate
5. Test on device
6. Deploy

Steps 1 and 2 should be pretty familiar to you because they parallel traditional development in just about any compiled programming language. Steps 3 and 4 are where things look a little different. You already know that a preverification step is required to ensure that a MIDlet isn't trying to do something dangerous such as trample device memory. Step 4 is where you test a MIDlet with a special tool called an *emulator*.

The J2ME emulator does exactly what its name implies: It emulates a physical mobile device on your desktop computer. This allows you to test MIDlets within the comforts of your desktop computer without having to download the code onto a device. Debugging is also made much simpler when a MIDlet is running within an emulator.

Step 5 in the MIDlet game development process is testing the MIDlet on a physical device. In reality, you will probably test your games on several different phones to make sure that they perform as expected on each. This testing phase typically takes place after you've ironed out the bugs in a MIDlet game, and you're very close to shipping it as a final product. In other words, the bulk of the game testing takes place in the J2ME emulator before the physical device enters the picture.

The final step in the MIDlet game creation process is deploying the game for others to purchase and enjoy. Game deployment can be as simple as emailing a ZIP file to your friend to directly install on his phone, or as involved as offering the game for over-the-air purchase and installation from a wireless carrier. In the latter scenario, you must jump through a few technical hoops to ensure that your game meets security standards, such as digitally signing the final downloadable file with a valid security certificate. You learn more about deploying mobile games in Chapter 16, "Debugging and Deploying Mobile Games."

Gamer's Garage

Because mobile games typically put a heavy burden on the processing capabilities of mobile phones, you may find that you have to develop slightly different versions of your games for different phones; for example, you may need to remove some game features for less powerful phones. The varying screen sizes on different phones also need to be accommodated. Just keep in mind that while testing a game on different physical phones, you may run into issues that require tweaking the game code to accommodate specific phones.

Now that you have an idea of how a MIDlet game is developed, I'd like to shift gears and take a look at the tools required to assemble a MIDlet:

- ▶ Java 2 SDK
- ▶ J2ME Wireless Toolkit

The Java 2 SDK is the standard development toolkit for Java development. The J2ME Wireless Toolkit serves as an add-on to be used in conjunction with the Java 2 SDK, and includes a bytecode verifier and several J2ME emulators for verifying and testing MIDlets. In addition to the standard J2ME Wireless Toolkit, several mobile device manufacturers offer their own toolkits that include additional tools for MIDlet development. For example, Nokia provides several different MIDP SDKs to target each line of their Java-powered mobile phones. Motorola also offers an SDK for J2ME that is specifically targeted at Motorola phones.

Typically, a toolkit specific to a particular manufacturer offers device profiles to assist you in emulating MIDlets on its devices, along with API extensions tailored exclusively to its devices. Although these APIs are often powerful, I encourage you to stick with the standard MIDP API whenever possible so that your games can be more easily ported across the widest range of mobile phones.

Gamer's Garage

> Optional standard APIs are available for some phones that have capabilities beyond the limited MIDP requirements. For example, the Location API for J2ME provides classes and interfaces for determining the physical location of a mobile phone based on either the Global Positioning System (GPS) or the phone's proximity to a base transceiver station for the wireless network.

Getting to Know the J2ME Wireless Toolkit

The J2ME Wireless Toolkit is a set of development tools made available by Sun that allows MIDlet development when used with the Java 2 SDK. The J2ME Wireless Toolkit is included on the accompanying CD-ROM, but you may want to double check http://java.sun.com/products/j2mewtoolkit/ for the latest version. The toolkit essentially boils down to the following tools:

- Bytecode verifier
- J2ME emulator
- KToolbar
- Provisioning server

You've already learned that the bytecode verifier checks the Java classes that go into a game before they are packaged up for distribution. You also know that the J2ME emulator is used to test mobile games on your desktop computer without the hassle of downloading and running them on a physical mobile phone. A useful feature of the emulator allows you to tweak the default emulation devices to match a target physical phone. For example, you might want to emulate a mobile phone with a certain screen size that isn't reflected in any of the default devices, in which case you can easily create a new configuration to match the phone's parameters. The J2ME emulator also does a good job of emulating the security settings on physical phones, which provides a more realistic emulation environment.

KToolbar is a visual development environment that allows you to build, compile, package, and test J2ME applications with a graphical user interface. This is in contrast to the other J2ME tools, which are all command-line tools that must be run from a command prompt. You'll use KToolbar later in this chapter and throughout the book to build and test mobile games.

New to version 2.0 of the MIDP platform is support for Over The Air provisioning, or OTA, which provides a mechanism for downloading mobile applications over a wireless network connection. The J2ME Wireless Toolkit includes a provisioning server that allows you to perform test installations of mobile games to an emulator device just as users will download the games online.

Gamer's Garage

> Provisioning is the process of verifying and installing a MIDlet to a Java-powered phone. Unfortunately, prior to MIDP 2.0 there was no standard approach to MIDlet provisioning, so it was up to each device manufacturer to provide their own over-the-air download and installation routine.

Using KToolbar

Throughout this lesson I've alluded several times to visual development environments and how they improve and enhance the process of designing and building MIDlets. KToolbar is by far the simplest of the visual development environments that currently support MIDlet development with J2ME. In fact, it is so simple that it doesn't even include an editor for editing source code. Instead, KToolbar focuses on the task of managing source code files and automating the build and test process. Using the KToolbar application, you can forego the command-line J2ME tools and perform the compile, verification, and emulation steps from a single environment. Figure 2.1 shows the KToolbar application with an open J2ME game project.

FIGURE 2.1
KToolbar provides a minimalist approach to visual J2ME game development.

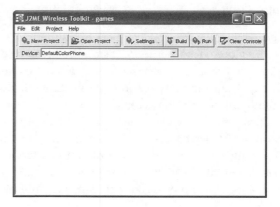

Although the KToolbar tool is admittedly a minimalist visual environment, the upside is that it is included free with the J2ME Wireless Toolkit. Just keep in mind that you'll need to find a suitable text editor (such as Notepad on Windows computers) for editing the source code files. On the other hand, if you already have a visual Java development environment, even if it doesn't support J2ME, you might still find it useful for editing J2ME source code files.

Managing MIDlet Game Projects

KToolbar provides a straightforward approach to managing MIDlet projects and build settings. When you create a new project in KToolbar, it is automatically created within the apps folder beneath the default J2ME Wireless Toolkit installation folder. So, for example, if the Wireless Toolkit is installed in a folder named WTK21, then all new projects will be created in WTK21\apps. To create a new project, click the New Project button on the toolbar. Figure 2.2 shows the New Project dialog box that prompts you for a project name and a MIDlet class name.

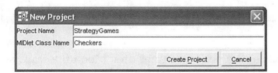

FIGURE 2.2
To create a new project in KToolbar, you simply provide the project name and MIDlet class name.

The project name specified in KToolbar is used to name the final JAR file that is installed onto a phone. Keep in mind that the project name might apply to an entire MIDlet suite, whereas the MIDlet class name identifies an individual MIDlet game within the suite. In most cases where there is only a single MIDlet in a project, you'll probably match the project name and the MIDlet class name.

To open an existing project in KToolbar, just click the Open Project button on the toolbar. The only projects displayed are those that have been created within the apps folder beneath the main J2ME Wireless Toolkit installation folder. Figure 2.3 shows the Open Project dialog box that allows you to select a project from within the apps folder.

FIGURE 2.3
Only projects created in the J2ME Wireless Toolkit apps folder are available for opening in KToolbar.

After a project is open in KToolbar, you can tweak its settings by clicking the Settings button on the toolbar. You are then presented with the Settings dialog box shown in Figure 2.4.

FIGURE 2.4
The Settings dialog
box in KToolbar
provides you plenty
of options for fine-
tuning a MIDlet
project.

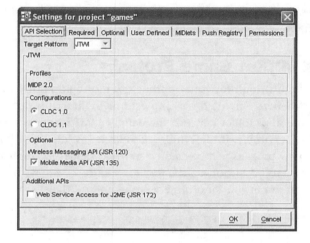

For now, the details of the project settings aren't too important because the defaults work fine in most cases. Possibly the only thing worth paying attention to at the moment is the MIDlets tab, which shows the MIDlets that are part of the current project. Figure 2.5 shows how three different mobile game MIDlets are contained within the single games project.

The games project shown in the figure is included with the J2ME Wireless Toolkit, and includes two puzzle games and a worm game. Let's use KToolbar to compile and package up these games so we can test them out!

FIGURE 2.5
A project in
KToolbar can con-
sist of multiple
MIDlets, in which
case the project
represents a
MIDlet suite.

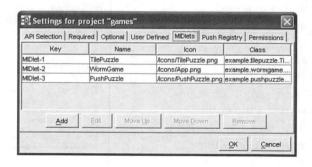

Building a Game MIDlet

You've now arrived at what could very well be the most difficult part of the chapter: compiling a complete example MIDlet game. In fact, you're going to compile all three of the example MIDlet games that are part of the games project in the standard J2ME Wireless Toolkit installation. I'm actually kidding about this process being difficult—just click the Build button on the toolbar to build the games project. Figure 2.6 shows the build process taking place in KToolbar.

Although the build process involves several discrete steps, they often take place so fast that it's hard to distinguish between them; the figure shows the compile part of the MIDlet build sequence. You now have a verified, compiled, and packaged MIDlet suite of games ready to install and run on a real mobile phone or test in the J2ME emulator.

Testing a Game MIDlet

The J2ME emulator plays an invaluable role in testing MIDlet games during development. The reason for using an emulator has to do with the practical difficulties of downloading code onto a physical device over and over as you diagnose bugs and make changes. It is much more effective and efficient to test MIDlet games in a desktop environment, and resort to testing on a physical device only in the later development stages.

FIGURE 2.7
The default phone in the J2ME emulator has a multi-colored faceplate and a screen size of 180×210.

FIGURE 2.8
The example Worm game is a good example of a basic MIDlet game.

To use KToolbar to run a MIDlet in the J2ME emulator, just click the Run button in the toolbar. Figure 2.7 shows the example games MIDlet suite as it first appears in the J2ME emulator.

As Figure 2.7 reveals, the J2ME emulator displays an image of a phone with the MIDlet suite visible in the screen area. To run one of the MIDlet games, just click the up and down arrow keys on the phone with the mouse, and then click the Launch key; you may also use the arrow keys and Enter (Return) key on the keyboard. Figure 2.8 shows the Worm game as it executes within the emulator with the default color phone configuration.

The Worm example game is a variation on the classic Snake game that you learned about in the previous chapter. Take some time playing the game and experimenting with the emulator. When you're finished and you close the emulator window, try out one of the other device configurations offered by KToolbar in the drop-down Device list. Figure 2.9 shows the PushPuzzle example game as it is being emulated in the Qwerty device configuration.

As you can see, the emulator is quite flexible in the types of mobile devices it allows you to use as the basis for MIDlet game testing.

As with all the J2ME development tools, the emulator can be run directly from a command prompt. However, KToolbar makes it considerably easier to use the emulator and keeps you from having to bother with the command-line approach.

Although you may be tempted to click directly on the screen of the emulator phone to make selections, keep in mind that you must control the phone entirely through its keys via mouse clicks and key presses.

Gamer's Garage

FIGURE 2.9
The Qwerty device configuration allows you to emulate games on a device that mimics a mobile phone with a full keyboard.

If you'd like to test the example games on a real mobile phone, you'll need to refer to the documentation for your phone. Without performing the setup required for over-the-air provisioning, which would be a bit of a distraction at this stage of the book, you may be able to quickly download the MIDlets to your phone with a serial/USB cable or a wireless Bluetooth connection. Again, it depends entirely on your specific phone.

Gamer's Garage

The J2ME Emulator and Physical Devices

The J2ME Wireless Toolkit is designed as an all-purpose J2ME development tool suite that is geared toward a wide range of wireless mobile devices. For this reason, you won't find any mention of a specific manufacturer's name or mobile phone model in the J2ME Wireless Toolkit. Instead, general device types are supported. More specifically, the J2ME Wireless Toolkit includes emulation support for the following generic devices:

- ▶ Default gray phone
- ▶ Default color phone
- ▶ Media control skin
- ▶ Qwerty device

The first two default devices are the most important for emulating games on mobile phones, although you might find a reason to try a game out on the other devices. Table 2.1 lists the specific attributes of each of these devices.

TABLE 2.1   Mobile Devices Supported in the J2ME Wireless Toolkit

Device Name	Screen Size	Colors	Key Set
Default gray phone	180×208	256 grayscale	ITU-T
Default color phone	180×208	256 colors	ITU-T
Media control skin	180×208	256 colors	ITU-T
Qwerty device	640×240	256 colors	QWERTY

The table reveals how much variance is possible in J2ME devices. Notice that the phones and media control skin have vertically oriented screens, whereas the Qwerty device has a horizontal screen. Also, the gray phone supports 256 shades of gray, whereas the remaining devices support 256 colors. The key sets on the devices vary as well. The Qwerty device includes a full QWERTY key set similar to your computer keyboard—this corresponds to larger mobile devices that include keyboards, such as those produced by Research In Motion (RIM). The ITU-T key set is based upon the familiar keypad commonly found on most mobile phones in use today.

Although the general devices in the J2ME Wireless Toolkit are valuable for testing MIDlet games without regard for specific brands and models of devices, you will likely need to specifically target a popular phone for testing. In this case, you'll need to customize the emulator for the device. The simplest way to accomplish this is to use the J2ME toolkit made available by the manufacturer of the device in question. As an example, Motorola and Nokia J2ME toolkits are available with emulation devices for all their major Java-powered phones. By testing a MIDlet game on these devices within the J2ME emulator, you can more accurately approximate how the MIDlet will function on the real device—particularly how it will look on the device display.

Summary

Before digging into the details of the J2ME Wireless Toolkit, this chapter presented you with general game design ideas. Although not etched in stone, these ideas and suggestions serve as good guidelines when you start working out your masterpiece. The chapter then shifted its focus to the J2ME Wireless Toolkit, and the specific tools within it that give you the power to assemble mobile Java games.

You found out that the J2ME emulator is a critical part of J2ME development because it enables you to test MIDlet games on your desktop computer without a physical mobile phone. You certainly need to test all your games on real phones, but the emulator dramatically speeds up the development process by allowing you to test on a real device only when absolutely necessary. You learned about the standard J2ME emulator that ships with the J2ME Wireless Toolkit, as well as how it can be extended with specific emulation devices that match real phones.

Field Trip

Take some time to tinker with the J2ME emulator and the three games that are included with the J2ME Wireless Toolkit. If you're feeling particularly adventurous, take an online stroll to the website of a mobile phone manufacturer such as Motorola or Nokia, and download a J2ME SDK specific to one of their phones. You'll be able to use an emulation device for a production phone, which is a little more interesting than the generic phone profiles included in the base J2ME Wireless Toolkit.

CHAPTER 3

Constructing a Mobile Game Skeleton

Arcade Archive

Released by Namco in 1979, Galaxian was the first major space shooter to serve as a legitimate successor to Space Invaders. Galaxian is also the predecessor to Galaga, which is perhaps the most successful space shooter game of all time. In Galaxian, as in most games of the genre, you control a space ship that can move horizontally along the bottom of the screen and fire vertically at attacking aliens. Galaxian holds a special place in video game history because it is the first arcade game to use true RGB (Red Green Blue) color throughout all its graphics.

Java development of any kind revolves around the Java programming language and a set of APIs that provide support for application services such as GUI components, networking, and input/output. Mobile Java game development is no different in that it relies on a set of APIs for supporting the various pieces of functionality required for MIDlet games that must run in a wireless mobile environment. Understanding these APIs and what they have to offer is critical to becoming a mobile Java game developer. This chapter introduces you to the mobile Java APIs and guides you through the creation of a mobile game skeleton. This skeleton MIDlet serves as a template for you to reuse as you continue to develop games throughout the book.

In this chapter, you'll learn

- ▶ How J2ME programming is broken down into a few different APIs
- ▶ About the internal structure of MIDlets
- ▶ How to build a MIDlet from scratch that displays important game-related information about a mobile phone
- ▶ Prepare a MIDlet for distribution

Exploring the J2ME APIs

Before getting into the coding details of your first mobile phone program, you need a quick primer on the APIs that go into building MIDlets. The MIDP (Mobile Information Device Profile) specification is a set of rules that describe the capabilities and limitations of Java with respect to mobile devices. A significant aspect of these capabilities and limitations is the standard set of classes and interfaces that are available for MIDlet programming. Although the MIDP specification provides a detailed description of the API available for MIDlet development, an additional API is provided by the CLDC (Connected Limited Device Configuration). The MIDP API builds on the CLDC API to provide classes and interfaces that are more specific to mobile information devices. You can think of the CLDC as providing a general Java API for networked devices, whereas the MIDP goes a step further in providing a more detailed API that fills in the specifics left out of the CLDC API for compact wireless devices such as phones and pagers.

FIGURE 3.1
A MIDlet must make calls to the CLDC and MIDP APIs to carry out most of its functions.

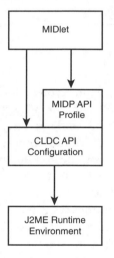

Why should you care about any of these specifications and APIs? The CLDC and MIDP specifications are important because they explicitly define what classes and interfaces can be used to build MIDlets. Mobile devices are nimble machines that don't have the luxury of megabytes of memory to pack full of application overhead. Knowing this, Sun had to figure out a way to provide a core set of functionality with a useful feature set but without bloating the runtime requirements of mobile devices. Their answer is the two-tier approach that consists of a configuration layered with a more detailed profile. The CLDC API describes the core classes and interfaces required by a general network device, whereas the MIDP API adds the classes and interfaces required by a mobile information device such as a mobile phone. Figure 3.1 shows the relationship between a MIDlet and the respective CLDC and MIDP APIs.

Keep in mind that although the CLDC and MIDP APIs have been carefully thought out to trade off functionality against the memory and resource constraints of mobile devices, they will inevitably come up short in certain situations.

This means that you will sometimes have to work a little harder as a MIDlet game developer because you don't have as rich an API to work with as you would if you were doing traditional game programming.

The CLDC API

The majority of the classes in the CLDC API are directly included from the standard J2SE API. These classes and interfaces are practically identical to those that you may be familiar with from traditional Java programming. This portion of the CLDC API is located in packages with familiar J2SE names such as `java.lang` and `java.util`. In addition to the classes and interfaces that are borrowed directly from the J2SE API, a few interfaces are unique to the CLDC API. These interfaces deal primarily with networking, which is an area of the J2SE API that is particularly difficult to scale down for the needs of network devices.

The CLDC defines a set of interfaces that facilitate generic networking, and leaves the specifics of implementing these interfaces to the MIDP API. So the CLDC API is logically divided into two parts:

▶ A series of packages that serve as a subset of the J2SE API

▶ A set of generic networking interfaces

The bulk of the classes and interfaces in the CLDC API are inherited directly from the J2SE API. J2ME requires that any classes or interfaces inherited directly from J2SE must not be changed in any way, which means that the methods and fields are identical to the versions found in J2SE. This makes it easier to learn how to program in J2ME, and it also makes Java code more portable between J2SE and J2ME.

Where the CLDC veers away from the J2SE API is in its support for networking, which is outlined in a generic network framework known as the Generic Connection Framework (GCF). The purpose of the GCF is to define a general network architecture that supports networked I/O and is extremely flexible, and is therefore extensible. The GCF is designed as a functional subset of the J2SE networking classes, which means that features described in the GCF are available in J2SE. The GCF consists primarily of a set of connection interfaces, along with a `Connector` class that is used to establish the different connections. Both the `Connector` class and the connection interfaces are located in the `javax.microedition.io` package. You learn much more about network mobile game programming in Chapter 14, "Mobile Game Networking Essentials."

The MIDP API

A device profile picks up where a configuration leaves off by providing detailed functionality to carry out important tasks on a given type of device. In the case of the Mobile Information Device Profile (MIDP), the type of device is a wireless mobile device such as a mobile phone or pager. It is therefore the job of the MIDP API to take the CLDC API and build on top of it the necessary classes and interfaces that make it possible to build compelling MIDlets such as games.

Similar to the CLDC API, the MIDP API can be divided into two parts:

► Two classes that are inherited directly from the J2SE API

► A series of packages that include classes and interfaces unique to MIDP development

Like the CLDC API, the MIDP API borrows from the standard J2SE API. Not surprisingly, the bulk of the MIDP API is new classes and interfaces designed specifically for use in MIDlet programming. Although these classes and interfaces can play a similar role as some of the classes and interfaces in the J2SE API, they are entirely unique to the MIDP API and therefore are carefully designed to solve MIDlet-specific problems. This portion of the MIDP API is divided among several packages, all of which are prefixed with the javax.microedition name:

► javax.microedition.midlet

► javax.microedition.lcdui

► javax.microedition.lcdui.game

► javax.microedition.media

► javax.microedition.media.control

► javax.microedition.io

► javax.microedition.pki

► javax.microedition.rms

The javax.microedition.midlet package is the central package in the MIDlet API, and contains only one class: the MIDlet class. The MIDlet class provides the basic functional overhead required of a MIDP application (MIDlet) that can execute on a mobile device. You will continue to learn more about the MIDlet class as you progress through the book and construct more complex MIDlet examples and games.

The `javax.microedition.lcdui` and `javax.microedition.lcdui.game` packages include classes and interfaces that support GUI components specially suited for the small screens found in mobile devices. Additionally, there are classes and interfaces that specifically target the development of mobile games. Unique features such as sprite animation and layer management make these packages extremely valuable for mobile game programming. You begin learning about some of the classes in these packages later in this chapter, and continue to dig deeper into them throughout the book.

Gamer's Garage

If you happen to have used J2ME before, you'll be interested to know that the `javax.microedition.lcdui.game` package is entirely new to MIDP 2.0. This is why MIDP 2.0 represents a significant leap forward in making J2ME a viable mobile game technology.

The `javax.microedition.media` and `javax.microedition.media.control` packages include classes and interfaces for managing audio within a MIDlet. These packages represent the MIDP 2.0 Media API, which is a subset of the larger Mobile Media API; the full Mobile Media API supports a wide range of media objects such as images, sounds, music, and videos. The media features in the MIDP 2.0 Media API are limited to tone generation and the playback of digital audio effects via wave files. You find out the specifics of playing sound in MIDlet games in Chapter 8, "Making Noise with Tones."

You learned earlier that the CLDC lays the groundwork for networking and I/O with the Generic Connection Framework (GCF). The MIDP API builds on this support with the `javax.microedition.io` package, which includes several interfaces and classes for establishing wireless network connections and shuttling data back and forth across them. The `javax.microedition.pki` package is used in concert with the `javax.microedition.io` package to provide secure network communications. You learn how to carry out game basic networking tasks in Chapter 14, "Mobile Game Networking Essentials."

Because mobile phones don't have hard drives or any tangible file system (yet), you probably won't rely on files to store away persistent MIDlet data. Instead, the MIDP API describes an entirely new approach to store and retrieve persistent MIDlet data: the Record Management System (RMS). The MIDP RMS provides a simple record-based database API for persistently storing data such as high score lists and saved game data. The classes and interfaces that comprise the RMS are all located in the `javax.microedition.rms` package.

Understanding MIDlets

Sun Microsystems uses the "let" suffix to name several different types of programs that fall within the Java technology umbrella. Applets, servlets, spotlets, and now MIDlets are some of these. Sun might have even tried to use the term "sniglets" had comedian Rich Hall not already worn it out on the HBO television show *Not Necessarily the News* in the 1980s. MIDlets are programs that are developed with the J2ME APIs, and that are used in a mobile computing environment. MIDlets require a special runtime environment to run. This environment primarily consists of an application manager that provides a means of selecting and launching MIDlets on a mobile device. The application manager for a MIDlet is responsible for establishing a frame window for the MIDlet.

Inside a MIDlet

It probably won't come as too much of a surprise that every MIDlet must derive from a standard class that is part of the MIDP API. This class is located in the `javax.microedition.midlet` package, and is named `MIDlet`. Although the `MIDlet` class defines several methods, three are particularly important to developing your own MIDlets:

- ▶ `startApp()`—Starts a MIDlet
- ▶ `pauseApp()`—Pauses a MIDlet
- ▶ `destroyApp()`—Destroys a MIDlet

To better understand how these methods impact a MIDlet, it's important to clarify that a MIDlet has three distinct states that determine how it functions: Active, Paused, and Destroyed. These states correspond directly with the three methods, which are usually called directly by the runtime environment's application manager; in some cases you can call them yourself, particularly the `destroyApp()` method. These methods are collectively referred to as *life cycle methods* because they control the life cycle of a MIDlet. They are ultimately what allow the application manager to manage multiple MIDlets and provide each of them with shared access to device resources.

MIDlet Life Cycle

The life cycle of a MIDlet is spent between the three states you just learned about. In a typical MIDlet, most of the time is spent in the Active or Paused states, and then when the MIDlet closes it enters the Destroyed state until it is completely removed from memory. You override the relevant MIDlet life cycle methods in most game MIDlets because it is important to allocate and free resources based on the state of the MIDlet. For example, when a game MIDlet starts, you will probably need to create objects and/or load data. When the MIDlet pauses, it will probably make sense to free up some resources, close any network connections, and pause game music. And finally, upon destruction it is important to free up any resources you've allocated, as well as to save any pertinent game data.

Keep in mind that a MIDlet can enter and exit the Active and Paused states several times throughout its lifetime. However, after a MIDlet enters the Destroyed state it cannot return. In this regard, an individual game MIDlet only has one life to live.

MIDlet Commands

In addition to overriding the life cycle methods, most MIDlets implement the commandAction() method, an event response method defined in the javax.microedition.lcdui.CommandListener interface. Commands are used to control game MIDlets and initiate actions such as pausing a game, saving game data, tweaking game settings, and quitting a game. MIDlet commands are accessible through a soft button or a menu, and must be handled by the commandAction() method.

Soft buttons are special buttons located near the screen on a mobile phone that are used to issue commands specific to a particular MIDlet. Clicking a soft button initiates the command on the screen just above the button. Buttons used to control game play are handled in a different manner than soft button commands, as you learn in Chapter 6, "Handling Mobile User Input."

Gamer's Garage

The Display, Screens, and Canvases

One other important MIDlet concept worth tackling at this point is the Display class, which represents the display manager for a device. The Display class is defined in the javax.microedition.lcdui package, along with other GUI classes, and is responsible for managing the display and user input for the device.

You don't ever create a `Display` object; you typically obtain a reference to the `Display` object in the `startApp()` method for a game MIDlet, and then use it to establish the game screen and user interface. There is exactly one instance of `Display` for each MIDlet that is executing on a device.

Another important display-related class is `javax.microedition.lcdui.Canvas`, which represents an abstract drawing surface the size of the device screen. A canvas is used to perform direct graphics operations such as drawing lines and curves or displaying images. As you might suspect, canvases form the basis for game screens. In fact, there is a special `javax.microedition.lcdui.game.GameCanvas` class devoted solely to drawing efficient graphics for games. The `GameCanvas` class differs from the `Canvas` class in that it supports a highly efficient means of drawing animated graphics, which are often used in games.

Gamer's Garage

If you create a game that has customizable settings or otherwise needs to retrieve information from the user, you probably need to use the `javax.microedition.lcdui.Screen` class. A *screen* is a generic MIDlet GUI component that serves as a base class for other important components. The significance of screens is that they represent an entire screen of information; only one screen can be displayed at a time. You can think of multiple screens as a stack of cards that you can flip through. Most MIDlets utilize subclasses of the Screen class such as `javax.microedition.lcdui.Form`, `javax.microedition.lcdui.TextBox`, or `javax.microedition.lcdui.List` because they provide more specific functionality. Screens can be used with `Canvas` objects to provide a comprehensive GUI for a game MIDlet. You can't show a screen and a canvas at the same time, but you can alternate between the two.

The Basics of MIDlet Development

To get started developing MIDlets, you first need to install the J2ME Wireless Toolkit, which is available on the accompanying CD-ROM. You can also use a third-party mobile Java development tool if you want to target a specific mobile phone, but you can stick with the J2ME Wireless Toolkit for now if you want to stick with emulating Java-powered phones on your PC.

To take a MIDlet game from concept to reality, you need to take the following steps:

1. Develop the source code files.

2. Compile the source code files into bytecode classes.

3. Preverify the bytecode classes.

4. Package the bytecode classes into a JAR (Java archive) file with any additional resources and a manifest file (more on this in a moment).

5. Develop a JAD (application descriptor) file to accompany the JAR file.

6. Test and debug the MIDlet.

Step 1 is carried out with a simple text editor. If you don't have a programming text editor, you can use a simple editor such as Notepad in Windows. Step 2 involves using the standard Java compiler to compile the source code files for your MIDlet. In step 3 you are required to preverify the compiled bytecode classes with a special preverification tool. Step 4 involves using the Java archive (JAR) tool to compress the MIDlet source code files, resources, and manifest file into a JAR file. Step 5 requires you to create a special application descriptor file, which is a text file containing information about your MIDlet. And finally, in step 6 you get to enjoy your hard work and test out the MIDlet with the J2ME emulator.

Although you could carry out each of these individual development steps with the command-line tools included in the J2ME Wireless Toolkit, you saw in the previous chapter how Sun's KToolbar visual tool simplifies the build/test process into a couple of mouse clicks.

Building the Skeleton Example Program

Although I'd love to lead you through the creation of a real-time 3D multiplayer game as your first MIDlet game, I don't think it would serve as a best first impression of how MIDlets are structured and coded because of the overwhelming complexity. Instead, you learn here how to build a very simple MIDlet called Skeleton that displays information about the mobile phone as lines of text onscreen. Because this information includes important device parameters such as the game screen size and color depth, you'll find it useful in double checking the parameters of real phones.

In building the Skeleton MIDlet, you go through the same sequence of steps outlined in the previous section. This process will be very similar for every MIDlet game that you develop. Following are the steps involved in creating the Skeleton MIDlet:

1. Code the MIDlet.
2. Compile the MIDlet.
3. Preverify the MIDlet.

4. Package the MIDlet.
5. Test the MIDlet.

The next few sections tackle each of these steps in succession, culminating in the completion of your first J2ME MIDlet.

Writing the Program Code

In this section you assemble the code for the Skeleton MIDlet a section at a time, with the complete source code listing appearing at the end. The first code for your MIDlet is the code that imports a couple of important J2ME packages. Although you can certainly avoid importing any packages and reference every J2ME class and interface with its fully qualified name (javax.microedition.midlet.MIDlet, for example), this can be quite cumbersome and ultimately makes the code hard to read. So the first two lines of your MIDlet import the two primary packages associated with MIDlet development:

```
import javax.microedition.midlet.*;
import javax.microedition.lcdui.*;
```

Construction Cue

Most Java programmers frown on importing entire packages via the * wildcard because it doesn't reveal much about what specific classes you're importing. However, it is a quick and easy way to import all the classes in a package, and for the purposes of this book, I went the easy route to keep the code as simple as possible. Feel free to import classes one at a time in your own code to make your code more explicit.

The javax.microedition.midlet package includes support for the MIDlet class itself, whereas the javax.microedition.lcdui package includes support for the GUI classes and interfaces that are used to construct MIDlet GUIs, such as the Display class. With those two packages imported, you're ready to declare the SkeletonMIDlet class, which is derived from MIDlet:

```
public class SkeletonMIDlet extends MIDlet implements CommandListener {
```

The fact that SkeletonMIDlet extends MIDlet is no surprise, but the implementation of the CommandListener interface might seem a little strange. This interface is necessary to create an Exit command that allows the user to exit the MIDlet. More specifically, the CommandListener interface is implemented so that the MIDlet can respond to command events.

The only member variable in the SkeletonMIDlet class is an SCanvas object that represents the main screen:

```
private SCanvas canvas;
```

The SCanvas class type is a custom MIDlet-specific canvas class you see in a moment that is derived from Canvas. The canvas is initialized in the startApp() method, which follows:

```
public void startApp() {
  if (canvas == null) {
    canvas = new SCanvas(Display.getDisplay(this));
    Command exitCommand = new Command("Exit", Command.EXIT, 0);
    canvas.addCommand(exitCommand);
    canvas.setCommandListener(this);
  }

  // Start up the canvas
  canvas.start();
}
```

The Exit command is created and added to the canvas so that the canvas can respond to it.

The startApp() method is called whenever the MIDlet enters the Active state, and the first step in the method is to create a canvas. The Display object for the MIDlet is obtained and passed into the canvas as part of its creation. The Exit command is then created when you pass three arguments to the Command constructor that specify the name of the command, its type, and its priority. The name of the command is user defined and appears above one of a phone's soft buttons or on a menu, depending on its priority and how many buttons are available. The command type must be one of several built-in Command constants such as EXIT, OK, or CANCEL.

The command is added to the canvas so that it becomes active. It is still necessary to designate a command listener to receive and process command events. You accomplish this by calling the setCommandListener() method and passing this, which makes the MIDlet class (SkeletonMIDlet) the command listener. That's perfect because earlier you made the class implement the CommandListener interface.

The priority of a command is used to determine the placement of the command for user access. This is necessary because most devices have limited buttons available for MIDlet-specific usage. Therefore, only the most important commands are mapped to these soft buttons. Other commands are still available, but only from menus within the MIDlet that aren't as easily accessible as a soft button. The priority value of a command decreases with the level of importance; that is, a value of 1 is assigned to a command with the highest priority. In the Skeleton example, the Exit command is given a priority of 2, which means that it has a high priority. Of course, priority values are entirely relative, and because no other commands are in this example the value doesn't matter.

Construction Cue

The Exit command for the Skeleton MIDlet is handled in the commandAction() method, which follows:

```
public void commandAction(Command c, Displayable s) {
  if (c.getCommandType() == Command.EXIT) {
    destroyApp(true);
    notifyDestroyed();
  }
}
```

The two arguments passed into the `commandAction()` method are the command and the screen on which the command was generated. Only the command is of interest in this particular example. The Command object is compared with the `Command.EXIT` member constant to see whether the `Exit` command is indeed the command being handled. If so, the `destroyApp()` method is called to destroy the MIDlet. The `true` argument to this method indicates that the destruction is unconditional, which means that the MIDlet is destroyed even if some error or exception occurs during the destruction process. The `notifyDestroyed()` method is called afterward to notify the application manager that the MIDlet has entered the Destroyed state.

The Skeleton MIDlet doesn't have any use for the `pauseApp()` and `destroyApp()` methods, but you must provide empty implementations for them nonetheless:

```
public void pauseApp() {}
public void destroyApp(boolean unconditional) {}
```

Although you've seen the bits and pieces separately, the complete code for the `SkeletonMIDlet.java` source code file is shown in Listing 3.1.

LISTING 3.1　The Source Code for the `SkeletonMIDlet` Class Is Located in SkeletonMIDlet.java

```java
import javax.microedition.midlet.*;
import javax.microedition.lcdui.*;

public class SkeletonMIDlet extends MIDlet implements CommandListener {
  private SCanvas canvas;

  public void startApp() {
    if (canvas == null) {
      canvas = new SCanvas(Display.getDisplay(this));
      Command exitCommand = new Command("Exit", Command.EXIT, 0);
      canvas.addCommand(exitCommand);
      canvas.setCommandListener(this);
    }

    // Start up the canvas
    canvas.start();
  }

  public void pauseApp() {}

  public void destroyApp(boolean unconditional) {}

  public void commandAction(Command c, Displayable s) {
    if (c.getCommandType() == Command.EXIT) {
      destroyApp(true);
      notifyDestroyed();
    }
  }
}
```

You don't use these methods for anything in this example, but you must provide empty implementations to satisfy the MIDlet class.

To be thorough, you need to call the destroyApp() method, although notifyDestroyed() is what is really ending the MIDlet.

The remaining code for the Skeleton MIDlet example is associated with the SCanvas class, which is shown in Listing 3.2.

LISTING 3.2   The SCanvas Class Serves as a Customized Canvas for the Skeleton MIDlet

```
import javax.microedition.lcdui.*;

public class SCanvas extends Canvas {
  private Display display;

  public SCanvas(Display d) {
    super();
    display = d;
  }

  void start() {
    display.setCurrent(this);
    repaint();
  }

  public void paint(Graphics g) {
    // Clear the canvas
    g.setColor(0, 0, 0);         // black
    g.fillRect(0, 0, getWidth(), getHeight());
    g.setColor(255, 255, 255);   // white

    // Draw the available screen size
    int y = 0;
    String screenSize = "Screen size: " + Integer.toString(getWidth())
 + " x " +
      Integer.toString(getHeight());
    g.drawString(screenSize, 0, y, Graphics.TOP | Graphics.LEFT);

    // Draw the number of available colors
    y += Font.getDefaultFont().getHeight();
    String numColors = "# of colors: " +
Integer.toString(display.numColors());
    g.drawString(numColors, 0, y, Graphics.TOP | Graphics.LEFT);

    // Draw the number of available alpha levels
    y += Font.getDefaultFont().getHeight();
    String numAlphas = "# of alphas: " +
      Integer.toString(display.numAlphaLevels());
    g.drawString(numAlphas, 0, y, Graphics.TOP | Graphics.LEFT);

    // Draw the amount of total and free memory
    Runtime runtime = Runtime.getRuntime();
    y += Font.getDefaultFont().getHeight();
    String totalMem = "Total memory: " +
      Long.toString(runtime.totalMemory() / 1024) + "KB";
    g.drawString(totalMem, 0, y, Graphics.TOP | Graphics.LEFT);
    y += Font.getDefaultFont().getHeight();
    String freeMem = "Free memory: " + Long.toString(runtime.freeMemory()
 / 1024) + "KB";
    g.drawString(freeMem, 0, y, Graphics.TOP | Graphics.LEFT);
  }
}
```

This line of code is extremely important because it sets this canvas as the current canvas for the MIDlet.

It's important to clear the background before you begin drawing content.

The SCanvas class is derived from the Canvas class, and accepts a Display object as the only parameter to its constructor. The constructor simply sets the display member variable so that the MIDlet display is accessible throughout the canvas code. The start() method calls the setCurrent() method on the Display object to set the canvas as the current screen. It's possible to have multiple screens in a MIDlet, in which case you can use the setCurrent() method to switch between them. The start() method calls repaint() to force a paint of the canvas so that it is initially painted properly.

Construction Cue

Although the SCanvas class in the Skeleton MIDlet is derived from Canvas, most of the examples throughout the book actually use canvas classes derived from GameCanvas, which provides game-specific features such as double-buffered graphics and efficient key handling. These features aren't necessary in the Skeleton example.

The painting of the canvas represents the majority of the code in the Skeleton MIDlet, and is handled by the paint() method. It isn't important for you to understand the details of this graphics code right now—the next chapter tackles mobile game graphics in detail. I will give you a quick summary, however, just in case you want to try and follow along as a look-ahead to the next chapter.

The method begins by clearing the canvas with a solid color fill in black. The paint color is then changed to white to draw the text. The screen size is obtained first, and then drawn, centered horizontally near the top of the screen. The number of available colors and alpha levels are obtained next and displayed below the screen size. Finally, the amounts of total and free memory are determined, and displayed last.

Gamer's Garage

The number of alpha levels supported by a phone determine how much control you have over transparent areas in graphical images. For example, all phones support at least two alpha levels, which correspond to a pixel being either fully opaque or fully transparent. Some phones support as many as 256 alpha levels, which allow you to create graphics with partial transparency, where you can see through an object in varying amounts.

Now that the source code is complete, you're almost ready to build and test the Skeleton MIDlet. But first you need to create a couple of important support files that are required for packaging the MIDlet for distribution.

Preparing the MIDlet for Distribution

Packaging a MIDlet game for distribution involves compressing the various files used by the MIDlet into an archive known as a JAR file. In addition to compressing the preverified class files for a MIDlet into a JAR file, you must also include in the JAR file any resources associated with the MIDlet, as well as a manifest file that describes the contents of the JAR file.

In the case of the Skeleton MIDlet, the only resource is an icon that is displayed next to the MIDlet name on a device. I explain about the icon in just a moment. For now, let's focus on the *manifest file*. The manifest file is a special text file that contains a listing of MIDlet properties and their respective values. This information is very important because it identifies the name, icon, and classname of each MIDlet in a JAR file, as well as the specific CLDC and MIDP version targeted by the MIDlets in the JAR file. Remember that multiple MIDlets can be stored in a single JAR file, in which case the collection is known as a MIDlet suite.

All the examples throughout the book target MIDP 2.0 and CLDC 1.0. Although some mobile phones support CLDC 2.0, CLDC 1.0 is sufficient for most game programming. However, MIDP 2.0 is extremely important because game features were added to the MIDP API as of version 2.0.

Construction Cue

The manifest file for a MIDlet suite must be named `Manifest.mf`, and must be placed in the JAR file with the MIDlet classes and resources. Following is the code for the Manifest file associated with the Skeleton MIDlet:

```
MIDlet-1: Skeleton, /icons/Skeleton_icon.png, SkeletonMIDlet
MIDlet-Name: Skeleton
MIDlet-Description: Skeleton Example MIDlet
MIDlet-Vendor: Stalefish Labs
MIDlet-Version: 1.0
MicroEdition-Configuration: CLDC-1.0
MicroEdition-Profile: MIDP-2.0
```

The first entry in the manifest file is by far the most important because it specifies the name of the MIDlet, along with its icon file and its executable class name. You might notice that the property is named `MIDlet-1`; if you were to include additional MIDlets in this MIDlet suite, you would reference them as `MIDlet-2`, `MIDlet-3`, and so on. The `MIDlet-Name`, `MIDlet-Description`, `MIDlet-Vendor`, and `MIDlet-Version` properties all refer to the MIDlet suite as a whole. However, in this case the Skeleton MIDlet is the only MIDlet in the suite, so it's okay to refer to the entire suite as Skeleton. The last two properties identify the versions of the configuration and profile that the MIDlet suite targets, which in this case are CLDC 1.0 and MIDP 2.0.

Earlier I mentioned that you must include any resources in a JAR file along with the MIDlet classes and the manifest file. At the very least a MIDlet will have an icon as a resource. This icon is simply a 12×12 pixel image that is stored in the PNG image format. It can be a color or black-and-white image, depending on whether or not the mobile phone you're targeting has a color screen. I created a small picture of a skull to use as the Skeleton icon, and stored it in a file called Skeleton_icon.png.

One small caveat in regard to the icon for a MIDlet is that it must be stored in a folder named icons within the MIDlet JAR file. Similar to ZIP files, JAR files enable you to store files within folders inside of the archive. To place a file in such a folder inside a JAR file, you must reference it from a subfolder when you add it to the JAR file. It is somewhat standard convention to place MIDlet resources in a folder named res beneath the folder where the source code files are located. Knowing this, a simple solution for the icon is to place it in an icons folder located beneath the res folder.

FIGURE 3.2
Adhering to a simple folder structure for your MIDlet source files helps keep things organized.

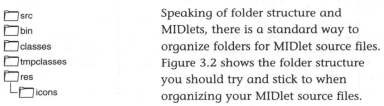

Speaking of folder structure and MIDlets, there is a standard way to organize folders for MIDlet source files. Figure 3.2 shows the folder structure you should try and stick to when organizing your MIDlet source files.

The different folders in the figure are used to store the following:

- src—Java source code files
- bin—Manifest file, JAD file, and JAR file
- classes—Compiled Java bytecode files
- tmpclasses—Compiled and verified Java bytecode files
- res—Resource files other than icons (images, sounds, and so on)
- res/icons—Icon files

Construction Cue

> The example MIDlets included in the J2ME Wireless Toolkit, including the example games you saw in the previous chapter, adhere to this same folder structure.

In addition to the manifest file that resides in the JAR file for a MIDlet, an additional application descriptor file is required for distributing a MIDlet. An *application descriptor* file, or JAD file, contains information similar to that found in a manifest file. The JAD file is used by the Java emulator when you test a MIDlet suite. Following is the JAD file for the Skeleton MIDlet:

```
MIDlet-1: Skeleton, /icons/Skeleton_icon.png, SkeletonMIDlet
MIDlet-Name: Skeleton
MIDlet-Description: Skeleton Example MIDlet
MIDlet-Vendor: Stalefish Labs
MIDlet-Version: 1.0
MicroEdition-Configuration: CLDC-1.0
MicroEdition-Profile: MIDP-2.0
MIDlet-Jar-Size: 2706
MIDlet-Jar-URL: Skeleton.jar
```

This is your own version number for the MIDlet, which in this case means Skeleton 1.0.

If this size (in bytes) doesn't match the exact size of the JAR file, the MIDlet won't run.

With the exception of the last two entries, the JAD file contains information with which you are already quite familiar. The last two entries specify the size of the JAR file (in bytes) for the MIDlet and the name of the JAR file. It is important that you update the size of the JAR file any time you repackage the MIDlet because the size is likely to change each time you rebuild the MIDlet.

Building and Testing the Finished Product

The previous chapter introduced you to the KToolbar visual development tool that allows you to build and run MIDlets with very little effort. To build the Skeleton MIDlet with KToolbar, you must first copy the entire Skeleton MIDlet folder to the apps folder beneath the J2ME Wireless Toolkit installation folder. After the Skeleton folder has been copied, you can open the Skeleton project from within KToolbar by clicking the Open Project button on the toolbar.

After the project opens, just click the Build button on the toolbar to build the Skeleton MIDlet. After the project is built, click the Run button on the toolbar to run it in the J2ME emulator. Figure 3.3 shows the Skeleton MIDlet available to be run within the emulator.

FIGURE 3.3
The Skeleton MIDlet is made available for running within the application manager of the J2ME emulator.

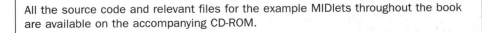

FIGURE 3.4
The Skeleton MIDlet displays information about the mobile phone such as the screen size and number of available colors.

Because Skeleton is the only MIDlet in the MIDlet suite, it is already highlighted and ready to be launched. To run it, click the Action button on the device keypad, which appears between the arrow keys, or the Launch soft button; you can also press Enter on your computer keyboard. Figure 3.4 shows the Skeleton MIDlet executing in the emulator.

To exit the Skeleton MIDlet, click the soft button beneath the word *Exit*. This invokes the Exit command and results in the MIDlet being destroyed. You can also exit a MIDlet by clicking the red End button, which is used on a real device to end a phone call.

Summary

In this chapter you finally got to see some Java code for a real MIDlet. Although the MIDlet wasn't quite a mobile game, you got to build it from scratch and go from source code files to a distributable JAR file. Before you dove into the coding, however, this chapter made sure to lay the groundwork for what exactly constitutes a MIDlet, as well as the general layout of the J2ME APIs. You also learned about the life cycle of a MIDlet and the methods in the MIDlet class that manage this life cycle.

This chapter introduced you to several classes and interfaces that are entirely unique to mobile phone programming in Java. The next chapter takes you an important step closer to mobile game development by digging into mobile game graphics.

Extreme Game Makeover

I want to start you off with some baby steps to get you comfortable with MIDlet development, so this first makeover is fairly simple. Follow these steps to change the icon in the Skeleton MIDlet:

1. Create a different icon for the Skeleton example MIDlet; make sure that it's in the PNG format, it's 12×12 pixels in size, and it's located in the res/icons folder.

2. Modify the manifest and JAD files so that the MIDlet uses the new icon file.

3. Rebuild the MIDlet and test it using KToolbar.

If all goes well, you'll see your replacement icon when the MIDlet is first displayed in the J2ME emulator.

PART II

Mobile Game Programming Essentials

CHAPTER 4

Mobile Game Graphics 101

Arcade Archive

Atari released Lunar Lander in 1979 as its first attempt at an arcade game with vector graphics. Although Lunar Lander wasn't nearly as successful as Asteroids, which followed soon after, it nevertheless holds an important place in video game history. Lunar Lander has been remade in a variety of different formats on a wide range of computer systems. What makes the original arcade version unique, however, is the massive thruster control used to carefully manage the thrust on the Eagle lander as it approaches the moon's surface.

A computer game consists of many different pieces, all of which must come together to form a unique entertainment experience for the player. By far the most important piece of any game is the graphics. Graphics are used to represent the characters and creatures in a game, as well as background worlds and other interesting objects that factor into the overall game design. Granted, some games have certainly done well because of factors outside of graphics, such as game play and sound quality, but those games are very rare. Besides, nowadays game players expect to see high-quality graphics just as we all expect to see high-quality visual effects in Hollywood movies. This is even true of mobile games that run on small mobile phone screens. So it's important to develop a solid understanding of graphics programming and how to use graphics wisely in your games.

In this chapter, you'll learn

▶ About the MIDP graphics coordinate system

▶ Why color is so important in MIDP graphics

▶ How to use the Graphics and Canvas classes

▶ How to construct graphical MIDlets that draw primitives, text, and images

Mobile Graphics Basics

With the exception of trivia and word games, even the simplest of mobile games rely on graphics to some degree. Fortunately, it isn't difficult at all to draw graphics in MIDlets. Before jumping into the details of how graphics work in J2ME and how they are applied to mobile games, however, it's important to establish some ground rules and gain an understanding of how computer graphics work in general. More specifically, you need to have a solid grasp on what a graphics coordinate system is, as well as how color is represented in computer graphics. The next couple of sections provide you with this knowledge, which you'll put to practical use a little later in the chapter.

Understanding the Graphics Coordinate System

All graphical computing systems use some sort of graphics coordinate system to specify how points are arranged in a window or on the screen. Graphics coordinate systems typically spell out the origin (0, 0) of the system, as well as the axes and directions of increasing value for each of the axes. If you're not a big math person, this simply means that a coordinate system describes how to pinpoint any location on the screen as an XY value. The traditional mathematical coordinate system familiar to most of us is shown in Figure 4.1.

FIGURE 4.1
The traditional XY coordinate system is commonly used in math.

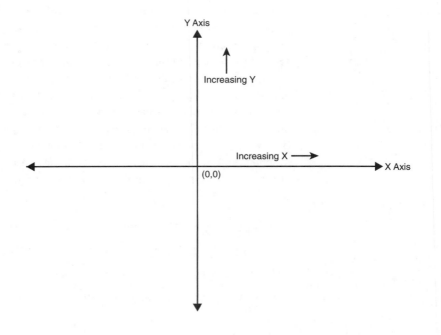

MIDP graphics rely on a similar coordinate system to specify how and where drawing operations take place. Because all drawing in a MIDlet takes place within the confines of a canvas, the MIDP coordinate system is applied relative to the canvas. The MIDP coordinate system has an origin that is located in the upper-left corner of the canvas, with positive X values increasing to the right and positive Y values increasing down. All values in the MIDP coordinate system are positive integers. Figure 4.2 shows how this coordinate system looks.

The canvas area used to draw graphics in a MIDlet doesn't include the MIDlet title bar and menu. The screen size reported in the Skeleton MIDlet from the previous chapter reflects the maximum canvas area available for drawing graphics in a MIDlet. In the case of games, you can think of the canvas area of the MIDlet as the game screen.

Gamer's Garage

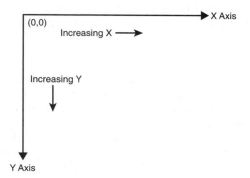

FIGURE 4.2
The MIDP XY coordinate system is similar to the traditional math coordinate system except that it applies to the game canvas of a MIDlet.

If the MIDP graphics coordinate system sounds a little complicated, just think of it in terms of a classic game of Battleship. In Battleship, you try to sink enemy ships by firing torpedoes at specific locations on a grid. Battleship uses its own coordinate system to allow you to specify locations on the grid where ships might be located. Similarly, when you draw graphics in a MIDlet, you specify locations in the canvas area, which is really just a grid of little squares called pixels.

One interesting thing to note about the MIDP coordinate system is that it represents locations between pixels, as opposed to pixels themselves. In other words, the pixel in the upper-left corner of a canvas has its upper-left corner at (0,0) and its lower-right corner at (1,1). This helps to remove any doubts when filling a primitive graphics shape such as a rectangle: The coordinates specified for the rectangle serve as the bounds of the filled area.

Learning the Basics of Color

A topic that impacts almost every aspect of game graphics is color. Fortunately, most computer systems take a similar approach to representing color. The main function of color in a computer system is to accurately reflect the physical nature of color within the confines of a computer. This physical nature isn't hard to figure out; anyone who has experienced the joy of Play-Doh can tell you that colors react in different ways when they are combined with each other. Like Play-Doh, a computer color system needs to be capable of mixing colors with accurate, predictable results.

Color computer monitors provide possibly the most useful insight into how software systems implement color. A color monitor has three electron guns: red, green, and blue. The output from these three guns converges on each pixel on the screen, stimulating phosphors to produce the appropriate color. The combined intensities of each gun determine the resulting pixel color. This convergence of different colors from the monitor guns is very similar to the convergence of different colored Play-Doh. Although the LCD screen on a mobile phone uses a different physical process to display colors, the concept of blending three component colors is still valid.

Gamer's Garage

> Technically speaking, the result of combining colors on a monitor is different from that of combining similarly colored Play-Doh. The reason for this is that color combinations on a monitor are additive, meaning that mixed colors are added together to become white; Play-Doh color combinations are subtractive, meaning that mixed colors are subtracted from each other to become black. Whether the color combination is additive or subtractive depends on the physical properties of the particular medium involved.

The Java color system is very similar to the physical system used by color monitors; it forms unique colors by using varying intensities of the colors red, green, and blue. Therefore, Java colors are represented by the combination of the numeric intensities of these colors (red, green, and blue). This color system is known as RGB (Red Green Blue) and is standard across most graphical computer systems.

Table 4.1 shows the numeric values for the red, green, and blue components of some basic colors. Notice that the intensities of each color component range from 0 to 255 in value.

TABLE 4.1   Numeric RGB Color Component Values for Commonly Used Colors

Color	Red	Green	Blue
White	255	255	255
Black	0	0	0
Light Gray	192	192	192
Medium Gray	128	128	128
Dark Gray	64	64	64
Red	255	0	0
Green	0	255	0
Blue	0	0	255
Yellow	255	255	0
Purple	255	0	255

Notice in the table that the intensities of each color component range from 0–255 in value. This means that each color is given 8 bits of storage in memory. This also means that when the color components are combined to form a complete color, the color takes up 24 bits of storage. For this reason, the MIDP color system is referred to as 24-bit color. Of course, that doesn't mean a whole lot for displays that render only shades of gray, but it matters a great deal when it comes to MIDP graphics programming.

It's worth pointing out that the MIDP graphics API doesn't include the familiar Color class that is a part of standard Java Advanced Windowing Toolkit (AWT) graphics. Eliminating the Color class is part of the streamlining that took place in trying to make the MIDP API as compact as possible. In reality, the Color class just served as an organizational structure for the red, green, and blue color components. In MIDP graphics programming, you just reference these color components as individual integers, as opposed to using a Color object.

Most image editing applications allow you to experiment with RGB color combinations to create colors. For example, in the standard Paint program in Windows you can double-click one of the colors in the color palette to find out its color components. Just click the Define Custom Colors button in the Edit Colors dialog box. You can then either type numbers into the Red, Green, and Blue edit fields or click to select a color and intensity (see Figure 4.3).

FIGURE 4.3
The standard Windows Paint program allows you to specify colors via RGB values.

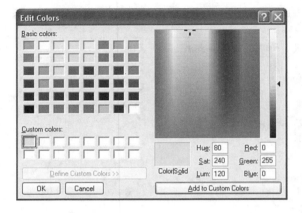

Gamer's Garage

For a more esoteric take on RGB colors, check out the online RGB Game at http://www.rgb-game.com/.

Working with Graphics in J2ME

If you've done any programming with standard Java, you are no doubt familiar with the Graphics class, which provides the capability of drawing graphics primitives (lines, rectangles, and so on), text, and images either to the display or to an offscreen memory buffer. You perform graphics operations by calling methods on a Graphics object, which is a parameter of a MIDlet's paint() method. A Graphics object is passed into the paint() method and is then used to perform graphical output to the MIDlet's screen or an offscreen buffer. Because the Graphics object is automatically passed into paint(), you never explicitly create a Graphics object.

Construction Cue

The paint() method is actually part of the Canvas class, which represents an abstract drawing surface. To use the Graphics class to draw graphics, you must create a Canvas object and set it as the screen for your MIDlet, as you did in the Skeleton MIDlet in the previous chapter.

The Graphics class has a few attributes that determine how different graphical operations are carried out. The most important of these attributes is the color attribute, which determines the color used in graphics operations such as drawing lines. You set this attribute by using the setColor() method defined in the Graphics class.

setColor() takes three integer parameters that represent the three primary color components. Similar to setColor() is setGrayScale(), which takes a single integer parameter that establishes a shade of gray within the range 0 to 255. If a grayscale color is created on a color display, all three color components are set to the same level, which is always a gray color.

Graphics objects also have a font attribute that determines the size and appearance of text. The setFont() method, which takes a Font object as its only parameter, is used to set this attribute. You learn more about drawing text and using the Font object in the section "Drawing Text," later in this chapter.

> Another version of the setColor() method takes a single integer parameter containing the complete color. The individual red, green, and blue color components are specified within this color value according to the following hexadecimal format: 0x00RRGGBB. In other words, the red (RR), green (GG), and blue (BB) components are stored as the lower three bytes of the 32-bit integer value.

Construction Cue

Most of the graphics operations provided by the Graphics class fall into one of the following categories:

- Drawing graphics primitives
- Drawing images
- Drawing text

The next few sections dig a little deeper into these graphics operations and show you exactly how to perform each of them.

Drawing Graphics Primitives

Graphics primitives consist of lines, rectangles, and arcs. You can create pretty impressive graphics by mixing these primitives; the Graphics class provides methods for drawing these primitives. You can also use the methods defined in the Graphics class to fill the area defined by a primitive with a particular color. Although primitive graphics may sound limiting when compared to bitmapped images, you'd be surprised what can be accomplished by getting creative with primitive graphics.

Lines

A line is the simplest of the graphics primitives and is therefore the easiest to draw. Even so, some of the most popular arcade games of all time, such as Asteroids, use vector graphics, which consist of nothing more than lines. The drawLine() method handles drawing lines and is defined as follows:

```
void drawLine(int x1, int y1, int x2, int y2)
```

The first two parameters, x1 and y1, specify the starting point for the line; the x2 and y2 parameters specify the ending point. It's important to understand that these coordinates represent the bounds of the starting and ending points for a line. Assuming that you're drawing a line in positive X and Y directions, x1 and y1 pinpoint the upper-left corner of the first pixel in the line, and x2 and y2 define the lower-right corner of the last pixel in the line. To draw a line in a MIDlet, call drawLine() in the MIDlet's paint() method, as in this example:

```
public void paint(Graphics g) {
  g.drawLine(5, 10, 15, 55);
}
```

This code results in a line being drawn from the point (5,10) to the point (15,55). You can change the style of the line via the setStrokeStyle() method. This method accepts one of two constant values, Graphics.SOLID and Graphics. DOTTED, which determine whether a solid or dotted line is drawn. The Graphics.SOLID stroke style is used by default if you don't specify a stroke style.

Construction Cue

> The MIDP API doesn't include direct support for drawing polygons. Instead, you must draw a polygon by drawing multiple lines with the drawLine() method.

Rectangles

Rectangles are also very easy to draw in MIDlets. The drawRect() method enables you to draw rectangles by specifying the upper-left corner and the width and height of the rectangle. The drawRect() method is defined in the Graphics class as follows:

```
void drawRect(int x, int y, int width, int height)
```

The x and y parameters specify the location of the upper-left corner of the rectangle, and the width and height parameters specify their namesakes, in pixels. To use drawRect() to draw a rectangle, just call it from the paint() method like this:

```
public void paint(Graphics g) {
  g.drawRect(5, 10, 15, 55);
}
```

This code draws a rectangle that is 15 pixels wide, 55 pixels tall, and has its upper-left corner at the point (5,10). There is also a drawRoundRect() method that enables you to draw rectangles with rounded corners:

```
void drawRoundRect(int x, int y, int width, int height, int arcWidth,
  int arcHeight)
```

The drawRoundRect() method requires two more parameters than drawRect(): arcWidth and arcHeight. These parameters specify the width and height of the arc forming the rounded corners of the rectangle. If you were to draw an oval that is arcWidth wide and arcHeight tall and then divide the oval into four sections, each section would represent the rounded corner of a rectangle. Following is an example that uses drawRoundRect() to draw a rectangle with rounded corners:

```
public void paint(Graphics g) {
 g.drawRoundRect(5, 10, 15, 55, 6, 12);
}
```

In this example, a rectangle that is 15 pixels wide and 55 pixels tall is drawn at the point (5,10). The corners are rounded and have arcs equivalent to a curved section of an oval that is 6 pixels wide by 12 pixels tall. The Graphics class also provides versions of each of these rectangle-drawing methods that fill the interior of a rectangle with the current color, in addition to drawing the rectangle itself. These methods are fillRect() and fillRoundRect().

To draw a perfect square with either of the rectangle-drawing methods, simply use an equal width and height.

Construction Cue

Arcs

Arcs are more complex than lines and rectangles. An arc is a section of an oval; erase part of an oval and what you have left is an arc. If you're still having trouble visualizing an arc, just think of the outline around Pac-Man when he has his mouth open. You draw an arc in relation to the complete oval it is a part of. To specify an arc, you must specify a complete oval and what section of the oval the arc comprises. The method for drawing an arc is as follows:

```
void drawArc(int x, int y, int width, int height, int startAngle, int arcAngle)
```

The first four parameters of the drawArc() method define the oval of which the arc is a part. The remaining two parameters define the arc as a section of this oval. Figure 4.4 shows an arc as a section of an oval.

As you can see in Figure 4.4, an arc is defined within an oval by specifying the starting angle for the arc in degrees, as well as the number of degrees to sweep in a particular direction. The sweep direction is counterclockwise, meaning that positive arc angles are counterclockwise and negative arc angles are clockwise. The arc shown in Figure 4.4 has a starting angle of 95° and an arc angle of 115°. The resulting angle is the sum of these two angles, which is 210°.

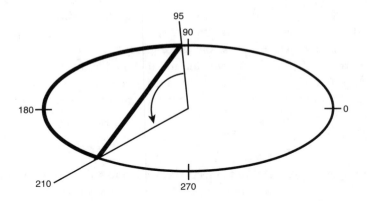

Following is an example of using the drawArc() method to draw an arc:

```
public void paint(Graphics g) {
  g.drawArc(5, 10, 150, 75, 95, 115);
}
```

This code draws an arc that is a section of an oval 150 pixels wide and 75 pixels tall, located at the point (5,10). The arc starts at 95° within the oval, and sweeps counterclockwise for 115°.

You may be surprised to learn that there is no drawOval() method defined in the MIDP Graphics class. Instead, you must draw ovals using the drawArc() method. To draw an oval, simply specify a sweep angle of 360° as the last parameter to the drawArc() method. This means that the arc is to sweep the entire oval, which effectively draws the complete oval.

The method for drawing filled arcs is fillArc(). This is very useful because you can use it to draw pie-shaped pieces of a circle or oval. For example, maybe you want to create a mobile version of the classic Food Fight arcade game, in which case you might use fillArc() to draw the pies being thrown by the comical chefs in the game.

Construction Cue

To draw a perfect circle using the drawArc() or fillArc() methods, simply use an equal width and height and set the sweep angle of the arc to 360°.

Drawing Text

Although text usually isn't central in games other than trivia and words games, it still comes in handy. If nothing else, most games display a score, and graphics code must be used somehow to draw it. In MIDlet graphics programming, text is always drawn with the currently selected font. The default font is of a medium size, but there will be times when you'll want to use a larger or smaller font or bold or italicize the text. To accomplish this, you first must create a font and select it before drawing any text. The setFont() method is used to select a font and is defined as follows:

```
void setFont(Font font)
```

The Font object models a textual font and includes the face, style, and size of the font. The Font object supports four different font styles, which are represented by the following constant members: STYLE_PLAIN, STYLE_BOLD, STYLE_ITALIC, and STYLE_UNDERLINED. These styles are really just constant numbers, and the last three can be used together to yield a combined effect; the STYLE_PLAIN style is the absence of the other three styles. To create a Font object, you call the static getFont() method and pass in the face, style, and size parameters as integer constants:

```
static Font getFont(int face, int style, int size)
```

Because fonts are somewhat limited in MIDlets, you must use predefined integer constants for each of these parameters. For example, the font face must be one of the following values: FACE_SYSTEM, FACE_MONOSPACE, or FACE_PROPORTIONAL. Likewise, the style of font must be one of the constants I mentioned earlier: STYLE_PLAIN or a combination of STYLE_BOLD, STYLE_ITALIC, and STYLE_UNDERLINED. Finally, the font size is specified as one of the following predefined constants: SIZE_SMALL, SIZE_MEDIUM, or SIZE_LARGE. Following is an example of obtaining a large, bold, underlined font with a monospace face:

```
Font myFont = Font.getFont(Font.MONOSPACE, Font.LARGE,
  Font.BOLD | Font.UNDERLINED);
```

Notice that in MIDP graphics, you don't have the freedom to create fonts of any point size. This makes sense given the limited size of mobile device displays. Also keep in mind that there is no guarantee that a font is available on a given mobile phone, which is a good example of why it's important to test your MIDlets on a real phone.

If you ever need to obtain the default system font, you can retrieve it by calling the static getDefaultFont() method of the Font class.

Construction Cue

After you've obtained a font with the getFont() method, you must select it for drawing text by calling the setFont() method, as in the following example:

```
g.setFont(myFont);
```

Now you're ready to draw some text that uses the font you've obtained and selected. The drawString() method, defined in the Graphics class, is exactly what you need. drawString() is defined as follows:

```
void drawString(String str, int x, int y, int anchor)
```

The drawString() method takes a String object as its first parameter, which contains the text to be drawn. The next two parameters, x and y, specify the location at which the string is drawn. The specific meaning of this location is determined by the last parameter, anchor. To help simplify the positioning of text and images, the MIDP API introduces anchor points, which help a great deal in positioning text and images without having to perform any calculations. An *anchor point* is associated with a horizontal constant and a vertical constant, each of which determines the horizontal and vertical positioning of the text with respect to the anchor point. The horizontal constants used to describe an anchor point are LEFT, HCENTER, and RIGHT. One of these constants is combined with a vertical constant to fully describe an anchor point. The vertical constants are TOP, BASELINE, and BOTTOM.

As an example of how to use anchor points, if you wanted a string of text containing the score of a game to appear centered along the top edge of the screen, you might call the drawString() method with the following values:

```
g.drawString("Look up here!", getWidth() / 2, 0,
  Graphics.HCENTER | Graphics.TOP);
```

In this code, the text's x,y position is specified at the top of the display and halfway across (getWidth() / 2). Incidentally, I'm assuming this code is placed within a Canvas-derived class, which is why I'm able to call the getWidth() method to get the size of the display. The meaning of this x,y position is established by the anchor parameter, which is specified as the combination of the Graphics.HCENTER and Graphics.TOP constants. This means that the text is drawn centered horizontally on the x part of the x,y position. It also means that the top of the text is placed at the y part of the x,y position.

In addition to the drawString() method, several other methods are used to draw text. The drawChar() and drawChars() methods are used to draw individual text characters:

```
void drawChar(char character, int x, int y, int anchor)
void drawChars(char[] data, int offset, int length, int x, int y,
  int anchor)
```

Both of these methods work similarly to drawString() in that they rely on an x,y position and an anchor to specify precisely where the text is drawn. There is also a drawSubstring() method that enables you to draw a substring of text located within a string:

```
void drawSubstring(String str, int offset, int len, int x, int y,
  int anchor)
```

This method includes the additional parameters offset and len for specifying the substring of text within the string passed as the str parameter.

Drawing Images

With the exception of word games and games that utilize vector graphics, images are extremely important to game programming. Images are rectangular graphical objects composed of colored or grayscale pixels. Each pixel in an image describes the color at that particular location of the image. Pixels can have unique colors that are described with the RGB color system. Color images in MIDP graphics are 24-bit images, which means that each pixel in an image is described by 24 bits. The red, green, and blue components of a pixel's color are stored in these 32 bits as individual 8-bit values.

Gamer's Garage

You may have also heard of 32-bit color graphics, where the extra 8 bits are used for the alpha component of the color, which determines the transparency of a pixel. MIDP supports transparency, and is therefore capable of using an extra 8 bits for the alpha component on phones that support 8-bit alpha transparency. If you recall, the Skeleton MIDlet in the previous chapter reports how many alpha levels a phone supports. Throughout this book you effectively use 1-bit alpha transparency, which simply means that you rely on one color in an image to serve as a transparent color.

Before we get into the details of how to draw an image, you must first learn how to load images. Because images are typically stored in external files, you must load them from a file before you can draw them. A special static method of the Image class called createImage() is used to load and create images:

```
public static Image createImage(String name) throws IOException
```

To use the createImage() method to create an image, you specify the name of the image file as the only parameter to createImage():

```
Image img = Image.createImage("Explosion.png");
```

The createImage()method returns an Image object, which can then be used to work with the image within the MIDP graphics API. It is also possible to create a blank Image object from scratch by calling a different version of the createImage() method that accepts the width and height of the image. The Image class represents a graphical image, such as a PNG, GIF, or JPEG file image, and provides a few methods for determining the width and height of the image. Image also includes a method for retrieving a Graphics object for the image, which enables you to draw directly onto the image.

Gamer's Garage

In case you aren't familiar with it, the Portable Network Graphics (PNG) image format is an improvement over the GIF format, and is slowly catching on as an alternative to GIF images. PNG images compress better than GIF images, resulting in smaller image files. PNG images also offer more flexibility for game graphics by supporting variable transparency (alpha levels). The Image class fully supports the PNG image format.

The Graphics class provides a single method, drawImage(), for drawing images:

```
boolean drawImage(Image img, int x, int y, int anchor)
```

This method probably looks somewhat familiar to you because it uses the same anchor point approach as the drawString() method you learned about in the previous section. Similar to drawString(), the drawImage() method draws the image at the x,y position as determined by the anchor parameter. The same horizontal and vertical anchor constants that you learned about earlier apply to images as well.

To summarize, the process of drawing an image involves first calling the static Image.createImage() method to create and load the image, followed by a call to drawImage(), which actually draws the image on the display. Following is an example of code that loads and draws a centered image within the paint() method of a MIDlet:

```
public void paint(Graphics g) {
  // Clear the display
  g.setColor(255, 255, 255);  // White
  g.fillRect(0, 0, getWidth(), getHeight());

  // Create and load the image
  Image img = Image.createImage("Splash.png");

  // Draw the image
  g.drawImage(img, getWidth() / 2, getHeight() / 2,
    Graphics.HCENTER | Graphics.VCENTER);
}
```

The image is drawn in the middle of the canvas with the HCENTER and VCENTER attributes.

In this example, you first clear the display by setting the color to white and filling the entire display. This is necessary so that you have a clean surface on which to draw. After that, the image `Splash.png` is loaded and created via the `createImage()` method. After the image is created, the `drawImage()` method is used to draw the image centered on the display; the `HCENTER` and `VCENTER` constants are used to specify the image's anchor point.

Building the Olympics Example Program

You now have a solid understanding of MIDP graphics and are probably anxious to see them at work within the context of a real MIDlet. You learned throughout this chapter that graphics are handled in the `paint()` method of a MIDlet. However, the MIDlet class doesn't include a `paint()` method; instead, you must use the `Canvas` class to perform all graphics operations. The `Canvas` class represents an abstract drawing surface and must be subclassed in a MIDlet to perform any drawing operations; these operations are carried out via the `Graphics` class. You then establish your derived `Canvas` class as the screen for a MIDlet to display it to the user.

To get started with a graphical MIDlet, you must follow these steps:

1. First create a `Canvas`-derived class that is associated with your MIDlet.

2. Then create an object of this canvas class as a member variable of the MIDlet class.

3. Set the `Canvas` object as the current screen for the MIDlet through a call to the `setCurrent()` method.

The best way to understand this process is to work through a simple example. A good example of basic MIDP graphics programming is to draw the Olympics symbol, which consists of five interlocking rings of different colors.

Writing the Program Code

Let's get started with the `OCanvas` class, which provides a canvas for the Olympics MIDlet. The code for the `OCanvas` class is shown in Listing 4.1.

LISTING 4.1 The OCanvas Class Serves as a Customized Canvas for the Olympics MIDlet

```
import javax.microedition.lcdui.*;

public class OCanvas extends Canvas {
  private Display display;

  public OCanvas(Display d) {
    super();
    display = d;
  }

  void start() {
    display.setCurrent(this);
    repaint();
  }

  public void paint(Graphics g) {
    // Clear the display
    g.setColor(255, 255, 255);  // White
    g.fillRect(0, 0, getWidth(), getHeight());

    // Draw the first row of circles
    g.setColor(0, 0, 255);      // Blue
    g.drawArc(5, 5, 25, 25, 0, 360);
    g.setColor(0, 0, 0);        // Black
    g.drawArc(35, 5, 25, 25, 0, 360);
    g.setColor(255, 0, 0);      // Red
    g.drawArc(65, 5, 25, 25, 0, 360);

    // Draw the second row of circles
    g.setColor(255, 255, 0);    // Yellow
    g.drawArc(20, 20, 25, 25, 0, 360);
    g.setColor(0, 255, 0);      // Green
    g.drawArc(50, 20, 25, 25, 0, 360);
  }
}
```

All the arcs are drawn as perfect circles when you specify equal widths and heights (25), and sweep from 0 to 360 degrees.

This class extends the Canvas class and takes care of establishing itself as the current screen for the MIDlet. The constructor calls the parent Canvas constructor and sets the display member variable. The start() method sets the canvas as the current MIDlet screen, and forces a repaint. The most important code is located in the paint() method, which calls the setColor() and drawArc() methods to draw the Olympics symbol. Notice that all the angle arguments to the drawArc() methods are 0 and 360, which results in complete ovals being drawn.

With the OCanvas class in place, you can declare a member variable of type OCanvas in the OlympicsMIDlet class:

```
private OCanvas canvas;
```

This member variable must be initialized in the constructor for the
OlympicsMIDlet class, as the following code demonstrates:

```
canvas = new OCanvas(Display.getDisplay(this));
```

That's really all the graphics-specific code required in the Olympics MIDlet. Just
so you see how it all goes together, Listing 4.2 contains the complete source code
for the OlympicsMIDlet class.

LISTING 4.2   The Source Code for the OlympicsMIDlet Class Is Located
in OlympicsMIDlet.java

```
import javax.microedition.midlet.*;
import javax.microedition.lcdui.*;

public class OlympicsMIDlet extends MIDlet implements CommandListener {
  private OCanvas canvas;

  public void startApp() {
    if (canvas == null) {
      canvas = new OCanvas(Display.getDisplay(this));
      Command exitCommand = new Command("Exit", Command.EXIT, 0);
      canvas.addCommand(exitCommand);
      canvas.setCommandListener(this);
    }

    // Start up the canvas
    canvas.start();
  }

  public void pauseApp() {}

  public void destroyApp(boolean unconditional) {}

  public void commandAction(Command c, Displayable s) {
    if (c.getCommandType() == Command.EXIT) {
      destroyApp(true);
      notifyDestroyed();
    }
  }
}
```

*The start() method
for the canvas is
what really gets the
MIDlet going.*

As you progress through the book, you will find that this code becomes somewhat
of a standard boilerplate MIDlet template for all games. The vast majority of
game-specific code resides in canvas classes and other support classes.

FIGURE 4.5
The Olympics
MIDlet demon-
strates how to draw
basic graphics
shapes with the
MIDP API.

Testing the Finished Product

To build and test the Olympics MIDlet, just copy the entire Olympics folder to the apps folder beneath your J2ME Wireless Toolkit installation. Click the Build button to build the MIDlet, and then click Run to run it in the J2ME emulator. Figure 4.5 shows the Olympics MIDlet in all its graphical glory.

Building the Slideshow Example Program

Although the Olympics MIDlet example is pretty interesting and definitely helped to get your feet wet with MIDP graphics programming, you're probably still craving a little more. Wouldn't it be nice to see how images and text are drawn within the context of a MIDlet? In this section you work through the details of a slide show MIDlet that serves as a practical example of how to draw images and text. Granted, the Slideshow MIDlet isn't exactly a game, but it is starting to demonstrate basic game programming tasks such as combining images and text and altering them in response to user input.

Writing the Program Code

The Slideshow MIDlet loads several images, along with associated text captions, and displays them one at a time. The user can flip through the "slides" by using the left and right arrow keys on a mobile phone. Because virtually all the slide show functionality of the MIDlet is graphical, the majority of the code appears in the SSCanvas class, which is derived from Canvas and serves as the canvas for displaying a slide. Following are the member variables defined for the SSCanvas class, which store the slide images and their respective captions, along with the current slide:

```
private Display display;
private Image[] slides;
private String[] captions = { "Love Circle Bowl", "Double Wide Spine",
                              "Flume Zoom Over-vert", "Kulp De Sac Bowl",
                              "Louie's Ledge" };
private int curSlide = 0;
```

The slides variable is an array of Image objects that is initialized in the constructor for the SSCanvas class. The following is the code for this constructor:

```
public SSCanvas(Display d) {
  super();
  display = d;

  // Load the slide images
  try {
    slides = new Image[5];
    slides[0] = Image.createImage("/LoveCircle.jpg");
    slides[1] = Image.createImage("/DoubleWide.jpg");
    slides[2] = Image.createImage("/FlumeZoom.jpg");
    slides[3] = Image.createImage("/KulpDeSac.jpg");
    slides[4] = Image.createImage("/LouiesLedge.jpg");
  }
  catch (IOException e) {
    System.err.println("Failed loading images!");
  }
}
```

This code is pretty straightforward in that it creates an Image array and then initializes each of its elements by loading an image with the Image.createImage()
method. It's important to note that each image filename is preceded by a forward
slash (/), which indicates that it appears in the root directory where the MIDlet is
located. This is important because these images are packaged into the JAR file
with the MIDlet class and therefore must be readily accessible.

If you're wondering about the slide show images, they are pictures of a public skate
park under construction where I live in Nashville, Tennessee. I helped document the
construction of the park for our local skateboarding community.

*Gamer's
Garage*

The real work in the SSCanvas class takes place in the paint() method, which
draws the current slide image and caption on the display. Following is the code
for the paint() method:

```
public void paint(Graphics g) {
  // Clear the display
  g.setColor(255, 255, 255);  // White
  g.fillRect(0, 0, getWidth(), getHeight());
```

```
// Draw the current image
g.drawImage(slides[curSlide], getWidth() / 2, getHeight() / 2,
  Graphics.HCENTER | Graphics.VCENTER);

// Set the font for the caption
Font f = Font.getFont(Font.FACE_PROPORTIONAL, Font.STYLE_BOLD,
  Font.SIZE_MEDIUM);
g.setFont(f);

// Draw the current caption
g.setColor(0, 0, 0);           // Black
g.drawString(captions[curSlide], getWidth() / 2, 0,
  Graphics.HCENTER | Graphics.TOP);
}
```

The current slide image is drawn centered on the screen.

The current slide caption is drawn centered horizontally and at the top of the screen.

The paint() method first clears the display so that the remnants of the previous slide are erased. The current slide image is then drawn, centered on the display. A bold, medium, proportional font for the text is then obtained for use in drawing the slide caption. Finally, the color is set back to black and the slide caption is drawn centered along the top edge of the display.

With all the painting out of the way, the last chore for the SSCanvas class is to process key presses for the left and right arrow buttons, which allow the user to navigate back and forth through the slide show. You don't technically learn about processing game input until Chapter 6, "Handling Mobile User Input," but I don't think it hurts anything to provide a bit of foreshadowing here. Following is the code for the keyPressed() method, which carries out this chore:

```
public void keyPressed(int keyCode) {
  // Get the game action from the key code
  int action = getGameAction(keyCode);

  // Process the left and right buttons
  switch (action) {
    case LEFT:
      if (--curSlide < 0)
        curSlide = slides.length - 1;
      repaint();
      break;

    case RIGHT:
      if (++curSlide >= slides.length)
        curSlide = 0;
      repaint();
      break;
  }
}
```

Wrap to the last slide if you go past the beginning.

Wrap to the first slide if you go past the end.

The keyPressed() method reveals something in MIDP programming: game actions. A game action is a special key event that is associated with keys typically used in games. The idea is that you can map game actions to different keys and enable the user to customize the user interface for games. In the keyPressed() method, the game action associated with the key code is first obtained with a call to getGameAction(). The LEFT and RIGHT constants are then used to check for the Left and Right game actions. If one of these constants produces a match, then the current slide is incremented or decremented, and the display is repainted.

That wraps up the SSCanvas class, which represents the majority of the work involved in the Slideshow MIDlet. Take a look at Listing 4.3 to see the complete code for this class.

LISTING 4.3 The SSCanvas Class Serves as a Customized Canvas for the Slideshow MIDlet

```
import javax.microedition.lcdui.*;
import java.io.*;

public class SSCanvas extends Canvas {
  private Display display;
  private Image[] slides;
  private String[] captions = { "Love Circle Bowl", "Double Wide Spine",
                                "Flume Zoom Over-vert", "Kulp De Sac Bowl",
                                "Louie's Ledge" };
  private int curSlide = 0;

  public SSCanvas(Display d) {
    super();
    display = d;

    // Load the slide images
    try {
      slides = new Image[5];
      slides[0] = Image.createImage("/LoveCircle.jpg");
      slides[1] = Image.createImage("/DoubleWide.jpg");
      slides[2] = Image.createImage("/FlumeZoom.jpg");
      slides[3] = Image.createImage("/KulpDeSac.jpg");
      slides[4] = Image.createImage("/LouiesLedge.jpg");
    }
    catch (IOException e) {
      System.err.println("Failed loading images!");
    }
  }

  void start() {
    display.setCurrent(this);
    repaint();
  }
```

The array indexes of these captions is aligned with the images in the slides array.

LISTING 4.3 Continued

```
public void keyPressed(int keyCode) {
  // Get the game action from the key code
  int action = getGameAction(keyCode);

  // Process the left and right buttons
  switch (action) {
    case LEFT:
      if (--curSlide < 0)
        curSlide = slides.length - 1;
      repaint();
      break;

    case RIGHT:
      if (++curSlide >= slides.length)
        curSlide = 0;
      repaint();
      break;
    }
}

public void paint(Graphics g) {
  // Clear the display
  g.setColor(255, 255, 255);  // White
  g.fillRect(0, 0, getWidth(), getHeight());

  // Draw the current image
  g.drawImage(slides[curSlide], getWidth() / 2, getHeight() / 2,
    Graphics.HCENTER | Graphics.VCENTER);

  // Set the font for the caption
  Font f = Font.getFont(Font.FACE_PROPORTIONAL, Font.STYLE_BOLD,
    Font.SIZE_MEDIUM);
  g.setFont(f);

  // Draw the current caption
  g.setColor(0, 0, 0);          // Black
  g.drawString(captions[curSlide], getWidth() / 2, 0,
    Graphics.HCENTER | Graphics.TOP);
  }
}
```

To integrate the canvas with the MIDlet, an instance of the SSCanvas class is created as a member variable of the SlideshowMIDlet class:

```
private SSCanvas canvas;
```

This variable is then initialized in the SlideshowMIDlet constructor, which is shown in the complete Slideshow MIDlet code in Listing 4.4.

LISTING 4.4   The Source Code for the `SlideshowMIDlet` Class Is Located in `SlideshowMIDlet.java`

```java
import javax.microedition.midlet.*;
import javax.microedition.lcdui.*;

public class SlideshowMIDlet extends MIDlet implements CommandListener {
  private SSCanvas canvas;

  public void startApp() {
    if (canvas == null) {
      canvas = new SSCanvas(Display.getDisplay(this));
      Command exitCommand = new Command("Exit", Command.EXIT, 0);
      canvas.addCommand(exitCommand);
      canvas.setCommandListener(this);
    }

    // Start up the canvas
    canvas.start();
  }

  public void pauseApp() {}

  public void destroyApp(boolean unconditional) {}

  public void commandAction(Command c, Displayable s) {
    if (c.getCommandType() == Command.EXIT) {
      destroyApp(true);
      notifyDestroyed();
    }
  }
}
```

The usage of the custom canvas class is the only thing unique about this MIDlet code

As you may notice, this code is virtually identical to the MIDlet class for the Olympics MIDlet, which confirms that most of the functionality of MIDlets is contained within the specialized canvas class.

Testing the Finished Product

After building the Slideshow MIDlet, you will definitely want to try it out in the J2ME emulator. Don't forget that the left and right arrow buttons are used to navigate back and forth through the slide show. Figure 4.6 shows the Slideshow MIDlet in action.

FIGURE 4.6
The Slideshow MIDlet provides an interactive slide show that draws both images and text to the display.

Summary

This chapter bombarded you with a great deal of information about graphics support in the MIDP API. Most of it was centered on the Graphics and Canvas objects, which are very straightforward to use. You began by learning about the MIDP graphics coordinate system and how it affects MIDlet graphics programming. You then moved on to draw a variety of different graphics primitives. From there, you found out how text is drawn through the use of fonts and anchor points. Finally, you concluded the chapter by taking a look at images and how they are drawn. Perhaps the most important aspects of this chapter are the two sample MIDlets that demonstrated most of the graphics concepts you learned.

I know you're probably getting fed up with all this ground work and are ready to dig into some real games. Trust me, you're getting much closer. The next chapter explores the most important topic related to game programming: sprite animation.

Extreme Game Makeover

One of the biggest challenges facing any mobile game developer is dealing with the wide range screen sizes across mobile phones. If you stick with primitive graphics in your games, this challenge becomes a bit easier because you don't have to worry about scaling and providing different sizes of images. The Olympics example MIDlet is a good MIDlet to use as an example of how you can scale graphics to fit any mobile phone screen size. As you've already seen the MIDlet, it draws the Olympics symbol in a fixed size at a fixed position regardless of screen size. Following are the steps required to alter the Olympics MIDlet so that the symbol fills the screen regardless of screen size:

1. Call the getWidth() and getHeight() canvas methods to determine the size of the screen (canvas).

2. Calculate a circle size for each circle in the symbol that is one-fourth the screen width (or one-third of the height if the device screen is oriented horizontally).

3. Modify the code in the paint() method so that the circles are drawn relative to the calculated circle size, and positioned accordingly, as opposed to being drawn at fixed sizes and positions; the symbol should be centered on the screen.

4. Build and run the MIDlet in the J2ME emulator. Change the emulation device to QwertyDevice in the emulator to see how the symbol is drawn on a larger device screen.

This is an important makeover because it demonstrates the significance of developing game graphics that can scale to different mobile phone screen sizes. It isn't always realistic to target a wide range of screen sizes in a single version of a MIDlet, but in this case the primitive graphics made it easier to pull off.

CHAPTER 5

Using Sprite Animation

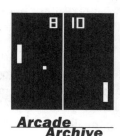

Arcade Archive

Unanimously considered a classic by virtually all arcade aficionados, Battlezone was released in 1980 by Atari. Battlezone relies on wireframe vector graphics as seen through a viewfinder that simulates the scope on a tank. The first-person 3D perspective offered by Battlezone was uniquely appealing to gamers at the time of the game's peak success. Legend has it that a military version of Battlezone was developed as a training aid for the U.S. Army's Bradley fighting vehicle. Although there is no formal acknowledgement from Atari or the U.S. military, a military version of the game with a specially designed cabinet was spotted at Atari years after Battlezone's heyday.

The heart of graphics in almost all computer games is animation. Without animation, there would be no movement, and without movement, we'd all be stuck playing word games and trivia games. This chapter presents the fundamental concepts surrounding animation in mobile games and, more specifically, sprite animation. After the animation theory is out of the way, this chapter shows you how to use the sprite features built into the MIDP 2.0 API. You'll continue to build on your sprite animation knowledge throughout the book, but this chapter lays the groundwork for mobile game animation and what it takes to make it happen.

In this chapter, you'll learn

▶ The basics of animation and how it works in games

▶ The difference between 2D and 3D animation

▶ The different types of 2D animation, and when to use each one in games

▶ How to use the MIDP `Sprite` class to develop animated MIDlets

▶ How to use the MIDP `GameCanvas` class to ensure that your MIDlet animations run smoothly

Understanding Animation

Before getting into animation as it relates to mobile games, it's important to understand the basics of what animation is and how it works. Let's begin by asking this fundamental question: What is animation? Put simply, animation is the illusion of movement. Could it be that every animation you've ever seen is really just an illusion? That's exactly right! And probably the most surprising animated illusion is one that captured attentions long before computers—the television. When you watch television, you see a lot of things moving around. But what you perceive as movement is really just a trick being played on your eyes.

Animation and Frame Rate

In the case of television, the illusion of movement is created when a rapid succession of images is displayed with slight changes in their appearance. The human eye perceives these changes as movement because of its low visual acuity, which means that your eyes are fairly easy to trick into believing the illusion of animation. More specifically, the human eye can be tricked into perceiving animated movement with as low as 12 frames of movement per second. It should come as no surprise that this animation speed is the minimum target speed for most computer games. Animation speed is measured in frames per second (fps).

Although 12fps is technically enough to fool your eyes into seeing animation, animations at speeds this low often end up looking somewhat jerky. Therefore, most professional animations use a higher frame rate. Television, for example, uses 30fps. When you go to the movies, you see motion pictures at about 24fps. It's pretty apparent that these frame rates are more than enough to captivate your attention and successfully create the illusion of movement.

Gamer's Garage

The reason for the difference between film and television frame rates has to do more with technical necessity than careful design or planning. In its early days, film speeds were as low as 16fps, but were eventually standardized at 24fps, which turned out being a good frame rate to accommodate sound reproduction. American television, also known as NTSC (National Television Standards Committee), came along later, and relied on the power line frequency as a timing reference. This frequency was (and still is) 60Hz, which results in a frame rate of 30fps. The fact that film and television frame rates are different means that films have to be converted to be shown on television.

Unlike television and motion pictures, mobile games are considerably more limited when it comes to frame rate. Higher frame rates in games correspond to much higher processor overhead, so mobile game developers are left to balance the frame rate against the limited system speed and resources. You may find yourself in the position of having to use simpler graphics in a game so that you can increase its frame rate and generate smoother animations.

When programming animation in mobile games, you typically can manipulate the frame rate a reasonable amount. The most obvious limitation on frame rate is the speed at which the mobile phone can generate and display the animation frames. Actually, the same limitation must be dealt with by game developers, regardless of the programming language or platform. When determining the frame rate for a game, you usually have some give and take in establishing a low enough frame rate to yield a smooth animation, while not bogging down the processor and overloading the system. But don't worry too much about this right now. For now, just keep in mind that when programming animation for games, you are acting as a magician creating the illusion of movement.

Making the Move to Computer Animation

Most of the techniques used in computer animation have been borrowed or based on traditional animation techniques developed for animated films. The classic approach to handling traditional animation is to draw a background image separately from the animated objects that will be moving in the foreground. The animated objects are then drawn on clear celluloid sheets so that they can be overlaid on the background and moved independently. This type of animation is referred to as *cel animation*. Cel animation enables artists to save a great deal of time by drawing only the specific objects that change shape or position from one frame to the next. This explains why so many animated movies have detailed backgrounds with relatively simple animated characters. Computer game sprites, which you learn about a little later in the chapter, directly correspond to traditional cel animated objects.

As computer power improved in the last two decades, traditional animators saw the potential for automating many of their hands-on techniques. Computers enabled them to scan in drawings and overlay them with transparency, for example. This is a similar approach to cel animation, but with one big difference: The computer imposes no limitations on the number of overlaid images. Cel animation is limited because only so many cel sheets can be overlaid. The technique of overlaying objects with transparency is a fundamental form of computer game animation, as you soon find out.

Gamer's Garage

Modern animated movies have officially proven that computer animation is for more than just games. Popular movies such as *Toy Story*, *Ice Age*, *Monsters, Inc.*, *Finding Nemo*, and *The Incredibles* are great examples of how traditional animated movies are now being created solely on computers. Perhaps an even more advanced example of computer animation in movies is *Final Fantasy*, which is one of the first movies to use computer animation to simulate live action graphics throughout an entire film.

Although computers have certainly improved upon traditional animation techniques, the animation potential available to the game programmer is far more flexible than traditional techniques. As a programmer, you have access to each individual pixel of each bitmap image, and you can manipulate each of them to your heart's desire.

2D Versus 3D Animation

There are two fundamental types of animation that you might consider using when creating mobile games: 2D and 3D. 2D animation involves objects moving or being manipulated within two dimensions. Objects in a 2D animation can still have a 3D look to them—they just can't physically move in three dimensions. Many 2D animation techniques simulate 3D animation by altering the look of objects to simulate depth, but they aren't truly 3D. As an example, an animation of a car driving off into the distance would involve the car getting smaller as it gets farther away. However, this isn't necessarily a 3D animation because you can achieve the 3D effect by making the car image get smaller as it moves away. Although the end result is three-dimensional, the car is very much a 2D object.

Unlike 2D animation, 3D animation involves placing and manipulating objects in a three-dimensional virtual world. A 3D object is defined by a model rather than an image because an image is inherently two-dimensional. A 3D model specifies the shape of an object by a series of points, or vertices, in 3D space. In other words, a 3D model is a mathematical representation of a physical object. For this reason, 3D graphics and animation can get extremely complicated because they often rely on heavy-duty mathematical processing.

In reality, many games make use of a mixture of 2D and 3D graphics and animation. For example, the original Doom game uses 3D graphics for the building interiors. However, the monsters in the game are 2D graphics objects. The monsters have a 3D appearance, but they are represented by flat images on the screen.

This mixture of 2D and 3D graphics works great in Doom because the 2D monsters look realistic enough when blending into 3D surroundings. Of course, things have evolved since the original Doom game. Quake and other more modern 3D first-person shooters (FPS) now use 3D objects throughout the game.

The remainder of this chapter, and the book in general, focuses on 2D animation because it is the more straightforward and efficient technique of the two, and is therefore better suited to games for mobile phones. The good news is that you can still do some pretty powerful things with 2D animation.

Analyzing 2D Sprite Animation

Although the focus of this chapter is ultimately on sprite animation, it is important to understand the primary types of animation used in game programming. Actually, a lot of different types of animation exist—all of which are useful in different instances. However, for the purposes of implementing animation in mobile games, I've broken animation down into two basic types: *frame-based* and *cast-based animation*. Technically speaking, there is also a third animation type known as *palette animation*, which involves animating the colors in a graphic object, but I think of it as more of a graphics effect rather than a fundamental type of animation.

Frame-Based Animation

The most simple animation technique is frame-based animation, which finds a lot of usage in nongaming animations. Frame-based animation involves simulating movement by displaying a sequence of pregenerated, static frame images. A movie is a perfect example of frame-based animation: Each frame of the film is a frame of animation, and when the frames are shown in rapid succession, they create the illusion of movement.

Frame-based animation has no concept of a graphical object distinguishable from the background; everything appearing in a frame is part of that frame as a whole. The result is that each frame image contains all the information necessary for that frame in a static form. This is an important point because it distinguishes frame-based animation from cast-based animation, which you learn about in the next section. Figure 5.1 shows a few frames in a frame-based animation.

FIGURE 5.1
In frame-based ani-
mation, the entire
frame changes to
achieve the effect
of animation.

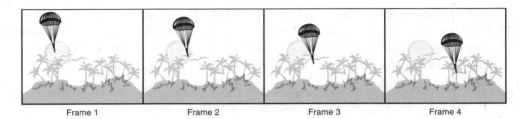

| Frame 1 | Frame 2 | Frame 3 | Frame 4 |

Figure 5.1 shows how a paratrooper is drawn directly onto each frame of animation, so there is no separation between the paratrooper object and the sky background. This means that the paratrooper cannot be moved independently of the
background. The illusion of movement is achieved as each frame is redrawn with
the paratrooper in a slightly different position. This type of animation is of limited use in games because games typically require the ability to move objects
around independently of the background.

Cast-Based Animation

A more powerful animation technique employed by many games is cast-based
animation, which is also known as sprite animation. Cast-based animation
involves graphical objects that move independently of a background. At this
point, you might be a little confused by the usage of the term "graphical object"
when referring to parts of an animation. In this case, a graphical object is something that logically can be thought of as a separate entity from the background
of an animation image. For example, in the animation of a space shoot-em-up
game, the aliens are separate graphical objects that are logically independent of
the star field background.

Gamer's Garage

The term "cast-based animation" comes from the fact that sprites can be thought of
as cast members moving around on a stage. This analogy of relating computer animation to theatrical performance is very useful. By thinking of sprites as cast members and the background as a stage, you can take the next logical step and think
of an animation as a theatrical performance. In fact, this isn't far from the mark
because the goal of theatrical performances is to entertain the audience by telling a
story through the interaction of the cast members. Likewise, cast-based animations
use the interaction of sprites to entertain the user, while often telling a story.

Each graphical object in a cast-based animation is referred to as a *sprite*, and has a position that can vary over time. In other words, a sprite can have a velocity associated with it that determines how its position changes over time. Almost every video game uses sprites to some degree. For example, every object in the classic Asteroids game is a sprite that moves independently of the background; even though Asteroids relies on vector graphics, the objects in the game are still sprites. Figure 5.2 shows an example of how cast-based animation simplifies the paratrooper example you saw in the previous section.

In this example, the paratrooper is now a sprite that can move independently of the background sky image. So, instead of having to draw every frame manually with the paratrooper in a slightly different position, you can just move the para-trooper image around on top of the background. This is the same approach you'll be using to inject animation into games throughout the remainder of the book.

Even though the fundamental principle behind sprite animation is the positional movement of a graphical object, there is no reason you can't incorporate frame-based animation into a sprite. This enables you to change the image of the sprite as well as alter its position. This hybrid type of animation is actually built into the sprite support in the MIDP 2.0 API, as you soon learn.

I mentioned in the frame-based animation discussion that television is a good example of frame-based animation. But can you think of something on television that is created in a manner similar to cast-based animation (other than animated movies and cartoons)? Have you ever wondered how weather people magically appear in front of a computer-generated map showing the weather? The news station uses a technique known as blue-screening or green-screening, which enables them to overlay the weatherperson on top of the weather map in real time. It works like this: The person stands in front of a solid colored backdrop (blue or green), which serves as a transparent background. The image of the weatherperson is overlaid onto the weather map; the trick is that the colored background is filtered out when the image is overlaid so that it is effectively transparent. In this way, the weatherperson is acting exactly like a sprite!

FIGURE 5.2
In cast-based ani-
mation, a graphical
object can move
independently of
the background to
achieve the effect
of animation.

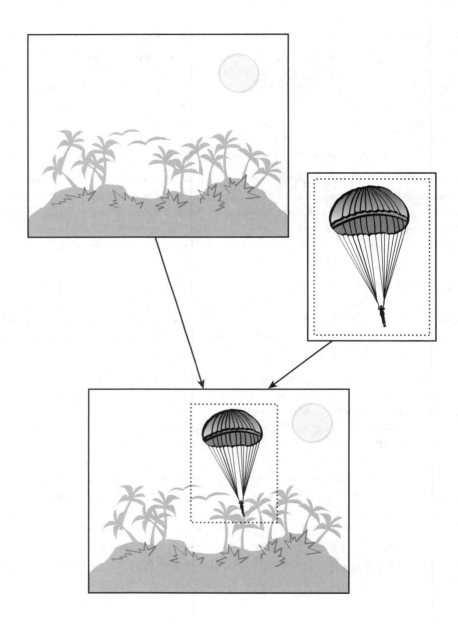

Seeing Through Objects with Transparency

The weatherperson example brings up a very important point regarding sprites: transparency. Because bitmapped images are rectangular by nature, a problem arises when sprite images aren't rectangular in shape. In sprites that aren't rectangular in shape, which is the majority of them, the pixels surrounding the sprite image are unused. In a graphics system without transparency, these unused pixels are drawn just like any others. The end result is sprites that have visible rectangular borders around them, which completely destroys the effectiveness of having sprites overlaid on a background image.

What's the solution? Well, one solution is to make all your sprites rectangular. Because this solution isn't very practical, a more realistic solution is transparency, which allows you to define a certain color in an image as unused, or transparent. When drawing routines encounter pixels of this color, they simply skip them, leaving the original background showing through. Transparent colors in images act exactly like the weatherperson's colored screen in the earlier example.

Adding Depth with Z-Order

In many instances, you will want some sprites to appear on top of others. For example, in a war game you might have planes flying over a battlefield dropping bombs on everything in sight. If a plane sprite happens to fly over a tank sprite, you obviously want the plane to appear above the tank and, therefore, hide the tank as it passes over. You handle this problem by assigning each sprite a screen depth, which is also referred to as *Z-order*.

Z-order is the relative depth of sprites on the screen. The depth of sprites is called Z-order because it works sort of like another dimension—like a z axis. You can think of sprites moving around on the screen in the XY axis. Similarly, the z axis can be thought of as another axis projected into the screen that determines how the sprites overlap each other. To put it another way, Z-order determines a sprite's depth within the screen. Because they make use of a z axis, you might think that Z-ordered sprites are 3D. The truth is that Z-ordered sprites can't be considered 3D because the z axis is a hypothetical axis only used to determine how sprite objects hide each other.

The easiest way to control Z-order in a game is to pay close attention to the order in which you draw the game graphics. Fortunately, the MIDP API provides a class called LayerManager that simplifies the task of managing multiple graphics objects (layers) and their respective Z-orders. You learn how to use the LayerManager class in Chapter 11, "Managing Multiple Game Layers."

Construction Cue

Just to make sure that you get a clear picture of how Z-order works, let's go back for a moment to the good old days of traditional animation. You learned earlier that traditional animators, such as those at Disney, used celluloid sheets to draw animated objects. They drew on celluloid sheets because the sheets could be overlaid on a background image and moved independently; cel animation is an early version of sprite animation. Each cel sheet corresponds to a unique Z-order value, determined by where in the pile of sheets the sheet is located. If a sprite near the top of the pile happens to be in the same location on the cel sheet as any lower sprites, it conceals them. The location of each sprite in the stack of cel sheets is its Z-order, which determines its visibility precedence. The same thing applies to sprites in cast-based animations, except that the Z-order is determined by the order in which the sprites are drawn, rather than the cel sheet location.

Detecting Collisions between Objects

No discussion of animation as it applies to games would be complete without covering collision detection. Collision detection is the method of determining whether sprites have collided with each other. Although collision detection doesn't directly play a role in creating the illusion of movement, it is tightly linked to sprite animation and extremely crucial in games.

Collision detection is used to determine when sprites physically interact with each other. In an Asteroids game, for example, if the ship sprite collides with an asteroid sprite, the ship is destroyed and an explosion appears. Collision detection is the mechanism employed to find out whether the ship collided with the asteroid. This might not sound like a big deal; just compare their positions and see whether they overlap, right? Correct, but consider how many comparisons must take place when a lot of sprites are moving around—each sprite must be compared to every other sprite in the system. It's not hard to see how the processing overhead of effective collision detection can become difficult to manage.

Not surprisingly, there are many approaches to handling collision detection. The simplest approach is to compare the bounding rectangles of each sprite with the bounding rectangles of all the other sprites. This method is efficient, but if you have objects that are not rectangular, a certain degree of error occurs when the objects brush by each other. Corners might overlap and indicate a collision when really only the transparent areas are overlapping. The less rectangular the shape of the sprites, the more error typically occurs. Figure 5.3 shows how simple rectangle collision works.

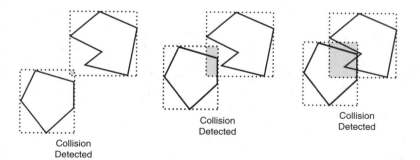

Collision
Detected

Collision
Detected

Collision
Detected

FIGURE 5.3
Collision detection
using rectangle col-
lision simply
involves checking
to see whether the
bounding rectan-
gles of two objects
overlap.

In the figure, the areas determining the collision detection are shaded. You can
see how simple rectangle collision detection isn't very accurate unless you're dealing with sprites that are rectangular in shape. An improvement upon this technique is to shrink the collision rectangles a little, which reduces the error. This
method improves things a little, but it has the potential of causing error in the
reverse direction by allowing sprites to overlap in some cases without signaling a
collision. Figure 5.4 shows how shrinking the collision rectangles can improve the
error on simple rectangle collision detection. Shrunken rectangle collision is just
as efficient as simple rectangle collision because all you are doing is comparing
rectangles for intersection.

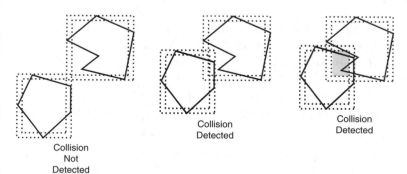

Collision
Not
Detected

Collision
Detected

Collision
Detected

FIGURE 5.4
Collision detection
using shrunken rec-
tangle collision
involves checking
to see whether
shrunken versions
of the bounding
rectangles of two
objects overlap.

The most accurate collision detection technique is to detect collision based on the
sprite image data, which involves actually checking to see whether transparent
parts of the sprite or the sprite images themselves are overlapping. In this case,
you get a collision only if the actual sprite images are overlapping. This is the
ideal technique for detecting collisions because it is exact and enables objects of
any shape to move by each other without error. Figure 5.5 shows collision detection that uses the sprite image data.

FIGURE 5.5
Collision detection
that uses image
data collision
involves checking
the specific pixels
of the images for
two objects to
see whether they
overlap.

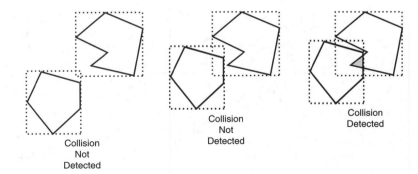

Unfortunately, the technique shown in Figure 5.5 requires more processing overhead than rectangle collision detection and can be a bottleneck in game performance. It really depends on the importance of extremely accurate collision detection
in your specific game, and how much room you have to carry out the processing
without killing your frame rate. You'll find that shrunken rectangle collision
detection is sufficient in a lot of games.

Applying Sprite Animation to Mobile Games

Now that you have a basic understanding of the fundamental types of animation, you're probably wondering which is best for games. I've already alluded to
the fact that cast-based animation is more efficient and often gives you more control over game graphics, but the truth is that most games use a combination of
the two animation techniques. Each technique offers its own unique benefits, so
combining the techniques gives you capabilities that would be hard to get by
using one of them alone.

A good example of how games often require the use of more than one animation
technique is an animation of a person walking. You obviously need to be able to
alter the position of the person so that he appears to be moving across a landscape. This requires cast-based animation because you need to move the person
independently of the background on which he appears. However, if we let it go at
this, the person would appear to just be sliding across the screen because he isn't
making any movements that simulate walking. To effectively simulate walking,
the person needs to move his arms and legs as a real person does when walking.

This requires frame-based animation because you need to show a series of frames of the leg and arm movements. The end result is an object that can both move and change its appearance, which is where the two animation techniques come together.

Sprites are incredibly important in virtually all two-dimensional games because they provide a simple, yet effective means of conveying movement while also enabling objects to interact with one another. By modeling the objects in a game as sprites, you can create some surprisingly interesting games in which the objects interact with each other in different ways. The simplest example of a sprite used in a game is Pong, which involves a total of three sprites: the ball and the two paddles (vertical bars) along each side of the screen. All these objects must be modeled as sprites because they all move and interact with each other. The ball flies around on its own and bounces off the paddles, which are controlled by each of the two players.

As games get more complex, the role of sprites changes slightly, but their importance only increases. For example, a tank battle game would obviously use sprites to model the tanks and bullets that they shoot at each other. However, you could also use sprites to represent stationary objects such as walls and buildings. Even though the stationary objects don't move, they benefit from being modeled as sprites because you can detect a collision between them and a tank and limit the tank's movement accordingly. Similarly, if a bullet strikes a building, you would want to destroy it or make it ricochet off the building at an angle; modeling the building as a sprite allows you to detect the bullet collision and respond accordingly.

Working with the `Layer` and `Sprite` Classes

I mentioned earlier that the MIDP 2.0 API includes support for sprite animation. The two primary classes that make sprite animation possible in MIDP programming are the `Layer` and `Sprite` classes. The `Layer` class models a general graphical object known as a *layer*, which serves as the foundation for sprites and other graphical game objects. You can think of any discrete visual element in a game as being a distinct layer. From a programming perspective, the `Layer` class keeps track of information such as the position, width, height, and visibility of a visual element.

It's important to note that the `Layer` class is an abstract class, which means you can never directly create an instance of a `Layer` object. Instead, you create instances of objects derived from `Layer`, such as `Sprite` or your own `Sprite`-derived class. Subclasses of the `Layer` class must implement their own `paint()` methods so that they can be drawn.

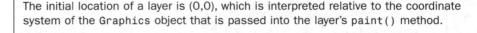

Construction
Cue

The initial location of a layer is (0,0), which is interpreted relative to the coordinate system of the `Graphics` object that is passed into the layer's `paint()` method.

Following are the methods defined in the `Layer` class, all of which are important when it comes to working with layers and sprites:

▶ `getX()`—Gets the X position of the layer's upper-left corner

▶ `getY()`—Gets the Y position of the layer's upper-left corner

▶ `getWidth()`—Gets the layer's width

▶ `getHeight()`—Gets the layer's height

▶ `setPosition()`—Sets the XY position of the layer's upper-left corner

▶ `move()`—Moves the layer by a specified XY amount

▶ `isVisible()`—Gets the layer's visibility

▶ `setVisible()`—Sets the layer's visibility

▶ `paint()`—Overridden in derived layer subclasses

The `Sprite` class builds on the `Layer` class by providing additional functionality required of animated two-dimensional graphical objects. The primary functional additions in the `Sprite` class are as follows:

▶ Sprites are based on images, and support multiple frame images.

▶ The image(s) for a sprite can be transformed (rotated, mirrored, and so on).

▶ You can define a reference pixel, which serves as the basis for sprite transformations and positioning.

▶ For sprites with multiple frame images, the sequence in which the images are displayed can be set precisely.

▶ Collisions can be detected between sprites through the use of rectangle, shrunken rectangle, or image data collision detection.

As you can see, the `Sprite` class offers a considerable number of features for mobile game programming. You don't tackle all these aspects of the `Sprite` class in this chapter, but you will soon enough. For now, let's focus on the basics of getting a sprite up and running. To create a sprite based on a single image, just pass a newly created `Image` object into the `Sprite` constructor, like this:

```
Sprite monsterSprite = new Sprite(Image.createImage("/Monster.png"));
```

In this example, a monster image is used as the basis for creating a monster sprite. The problem is, if you placed this code by itself into a MIDlet, you would get compile errors because an I/O exception is not being caught. This exception can be thrown by the createImate() method in response to a failure loading an image. Here's how to package the code in a try-catch clause to get it running smoothly:

```
try {
  monsterSprite = new Sprite(Image.createImage("/Monster.png"));
  monsterSprite.setPosition(0, 0);
}
catch (IOException e) {
  System.err.println("Failed loading image!");
}
```

Even though the Layer class defaults the position of every layer to (0,0), it's still a good idea to get in the habit of initializing the position of all your sprites, as this code shows. With your sprite loaded and ready, all you must do to move it around on the screen is call its setPosition() or move() methods. Then you follow that code with a call to the paint() method to draw the sprite. The following steps show exactly how to accomplish these tasks:

1. Following is an example of using the setPosition() method to center a sprite on the screen:

   ```
   monsterSprite.setPosition((getWidth - monsterSprite.getWidth()) / 2,
     (getHeight - monsterSprite.getHeight()) / 2);
   ```

   This code uses the canvas width and height in conjunction with the sprite's width and height to center the sprite on the screen.

2. Moving a sprite works a little differently in that you simply provide the amount you'd like to move the sprite in each direction:

   ```
   monsterSprite.move(-5, 10);
   ```

   In this example, the sprite is moved 5 pixels to the left and 10 pixels down. Negative offset values indicate left or up directions, whereas positive values indicate right or down.

3. Because every Sprite object has an image associated with it, a paint() method is provided that paints the sprite at its current position. All you have to do is pass the paint() method a Graphics object, like this:

   ```
   monsterSprite.paint(g);
   ```

   This code assumes that you have a Graphics object named g, but you always have a Graphics object handy in game painting code.

You've now seen the essentials of sprite animation with the MIDP API. All you're missing is a quick look at the GameCanvas class, which is uniquely suited to animation thanks to its double-buffered graphics support.

Achieving Smooth Animation with the GameCanvas Class

If you were to use everything you've learned thus far to build an animated MIDlet using the regular MIDP Canvas class, you would find that the resulting animation has an annoying flicker. This flicker occurs because the game screen is cleared before the animated graphics are painted. In other words, animated graphics objects are erased and repainted each time they are moved. Because the erase and repaint process takes place directly on the game screen, the animation appears to flicker. To better understand the problem, imagine a movie in which a blank background is displayed quickly in between each frame containing actors that move. Although the film is cooking along at a fast enough pace to give the illusion of movement, you would still see a noticeable flicker because of the blank backgrounds.

You can solve the flicker problem associated with sprite animation by using a technique known as *double buffering*. In double buffering, you perform all your erasing and drawing on an offscreen drawing surface that isn't visible to the user. After all the drawing is finished, the end result is painted straight to the game screen in one pass. Because no visible erasing is taking place, the end result is flicker-free animation. Figure 5.6 shows the difference between traditional single-buffer animation and double-buffer animation that eliminates flicker.

Gamer's Garage

A *buffer* is simply an area in memory to which you are drawing graphics. The buffer in traditional single-buffer animation is the game screen itself, whereas double-buffer animation adds an offscreen memory buffer to the equation.

Figure 5.6 reveals how an offscreen memory buffer is used to perform all the incremental animation drawing, with only the finished image being drawn to the game screen. This might sound like a tricky programming problem, but double-buffering is extremely easy to incorporate into your mobile games thanks to the MIDP 2.0 API.

In addition to the standard Canvas class, the MIDP API offers the GameCanvas class, which supports double-buffered graphics. To take advantage of this feature in the GameCanvas class, you simply derive your game-specific canvas from the GameCanvas class and paint the graphics just as you would in a normal MIDlet. However, all the painting you perform is actually being done to an offscreen buffer. To commit the offscreen painting to the actual screen, you must call the flushGraphics() method.

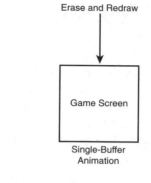

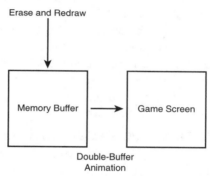

Erase and Redraw

Game Screen

Single-Buffer Animation

Erase and Redraw

Memory Buffer → Game Screen

Double-Buffer Animation

FIGURE 5.6
Double-buffer animation eliminates the annoying flicker associated with drawing directly to the game screen with a single buffer.

To recap how the offscreen buffer works in the GameCanvas class, a game canvas has an offscreen buffer image that is associated with the canvas. When you perform any graphics operations on the Graphics object associated with the canvas, the graphics are actually drawn to the offscreen buffer; nothing on the screen changes. A call to the flushGraphics() method is what results in the offscreen buffer being drawn to the screen in one single operation. Flushing the offscreen buffer doesn't change its contents or clear it; it just paints the buffer to the screen.

When you first create a GameCanvas object, the offscreen buffer is initially filled with all white pixels.

Gamer's Garage

The GameCanvas class includes a few other interesting features that come in handy for mobile games, such as efficient key input processing, which you learn about in the next chapter. For now, however, you know enough to use the GameCanvas class to create a smooth little animation MIDlet.

Building the UFO Example Program

Although any number of good themes can be used for an example of sprite animation, UFOs never get old. If you're ever stuck with a game design that just seems as if something is missing, try adding a flying saucer! Seriously, in this section you learn how to use the MIDP sprite features to build a MIDlet that demonstrates how to animate a flying saucer sprite around the screen. This UFO example demonstrates the basics of sprite animation and how it works in a practical example. You will continue to squeeze more interesting functionality out of the MIDP animation classes as you progress through the book.

The UFO example uses a single sprite of a UFO that flies randomly around a black background. The UFO sprite relies on a single image of a flying saucer, and makes use of the positioning features of the Sprite class to update the sprite's position over time. Perhaps the most important aspect of the UFO example is how it establishes an animation thread that updates and draws the UFO sprite on regularly scheduled intervals. This animation thread is also known as a *game loop*, and is the heart and soul of any mobile game that relies on animation.

Writing the Program Code

As with most graphical MIDlets, the interesting code begins with a specialized canvas class, which in this case is named UFOCanvas. Following are the member variables declared in the UFOCanvas class:

```
private Display display;
private boolean sleeping;
private long    frameDelay;
private Random  rand;
private Sprite  ufoSprite;
private int     ufoXSpeed, ufoYSpeed;
```

The display member should be familiar to you from earlier examples—it stores away the main display for the MIDlet, and is necessary to set the canvas as the main screen. The sleeping member variable determines whether or not the MIDlet's animation loop is running. You can effectively pause the animation by setting the sleeping variable to true. The frameDelay member is closely linked to the animation loop in that it controls how frequently the loop cycles. More specifically, the frameDelay member sets the amount of time, in milliseconds, that the loop waits between iterations. You can easily translate this value into a frame rate by dividing 1 by it. So, for example, if the frameDelay member is set to 40 (milliseconds), convert it to 0.04 seconds, and then divide it into 1 to get 25fps.

Similarly, you can convert backward from a target frame rate by inverting the frame rate (dividing it into 1), and then multiplying by 1,000. Here's an example:

$^1/_{30}$fps = 0.0333 seconds = 33 milliseconds

The rand member variable is an instance of the standard MIDP random number generator, which is used in the UFO MIDlet to randomly alter the UFO's speed. The UFO sprite is stored in the ufoSprite member, which is a Sprite object. The speed of the UFO sprite is stored independently of the Sprite object in the ufoXSpeed and ufoYSpeed members.

> Practically speaking, it is usually better to create your sprites as classes derived from the Sprite class. However, in the case of the UFO sprite, it is simple enough that creating a custom class would be overkill. Most of the sprites you encounter throughout the remainder of the book are created as custom-derived sprite classes.

Construction Cue

A bit earlier I mentioned that the frameDelay member variable controls the frame rate for the animation of the UFO MIDlet. This variable is initialized in the MIDlet constructor with a single line of code:

```
frameDelay = 33;
```

Going back to the equation from earlier, you can see that this frame delay value of 33 results in a frame rate of 30fps. If you recall from earlier in the chapter in the discussion of animation basics, 30fps is plenty high to result in a smooth animation, assuming real mobile phones can keep up. This is where testing on a physical phone becomes very important as you develop games with more complex animation code.

The majority of the initialization for the UFO MIDlet takes place in the start() method. Following is the section of code in this method that sets up the UFO sprite:

```
ufoXSpeed = ufoYSpeed = 3;
try {
  ufoSprite = new Sprite(Image.createImage("/Saucer.png"));
  ufoSprite.setPosition(0, 0);
}
catch (IOException e) {
  System.err.println("Failed loading image!");
}
```

The X and Y components of the sprite's speed are set to 3, which means the sprite will start off moving down and to the right at a rate of 3 pixels per animation cycle; negative values for the speed would reverse the direction of movement. To create the UFO Sprite object, just pass a newly created image into the Sprite constructor. The sprite's position is then set to (0,0), which is the upper-left corner of the screen.

The animation thread is also established in the start() method, as the following code reveals:

```
sleeping = false;
Thread t = new Thread(this);
t.start();
```

The sleeping variable is first set to false to indicate that the animation loop is to be let loose. A Thread object is then created with the canvas passed into it, as evident by the this parameter. The thread is then started with a call to the start() method, which is ultimately what gets the animation loop off and running.

It's important to provide the canvas with a means of stopping the animation loop. This is accomplished by the stop() method, whose code follows:

```
public void stop() {
  // Stop the animation
  sleeping = true;
}
```

As you might have guessed, stopping the animation loop is as simple as setting the sleeping variable to true. Speaking of the animation loop, it resides in the run() method. Following is the code for the animation loop within this method:

```
while (!sleeping) {
  update();
  draw(g);
  try {
    Thread.sleep(frameDelay);
  }
  catch (InterruptedException ie) {}
}
```

The animation loop is a very simple while loop that continues to loop as long as the sleeping variable isn't true. Within the loop, the update() method is called to update the animation, and then the draw() method is called to draw the updated graphics. The static sleep() method of the Thread class is used to establish the timing of the animation thread accepting the frameDelay value as the amount of time for the thread to sleep before continuing execution. This section of code is what drives the entire timing mechanism of the animation in the UFO MIDlet.

The update() method is called once every time through the animation loop, and is therefore responsible for updating each frame of animation. In other words, the update() method is called 30 times per second because the UFO MIDlet is set up to run at 30fps. In this case, the update() method is responsible for randomly altering the speed of the flying saucer, and then changing its position based on its current speed. Following is the code that randomly changes the flying saucer's speed:

```
if (rand.nextInt() % 5 == 0) {
  ufoXSpeed = Math.min(Math.max(ufoXSpeed + rand.nextInt() % 2, -8), 8);
  ufoYSpeed = Math.min(Math.max(ufoYSpeed + rand.nextInt() % 2, -8), 8);
}
```

> The update() method is the single most important method you will encounter as you develop mobile games with J2ME. Every pass through the update() method is equal to one game cycle, so this method controls every beat of your game's heart. For this reason, you should do all you can to make sure that every line of code in the update() method is carefully planned and thought out, as well as being optimized for efficiency. You learn some tricks about how to optimize your games in Chapter 17, "Optimizing Mobile Java Games."

Construction Cue

The nextInt() method of the Random class is used to obtain a random integer. If the random integer is divisible by 5, the speed of the flying saucer is changed. This might seem like a curious test to perform to see whether the saucer speed should change, but the idea is to not have the speed changing in every animation cycle. By mod'ing (%) the random number with 5, and then comparing the result to 0, you're effectively changing the speed only one fifth of the time, on average. To cause the speed to change more frequently, just lower the mod number (5). For example, if you want the speed changed one third of the time, change the code to rand.nextInt() % 3.

The speed of the flying saucer is also changed by a random amount. At most, the speed can be increased by a value of only 2 or -2. Furthermore, the Math.min() and Math.max() methods are used to prevent the speed from going above -8 or 8. I say "above -8" because the negative part of the number simply means the speed is in the left direction; the magnitude is all that matters in terms of capping the actual speed. In other words, -8 means the saucer is traveling 8 pixels per cycle in the left direction, whereas 8 means it is traveling the same speed in the right direction.

> Feel free to try other values for the maximum flying saucer speed—there is no magical meaning to the maximum speed of 8 that I used.

Construction Cue

After randomly altering the speed of the saucer, the update() method takes care of moving the saucer to its new position:

```
ufoSprite.move(ufoXSpeed, ufoYSpeed);
```

The move() method of the Sprite class moves a sprite by a specified amount. In this case, the values of the individual X and Y speed components for the sprite are exactly what are needed to move the sprite.

But there's a hitch! What happens when the sprite reaches the edge of the screen? Although you could certainly let it keep on flying into the nether regions of a mobile phone off the extents of the visible screen, it makes a bit more sense to have it wrap around to the other side of the screen a la Asteroids. Following is the code that takes care of wrapping the flying saucer:

Wrap the flying saucer horizontally.

```
if (ufoSprite.getX() < -ufoSprite.getWidth())
  ufoSprite.setPosition(getWidth(), ufoSprite.getY());
else if (ufoSprite.getX() > getWidth())
  ufoSprite.setPosition(-ufoSprite.getWidth(), ufoSprite.getY());
```

Wrap the flying saucer vertically.

```
if (ufoSprite.getY() < -ufoSprite.getHeight())
  ufoSprite.setPosition(ufoSprite.getX(), getHeight());
else if (ufoSprite.getY() > getHeight())
  ufoSprite.setPosition(ufoSprite.getX(), -ufoSprite.getHeight());
```

There is nothing too magical about this code; it basically checks to see whether the flying saucer has gone past the edge of the screen in any of the four directions (top, right, bottom, left). If so, the saucer is wrapped around to the opposite edge, giving the familiar wrapping effect.

Construction Cue

If you didn't want to go the Asteroids route and wrap the flying saucer, you could instead go the Pong route and have it bounce off the edges of the screen. Rather than change the position when the saucer goes past an edge, you would simply reverse its speed. More specifically, you would negate the ufoXSpeed variable if the saucer wrapped off the left or right edge of the screen, and negating the ufoYSpeed variable would take care of the top and bottom edges.

The final piece of the UFOCanvas puzzle is the draw() method, which is called upon once each animation cycle to draw the animation:

```
private void draw(Graphics g) {
  // Clear the display
  g.setColor(0x000000);
  g.fillRect(0, 0, getWidth(), getHeight());

  // Draw the UFO sprite
  ufoSprite.paint(g);

  // Flush the offscreen graphics buffer
  flushGraphics();
}
```

The method first clears the screen with a solid black fill, and then calls the paint() method on the UFO sprite. The resulting graphics are then committed to the screen with a call to the flushGraphics() method. This is the beauty of double-buffered graphics—all the drawing takes place offscreen until you perform a final draw in one swoop by flushing the graphics. Without this, your games would be a flickery mess...trust me.

To pull everything together and see how it fits into a complete class, check out
Listing 5.1, which shows all the code for the UFOCanvas class.

LISTING 5.1   The UFOCanvas **Class Serves as a Customized Canvas for
the UFO MIDlet**

```
import javax.microedition.lcdui.*;
import javax.microedition.lcdui.game.*;
import java.util.*;
import java.io.*;

public class UFOCanvas extends GameCanvas implements Runnable {
  private Display  display;
  private boolean sleeping;
  private long     frameDelay;
  private Random   rand;
  private Sprite   ufoSprite;
  private int      ufoXSpeed, ufoYSpeed;

  public UFOCanvas(Display d) {
    super(true);
    display = d;

    // Set the frame rate (30fps)
    frameDelay = 33;
  }

  public void start() {
    // Set the canvas as the current screen
    display.setCurrent(this);

    // Initialize the random number generator
    rand = new Random();

    // Initialize the UFO sprite
    ufoXSpeed = ufoYSpeed = 3;
    try {
      ufoSprite = new Sprite(Image.createImage("/Saucer.png"));
      ufoSprite.setPosition(0, 0);
    }
    catch (IOException e) {
      System.err.println("Failed loading image!");
    }

    // Start the animation thread
    sleeping = false;
    Thread t = new Thread(this);
    t.start();
  }

  public void stop() {
    // Stop the animation
    sleeping = true;
  }
```

*The flying saucer
starts out in the
upper-left corner
of the screen.*

LISTING 5.1   Continued

```
public void run() {
  Graphics g = getGraphics();

  // The main game loop
  while (!sleeping) {
    update();
    draw(g);
    try {
      Thread.sleep(frameDelay);
    }
    catch (InterruptedException ie) {}
  }
}

private void update() {
  // Randomly alter the UFO's speed
  if (rand.nextInt() % 5 == 0) {
    ufoXSpeed = Math.min(Math.max(ufoXSpeed + rand.nextInt() % 2, -8), 8);
    ufoYSpeed = Math.min(Math.max(ufoYSpeed + rand.nextInt() % 2, -8), 8);
  }

  // Move the sprite
  ufoSprite.move(ufoXSpeed, ufoYSpeed);

  // Wrap the UFO around the screen if necessary
  if (ufoSprite.getX() < -ufoSprite.getWidth())
    ufoSprite.setPosition(getWidth(), ufoSprite.getY());
  else if (ufoSprite.getX() > getWidth())
    ufoSprite.setPosition(-ufoSprite.getWidth(), ufoSprite.getY());
  if (ufoSprite.getY() < -ufoSprite.getHeight())
    ufoSprite.setPosition(ufoSprite.getX(), getHeight());
  else if (ufoSprite.getY() > getHeight())
    ufoSprite.setPosition(ufoSprite.getX(), -ufoSprite.getHeight());
}

private void draw(Graphics g) {
  // Clear the display
  g.setColor(0x000000);
  g.fillRect(0, 0, getWidth(), getHeight());

  // Draw the UFO sprite
  ufoSprite.paint(g);

  // Flush the offscreen graphics buffer
  flushGraphics();
}
}
```

Randomly change the flying saucer's speed to XY values in the range of -8 (left/up) to 8 (right/down).

Drawing a sprite is surprisingly simple, thanks to the paint() method.

With the UFOCanvas code in place, you're ready to plug the canvas into a MIDlet. Listing 5.2 contains the code for the UFOMIDlet class, which does little more than harness the power of the UFOCanvas class.

LISTING 5.2   The Source Code for the UFOMIDlet Class Is Located in UFOMIDlet.java

```java
import javax.microedition.midlet.*;
import javax.microedition.lcdui.*;

public class UFOMIDlet extends MIDlet implements CommandListener {
  private UFOCanvas canvas;

  public void startApp() {
    if (canvas == null) {
      canvas = new UFOCanvas(Display.getDisplay(this));
      Command exitCommand = new Command("Exit", Command.EXIT, 0);
      canvas.addCommand(exitCommand);
      canvas.setCommandListener(this);
    }

    // Start up the canvas
    canvas.start();
  }

  public void pauseApp() {}

  public void destroyApp(boolean unconditional) {
    canvas.stop();
  }

  public void commandAction(Command c, Displayable s) {
    if (c.getCommandType() == Command.EXIT) {
      destroyApp(true);
      notifyDestroyed();
    }
  }
}
```

The custom canvas class is all that separates this MIDlet class from earlier examples.

As the listing reveals, the UFOMIDlet class primarily consists of boilerplate MIDlet code that is starting to look familiar. The MIDlet class is certainly still responsible for creating the canvas and starting and stopping it, but this is nothing ground-breaking. You should be getting the point that most of the game-specific code in your mobile games will lie in the canvas class and other support classes.

FIGURE 5.7
The flying saucer in the UFO MIDlet immediately starts flying around when the MIDlet is executed.

FIGURE 5.8
Like the Energizer Bunny, the flying saucer in the UFO MIDlet never gets tired.

Testing the Finished Product

After building the UFO MIDlet, take it for a test spin in the J2ME emulator. Upon being executed, the flying saucer immediately starts flying around within the MIDlet, as shown in Figure 5.7.

Because it's difficult to convey animation on the printed page, check out Figure 5.8, which shows the flying saucer cruising around in a different area of the screen.

About all the UFO MIDlet is missing are a few asteroids and the ability to control the flying saucer. Don't worry, that stuff is coming up in the next chapter!

Summary

This chapter introduced you to animation and how it applies to mobile games. You found out how animation is what makes many forms of modern entertainment work, including movies, television, and video games. Two primary types of animation are used in the development of most computer games, and this chapter explored how they work and when you would want to use them. You then explored the basic sprite animation features that are built into the MIDP API, along with how to use them. The chapter concluded by leading you through the development of an animated MIDlet that demonstrates the basics of sprite animation.

The next chapter builds on your animation knowledge by allowing you to control animated objects with keys on a mobile phone.

Extreme Game Makeover

Seeing as the UFO MIDlet is your first foray into mobile animation, it's worthwhile to spend some time tweaking with the animation properties. More specifically, I'm referring to the frame rate of the animation and UFO sprite speed. Following are the steps required to tinker with the animation to see how different values affect the MIDlet:

1. Try setting the `frameDelay` member variable to a higher number such as 100 (10fps), as well as a lower number such as 20 (50fps). Notice not only how much slower/faster the animation runs at each setting, but also how choppy/smooth it appears.

2. Change the frequency at which the flying saucer's speed is changed so that it happens more frequently. This involves changing the line of code that says `rand.nextInt() % 5` to something like `rand.nextInt() % 2`.

3. Change the cap on the flying saucer's speed so that it can go much faster. This involves changing the `min()` and `max()` method calls so that the speed limits are higher than -8 and 8.

These changes can dramatically impact the speed and performance of the animation, especially the first step. It's definitely worth spending some time tweaking the various values to see how it changes the animation.

Handling Mobile User Input

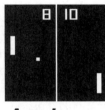

Arcade Archive

Released in 1980 by Stern, Berzerk is a simple shoot-em-up maze game where you guide a humanoid character through a maze of rooms blasting away at robots. Berzerk is one of the first games to make use of a "boss," which is a tough enemy that appears at the end of a level. In the case of Berzerk, the boss is Evil Otto, who resembles a bouncing smiley face, and serves as somewhat of a timer to encourage the player to exit a particular room quickly. Berzerk is known for the robots in the game making human mistakes such as shooting each other with "friendly fire." Berzerk is also known as the first arcade game to be blamed for a player's death—in 1981 a man died of a massive heart attack immediately after playing the game. In 1982, another man died of a heart attack after playing the game and reaching the high score list. Play Berzerk at your own risk!

No matter how much time and energy you put into the storyline and graphics for a mobile game, none of it will matter if you don't get the game play right. And getting the game play right largely revolves around giving the user a responsive and well-thought-out set of controls for playing the game. From a programming perspective, this is both easy and difficult for the mobile game developer. It's easy because the controls on mobile phones are so simplified as compared to desktop computer and console game controls. On the other hand, this can make the user input handling in mobile games more difficult because you're extremely limited when it comes to how flexible the controls can be. This chapter shows you how to process user input efficiently for mobile games.

In this chapter, you'll learn

- ▶ Why user input is so important in mobile games
- ▶ How to efficiently detect and respond to mobile phone key presses

▶ How to control an animated graphical object via key presses

▶ How to detect collisions between sprites in a mobile game

▶ How to create sprites whose appearances change over time

Assessing Mobile Game Input

User input is the means by which a user interacts with a mobile game. Considering the fact that user input encompasses all communications between a player and a game, you would think that designing an intuitive, efficient interface for user input would be at the top of the list of key game design elements. However, that isn't always the case, especially when it comes to nonmobile computer games. With all the hype these days surrounding real-time, lifelike 3D graphics engines and positional 3D audio in games, effective user input support is often overlooked. In fact, user input is perhaps the most overlooked aspect of modern game design, which is truly a shame. User input support in a game directly impacts the playability of the game; when the user input isn't effective, the play suffers.

Gamer's Garage

I'm from the old school of game players, and I still remember paying homage to the gods of gaming with my hard-earned allowance in arcades, well before there was an option of playing anything other than Pong at home. In return for my quarter offerings, the game gods usually provided me with incredibly fun games that usually had to survive on their playability alone. Because the hardware at that time simply couldn't provide a very high level of graphic and sound intensity, game developers were forced to make up for it with game play. Of course, they didn't consider their focus on playability as making up for anything; with the limited graphics and sound capabilities at the time, they didn't have an option.

Let me give you a quick example of what I'm talking about in regard to playability and user input. One of my all-time favorite games is Ring King, which is a boxing game for the original Nintendo Entertainment System (NES). Ring King is definitely considered "old" by current gaming standards—possibly even ancient. Compared to current games, it has weak graphics, animation, and sound. However, I still play the game simply because it plays so well. And that playability is largely based on how the game handles user input; it allows for very subtle timing when you punch and dodge, which goes a long way in a boxing game! Ring King certainly has its limitations, but its designers got it right when they came up with the punch-dodge timing—try to throw a straight lunge punch, and you'll see what I mean.

Since then, I've tried to find a modern replacement for Ring King, but with no luck. Although there are plenty of modern games with fancy graphics and sound, the responsiveness of the controls in my old favorite are tough to find. I'm still looking, though.

The point of this discussion is that the mobile game programmer (you!) faces many of the same challenges that early arcade game programmers faced: mainly, limited hardware resources. You simply don't have the luxury of a microprocessor capable of running the latest and greatest 3D rendering engine. You have to make hard trade-offs when it comes to the complexity of your mobile game designs, and with these trade-offs you should always remember to put game play first. And as I mentioned in the introduction, this usually means taking a closer look at how user input is handled in your games.

Gamer's Garage

Although this chapter focuses on more primitive forms of user input, it's worth noting that researchers recently placed electrodes directly on the surfaces of the brains of several volunteers, and they were able to control a video game by thought alone. I know—it sounds like science fiction, but it's reality. It will likely be a long time before this technology could ever realistically trickle down to video games, but it could serve as an extremely important medical tool for people with paralysis and other physical impairments.

Your ultimate goal is to make your game input controls feel as natural as possible to the player. If you really want to see how well your user interface works, create an alternate set of really awful graphics with little or no sound and see whether your game is still fun to play. I encourage you to try this with some of the example games you encounter throughout the book, and see whether they are still fun to play with bad graphics and no sound. A game should be able to hold its own with solid game play and good input controls alone.

Handling Key Input with the GameCanvas Class

In Chapter 5, "Using Sprite Animation," you were introduced to the GameCanvas class, which offered a unique solution to animation flickering by supporting double-buffered graphics. The GameCanvas class doesn't stop there. In fact, it also supports highly efficient mobile key input processing that is specifically designed for mobile games. The traditional approach to processing key input in J2ME works fine for normal MIDlets, but isn't responsive enough for games. So the GameCanvas class provides a more efficient alternative in the getKeyStates() method.

The getKeyStates() method is used to retrieve a snapshot of the state of the keys on a mobile phone at any given time. This method doesn't report on all the keys on a phone, just the keys that potentially apply to games. Following are the key constants you can use with the getKeyStates() method to determine the status of individual game keys:

▶ UP_PRESSED—Up key

▶ DOWN_PRESSED—Down key

▶ LEFT_PRESSED—Left key

▶ RIGHT_PRESSED—Right key

▶ FIRE_PRESSED—Fire key

▶ GAME_A_PRESSED—Optional A key

▶ GAME_B_PRESSED—Optional B key

▶ GAME_C_PRESSED—Optional C key

▶ GAME_D_PRESSED—Optional D key

Gamer's Garage

The A, B, C, and D keys are optional keys that may or may not be available on all mobile phones. For this reason, you should try not to rely on these keys for critical game control features unless you are targeting a specific phone that you know supports them.

The getKeyStates() method returns an integer value that you can use to check which key was pressed, if any. To check for a specific key press, just call the getKeyStates() method and mask the return value against one of the preceding constants, like this:

```
int keyState = getKeyStates();
if ((keyState & LEFT_KEY) != 0) {
  // Move left
} else if ((keyState & RIGHT_KEY) != 0) {
  // Move right
}
```

This code should be placed in your animation loop (game loop) so that the key states are checked on a regular interval. It's important to clarify that the getKeyStates() method doesn't always reveal the live status of the game keys. If a key has been pressed and released since the last time the getKeyStates() method was called, the key is reported as being down. This ensures that rapid key presses aren't lost even if the game loop is running too slowly to catch them in real time.

Granted, you ideally don't want this scenario to take place, but at least you know that key presses won't be getting lost.

Some phones may support multiple key press combinations, but there is no guarantee of this support. If you are targeting a specific mobile phone and you know it supports multiple key presses, feel free to make use of it. Some popular commercial games such as Tony Hawk's Pro Skater would be virtually impossible to play without multiple key press support.

Another point worth making in regard to the getKeyStates() method is that it doesn't return meaningful information unless the game canvas is currently visible. If a game has multiple screens, the keys for the game canvas don't become active until the game canvas is selected as the current screen.

Revisiting the Sprite Class

Although this chapter is focused primarily on handling user input in mobile games, it's worth taking a brief detour and learning a bit more about sprite animation so that you can build a more interesting example that involves user input. More specifically, it's worth digging a little deeper into the Sprite class, and learning how to detect collisions between sprites and use sprites with multiple frame images.

Detecting Sprite Collisions

In the previous chapter you learned the theory behind sprite collision detection and the different approaches to handling it. If you recall, the following three collision detection approaches were discussed:

▶ Rectangle collision detection

▶ Shrunken rectangle collision detection

▶ Image data collision detection

These three collision detection techniques were presented in order of increasing accuracy but also increased processing overhead. In other words, rectangle collision isn't nearly as accurate as image data collision, but it puts significantly less demand on the processing overhead of your game loop. Knowing this, you should attempt to make careful decisions with how and when you use each collision detection approach.

To use the MIDP API to detect collisions, you must take advantage of a series of methods in the Sprite class, all of which are named collidesWith(). Although all of the three collidesWith() methods check for a collision between an object and the sprite on which they are called, they differ with respect to the object that is being checked. For example, the first collidesWith() method checks for a collision between the sprite and another sprite:

```
collidesWith(Sprite s, boolean pixelLevel)
```

To check for a collision, just call this method on a sprite and pass into it another sprite. The second parameter determines whether or not the collision detection is performed on a pixel-by-pixel basis, which equates to the image data collision detection approach. The following code shows how you might detect a collision between a space ship sprite and an asteroid sprite by using image data collision detection:

```
shipSprite.collidesWith(roidSprite, true);
```

If you wanted to go with simple rectangle collision to speed up the code, you could pass false into the collidesWith() method, like this:

```
shipSprite.collidesWith(roidSprite, false);
```

Yet another approach involves shrunken rectangle collision detection, which is identical to the rectangle collision detection approach you just saw, but it uses a smaller collision rectangle. To alter the collision rectangle for a sprite, call the defineCollisionRectangle() method and specify the new size. As an example, if the asteroid sprite in the previous example is 42×35 pixels in size, you might want to set its collision rectangle to a smaller 32×25 size, effectively shaving it by 10 pixels in each dimension. Following is the code to accomplish this:

```
alienSprite.defineCollisionRectangle(5, 5, 32, 25);
```

FIGURE 6.1
A shrunken collision rectangle is used to limit the portion of an asteroid sprite used for collision detection.

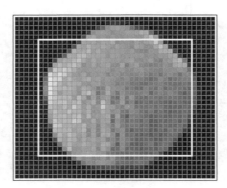

In this example, the collision rectangle is offset 5 pixels in each direction so that it remains centered on the sprite. Figure 6.1 shows the alien sprite with its shrunken collision rectangle defined.

One interesting thing about the defineCollisionRectangle() method is that it applies to both rectangle and image data collision detection. In the case of image data collision detection, only pixels within the collision rectangle are compared to detect collisions.

Earlier I mentioned that a total of three different collidesWith() methods are defined in the Sprite class, and you've already seen one of them. Following are the remaining two collidesWith() methods:

```
collidesWith(Image image, int x, int y, boolean pixelLevel)
collidesWith(TiledLayer t, boolean pixelLevel)
```

These two methods check a sprite for collision with an image and a tiled layer, respectively. In the case of an image, you specify the XY position of the image and a collision detection is performed on it and the sprite. Tiled layers are similar to sprites but utilize multiple tiled images to create a larger composite image. You could create a maze of walls using a tiled layer, and then perform a collision detection on it and a sprite character to keep the sprite within the maze. You learn how to carry out this exact task in Chapter 11, "Managing Multiple Game Layers."

Working with Frame-Animated Sprites

Another interesting feature of the Sprite class is support for frame animation. If you recall from the previous chapter, frame animation involves showing a sequence of frame images in succession to create animation. In the case of a sprite, frame animation simply means that the appearance of the sprite changes in addition to the position of the sprite. A good example of a frame-animated sprite is an asteroid tumbling through space. The motion of the sprite involves varying its position over time, and the tumbling effect is achieved by altering its image.

To specify frame images for a sprite, you simply arrange them in a single image as if they are in a filmstrip. Figure 6.2 shows an asteroid sprite with 14 frame images that simulate the asteroid tumbling.

Although it may be hard to see in the figure, the asteroid sprite images indeed provide a tumbling effect when displayed in rapid succession.

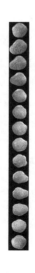

FIGURE 6.2
Multiple frame images are used to make an asteroid sprite appear to be tumbling.

You create a sprite based on frame images by passing the frame image into the `Sprite` constructor, along with the width and height of each frame image; the frame images must all be the same size. Following is an example of how to create the asteroid sprite based on the image in Figure 6.2.

```
roidSprite = new Sprite(Image.createImage("/Roid.png"), 42, 35);
```

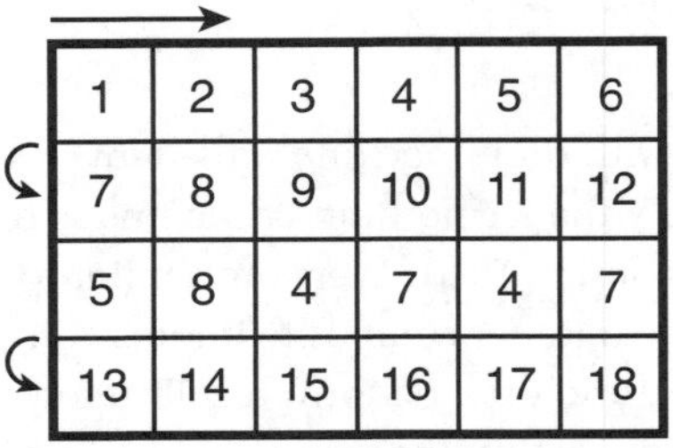

FIGURE 6.3
Arranging frames in a sprite image as a grid results in the frames being ordered from left to right and then top to bottom.

1	2	3	4	5	6
7	8	9	10	11	12
5	8	4	7	4	7
13	14	15	16	17	18

This code identifies the size of a single frame within the sprite image, which in this case is 42×35. The frames within a sprite image can be laid out horizontally, vertically, or in a two-dimensional grid. If you arrange the frames in a grid, the frames are ordered from left to right and then top to bottom, as shown in Figure 6.3.

To animate a sprite's appearance with frame animation, just call the `nextFrame()` or `prevFrame()` methods, like this:

```
roidSprite.nextFrame();
```

This method advances the animation frame to the next frame in the animation frame sequence. By default, this sequence is set to the ordering of the frames in the original sprite image, but you can change it to anything you want. When the `nextFrame()` or `prevFrame()` methods encounter the end of the frame sequence, they wrap back to the other end of the sequence and continue along. You can determine the index of the frame sequence at any given time by calling the `getFrame()` method. This method returns the current index of the frame sequence, not the actual animation frame. Consider the following frame sequence as an example:

```
int[] sequence = { 0, 1, 2, 3, 3, 3, 2, 1 };
```

The fifth index of this sequence is set to frame number 3. If the animation is currently on the fifth frame, a call to `getFrame()` returns 4 (zero-based index), not 3 (the actual frame number). The `setFrame()` method allows you to set the current frame index. Using the same example sequence, calling `setFrame(6)` would result in a frame number of 2 because 2 is set at the frame with an index of 6. Keep in mind that these frame numbers actually correspond to frame images. You can use frame sequences creatively to efficiently simulate animated motion in sprites such as wings flapping, fire balls exploding, asteroids tumbling, and so on.

You can change the frame sequence for a sprite with a call to the
setFrameSequence() method, which expects an array of integers. Following
is an example of how you could set the frame sequence for a bird sprite to the
previous example sequence:

```
birdSprite.setFrameSequence(sequence);
```

If you're struggling just a bit to fully comprehend frame-animated sprites, don't
worry because help is on the way. The remainder of the chapter focuses on you
revamping the UFO example from the previous chapter to take advantage of user
input and frame-animated sprites. This stuff will make more sense when you see
it in action.

Building the UFO 2 Example

The UFO example program from the previous chapter served as a great way to
get your feet wet with sprite animation. You're now going to take the example to
another level entirely by adding a means of controlling the UFO with keys on a
mobile phone, as well as adding some tumbling asteroids as obstacles for the UFO
to dodge. I'd stop short of officially calling the UFO 2 example a game, but it's
about as close as you can get!

The UFO 2 example program involves the following major additions with respect
to the original version of the program:

▶ User input for controlling the flying saucer

▶ Three frame-animated asteroid sprites that float around the screen

▶ Collision detection between the flying saucer and the asteroid sprites

You are already well equipped to tackle all these additions, so let's get to it.

Writing the Program Code

The MIDlet class for the UFO 2 example doesn't change at all from the previous
version, so let's jump straight into the modified UFOCanvas class. The first change
is the addition of three asteroid sprites, which are stored in a Sprite array:

```
private Sprite[] roidSprite = new Sprite[3];
```

You initialize these asteroid sprites in the start() method of the MIDlet by using the following code:

```
Image img = Image.createImage("/Roid.png");
roidSprite[0] = new Sprite(img, 42, 35);
roidSprite[1] = new Sprite(img, 42, 35);
roidSprite[2] = new Sprite(img, 42, 35);
```

As you can see, the asteroid image (Roid.png) is created only once, and then used as the sprite image for all three asteroid sprites. In addition to creating the three asteroid sprites, the start() method also initializes the position of the flying saucer sprite differently than the original version did:

```
ufoSprite.setPosition((getWidth() - ufoSprite.getWidth()) / 2,
  (getHeight() - ufoSprite.getHeight()) / 2);
```

Although it looks a bit messy, this code is simply centering the flying saucer sprite on the screen so that it isn't initially colliding with the asteroids, which are all three initially located in the upper-left corner of the screen at the default position (0,0).

The update() method is where most of the interesting new code lies in the UFO 2 MIDlet. All the key handling takes place in a single block of code, which looks like this:

```
int keyState = getKeyStates();
if ((keyState & LEFT_PRESSED) != 0)
  ufoXSpeed--;
else if ((keyState & RIGHT_PRESSED) != 0)
  ufoXSpeed++;
if ((keyState & UP_PRESSED) != 0)
  ufoYSpeed--;
else if ((keyState & DOWN_PRESSED) != 0)
  ufoYSpeed++;
ufoXSpeed = Math.min(Math.max(ufoXSpeed, -8), 8);
ufoYSpeed = Math.min(Math.max(ufoYSpeed, -8), 8);
```

The UFO's speed is randomly set somewhere in the range of -8 and 8.

Nothing too tricky here! The code simply checks the four directional keys and alters the UFO speed accordingly. Notice that the speed is still capped at a magnitude of 8 regardless of how much you pound on the keys. After altering the speed, the flying saucer is updated with another couple of lines of code:

```
ufoSprite.move(ufoXSpeed, ufoYSpeed);
checkBounds(ufoSprite);
```

The familiar sprite move() method is called to move the saucer, whereas the new checkBounds() method is called to perform any screen wrapping. The code in the checkBounds() method isn't new, but isolating it in a reusable method is. This is important because you need to be able to check the bounds of the UFO and asteroids sprites, and it wouldn't make much sense to duplicate the code unnecessarily.

The updating of the asteroid sprites takes place in a loop that takes care of several different tasks. Here's how the loop starts:

```
for (int i = 0; i < 3; i++) {
```

The first task within the loop is to move the asteroids and check their bounds in case they need to be wrapped around the screen:

```
roidSprite[i].move(i + 1, 1 - i);
checkBounds(roidSprite[i]);
```

The only tricky code here is the amount by which the asteroids are moved. To help give the asteroids their own unique speeds, the index of each asteroid is used as the basis for determining how fast it moves and in what direction. A similar approach is used to vary the animation frame directions of the asteroids, as this code reveals:

```
if (i == 1)
  roidSprite[i].prevFrame();
else
  roidSprite[i].nextFrame();
```

The idea behind this code is for the second asteroid to spin in an opposite direction as the first and third asteroids. You can accomplish this easily by moving the animation frames of the second sprite in the opposite direction as the others.

The remaining code in the asteroid update loop has to do with detecting a collision between the flying saucer and any of the asteroids:

```
if (ufoSprite.collidesWith(roidSprite[i], true)) {
  // Plan an alert sound
  AlertType.ERROR.playSound(display);

  // Reset the sprite positions and speeds
  ufoSprite.setPosition((getWidth() - ufoSprite.getWidth()) / 2,
    (getHeight() - ufoSprite.getHeight()) / 2);
  ufoXSpeed = ufoYSpeed = 0;
  for (int j = 0; j < 3; j++)
    roidSprite[j].setPosition(0, 0);

  // No need to continue updating the roid sprites
  break;
}
}
```

The sprite is centered on the game screen and its speed is reset to 0.

If a collision has indeed occurred, the AlertType object is used to play a standard error sound, which is determined by each individual phone. Later, in Chapter 8, "Making Noise with Tones," you learn how to make your games play more interesting sounds, but for now this approach will suffice. A collision in this program triggers a reset of the sprite positions, as is evident in the code. If this were a full-blown game, this is where you would decrement the number of lives and check to see whether the game is over. In this case, you just reposition the sprites and let the animation keep on trucking.

There is only a minor change to the draw() method in this version of the UFO example MIDlet. I'm referring to the code that draws the asteroids, which looks like this:

```
for (int i = 0; i < 3; i++)
  roidSprite[i].paint(g);
```

That wraps up the new chunks of code in the UFO 2 example. Listing 6.1 contains the complete code for the new UFOCanvas class, which helps add some context to the code you just learned about.

LISTING 6.1   The UFOCanvas **Class Serves as a Customized Canvas for the UFO 2 MIDlet**

```
import javax.microedition.lcdui.*;
import javax.microedition.lcdui.game.*;
import java.util.*;
import java.io.*;

public class UFOCanvas extends GameCanvas implements Runnable {
  private Display   display;
  private boolean   sleeping;
  private long      frameDelay;
  private Random    rand;
  private Sprite    ufoSprite;
  private int       ufoXSpeed, ufoYSpeed;
  private Sprite[]  roidSprite = new Sprite[3];

  public UFOCanvas(Display d) {
    super(true);
    display = d;

    // Set the frame rate (30fps)
    frameDelay = 33;
  }

  public void start() {
    // Set the canvas as the current screen
    display.setCurrent(this);

    // Initialize the random number generator
    rand = new Random();
```

There are 3 asteroid sprites in UFO 2. [

LISTING 6.1 Continued

```
  // Initialize the UFO and roids sprites
  ufoXSpeed = ufoYSpeed = 0;
  try {
    ufoSprite = new Sprite(Image.createImage("/Saucer.png"));
    ufoSprite.setPosition((getWidth() - ufoSprite.getWidth()) / 2,
      (getHeight() - ufoSprite.getHeight()) / 2);

    Image img = Image.createImage("/Roid.png");
    roidSprite[0] = new Sprite(img, 42, 35);
    roidSprite[1] = new Sprite(img, 42, 35);
    roidSprite[2] = new Sprite(img, 42, 35);
  }
  catch (IOException e) {
    System.err.println("Failed loading image!");
  }

  // Start the animation thread
  sleeping = false;
  Thread t = new Thread(this);
  t.start();
}

public void stop() {
  // Stop the animation
  sleeping = true;
}

public void run() {
  Graphics g = getGraphics();

  // The main game loop
  while (!sleeping) {
    update();
    draw(g);
    try {
      Thread.sleep(frameDelay);
    }
    catch (InterruptedException ie) {}
  }
}

private void update() {
  // Process user input to control the UFO speed
  int keyState = getKeyStates();
  if ((keyState & LEFT_PRESSED) != 0)
    ufoXSpeed--;
  else if ((keyState & RIGHT_PRESSED) != 0)
    ufoXSpeed++;
  if ((keyState & UP_PRESSED) != 0)
    ufoYSpeed--;
  else if ((keyState & DOWN_PRESSED) != 0)
    ufoYSpeed++;
  ufoXSpeed = Math.min(Math.max(ufoXSpeed, -8), 8);
  ufoYSpeed = Math.min(Math.max(ufoYSpeed, -8), 8);
```

The directional keys control the speed, and therefore the direction of the flying saucer.

LISTING 6.1   Continued

This line of code is responsible for wrapping the asteroids around the edges of the game screen.   [

The index of each asteroid is used to determine in which direction to cycle through the animation frames.   [

Because the second parameter to collidesWith() is true, collision detection takes place at the pixel level.   [

```
  // Move the UFO sprite
  ufoSprite.move(ufoXSpeed, ufoYSpeed);
  checkBounds(ufoSprite);

  // Update the roid sprites
  for (int i = 0; i < 3; i++) {
    // Move the roid sprites
    roidSprite[i].move(i + 1, 1 - i);
    checkBounds(roidSprite[i]);

    // Increment the frames of the roid sprites
    if (i == 1)
      roidSprite[i].prevFrame();
    else
      roidSprite[i].nextFrame();


    // Check for a collision between the UFO and roids
    if (ufoSprite.collidesWith(roidSprite[i], true)) {
      // Play an alert sound
      AlertType.ERROR.playSound(display);

      // Reset the sprite positions and speeds
      ufoSprite.setPosition((getWidth() - ufoSprite.getWidth()) / 2,
        (getHeight() - ufoSprite.getHeight()) / 2);
      ufoXSpeed = ufoYSpeed = 0;
      for (int j = 0; j < 3; j++)
        roidSprite[j].setPosition(0, 0);

      // No need to continue updating the roid sprites
      break;
    }
  }
}

private void draw(Graphics g) {
  // Clear the display
  g.setColor(0x000000);
  g.fillRect(0, 0, getWidth(), getHeight());

  // Draw the UFO sprite
  ufoSprite.paint(g);

  // Draw the roid sprites
  for (int i = 0; i < 3; i++)
    roidSprite[i].paint(g);

  // Flush the offscreen graphics buffer
  flushGraphics();
}

private void checkBounds(Sprite sprite) {
```

LISTING 6.1   Continued

```
    // Wrap the sprite around the screen if necessary
    if (sprite.getX() < -sprite.getWidth())
      sprite.setPosition(getWidth(), sprite.getY());
    else if (sprite.getX() > getWidth())
      sprite.setPosition(-sprite.getWidth(), sprite.getY());
    if (sprite.getY() < -sprite.getHeight())
      sprite.setPosition(sprite.getX(), getHeight());
    else if (sprite.getY() > getHeight())
      sprite.setPosition(sprite.getX(), -sprite.getHeight());
  }
}
```

You've already learned the ins and outs of this code, so I'll spare you more discussion. Let's see how it actually runs instead!

Testing the Finished Product

Testing the UFO 2 example MIDlet is considerably more interesting and entertaining than previous examples because you now get to use keys to control an animated graphical object (flying saucer). Figure 6.4 shows the UFO 2 MIDlet in all its glory as I carefully steer it around those pesky asteroids in the J2ME emulator.

It's not too hard to see the beginnings of an Asteroids-type game in this example. Take some time to play around with it and pay particularly close attention to how it handles collision detection. It's very apparent how using image data collision detection results in a great deal of accuracy, which translates into a flying saucer you can deftly guide between asteroids even when there is little room to spare.

FIGURE 6.4
The UFO 2 example MIDlet allows you to control a flying saucer and dodge asteroids by using mobile phone keys.

Summary

The ability to effectively communicate with the people who play your games is a critical factor of game design and development. It's very important for mobile game developers to master the fine art of responding to user input through the limited user interfaces made available by mobile phones. This chapter showed you how to respond to mobile phone key input, which is surprisingly simple. You also learned about sprite collision detection and how to use frame-animated sprites. Although it could certainly be improved, the UFO 2 example that was developed in this chapter demonstrates important elements of mobile game development.

The next chapter finally gets down to business and guides you through the creation of your first mobile game, Henway, which is somewhat of a tribute to the classic arcade game Frogger.

Extreme Game Makeover

It's time to get creative with these makeovers! I want you to dream up another type of sprite to add to the UFO 2 example that uses frame animation. It can be a satellite, a strange alien, or a comet cruising through the sky—whatever you want. Follow these steps to create your new sprite and integrate it into the MIDlet code:

1. Draw or otherwise obtain a sprite image, including a few frames of animation.
2. Create a member variable in the UFOCanvas class that stores a few instances of the new sprite.
3. Load the sprite image in the start() method of the MIDlet.
4. Also in the start() method, create the Sprite objects for the new sprites, making sure to pass in the sprite image and the size of each animation frame.
5. Add code to update the position of the new sprites, and check their bounds in the update() method. If you want to detect collisions between these sprites and any other sprites, feel free to do that here, too.
6. Add code to draw the new sprites in the draw() method.

Although several steps are involved, adding a new type of sprite to the UFO 2 example really isn't too terribly difficult. I guarantee you will find this makeover a worthy exercise because it will force you to dig into the code and experiment with adding something substantial to it.

CHAPTER 7

Henway: Paying Tribute to Frogger

Arcade Archive

Released in 1980 by Midway, Rally-X was a popular game that served as a combination racing game and maze game. You control a small car driving around a maze collecting flags while avoiding computer-controlled cars. The neat feature of Rally-X is the smoke screen you can emit from the back of your car to temporarily disable the enemy computer cars. However, the smoke screen uses up additional fuel, so you have to carefully manage your fuel while resisting the urge to go nuts with the smoke screen—a neat strategic touch! Another interesting feature of Rally-X is a zoomed-out map that shows your position, the flags you must collect, and the enemy cars with respect to the entire game area.

You've spent a fair amount of time throughout the book thus far learning the ins and outs of MIDlet programming and how to carry out mobile game-related programming tasks. But you haven't created a complete game yet. In this chapter, you embark on your first complete game, which takes what you've learned about sprites and puts it to very good use. The Henway game developed in this chapter uses several sprites and all the sprite features you've learned about in the preceding chapters. The game is somewhat of a takeoff on the classic Frogger game, and it represents a significant milestone in your game programming quest because it is such an interesting little game. This is the kind of game that you can use as the basis for your own game development efforts.

In this chapter, you'll learn

▶ Why modeling a mobile game on a classic arcade game is often a good idea

▶ How to design a mobile game called Henway that is somewhat of a takeoff on Frogger

▶ How to write the code for the Henway game

▶ Why testing a game of your own is often the most fun part of the development process

The Scoop on Henway

The original Frogger arcade game involved a frog whose goal was to make it safely across a highway and a river. Several obstacles appeared in the frog's path, including speeding cars, treacherous rushing water, and alligators, to name a few. Frogger played vertically, which means that you guided the frog from the bottom of the game screen to the top of the screen to reach safety. As you guided more and more frogs safely across, the game progressed to get more difficult by adding more cars and other obstacles to the mix. Although Frogger is certainly an incredibly simple game by modern gaming standards, it's a perfect example of a classic game with fun game play. This makes it a good candidate for creating a game of your own—just put a twist on the concept, and you can create your own Frogger-like masterpiece.

Gamer's Garage

In case you're wondering, I don't generally encourage basing all your games on existing classics, but I have found that popular games of the past can provide good ideas for new games. These days, everyone is busy trying to model computer games after movies, but not everyone is interested in playing a heavily scripted drama, especially on a mobile phone. Most of the time it's fun to fire up a mobile game and play for a few minutes as a light diversion; in which case, the classics are perfect.

The popularity of Frogger resulted in a variety of knockoff games being created to coattail Frogger's success. One of these games was called Freeway, which involved a chicken trying to cross a busy highway. Freeway was made by Activision for the Atari 2600 game system, which was the first console system to really hit it big. As a proud owner and player of Freeway, I thought it would be fun to create a similar game in this chapter. However, the game you create is called Henway, which comes from an old joke. If you've never heard the joke, it goes like this: You mention the word "henway" a few times in a conversation with a friend, and eventually he'll get up the nerve to say, "What's a henway?" And you immediately respond, "Oh, about three pounds." I know, it's a very bad joke, but it makes for a fun name for a game involving a chicken and a highway.

Unlike Frogger, the hero in Henway is a chicken who desperately needs to get from one side of a busy highway to the other. Also unlike Frogger, Henway plays horizontally, which means that you guide the chicken from the left side of the screen to the right side. So, the game screen looks something like the drawing in Figure 7.1.

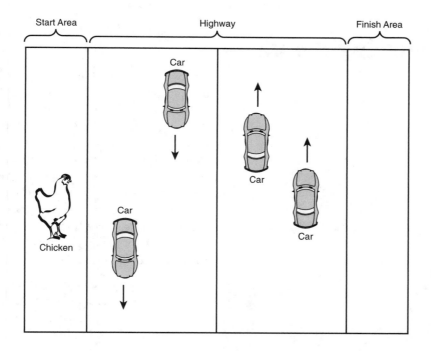

FIGURE 7.1
The Henway game consists of a Start Area, a Highway, and a Finish Area, along with chicken and car sprites.

As you can see, the obstacles working against the chicken are four cars cruising up and down four lanes of highway. The cars move at varying speeds, which makes it a little trickier to time the chicken's crossing. Unlike Frogger, which requires you to guide the frog into specific zones of the Finish Area, Henway just requires you to get the chicken across the road.

You'll notice that a common thread throughout all of the game examples in the book is simplicity. Although there are all kinds of enticing ways to improve on the games, I opted to leave it up to you to make the improvements. My goal is to provide you with a working mobile game that is simple enough to understand, and then you can jazz it up with extra features. In fact, I give you some great ideas for jazzing up the example games at the end of most of the chapters in the section titled "Extreme Game Makeover."

Gamer's Garage

You start the Henway game with a limited number of chickens: three. When all your chickens get run over, the game is over. It's important to show somewhere on the screen how many chickens you have remaining. Additionally, some kind of notification should take place to inform you when you lose a chicken, as well as when you successfully make it across the highway. It also wouldn't hurt to have some kind of scoring system for rewarding good game play.

Designing the Game

FIGURE 7.2
The chicken bitmap image shows two animation frames of a chicken walking to the right.

The overview of the Henway game has already given you a leg up on the game's design even if you don't realize it. For example, you already know how many sprites are required for the game. Can you hazard a guess? There are five sprites in the game: one chicken sprite and four car sprites. There is certainly the opportunity to include additional car sprites, possibly as a way to increase the difficulty of the game over time, but the basic game uses only four.

FIGURE 7.3
Each of the car bitmap images is oriented vertically so that the car appears to be traveling up or down.

Beyond the sprites, can you guess how many bitmap images the game needs? If you guessed six, you're very close. Following are the seven bitmap images required of the game:

FIGURE 7.4
The tiny chicken head bitmap image is sized to represent the number of lives remaining in the game.

- ▶ Background highway image
- ▶ Chicken image (see Figure 7.2)
- ▶ Four car images (see Figure 7.3)
- ▶ Small chicken head image (see Figure 7.4)

You probably factored in all these images except the last one. The small chicken head image is used to convey to the player how many chickens are left. As an example, when the game starts, three small chicken heads are displayed in the lower-right edge of the screen. As you sacrifice your chickens to the highway, the chickens disappear until you have none left and the game is over.

Now that you have a feel for the graphical objects involved in the game, let's consider other data that must be maintained by the game. First, it's pretty obvious that you'll need to keep track of how many chicken lives are remaining. You'll also want to keep a running score that is incremented each time a chicken makes it safely across the highway. A Boolean variable keeping track of whether the game is over is also required.

There is one last variable that would be hard for you to anticipate without actually developing the game and testing it out. I'm referring to an input delay variable, which helps to alter the key input response to improve the playability of the game. If you directly responded to the keys in every game cycle, which is how you would logically support input in the game, the chicken would zip around the game screen too fast. Simply too many game cycles are taking place to give user input that much attention, at least in this particular game. To slow down the input a little, you can use a delay variable and check for key input only every third game cycle.

Gamer's
Garage

Determining the appropriate input delay is somewhat of a trial-and-error process, so you're free to tinker with it and see what you like best. The point is that the game benefits dramatically if you put a leash on the speed of the user input handling. Also keep in mind that the input delay could possibly vary from one mobile phone to another one, depending on the specific hardware and MIDlet execution speed.

To recap, the design of the Henway game has led us to the following pieces of information that must be managed by the game:

- The number of chicken lives
- The score
- A Boolean "game over" variable
- An input delay variable

With this information in mind, you're now ready to move on and put the code together for the Henway game.

Developing the Game

By now, I hope you're getting antsy to see how the Henway game is put together. The next couple of sections explore the code development for the Henway game, which is relatively simple because much of the code builds on example code that you've already seen.

Writing the Game Code

Not surprisingly, the code for the Henway games begins in a customized canvas class, which is derived from the handy `GameCanvas` class. I'm referring to the `HCanvas` class, which is responsible for all the game logic in the Henway game. You see the complete code listing for the `HCanvas` in a moment, but for now let's focus on it a piece at a time. Following are the variables defined in the class:

```
private Display    display;
private boolean    sleeping;
private long       frameDelay;
private int        inputDelay;
private Random     rand;
private Image      background;
private Image      chickenHead;
private Sprite     chickenSprite;
private Sprite[]   carSprite = new Sprite[4];
private int[]      carYSpeed = new int[4];
private boolean    gameOver;
private int        numLives;
private int        score;
```

The sprites in the Henway game consist of a single chicken sprite and four car sprites.

Because the cars move only vertically, you only need to store their speeds in the Y direction.

The first three variables should already be somewhat familiar to you from the earlier UFO examples, along with the `rand` variable. The fourth variable, however, is entirely new. The `inputDelay` variable is used to carefully control the sensitivity of the user input controls in the game. It turns out that for this game in particular, the game play isn't as challenging if the player is allowed to rapidly move the chicken around at will. To help restrict the speed of the chicken's movements, you simply put a delay on the key input via the `inputDelay` variable.

The two `Image` variables represent the background highway image and the small chicken head image used to indicate the number of remaining lives. Although these images are important to the look of the game, the sprites are where the heart of the game lies. The `chickenSprite` variable stores away the sprite for the chicken while the `carSprite` array keeps track of the four car sprites. Because the chicken moves only a single position in response to each key press, there is no need to associate a speed with it. However, the cars do move at constant speeds, and therefore require their own `carYSpeed` variable, which is an array that indicates each car's speed along the Y axis.

The last three member variables are fairly common to most mobile games, and keep up with the status of the game, the number of remaining lives, and the score. The `gameOver` variable is used several places throughout the game code to determine whether or not the game is indeed over or still in play.

The numLives variable stores away the number of remaining chicken lives, and is used to help determine whether the game has ended, as well as how many chicken head images to draw on the screen. And finally, the score variable keeps up with the game's score, which is displayed at the end of the game.

As you know, the HCanvas constructor is called when the canvas object is initially created. In addition to establishing the frame rate for the game, the constructor also clears the input delay:

```
// Set the frame rate (30fps)
frameDelay = 33;

// Clear the input delay
inputDelay = 0;
```

> Remember that the frame rate is calculated as the inverse of the frame delay, in seconds. So, converting 33 milliseconds to seconds gives you 0.033. The inverse of 0.033 is approximately 30, which is how you end up with 30fps.

Construction Cue

The inputDelay variable makes much more sense a bit later in this discussion when you find out how it is actually used to control the key input.

The start() method has a lot of responsibility in the Henway game, and takes care of all the game-specific initialization tasks. For example, the following code initializes the three main game variables:

```
gameOver = false;
numLives = 3;
score = 0;
```

The start() method also handles loading images and creating the sprites for the game:

```
try {
  background = Image.createImage("/Highway.png");
  chickenHead = Image.createImage("/ChickenHead.png");

  chickenSprite = new Sprite(Image.createImage("/Chicken.png"), 22, 22);
  chickenSprite.setPosition(2, 77);

  carSprite[0] = new Sprite(Image.createImage("/Car1.png"));
  carSprite[0].setPosition(27, 0);
  carYSpeed[0] = 3;
  carSprite[1] = new Sprite(Image.createImage("/Car2.png"));
  carSprite[1].setPosition(62, 0);
  carYSpeed[1] = 1;
  carSprite[2] = new Sprite(Image.createImage("/Car3.png"));
  carSprite[2].setPosition(93, 67);
  carYSpeed[2] = -2;
```

The chicken sprite is carefully positioned to start out in the grass on the left side of the road.

This car, as well as the others, is carefully positioned within its lane on the road.

```
    carSprite[3] = new Sprite(Image.createImage("/Car4.png"));
    carSprite[3].setPosition(128, 64);
    carYSpeed[3] = -5;
}
catch (IOException e) {
  System.err.println("Failed loading images!");
}
```

This code first creates the background and chicken head images, and then gets down to business by creating the sprites. You will notice that each sprite is set to a specific position on the screen. Although you could use the width and height of the game screen and sprites to attempt to develop a generic equation to position the sprites, it is ultimately easier and more accurate to just hard-code the positions as I've done here. After the positions are nailed down, the speeds of the car sprites are set so that they travel at varying speeds and in different directions.

Construction Cue

This code brings up a good point about how the code in your games will vary according to your target mobile phone. In this case, the Henway game is targeting the J2ME emulator's default screen size of 180×177, so all the graphics positioning within the game is relative to that screen size. If you want to target a mobile phone with a different screen size, you have to tweak the sprite position values and likely the game images as well, especially the background image.

Although important, the significance of the start() method in mobile games pales in comparison to the role taken by the update() method, which essentially drives all the games in this book. In the Henway game, the update() method takes care of a variety of critical tasks, such as processing user input, moving the chicken sprite, updating the car sprites, and checking to see whether the chicken has been run over by a car or made it safely across the road. Before undertaking any of these tasks, however, the update() method first checks to see whether the game is being restarted:

```
if (gameOver) {
  int keyState = getKeyStates();
  if ((keyState & FIRE_PRESSED) != 0) {
    // Start a new game
    chickenSprite.setPosition(2, 77);
    gameOver = false;
    score = 0;
    numLives = 3;
  }

  // The game is over, so don't update anything
  return;
}
```

To start a new game, you just reposition the chicken and set a few game variables.

This code first looks to see whether the game is over, which is the only time where it makes sense to restart the game. The fire key is used to restart a game that is over; this key varies from phone to phone, but in the J2ME emulator it is the main Select key, which is mapped to the PC Enter key for emulation purposes. The game restart code in the update() method resets the position of the chicken sprite, clears the gameOver variable, resets the score to zero, and resets the number of remaining chicken lives to three. This is all it takes to start a new game.

The update()method is also responsible for handling user input and moving the chicken around the game screen accordingly. Following is the code that moves the chicken sprite in response to directional key presses:

```
if (++inputDelay > 2) {
  int keyState = getKeyStates();
  if ((keyState & LEFT_PRESSED) != 0) {
    chickenSprite.move(-6, 0);
    chickenSprite.nextFrame();
  }
  else if ((keyState & RIGHT_PRESSED) != 0) {
    chickenSprite.move(6, 0);
    chickenSprite.nextFrame();
  }
  if ((keyState & UP_PRESSED) != 0) {
    chickenSprite.move(0, -6);
    chickenSprite.nextFrame();
  }
  else if ((keyState & DOWN_PRESSED) != 0) {
    chickenSprite.move(0, 6);
    chickenSprite.nextFrame();
  }
  checkBounds(chickenSprite, false);

  // Reset the input delay
  inputDelay = 0;
}
```

In addition to being moved, the chicken's animation frame is changed in response to each directional key press.

The value of false passed into the second parameter indicates that the chicken should be prevented from moving past the edges of the game screen.

This code reveals how the inputDelay variable works—it is incremented in each game loop, and allows a key press to take place only every third game cycle. In other words, the responsiveness of the keys is reduced by a third, which happens to make the Henway game play a bit better in terms of limiting the chicken's movement to a more challenging level. After a key press is detected, this code moves the chicken sprite a specified distance and then changes its frame image with a call to nextFrame(). Because there are only two frames in the chicken sprite image, they are constantly alternated back and forth as you move the chicken around in the game. The net effect is that the chicken appears to be walking thanks to the simple frame animation.

> The usefulness of the inputDelay variable will certainly vary from game to game. In many games you will want the key input to perform with hair trigger responsiveness, in which case you would probably do away with the inputDelay variable entirely.

The other bit of code of interest in the key input handling code is the call to checkBounds(), which makes sure that the chicken stays within the bounds of the game screen. If you recall from the UFO 2 example, the checkBounds() method was used to wrap asteroids around the game screen. There is now a new version of checkBounds() in the Henway game that allows you to either wrap a sprite or restrict it from moving beyond the edges of the screen. The second parameter indicates which action should be taken; true results in the sprite wrapping, whereas false prevents the sprite from moving beyond the edges. You see the code for the revamped checkBounds() method a little later in this discussion.

The number 154 comes from the fact that the right edge of the road is 154 pixels across the game screen.

It's important for the update() method to check and see whether the chicken made it across the road after each move. Following is the code that looks for safe passage by the chicken:

```
if (chickenSprite.getX() > 154) {
    // Play a sound for making it safely across
    AlertType.WARNING.playSound(display);

    // Reset the chicken position and increment the score
    chickenSprite.setPosition(2, 77);
    score += 25;
}
```

The number 154 isn't magical; it's just the horizontal position on the game screen where the road ends. If the chicken's position is greater than this value, you know that it has made it safely across the road. In this case, a default "warning" sound is played to indicate a safe crossing, the chicken sprite's position is reset to the start position, and the score is incremented by 25 points.

The chicken isn't the only sprite in the Henway game that moves around. The update() method also takes care of moving the car sprites, as the following code reveals:

```
for (int i = 0; i < 4; i++) {
    // Move the car sprites
    carSprite[i].move(0, carYSpeed[i]);
    checkBounds(carSprite[i], true);

    // Check for a collision between the chicken and cars
    if (chickenSprite.collidesWith(carSprite[i], true)) {
        // Play a sound for losing a chicken
        AlertType.ERROR.playSound(display);
```

```
  // Check for a game over
  if (--numLives == 0) {
    gameOver = true;
  } else {
    // Reset the chicken position
    chickenSprite.setPosition(2, 77);
  }

  // No need to continue updating the car sprites
  break;
  }
}
```

If the game isn't over, the chicken is moved back to its start position to try another road crossing.

Each of the car sprites is moved in the Y direction via the carYSpeed variable, which is an array containing vertical speeds for the cars. The cars are then wrapped around the screen, if necessary: checkBounds() is called and a value of true is passed as the second parameter. The most important section of this code is the collision detection between the chicken sprite and the car sprites. If a collision occurs, a default "error" sound is played and the numLives variable is decremented. If the value of this variable has dropped to zero, you know the game is over so the gameOver variable is set to true. If not, the chicken sprite's position is reset and game play resumes. It's important to note that the loop breaks out when a collision occurs because there is no need to check and see whether the chicken has been hit more than once.

The draw() method in the HCanvas class is surprisingly straightforward, considering that there is a fair amount of graphical interest in the game. The first thing drawn in this method is the highway background image, which is accomplished in the following line of code:

```
g.drawImage(background, 0, 0, Graphics.TOP | Graphics.LEFT);
```

After the background, the number of remaining chicken lives is drawn, as this code reveals:

```
for (int i = 0; i < numLives; i++)
  g.drawImage(chickenHead, 180 - ((i + 1) * 8), 170, Graphics.TOP |
    Graphics.LEFT);
```

Perhaps the most important graphical object in the game, the chicken sprite, is actually the easiest thing to draw. It takes only one simple line of code to draw the chicken sprite:

```
chickenSprite.paint(g);
```

The car sprites aren't much tougher to draw; you just have to put the paint() method call in a loop so that each car gets drawn. This is how it's done:

```
for (int i = 0; i < 4; i++)
  carSprite[i].paint(g);
```

And finally, the last information to draw is the "game over" message and the score, but this drawing takes place only if the game is over. Following is the code that draws the "game over" information:

```
if (gameOver) {
  // Draw the game over message and score
  g.setColor(255, 255, 255); // white
  g.setFont(Font.getFont(Font.FACE_MONOSPACE, Font.STYLE_BOLD,
    Font.SIZE_LARGE));
  g.drawString("GAME OVER", 90, 40, Graphics.TOP | Graphics.HCENTER);
  g.setFont(Font.getFont(Font.FACE_MONOSPACE, Font.STYLE_BOLD,
    Font.SIZE_MEDIUM));
  g.drawString("You scored " + score + " points.", 90, 70, Graphics.TOP |
    Graphics.HCENTER);
}
```

A different sized font is used for each line of text so that the "game over" message appears larger than the score. Beyond that, there really isn't anything special about the code.

The final code I'd like to highlight in the HCanvas class is the code for the new and improved checkBounds() method, which either wraps or restricts a sprite based on whether or not the wrap parameter is set to true or false. Here's the code:

This code wraps a sprite around the edges of the game screen.

```
if (wrap) {
  // Wrap the sprite around the edges of the screen
  if (sprite.getX() < -sprite.getWidth())
    sprite.setPosition(getWidth(), sprite.getY());
  else if (sprite.getX() > getWidth())
    sprite.setPosition(-sprite.getWidth(), sprite.getY());
  if (sprite.getY() < -sprite.getHeight())
    sprite.setPosition(sprite.getX(), getHeight());
  else if (sprite.getY() > getHeight())
    sprite.setPosition(sprite.getX(), -sprite.getHeight());
}
else {
```

This code prevents a sprite from moving beyond the edges of the game screen.

```
  // Stop the sprite at the edges of the screen
  if (sprite.getX() < 0)
    sprite.setPosition(0, sprite.getY());
  else if (sprite.getX() > (getWidth() - sprite.getWidth()))
    sprite.setPosition(getWidth() - sprite.getWidth(), sprite.getY());
  if (sprite.getY() < 0)
    sprite.setPosition(sprite.getX(), 0);
  else if (sprite.getY() > (getHeight() - sprite.getHeight()))
    sprite.setPosition(sprite.getX(), getHeight() - sprite.getHeight());
}
```

The first block of code is identical to the code you saw for the checkBounds() method in the UFO 2 example. The second block is new, and acts to restrict a sprite from moving beyond the edges of the game screen. This functionality works perfectly for the chicken sprite because you don't want it to be able to wrap off the edges of the screen. You will find the checkBounds() method to be very useful as you continue to develop more interesting games throughout the book.

Although I hate to throw such a large code listing at you, it's worth seeing all the HCanvas code together in one place. Listing 7.1 contains the complete source code for the Henway game's HCanvas class.

LISTING 7.1 The HCanvas **Class Serves as a Customized Canvas for the Henway MIDlet Game**

```
import javax.microedition.lcdui.*;
import javax.microedition.lcdui.game.*;
import java.util.*;
import java.io.*;

public class HCanvas extends GameCanvas implements Runnable {
  private Display    display;
  private boolean    sleeping;
  private long       frameDelay;
  private int        inputDelay;
  private Random     rand;
  private Image      background;
  private Image      chickenHead;
  private Sprite     chickenSprite;
  private Sprite[]   carSprite = new Sprite[4];
  private int[]      carYSpeed = new int[4];
  private boolean    gameOver;
  private int        numLives;
  private int        score;

  public HCanvas(Display d) {
    super(true);
    display = d;

    // Set the frame rate (30 fps)
    frameDelay = 33;

    // Clear the input delay
    inputDelay = 0;
  }

  public void start() {
    // Set the canvas as the current screen
    display.setCurrent(this);

    // Initialize the random number generator
    rand = new Random();
```

LISTING 7.1 Continued

```
// Initialize the game variables
gameOver = false;
numLives = 3;
score = 0;

// Initialize the background image and chicken and car sprites
try {
  background = Image.createImage("/Highway.png");
  chickenHead = Image.createImage("/ChickenHead.png");

  chickenSprite = new Sprite(Image.createImage("/Chicken.png"), 22, 22);
  chickenSprite.setPosition(2, 77);

  carSprite[0] = new Sprite(Image.createImage("/Car1.png"));
  carSprite[0].setPosition(27, 0);
  carYSpeed[0] = 3;
  carSprite[1] = new Sprite(Image.createImage("/Car2.png"));
  carSprite[1].setPosition(62, 0);
  carYSpeed[1] = 1;
  carSprite[2] = new Sprite(Image.createImage("/Car3.png"));
  carSprite[2].setPosition(93, 67);
  carYSpeed[2] = -2;
  carSprite[3] = new Sprite(Image.createImage("/Car4.png"));
  carSprite[3].setPosition(128, 64);
  carYSpeed[3] = -5;
}
catch (IOException e) {
  System.err.println("Failed loading images!");
}

// Start the animation thread
sleeping = false;
Thread t = new Thread(this);
t.start();
}

public void stop() {
  // Stop the animation
  sleeping = true;
}

public void run() {
  Graphics g = getGraphics();

  // The main game loop
  while (!sleeping) {
    update();
    draw(g);
    try {
      Thread.sleep(frameDelay);
    }
    catch (InterruptedException ie) {}
  }
}
```

The last car is the fastest of the four cars.

LISTING 7.1   Continued

```
private void update() {
  // Check to see whether the game is being restarted
  if (gameOver) {
    int keyState = getKeyStates();
    if ((keyState & FIRE_PRESSED) != 0) {
      // Start a new game
      chickenSprite.setPosition(2, 77);
      gameOver = false;
      score = 0;
      numLives = 3;
    }

    // The game is over, so don't update anything
    return;
  }

  // Process user input to move the chicken
  if (++inputDelay > 2) {
    int keyState = getKeyStates();
    if ((keyState & LEFT_PRESSED) != 0) {
      chickenSprite.move(-6, 0);
      chickenSprite.nextFrame();
    }
    else if ((keyState & RIGHT_PRESSED) != 0) {
      chickenSprite.move(6, 0);
      chickenSprite.nextFrame();
    }
    if ((keyState & UP_PRESSED) != 0) {
      chickenSprite.move(0, -6);
      chickenSprite.nextFrame();
    }
    else if ((keyState & DOWN_PRESSED) != 0) {
      chickenSprite.move(0, 6);
      chickenSprite.nextFrame();
    }
    checkBounds(chickenSprite, false);

    // Reset the input delay
    inputDelay = 0;
  }

  // See whether the chicken made it across
  if (chickenSprite.getX() > 154) {
    // Play a sound for making it safely across
    AlertType.WARNING.playSound(display);

    // Reset the chicken position and increment the score
    chickenSprite.setPosition(2, 77);
    score += 25;
  }

  // Update the car sprites
  for (int i = 0; i < 4; i++) {
```

LISTING 7.1 Continued

A value of true as the second parameter indicates that the cars are wrapped around the edges of the game screen.

```java
    // Move the car sprites
    carSprite[i].move(0, carYSpeed[i]);
    checkBounds(carSprite[i], true);

    // Check for a collision between the chicken and cars
    if (chickenSprite.collidesWith(carSprite[i], true)) {
      // Play a sound for losing a chicken
      AlertType.ERROR.playSound(display);

      // Check for a game over
      if (--numLives == 0) {
        gameOver = true;
      } else {
        // Reset the chicken position
        chickenSprite.setPosition(2, 77);
      }

      // No need to continue updating the car sprites
      break;
    }
  }
}

private void draw(Graphics g) {
  // Draw the highway background
  g.drawImage(background, 0, 0, Graphics.TOP | Graphics.LEFT);
```

A series of small chicken head images are drawn in the lower-right corner of the game screen to indicate how many lives remain.

```java
  // Draw the number of remaining lives
  for (int i = 0; i < numLives; i++)
    g.drawImage(chickenHead, 180 - ((i + 1) * 8), 170, Graphics.TOP |
      Graphics.LEFT);

  // Draw the chicken sprite
  chickenSprite.paint(g);

  // Draw the car sprites
  for (int i = 0; i < 4; i++)
    carSprite[i].paint(g);

  if (gameOver) {
    // Draw the game over message and score
    g.setColor(255, 255, 255); // white
    g.setFont(Font.getFont(Font.FACE_MONOSPACE, Font.STYLE_BOLD,
      Font.SIZE_LARGE));
    g.drawString("GAME OVER", 90, 40, Graphics.TOP | Graphics.HCENTER);
    g.setFont(Font.getFont(Font.FACE_MONOSPACE, Font.STYLE_BOLD,
      Font.SIZE_MEDIUM));
    g.drawString("You scored " + score + " points.", 90, 70, Graphics.TOP |
      Graphics.HCENTER);
  }
```

LISTING 7.1 Continued

```
  // Flush the offscreen graphics buffer
  flushGraphics();
}

private void checkBounds(Sprite sprite, boolean wrap) {
  // Wrap/stop the sprite if necessary
  if (wrap) {
    // Wrap the sprite around the edges of the screen
    if (sprite.getX() < -sprite.getWidth())
      sprite.setPosition(getWidth(), sprite.getY());
    else if (sprite.getX() > getWidth())
      sprite.setPosition(-sprite.getWidth(), sprite.getY());
    if (sprite.getY() < -sprite.getHeight())
      sprite.setPosition(sprite.getX(), getHeight());
    else if (sprite.getY() > getHeight())
      sprite.setPosition(sprite.getX(), -sprite.getHeight());
  }
  else {
    // Stop the sprite at the edges of the screen
    if (sprite.getX() < 0)
      sprite.setPosition(0, sprite.getY());
    else if (sprite.getX() > (getWidth() - sprite.getWidth()))
      sprite.setPosition(getWidth() - sprite.getWidth(), sprite.getY());
    if (sprite.getY() < 0)
      sprite.setPosition(sprite.getX(), 0);
    else if (sprite.getY() > (getHeight() - sprite.getHeight()))
      sprite.setPosition(sprite.getX(), getHeight() - sprite.getHeight());
  }
}
}
```

I hope the length of this code listing doesn't intimidate you too much. If you take some time to study it, you'll realize that you've already covered all the code in isolated pieces; this listing just pulls it all together to show you how it fits into the complete HCanvas class.

The HenwayMIDlet class is a generic MIDlet class that simply creates an instance of the HCanvas class. For this reason, I'll spare you the details of the MIDlet class code here. Keep in mind that the complete source code for the Henway MIDlet, along with all the other example programs in the book, is located on the accompanying CD-ROM.

Testing the Game

You should find the Henway game to be much more fun to test than the UFO example from the previous two chapters. Henway is the first complete mobile game that you've created, which makes it considerably more interesting from a user perspective.

FIGURE 7.5
The Henway game begins with the chicken in the Start Area, ready to make an attempt at crossing the busy highway.

It is also an action game, which potentially makes testing a bit trickier; action games often require a greater deal of testing because it's hard to predict how moving sprites will react in every little situation. You should play your games a great deal to make sure that nothing out of the ordinary ever happens, or at least nothing detrimental that's out of the ordinary.

Figure 7.5 shows the Henway game at the start, with your lion-hearted chicken poised for a trip across the highway.

To get started with the game, just begin guiding your chicken through traffic with the directional keys on the mobile phone (arrow keys on your keyboard if you're using the J2ME emulator). If you successfully navigate the chicken across the highway, the game plays an alert sound and awards you with 25 points.

FIGURE 7.6
Getting hit by a car isn't as grisly as you might expect, but the game does lower the number of available lives to indicate that you've lost a chicken.

Of course, even the best Henway player eventually gets careless and steers the chicken into the path of an oncoming car. When this happens, a different alert sound is played and the chicken is repositioned at its start position. More importantly, the number of remaining lives is visibly reduced, as you can see in the lower-right corner of the screen in Figure 7.6.

If you find that the keyboard controls respond too sluggishly in the game, try lowering the value being tested against the `inputDelay` variable from 2 to 1. This speeds up the controls by a third.

When you eventually lose all three chickens, the game ends. Figure 7.7 shows the end of the game, which simply involves a "game over" message being displayed, along with your final score.

Although it might seem sad to steer three chickens to their demise in a highway full of busy traffic, it's all just a game. Despite its simplicity, I hope you can appreciate the Henway game in terms of it representing a culmination of much of what you've learned throughout the book thus far. Even so, there is much ahead as you continue to build more exciting games from here on.

FIGURE 7.7
When you've depleted all your chickens, the game ends.

Summary

It is a fact of life that book knowledge can get you only so far before you have to experience something yourself. This chapter showed you how to make book knowledge real when you assembled your first complete mobile game. The Henway game made use of the user input techniques you learned about in the previous chapter, as well as the sprite animation skills you've been continually developing. Hopefully it is now becoming apparent to you that the MIDP 2.0 API makes it possible to develop interesting mobile games with a minimal amount of suffering. The good news is that the example games only get more interesting from here on!

Although you played a few default phone sounds in the Henway game, the next chapter explores the sound features built into J2ME. You learn how to play custom digitized sounds, and in fact revisit the Henway game to take advantage of more appropriate game sounds.

Extreme Game Makeover

One interesting change that would make the Henway game more challenging is adding open manholes (sewage holes) in the streets that the chicken is capable of falling through. These manholes are created as sprites, and you use collision detection to see whether the chicken has collided with them and fallen to its death. Following are the steps required to add manholes of doom to the Henway game:

1. Create a sprite image for the new manhole sprite, which is basically just a black hole.

2. In the start() method, create the manhole sprites, making sure to provide the newly created manhole image as the sprites' image. Make sure to set the position of the sprites so that they appear in the lanes of the road.

3. Add code to the draw() method to draw the new manhole sprites, making sure to draw them after the background image but before you draw the chicken and car sprites. This is important because you want the manholes to appear below the chicken and cars.

4. Add a check in the update() function to see whether the chicken sprite has collided with any of the manhole sprites. If so, end the game as if the chicken had gotten run over by a car.

You'll find that this change to the Henway game makes the game considerably more challenging. It's even better if you add some randomness to the positioning of the manholes so that they appear in different locations with each new game.

CHAPTER 8

Making Noise with Tones

Arcade Archive

Released in 1981 by Midway, Gorf is one of the most popular space shoot-em-ups to come out after Space Invaders and Galaxian. Perhaps this is because Gorf directly incorporates elements of both of those games into its design. Gorf is known for its robotic speech synthesis, which is used to heckle the player at various points throughout the game. The strange title is not "Frog backwards," as some gamers thought, but is instead an acronym for Galactic Orbiting Robot Force. I kind of like the backwards Frog explanation better!

In 1977, a science fiction movie other than *Star Wars* created quite a stir and stamped in the memory of its viewers a familiar musical theme consisting solely of five notes. If you aren't sure of the movie, just hang in there because I'll get to it later in the chapter as an example of how to create game music using tones. This chapter explores tonal sound in general, and how J2ME makes it possible to play individual tones and sequences of tones. You can use tones for both sound effects and music in games, and the great thing is that tones are guaranteed to be supported in all MIDP 2.0 phones.

In this chapter, you'll learn

- ▶ About the support J2ME provides for adding sound to mobile games
- ▶ The basic theory behind tonal sound and music
- ▶ How to query a mobile phone for its audio capabilities
- ▶ How to play tones and tone sequences in mobile games

Sound and Mobile Games

Admittedly, sound has not been the strong suit of most mobile phones to date. Although it may be cute to download a ring tone that sounds like a tacky Muzak twist on a pop song, mobile phone sound hasn't been taken too terribly seriously just yet. Although phone speakers will likely continue to have some limitations (mainly due to size), headphones make it possible to hear high-quality sounds and music. So if you aren't already using your phone as an MP3 player, you probably will very soon. And if you can play MP3 music on a phone, you can hear high-quality sound effects and music in mobile games.

J2ME supports mobile audio through the Mobile Media API, which is a collection of classes and interfaces that supports varying degrees of multimedia based upon specific types of devices. More specifically, the Mobile Media API is divided into two distinct API sets:

▶ **Mobile Media API**—For devices with advanced sound and multimedia capabilities

▶ **MIDP 2.0 Media API**—For restricted devices that support only audio

Not surprisingly, most mobile phones currently fall under the MIDP 2.0 Media API, so that's what we're going to focus on for the purposes of adding sound to mobile games. So that you have a better understanding of what is possible when you use the MIDP 2.0 Media API, following is a list of what every MIDP 2.0 device must support in terms of a minimal multimedia feature set:

▶ Basic controls such as start, stop, pause, and so on

▶ Media-specific controls such as volume adjustment

▶ Generation of tones and tone sequences

Tones and tone sequences are what you may already be familiar with as *ring tones*. In terms of games, this means that you can use the MIDP 2.0 Media API to create custom tones and tone sequences as sound effects and music for games. The API doesn't stop there, however. It provides the flexibility for specific phones to support additional media types such as wave sounds, MIDI music, and MP3 audio. These more advanced media types aren't guaranteed to be available on all MIDP 2.0 phones, but some phones will certainly support them. As a game developer, you have the option of using tones or the more advanced sound options, or possibly even some combination of the two.

The MIDP 2.0 Media API is designed around three major components: a manager, a player, and a control. Together, these components make it possible to use a consistent programming interface to play a wide range of audio. The classes and interfaces that comprise the MIDP 2.0 Media API are located in the `javax.microedition.media` and `javax.microedition.media.control` packages. The `Manager` class, which is located in the `media` package, is the class that allows you to query a phone for its media capabilities, along with creating players for various media types. The `Player` interface, which is in the same package, provides a generic set of methods for manipulating the playback of audio. The `Control` interface serves as a base interface for specific types of media controls such as a volume control and a tone control. The `VolumeControl` and `ToneControl` interfaces are located in the `media.control` package.

The general approach involved in playing audio with the MIDP 2.0 Media API is as follows:

1. Use the `Manager` class to obtain a player for a specific media type.

2. Use the `Player` interface on the specific player to play the media.

3. Use the `Control` interface to alter the playback of the media, if necessary.

These steps are very general, and certainly vary according to the media type. For example, playing a single tone simply involves one call to a static method in the `Manager` class called `playTone()`. On the other hand, playing a tone sequence requires using the `ToneControl` interface to build a tone sequence and play it through a tone player. You learn how to play both tones and tone sequences in this chapter, whereas waves, MIDI music, and MP3 audio are covered in the next chapter.

A Tonal Sound and Music Primer

Before you start learning the specifics of how to play tones with the MIDP 2.0 Media API, it's important to cover some basic knowledge relating to tonal sound and music. You may already know that a physical sound is a wave that moves through the air, kind of like an air equivalent of an ocean wave. A sound wave is actually a result of the pressure of air expanding and contracting. In other words, a sound wave is a series of traveling pressure changes in the air. You hear sound because the traveling sound wave eventually gets to your ears, where the pressure changes are processed and interpreted by your eardrums. If your eardrums are rocky outcroppings on a beach, then you hear sound when an ocean wave crashes against the rocks. The softness or loudness of a sound is determined by the amount of energy in the wave, which corresponds to the height and force of an ocean wave.

The frequency of a sound wave is the speed at which the sound wave oscillates, or vibrates, as it travels through the air. The oscillation of a sound wave is known as its pitch, and can be easily heard if you hit a spoon on the rim of a glass of water. The amount of water in the glass affects the frequency of the sound waves, and therefore alters the pitch of the sound heard when you strike the glass.

Sound frequency is measured in Hertz (Hz), which is simply the number of oscillations occurring per second. Musical notes actually correspond to certain specific frequencies of sound. For example, middle C on a musical scale is approximately 262Hz. Rather than write sheet music in terms of a bunch of numbers in Hertz, musical notes were given letter names such as A, B, and C. Table 8.1 shows the "one-line c" octave, which contains the twelve notes and their respective frequencies.

TABLE 8.1   Frequency Values for Middle Octave Musical Notes

Musical Note	Frequency (Hz)
A	220
A#	233
B	247
C	262
C#	277
D	294
D#	311
E	330
F	349
F#	370
G	392
G#	416

You may know that musical notes repeat themselves as you go higher or lower in pitch; each set of 12 notes is known as an octave. A note that is an octave higher than another note is exactly two times the note in frequency. Similarly, a half-octave note is half the frequency of the original note. To put this into real numbers, the C note an octave higher than middle C has a frequency of 524Hz. Table 8.2 shows the relationship between C notes in different octaves.

If you're thinking that this musical discussion sounds a bit overkill for a chapter devoted to playing mobile phone tones, let me assure you that you will be putting all this knowledge to use by the end of the chapter. Like it or not, tones on mobile phones are musical in nature, so musical notation provides the best approach to specifying tones for games.

Gamer's Garage

TABLE 8.2 Frequency Values and Names for C Musical Notes in Different Octaves

Musical Note/Octave	Name	Frequency (Hz)
-2 Octave C	C2	66
-1 Octave C	C3	132
Middle C	C4	264
+1 Octave C	C5	528
+2 Octave C	C6	1056

The "name" given to each of the notes in Table 8.2 is significant because it provides a consistent means of referencing musical notes by their specific octave. In other words, you can specify a specific note at a specific frequency using a simple notation such as C5, A2, G4, and so on. This naming convention is important because you'll be using it later in the chapter when you learn how to create and play tone sequences. Before you get to that, however, let's find out how to query a phone for its audio support and play a tone in response.

Querying a Phone for Its Audio Capabilities

Before making a bunch of blind (or deaf) assumptions about what a phone can and cannot do in terms of playing audio, you might want to consider just asking the phone what it can do. The MIDP 2.0 Media API provides a very straightforward approach to querying a phone for its audio capabilities. You can then use this knowledge to enable and disable certain audio features in your games. For example, you might create alternate sounds for your games in tone versions and wave versions, and play one set or the other depending on whether or not a phone supports wave sounds.

> All MIDP 2.0 phones support tones and tone sequences, so you can always count on being able to use them for game sounds and music.

You use the `Manager` class to request a phone's media capabilities. More specifically, the static `getSupportedContentTypes()` method of the `Manager` class provides a list of the media content types supported by a phone. Because the method is static, you don't actually create a `Manager` object to call it. The method returns an array of strings that serves as a list of the supported content types. Following is an example of how you would call this method to ascertain the supported content types:

```
String[] contentTypes = Manager.getSupportedContentTypes(null);
```

I told you it was easy! After this call, the `contentTypes` array contains a list of the supported content types according to their MIME names. Following is a list of the more common audio MIME types supported by MIDP 2.0 mobile phones:

- ▶ `audio/x-tone-seq`—Tones and tone sequences
- ▶ `audio/x-wav`—Wave sounds
- ▶ `audio/midi`—MIDI music
- ▶ `audio/mpeg`—MP3 audio

Although it's interesting to theorize about what kinds of results the `getSupportedContentTypes()` method might return, it's even better to try it out on a real device. Listing 8.1 contains the code for the customized `SCCanvas` class in the SoundCheck MIDlet, which queries a phone for its sound capabilities and displays each supported media content type.

> The `Manager` class supports another method called `getSupportedProtocols()` that queries a device for the transfer protocols that can be used to acquire a specific content type. For example, a phone may allow you to load a wave file from a JAR file containing the MIDlet, but not load it from an HTTP connection. Because the games in this book are designed to have their media reside with the MIDlet files, it's not so important to query a phone for its supported media protocols.

LISTING 8.1   The SCCanvas Class Serves as a Customized Canvas for the SoundCheck MIDlet

```
import javax.microedition.lcdui.*;
import javax.microedition.media.*;
import javax.microedition.media.control.*;

public class SCCanvas extends Canvas {
  private Display  display;

  public SCCanvas(Display d) {
    super();
    display = d;
  }

  void start() {
    display.setCurrent(this);
    repaint();
  }

  public void paint(Graphics g) {
    // Clear the canvas
    g.setColor(0, 0, 0);         // black
    g.fillRect(0, 0, getWidth(), getHeight());
    g.setColor(255, 255, 255);  // white

    // Get the supported sound content types
    String[] contentTypes = Manager.getSupportedContentTypes(null);

    // Draw the supported sound content types
    int y = 0;
    for (int i = 0; i < contentTypes.length; i++) {
      // Draw the content type
      g.drawString(contentTypes[i], 0, y, Graphics.TOP | Graphics.LEFT);
      y += Font.getDefaultFont().getHeight();

      // Play a tone if tone generation is supported
      if (contentTypes[i] == "audio/x-tone-seq") {
        try {
          // play middle C (C4) for two seconds (2000ms) at maximum volume (100)
          Manager.playTone(ToneControl.C4, 2000, 100);
        }
        catch(MediaException me) {
        }
      }
    }
  }
}
```

A single line of code retrieves all the supported media content types.

A tone in middle C is played for 2 seconds at full volume if tone generation is supported.

The paint() method is responsible for displaying the list of supported media content types. As you can see, the Manager.getSupportedContentTypes() method is called to fill a string array with the available content types. A loop is then established that draws the available types to the screen, one at a time. Also notice that the two additional media packages are imported into this code in the first few lines.

FIGURE 8.1
The SoundCheck
example MIDlet
queries a mobile
phone for its audio
capabilities.

One interesting twist in the code is the check for the audio/x-tone-seq type, which results in a tone being played. The static playTone() method in the Manager class, which you learn about in the next section, is used to play the tone. For now, all you really need to know is that the second method parameter is the duration to play the note, in milliseconds, which means that the note is being played for 2 seconds, whereas the third parameter is the volume (100%).

Although the code is certainly interesting, seeing the results of the SoundCheck MIDlet is much more revealing. Figure 8.1 shows the SoundCheck MIDlet running in the J2ME Emulator.

As you can see in the figure, the mobile phone in the J2ME emulator supports tones, waves, MIDI music, and MP3 audio (mpeg). You could easily use these results to enable specific types of audio in your games if you wanted to allow them to scale smoothly across different mobile phones.

Playing Tones in Mobile Games

There are two fundamentally different approaches to playing tones in mobile games: using individual tones and using tone sequence. An individual tone is simply a single tone at a specific pitch played for a single unit of time. Although they are certainly limited in terms of what kinds of game events they can be applied to, individual tones are nonetheless an important part of mobile game development because of their simplicity and efficiency. It takes very little code to play a single tone, and more importantly, very little time and resources in most cases.

Tone sequences are much more versatile in terms of conveying more interesting sounds and music, and even establishing a level of emotion for different parts of a game. You can think of a tone sequence as being akin to a ring tone on your phone.

Tone sequences are just series of individual tones, but they are highly structured in terms of their pitches and durations. In fact, a tone sequence is really a piece of music. This explains why I hit you with such a thorough discussion of sound frequency and musical notes earlier in the chapter—it is critical in order to create tone sequences.

Playing Individual Tones

The Manager class in the javax.microedition.media package is what you use to play individual tones. This class includes a static method named playTone() that accepts the following parameters to play a single tone:

- **Note**—The pitch of the tone, in the range 0 to 127
- **Duration**—The duration of the tone, in milliseconds
- **Volume**—The volume of the tone, as a percentage of the current device volume level

Specifying the pitch of a note in the range 0 to 127 is admittedly a bit arbitrary, but you can use a tricky math equation to calculate the note value based upon a note frequency. Rather than get into that, however, I'd rather show you a much simpler way to determine the value of notes to be played. If you recall from earlier in the chapter, there are 12 musical notes in an octave (see Table 8.1). By arranging several octaves (sets of 12 notes) in order of increasing pitch, you come up with a set of 128 notes. That's where the 0 to 127 range comes from: Each note is one byte of data.

It so happens that the note middle C is at position 60 in the note range. Conveniently, the ToneControl interface in the javax.microedition.media. control package defines a constant for middle C named C4 (C in the fourth octave). Because you know the order of notes from basic music theory (or Table 8.1), you can easily calculate other notes by simply using the C4 constant and an offset. Following are some examples of how you might define variables to represent other notes based on the C4 constant:

```
byte C4 = ToneControl.C4;
byte C5 = (byte)(C4 + 12);
byte A6 = (byte)(C4 + 21);
byte B6 = (byte)(C4 + 23);
byte G5 = (byte)(C4 + 19);
byte G4 = (byte)(C4 + 7);
byte D5 = (byte)(C4 + 14);
```

The first variable is just a convenience variable to simplify the usage of the `ToneControl.C4` constant. The remaining variables are notes in various octaves that are calculated as offsets from middle C (`C4`). The `C5` variable is particularly interesting because it is exactly one octave higher than `C4`. Because there are 12 notes in an octave, you simply add 12 to `C4` to get `C5`; similarly, you subtract 12 from `C4` to get `C3`. Please refer back to the order of notes in Table 8.1 to better understand how adding or subtracting note positions to `C4` allows you to determine the values of other notes.

Now that you know how to determine the pitch of a note, all you must do is pass it into the `Manager.playTone()` method to play a tone, like this:

```
try {
  // play middle C (C4) for two seconds (2000ms) at maximum volume (100)
  Manager.playTone(ToneControl.C4, 2000, 100);
}
  catch(MediaException me) {
}
```

This code takes the easy way out by simply playing middle C, which requires no offset. You'll notice that the other two parameters establish that the note is played for two seconds at 100% of the current volume. You may also notice that the `playTone()` method is called within a `try-catch` clause. This is necessary because the method is capable of throwing a `MediaException` if something goes wrong during an attempt to play the tone. In this particular example, the code does nothing in response to a media exception, but you can choose to print an error message or otherwise log the error in your own code.

Playing a Tone Sequence

A tone sequence is just a series of tones played in order, but they are considerably more involved to construct and play in a mobile game. This mainly has to do with the fact that you are actually coding a musical score when you create a tone sequence, which is not a trivial task. Following are the basic steps required to play a tone sequence with the MIDP 2.0 Media API:

1. Create a player.

2. Realize the player.

3. Get the tone control for the player.

4. Set the tone sequence on the control.

5. Use the player to play the sequence.

6. Close the player.

This sounds like a lot of work, but it's really not too bad. The trickiest part is creating the data structure that represents the tone sequence. After the tone sequence is created, setting it up and playing it takes only a few lines of code.

A tone sequence is stored as an array of bytes, with each byte in the array having a very specific meaning. As long as you carefully construct this array with the information in the proper places, you'll find that creating and using tone sequences is no big deal. To construct a tone sequence as an array of bytes, you must use several constants defined in the ToneControl interface. Following are the most important ToneControl constants:

- VERSION—The version of the tone sequence (typically set to 1 for new sequences)
- TEMPO—The tempo of the tone sequence (how fast it plays)
- BLOCK_START—The start of a block of tones (a sub-sequence)
- BLOCK_END—The end of a block of tones
- PLAY_BLOCK—The notes to be played, including blocks

The version and the tempo shouldn't require too much explanation, although I'll come back to them in a moment. A *block* in a tone sequence is a sub-sequence of tones. For example, if you have a chorus in a song that you want to repeat several times throughout the song, you can put the notes for the chorus into a block. Then, rather than duplicate the notes over and over, you can just reference the block of notes. The PLAY_BLOCK constant is where you indicate which notes are to be played and in what order. You can specify individual notes or a block of notes when using the PLAY_BLOCK constant, or a combination of the two.

I realize that this discussion is probably a little difficult to grasp simply because it's hard to visualize how constants equate to a sequence of tones, so let's jump right in and take a look at a real example. Following is the code for a tone sequence array for a song you may find familiar:

```
byte[] marylambSequence = {
  ToneControl.VERSION, 1,
  ToneControl.TEMPO, 30,
  ToneControl.BLOCK_START, 0,
  E4,8, D4,8, C4,8, D4,8,
  E4,8, E4,8, E4,8, rest,8,
  ToneControl.BLOCK_END, 0,
  ToneControl.PLAY_BLOCK, 0,
```

The "A" section of the song, which acts as a chorus, is defined.

This code plays the "A" section.

Play the "B" section. [
```
    D4,8, D4,8, D4,8, rest,8,
    E4,8, G4,8, G4,8, rest,8,
```

Play the "A" section again. [
```
    ToneControl.PLAY_BLOCK, 0,
```

Play the "C" section. [
```
    D4,8, D4,8, E4,8, D4,8, C4,8
};
```

As you can see, the version is first set to 1 and the tempo is set to 30. Tempo is actually measured in beats per minute, or bpm, but when expressing the tempo as a byte value in a tone sequence you must divide the bpm value by 4. In other words, if you want to play a tone sequence at 120bpm, you would specify 30 as the value for the tempo, as in this example.

The BLOCK_START constant begins the "A" section of the tone sequence. The "A" has no special meaning other than to identify it separately from the other parts of the music. In this case, the song is "Mary Had a Little Lamb," and the sections of notes in the song are played as ABAC. In other words, the A block of notes is played twice: once at the beginning and once after the B section. Because the B and C sections of notes aren't repeated, there is no need to place them in their own blocks.

Each note in the sequence is defined by a pair of values, which identify the pitch of the note followed by its duration. For example, the first note in the A block is note E4, and its duration is set to 8. In fact, all the notes in this particular song are set to 8, which corresponds to an eighth note. Table 8.3 lists the duration values that you can use to represent common musical note lengths.

TABLE 8.3 Musical Note Lengths and Their Corresponding Duration Values

Musical Note Length	Duration Value
1/1 (Full note)	64
1/2 (Half note)	32
1/4 (Quarter note)	16
1/8 (Eighth note)	8

To help put all of this tone sequence information into perspective, take a look at Figure 8.2, which shows the sequence of notes being played and how they correspond to tone data.

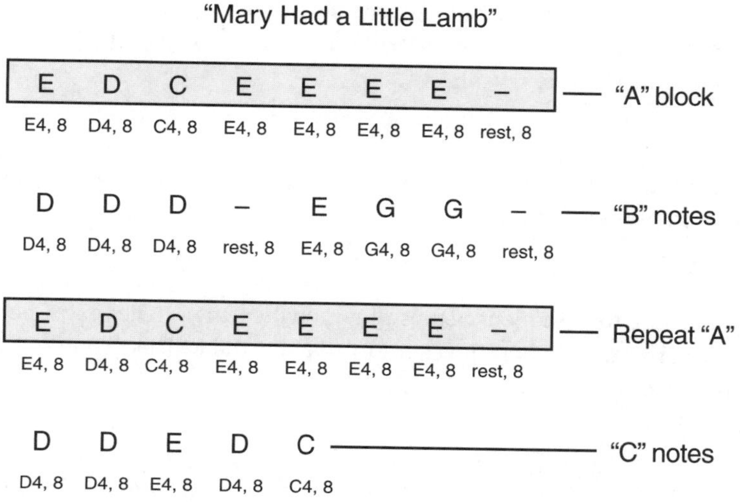

"Mary Had a Little Lamb"

FIGURE 8.2
The song "Mary Had a Little Lamb" can be coded as notes for inclusion in a tone sequence without too much trouble.

E	D	C	E	E	E	E	–	— "A" block
E4, 8	D4, 8	C4, 8	E4, 8	E4, 8	E4, 8	E4, 8	rest, 8	

D	D	D	–	E	G	G	–	— "B" notes
D4, 8	D4, 8	D4, 8	rest, 8	E4, 8	G4, 8	G4, 8	rest, 8	

E	D	C	E	E	E	E	–	— Repeat "A"
E4, 8	D4, 8	C4, 8	E4, 8	E4, 8	E4, 8	E4, 8	rest, 8	

D	D	E	D	C	— "C" notes
D4, 8	D4, 8	E4, 8	D4, 8	C4, 8	

Going back to the tone sequence code for this song, I didn't explain how the rest variable is used. The rest variable represents silence in the song, and is used to establish a pause between certain notes. The SILENCE constant in the ToneControl interface is used to indicate silence in a tone sequence. Following is how the rest variable is declared:

```
byte rest = ToneControl.SILENCE;
```

After you've constructed a tone sequence array of bytes, you can get down to the business of playing it with a player and a tone control. The first step in this process is creating a player that is capable of playing tones. Following is the code to carry this out:

```
Player tonePlayer = Manager.createPlayer(Manager.TONE_DEVICE_LOCATOR);
```

The TONE_DEVICE_LOCATOR constant is used to indicate that you want to create a player for playing tones. As soon as you have the player, you must "realize" it to secure resources for it so that you can begin playing tones:

```
tonePlayer.realize();
```

To set the tone sequence for playback, you must access the tone control within the player. A call to the getControl() method of the player is all that is required:

```
ToneControl toneControl = (ToneControl)tonePlayer.getControl("ToneControl");
```

With the tone control in hand, you call the setSequence() method on it to set the tone sequence. This is where the byte array that you created earlier comes into play, as the following code reveals:

```
toneControl.setSequence(marylambSequence);
```

And finally, to actually play the tone sequence, you must call the start() method on the player, like this:

```
tonePlayer.start();
```

To ensure that the tone sequence stops playing when the MIDlet exits, be sure to close the player somewhere in the cleanup code for the MIDlet. You do this by calling the close() method, as follows:

```
tonePlayer.close();
```

It's important to note that most of these media methods are capable of throwing exceptions, and must therefore be placed within a try-catch clause. Following is an example of how you might create a player and play a tone sequence in a single block of code:

```
try{
  Player tonePlayer = Manager.createPlayer(Manager.TONE_DEVICE_LOCATOR);
  tonePlayer.realize();
  ToneControl toneControl = (ToneControl)tonePlayer.getControl("ToneControl");
  toneControl.setSequence(marylambSequence);
  tonePlayer.start();
}
catch (IOException ioe) {
}
catch (MediaException me) {
}
```

Although there is certainly more to the MIDP 2.0 Media API and its handling of tones than I've shown here, I think you know enough to move on and see how to add a tone sequence to a real example MIDlet. Read on to find out how to add some spacey music to the UFO example from earlier in the book!

Building the UFO 3 Example Program

If you recall, the UFO example program from previous chapters involves a flying saucer that you can control as it moves around the game screen dodging asteroids.

This program has a lot of potential for sounds that use both individual tones and a tone sequence. The individual tones come in handy for denoting the movement of the flying saucer and a collision with an asteroid, whereas the tone sequence establishes some theme music. So you have three distinct sounds to add to the UFO 3 example:

- ▶ A tone to indicate a key press that moves the flying saucer
- ▶ A tone to indicate a collision between the flying saucer and an asteroid
- ▶ A tone sequence that serves as theme music

The next section digs into the code required to add these sounds to the UFO 3 example program.

Writing the Program Code

As you know from earlier in this chapter, it is possible to play a single tone with very little code. The UFO 3 example uses such code to play a tone in response to the user moving the flying saucer and the flying saucer colliding with an asteroid. A good tone I found to represent the movement of the flying saucer is G4, which is the note G in the same octave as middle C (C4). Following is the code that defines a G4 variable and then plays a tone that uses it:

```
byte G4 = (byte)(ToneControl.C4 + 7);
try {
  Manager.playTone(G4, 100, 50);
}
  catch (Exception e) {
}
```

The flying saucer's movement tone (G4) is played for a duration of 100 milliseconds, or 1/10 of a second, at 50% of the current device volume. The tone associated with a collision is played in a similar manner:

```
try {
  Manager.playTone(ToneControl.C4 - 12, 500, 100);
}
  catch (Exception e) {
}
```

In this case the explosion tone is C3, which is an entire octave below middle C (C4). Instead of declaring a variable to represent C3, its offset is calculated directly in the call to the playTone() method. The explosion tone is played for half a second (500 milliseconds) and at 100% volume; this is necessary because the lower pitch of the sound makes it a little more difficult to hear.

The code for playing individual tones is found in the update() method of the
UFOCanvas class in the UFO 3 MIDlet. This class also contains some of the code
responsible for playing a tone sequence in the MIDlet. Listing 8.2 contains the
code for this new and improved update() method.

LISTING 8.2   The update() Method in the UFOCanvas Class Plays Tone
Sounds in Response to Events in the UFO 3 MIDlet

```
private void update() {
  // Randomly play the "encounters" tone tune
  if (rand.nextInt() % 500 == 0)
    playTune();

  // Process user input to control the UFO speed
  byte G4 = (byte)(ToneControl.C4 + 7);
  int keyState = getKeyStates();
  if ((keyState & LEFT_PRESSED) != 0) {
    // Play a sound to indicate movement
    try {
      Manager.playTone(G4, 100, 50);
    }
    catch (Exception e) {
    }

    ufoXSpeed--;
  }
  else if ((keyState & RIGHT_PRESSED) != 0) {
    // Play a sound to indicate movement
    try {
      Manager.playTone(G4, 100, 50);
    }
    catch (Exception e) {
    }

    ufoXSpeed++;
  }
  if ((keyState & UP_PRESSED) != 0) {
    // Play a sound to indicate movement
    try {
      Manager.playTone(G4, 100, 50);
    }
    catch (Exception e) {
    }

    ufoYSpeed--;
  }
  else if ((keyState & DOWN_PRESSED) != 0) {
    // Play a sound to indicate movement
    try {
      Manager.playTone(G4, 100, 50);
    }
    catch (Exception e) {
    }

    ufoYSpeed++;
  }
```

The G4 tone is defined relative to middle C (C4).

Play the G4 tone for 1/10 of a second at 50% volume in response to the left directional key.

LISTING 8.2   Continued

```
ufoXSpeed = Math.min(Math.max(ufoXSpeed, -8), 8);
ufoYSpeed = Math.min(Math.max(ufoYSpeed, -8), 8);

// Move the UFO sprite
ufoSprite.move(ufoXSpeed, ufoYSpeed);
checkBounds(ufoSprite);

// Update the roid sprites
for (int i = 0; i < 3; i++) {
  // Move the roid sprites
  roidSprite[i].move(i + 1, 1 - i);
  checkBounds(roidSprite[i]);

  // Increment the frames of the roid sprites
  if (i == 1)
    roidSprite[i].prevFrame();
  else
    roidSprite[i].nextFrame();

  // Check for a collision between the UFO and roids
  if (ufoSprite.collidesWith(roidSprite[i], true)) {
    // Play a collision sound
    try {
      Manager.playTone(ToneControl.C4 - 12, 500, 100);
    }
    catch (Exception e) {
    }

    // Reset the sprite positions and speeds
    ufoSprite.setPosition((getWidth() - ufoSprite.getWidth()) / 2,
      (getHeight() - ufoSprite.getHeight()) / 2);
    ufoXSpeed = ufoYSpeed = 0;
    for (int j = 0; j < 3; j++)
      roidSprite[j].setPosition(0, 0);

    // No need to continue updating the roid sprites
    break;
  }
}
}
```

Play a low tone for half a second at full volume to indicate a collision.

If you pay close attention to the key handling code near the beginning of the method, you'll recognize the code that plays the single tone in response to flying saucer moves. The collision tone is played close to the end of the method in response to a collision occurring between the flying saucer and an asteroid. Perhaps the most interesting code in this method is at the very beginning, where a tone sequence is played at random intervals via a call to the playTune() method. Before you learn about the playTune() method, it's important to understand how the "tune" is first created.

The initTune() method is responsible for initializing the tone sequence in the UFO 3 MIDlet, as shown in Listing 8.3.

LISTING 8.3 The initTune() Method in the UFOCanvas Class Initializes the Tone Sequence in the UFO 3 MIDlet

Establish the tempo and note lengths.

Define a series of tones based on middle C, including a rest tone that represents silence.

This series of notes represents the Close Encounters tune.

```
private void initTune() {
  byte tempo = 30;  // 120bpm
  byte d4 = 16;     // 1/4 note
  byte d2 = 32;     // 1/2 note

  byte C4 = ToneControl.C4;
  byte A6 = (byte)(C4 + 21);
  byte B6 = (byte)(C4 + 23);
  byte G5 = (byte)(C4 + 19);
  byte G4 = (byte)(C4 + 7);
  byte D5 = (byte)(C4 + 14);
  byte rest = ToneControl.SILENCE;

  byte[] encountersSequence = {
    ToneControl.VERSION, 1,
    ToneControl.TEMPO, tempo,
    ToneControl.BLOCK_START, 0,
    A6,d4, B6,d4, G5,d4, G4,d4, D5,d2, rest,d2,
    ToneControl.BLOCK_END, 0,
    ToneControl.PLAY_BLOCK, 0,
    ToneControl.PLAY_BLOCK, 0,
  };

  try {
    // Create the tone player
    tonePlayer = Manager.createPlayer(Manager.TONE_DEVICE_LOCATOR);
    tonePlayer.realize();

    // Create the tone control and set the tone sequence
    ToneControl toneControl = (ToneControl)tonePlayer.getControl("ToneControl");
    toneControl.setSequence(encountersSequence);
  }
  catch (IOException ioe) {
  }
  catch (MediaException me) {
  }
}
```

This method starts out by establishing some important variables that are used to describe the tone sequence. The byte array for the tone sequence is then carefully constructed. At this point it's probably safe to let you in on the nature of this tone sequence—it's the five-note tune that was popularized in the movie *Close Encounters of the Third Kind,* where aliens used the tune to initially communicate with humans. The five notes are repeated twice in the encounterSequence tone sequence byte array. Figure 8.3 shows the *Close Encounters* theme as it is represented in the encountersSequence tone sequence.

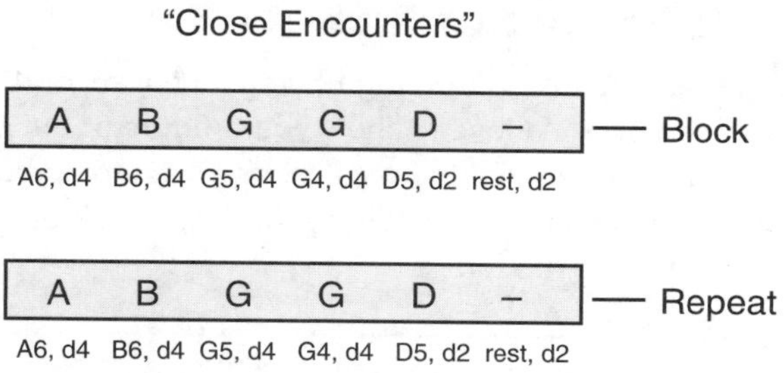

"Close Encounters"

FIGURE 8.3
The simple *Close Encounters* tune is coded as notes for inclusion in a tone sequence.

| A | B | G | G | D | – | — Block |

A6, d4   B6, d4   G5, d4   G4, d4   D5, d2   rest, d2

| A | B | G | G | D | – | — Repeat |

A6, d4   B6, d4   G5, d4   G4, d4   D5, d2   rest, d2

With the tone sequence data structure in place, the latter part of the `initTune()` method tackles the chores of creating a tone player, realizing it, obtaining a tone control, and then setting the tone sequence. When this method exits, the player is initialized with the tone sequence and ready to play the tune at a moment's notice.

The `playTune()` method plays the tone sequence, whereas the `cleanupTune()` method closes the player. Listing 8.4 shows these two methods.

LISTING 8.4   The `playTune()` and `cleanupTune()` Methods in the UFOCanvas **Class Play and Clean Up the Tone Sequence, Respectively**

```
private void playTune() {
  try {
    // Play the tone sequence
    tonePlayer.start();
  }
  catch (MediaException me) {
  }
}

private void cleanupTune() {
  // Close the tone player
  tonePlayer.close();
}
```

As you can see, the `playTune()` method plays the tone sequence by simply calling the `start()` method on the tone player. Similarly, a call to the player's `close()` method is all that is required to close the player and clean up the tone sequence.

Please refer to the CD-ROM for the complete source code for the UFO 3 example MIDlet. I deliberately focused on the most important pieces of code here so you wouldn't have to sift through pages and pages of repeated example code.

Testing the Finished Product

Testing the UFO 3 MIDlet involves cranking up your speakers and running the MIDlet in the J2ME emulator. I'd love to show you a figure of the MIDlet playing the *Close Encounters* tune and indicating a collision with a tone, but the printed page doesn't do a very good job of conveying sound. So you'll have to run the MIDlet yourself and listen for the tones.

Construction Cue

In a real game, you may want to provide a means of turning off all audio so that the user doesn't have to turn the phone's volume down. Some phones allow you to control the Java audio level independently from the main phone audio level, but this isn't a guaranteed feature on all phones. I know I sometimes don't want to hear the sounds for a game but I still want to be able to hear the ringer on my phone.

As you tinker with the UFO 3 MIDlet, pay particular attention to how the MIDlet sounds when multiple tones are playing at once. In the context of a real game, this will likely be a common occurrence, so you want to make sure that tones sound good when playing on top of each other. If you have a MIDP 2.0 mobile phone on hand, be sure to also test the UFO 3 MIDlet on it.

Summary

This chapter introduced you to mobile game sound. In addition to finding out how sound fits into the mobile game equation, you worked through a primer on tonal sound and music, which is a prerequisite for using the MIDP 2.0 Media API to produce tones. With some basic tone knowledge under your belt, you found out how to query a mobile phone for its audio capabilities. You then explored specific code that enables you to play individual tones as well as entire tone sequences. The chapter concluded by adding tones to the UFO example program from previous chapters, including a *Close Encounters* musical theme. The next chapter continues your education on sound in mobile games by digging into wave sounds, MIDI music, and MP3 audio.

Field Trip

If you've never seen the movie *Close Encounters of the Third Kind*, go rent it and take the time to watch it. It's a great movie, and more importantly, it will add some important context to the UFO 3 example you developed in this chapter and its tone sequence code. If you've already seen the movie, then I encourage you to expand on the tone sequence in the UFO 3 example to make it more interesting. If you recall, the aliens in the movie play some quite unusual tone sequences in addition to the familiar five-tone sequence.

CHAPTER 9

Playing Digitized Sound and Music

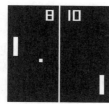

Arcade Archive

Another game from the class of 1981, Qix was created by Taito and is truly unique in design. In fact, I'm not sure a description of the game without playing it would appeal to more than math purists. However, Qix is a very fun and addictive game. Your job is to draw boxes on the screen while avoiding a spark (Sparx) that travels around previously drawn lines and a wavy line animation (Qix) that swirls and moves around the open area of the screen. Like I said, it doesn't sound fun on paper, but if you get a chance to play Qix somewhere, you'll likely find it to be uniquely challenging and addictive.

Although they are guaranteed to be supported on all MIDP 2.0 mobile phones, there's no arguing the limitations of tonal sounds. In an era where gamers are accustomed to CD-quality music and digitized sound effects, it would be nice to provide more interesting sounds and music than can be accomplished with tones alone. Fortunately, the MIDP 2.0 Media API supports several rich audio media types such as wave sounds, MIDI music, and MP3 audio. This chapter shows you how to incorporate these types of sounds into your mobile games.

In this chapter, you'll learn

- ▶ The basics of digitized sounds and how they are stored
- ▶ More details about the MIDP 2.0 Media API's `Player` interface
- ▶ How to play digitized wave sounds in your games
- ▶ How to play MIDI and MP3 music in your games
- ▶ How to modify the Henway game so that it uses wave sound effects and MIDI music

A Digitized Sound Primer

Although you could probably get away with playing digitized sounds in games without understanding how digitized sound works, I'm not going to let you off the hook that easy. It's important to at least have a basic understanding of digitized sound and how it relates to physical sound that we hear in the real world. You learned in the previous chapter that a physical sound is a wave that moves through the air, kind of like an air equivalent of an ocean wave. Unlike tone sounds that are based on a specific pitch, digitized sounds attempt to "record" a real world sound by converting a sound wave to a digital numeric value.

When a microphone converts sound waves to electrical signals, the resulting signal is an *analog* (or continuous) signal. Because computers are digital machines, it is necessary to convert this analog signal to a digital signal for a computer to process. Analog to digital (A/D) converters handle the task of converting analog signals to digital signals, which is also referred to as *sampling*. The process of converting an analog signal to a digital signal doesn't always yield exact results. How closely a digital wave matches its analog counterpart is determined by the frequency at which it is sampled, as well as the amount of information stored at each sample.

To sample a sound, you just store the amplitude of the sound wave at regular intervals. Taking samples at more frequent intervals causes the digital signal to more closely approximate the analog signal and, therefore, sound more like the analog wave when played. So, when sampling sounds, the rate (*frequency*) at which the sound is sampled is very important, as well as how much data is stored for each sample. The unit of measurement for frequency is Hertz (Hz), which specifies how many samples are taken per second. As an example, CD-quality audio is sampled at 44,000Hz (44KHz), which means that when you're listening to a music CD, you're actually hearing 44,000 digital sound samples every second.

In addition to the frequency of a sampled sound, the number of bits used to represent the amplitude of the sound impacts the sound quality, as well as whether the sound is a stereo or mono sound. Knowing this, it's possible to categorize the quality of a digital sound according to the following properties:

- ▶ Frequency
- ▶ Bits per sample
- ▶ Mono/stereo

The frequency of a sampled sound typically falls somewhere in the range of 8KHz to 44KHz, with 44KHz representing CD-quality sound. The bits per sample of a sound is usually either 8bps (bits per sample) or 16bps, with 16bps representing CD-quality audio; this is also known as 16-bit audio.

A sampled sound is then classified as being either mono or stereo—with mono meaning that there is only one channel of sound, whereas stereo has two channels. As you might expect, a stereo sound contains twice as much information as a mono sound. Not surprisingly, CD-quality audio is always stereo. Therefore, you now understand that a CD-quality sound is a 44KHz 16-bit stereo sound.

For you audiophiles out there, DVD-audio has raised the ante for digital audio quality, and is gaining in popularity. As a comparison to CD-quality sound, DVD-audio supports sampling rates up to 192KHz, bits-per-sample up to 24 bits, and up to six channels (as opposed to two channels for stereo CDs). The sheer amount of storage required for DVD-audio prevents it from being useful in mobile games for the foreseeable future.

Because mobile phones have both limited memory and communication bandwidth, you have to be very careful about the size of sounds used in your games. I'm not just talking about size with respect to the length of the sounds, but also the sample quality of the sounds. As an example, CD-quality sound sampled at 44KHz 16-bit stereo is way too memory hungry to be considered for most current mobile phones. For this reason, it's important to carefully choose a sound quality that sounds good without hogging too much memory.

Another issue you should consider with regard to using sound in games is that of copyrighted sounds: You can't use copyrighted sounds without written permission from the owner of the copyright. For example, sounds sampled from copyrighted movies or audio recordings can't be used without permission. It is technically no different than using copyrighted software without permission or a licensing agreement. So be careful when sampling sounds from copyrighted sources.

Some seemingly public domain sound collections are actually copyrighted and can get you into trouble. Most of these types of collections come in the form of an audio CD containing a variety of sound effects. Be sure to read the fine print on these CDs, and make sure that you can legally reuse the sounds or get explicit permission from the publisher.

Getting to Know Wave Sounds

A popular sound format that originated on the Windows platform is known as *wave sounds*, or *waves* for short. Waves are stored in files with a .wav file extension and can be stored in a wide range of formats to accommodate different sound qualities. More specifically, you can save waves in frequencies from 8KHz to 44KHz, with either 8 or 16 bits per sample and as either mono or stereo.

Just as with any other sampled digital audio, the size of a wave file is directly proportional to the quality of the wave sound. So, higher quality waves take up more memory than lower quality waves.

For mobile games, you'll want to go with the lowest quality sounds possible to help minimize memory usage and improve performance. It ultimately depends on the type of sound when it comes to how low you can go with the quality. I've found that 8-bit 8KHz mono sounds are suitable for many mobile game sounds, and provide the smallest file size possible. Don't forget that few mobile phones have speakers that are anywhere near the quality of desktop PC speakers, so trying to keep up with desktop game audio quality is not a realistic issue.

If you're using a Windows PC and you want to experiment a little with waves and how they work, you'll be glad to know that Windows includes a built-in tool for working with waves. It's called Sound Recorder, and you'll find it by following these steps in Windows XP:

1. Click the Start button.

2. Select All Programs, followed by Accessories, and then Entertainment.

3. Select Sound Recorder to launch the program.

Gamer's Garage

If you aren't using Windows XP, don't worry because Sound Recorder is included with all versions of Windows. Just poke around within the Accessories folder, and you'll be able to find it. If you aren't using Windows at all, you should still be able to find a suitable media player that supports waves.

FIGURE 9.1
The Sound Recorder program allows you to record sounds and then manipulate them to some degree.

The Sound Recorder program is shown in Figure 9.1.

You'll notice that the Sound Recorder tool includes a series of buttons that look like the buttons on a VCR. These buttons allow you to record new sounds with your computer's microphone or CD-ROM drive, as well as play, stop, rewind, and fast forward sounds. Feel free to try your hand at recording a sound with the microphone and playing it back with Sound Recorder. You might also want to experiment with some of the effects that can be applied to the sound, such as reversing it and hearing the sound backwards. Remember all the rumors about hidden messages in rock music when you play it backwards? Now you can create your own!

Clipping sounds down to exactly what you want is not only important for minimizing the storage of sounds, but it also makes sounds play more efficiently. If you perfectly clip a sound so that there is no silence at the beginning (and end), the sound plays very quickly in response to game actions. Otherwise, the silence has the effect of causing a noticeable and annoying delay in the sound.

Construction Cue

Creating and Editing Wave Sounds

As you prepare to create your own sounds, you have some decisions to make with respect to how you will obtain the sounds. For example, are you planning to record sounds yourself with a microphone, or sample sounds from a stereo cassette deck or VCR? The microphone is probably the easiest route because many multimedia computers come equipped with one. It's also the most creative route. However, you might already have some sounds in mind from a prerecorded audio cassette, videocassette, or DVD, which means that you probably need to look into connecting an external sound source to your computer.

Regardless of where you sample sounds from, the process of getting a sampled sound cleaned up for use in a game is basically the same. After you've sampled a sound, play it back to make sure that it sounds okay. It's likely that the sound will either be too loud or too soft. You can judge whether the volume of the sound is acceptable by looking at the waveform displayed in the sound editor. The *waveform* of a sound is the graphical appearance of the sound when plotted over time. If the sound amplitude goes beyond the top or bottom of the waveform display, you know it's definitely too loud. If you can barely hear it, it's probably too soft. To remedy this problem, you can either adjust the input level for the sound device and resample the sound or try to use amplification effects provided by the sound editor.

The best way to fix the volume problem is to adjust the input level of the sound device and resample the sound. After you have the volume of the sound at a level you like, you need to clip the sound to remove unwanted portions of it. *Clipping* a sound involves zooming in on the waveform in a sound editor and cutting out the silence that appears before and after the sound. This helps shorten the length of the sound and prevents unnecessary latency.

Latency is the amount of time between when you queue a sound for playing and when the user actually hears it. Latency should be kept to a minimum so that sounds are heard when you want them to be heard without any delay. Unnecessary silence at the beginning of a sound is a common cause of latency problems.

Construction Cue

After you have a sound clipped, it should be ready for prime time. You might want to check out the kinds of effects that are available with the sound utility you are using. Some simple effects range from reverse to echo, with more advanced effects including fading and phase shifts. It's all up to your imagination and your discerning ears.

Revisiting the `Player` Interface

In the previous chapter you found out how to use the `Player` interface to play tonal sounds. Although tones are useful in that they share broad support across all phones, digitized wave sounds and MIDI music are what truly take mobile game audio to the next level. Fortunately, the handy `Player` interface makes it possible to play these types of sounds with very little effort. Before you get into the coding details, however, let's take a moment to revisit the `Player` interface and learn a bit more about how it works.

In the MIDP 2.0 Media API, the `Player` interface acts as a remote control for playing all types of audio. Typically, using the `Player` interface to play audio involves the following steps:

1. Create a player via one of the `Manager.createPlayer()` methods.

2. Call the `prefetch()` method to start retrieving the audio and minimize latency.

3. Call the `start()` method to start playback.

4. Call the `stop()` method to stop playback, if necessary.

5. Call the `close()` method to close the player.

These method calls paint a fairly decent picture of the series of steps that are required to play audio with the `Player` interface. However, there is a bit more going on behind the scenes. More specifically, a player has five distinct "life-cycle" states in which it can exist at any given time: UNREALIZED, REALIZED, PREFETCHED, STARTED, and CLOSED. The significance of these states is that a player is constantly moving between them as you play sounds. Just as you spend different parts of your life sleeping, waking, eating, walking, and so on, so does a media player.

The reason for carefully defining life-cycle states for a media player is so that you can have better control over how audio is played. For example, if you develop a game that needs to download a large wave sound over a network connection, it would be handy to know the state of the download and whether the sound is ready for playback. Following is a step-by-step description of how a media player flows from one of these states to the next:

1. A player starts in the UNREALIZED state.

2. The player enters the REALIZED state when it has everything it needs to begin acquiring media resources.

3. The player enters the PREFETCHED state when media resources are acquired and playback is ready.

4. The player enters the STARTED state when playback begins.

5. The player returns to the PREFETCHED state when playback ends.

6. The player enters the CLOSED state when the player is closed.

After a player is up and running, it will spend most of its time alternating between the PREFETCHED and STARTED states, depending on whether a sound is actually being played. You can retrieve the state of a player at any time with a call to getState(), which returns one of the five state constants (UNREALIZED, REALIZED, PREFETCHED, STARTED, or CLOSED).

Now that you understand how the different player states work, let's take a quick look at some of the more important methods of the Player interface, along with how they control audio playback:

▶ realize()—Realizes the player without acquiring media resources (usually not necessary to explicitly call)

▶ prefetch()—Acquires media resources to help minimize playback latency (call to first initialize a player)

▶ getState()—Gets the state of the player (only necessary to call if you need to know the player's state)

▶ setLoopCount()—Sets the number of times a sound is looped when you play it (must be called prior to calling start())

▶ start()—Starts playing a sound

▶ stop()—Stops playing a sound

▶ getDuration()—Gets the duration of the sound (in milliseconds)

▶ getMediaTime()—Gets the current media time (in milliseconds)

▶ setMediaTime()—Sets the current media time (in milliseconds)

▶ close()—Closes the player

It's not terribly important for you to memorize or otherwise be intimately acquainted with how these methods work at this point. The next few sections put them into context and show you exactly how they are used to play both wave sounds and MIDI and MP3 music.

Playing Wave Sounds in Mobile Games

Thanks to the MIDP 2.0 Media API, playing wave sounds in mobile games isn't very difficult. The main decision you must make when it comes to playing a sound is where the sound is originating from. More specifically, is the wave file stored in the JAR file with the MIDlet, or is it accessed from across a network? It is obviously much more efficient to access a wave file from the MIDlet's JAR file, so that is the likely scenario for most mobile games. The next couple of sections explore how to play sounds with both approaches.

Gamer's Garage

In addition to playing a wave sound from a JAR file or from a network connection, you can also play a sound that is stored in a record store. If you aren't familiar with record stores, they are special databases that MIDlets can use to access and store data. Because the JAR approach to storing sounds is so straightforward, the vast majority of your games will probably be just fine accessing sounds from JAR files.

Playing a Wave from a JAR File

To access a wave sound from a MIDlet's JAR file, you must first make sure that the wave file is added to the JAR file when building the MIDlet. As long as you place the wave file in the res folder beneath your main MIDlet folder, it is included automatically in the JAR file when you build the MIDlet in the KToolbar development tool. With your wave file successfully included in the MIDlet JAR file, you can turn your attention to the code involved in playing the wave sound.

Playing a wave sound from a JAR file involves creating an input stream based on the wave file, and then using that stream as the basis for creating a player. This may sound complicated, but it really involves only a few lines of code. Following is an example of how you might play a "game over" wave sound that is stored in a JAR file:

The audio/X-wav MIME type is very important in identifying that this is a wave sound.

```
try {
  Player gameoverPlayer;
  InputStream is = getClass().getResourceAsStream("GameOver.wav");
  gameoverPlayer = Manager.createPlayer(is, "audio/X-wav");
  gameoverPlayer.prefetch();
  gameoverPlayer.start();
}
```

```
catch(IOException ioe) {
}
catch(MediaException e) {
}
```

An `InputStream` object is first obtained when the name of the wave file is passed into the `getResourceAsStream()` method; this method is called on the runtime object retrieved by `getClass()`. Although getting the input stream is a bit tricky, after you have it, all you have to do is pass it into the `Manager.createPlayer()` method, along with the MIME type of the wave sound. This gives you a new player object that is almost ready to play the "game over" wave sound. To make sure that the sound is prepped to play with minimum latency, the `prefetch()` method is called. Finally, the `start()` method is called to start playing the wave sound. Because several of these methods are capable of throwing exceptions, all the calls are contained within an exception handling clause.

Keep in mind that you can call the `start()` method as many times as you want to play the wave sound over again. However, calling the `start()` method while a sound is still playing does not restart the sound at its beginning. To restart a sound, you must call the `setMediaTime()` method and pass in 0 to indicate you want to set the media time to the beginning of the sound:

```
gameoverPlayer.setMediaTime(0);
```

> The `setMediaTime()` method can be used to restart any sounds played with the `Player` interface, including wave sounds, MP3 sounds, and MIDI music.

Construction Cue

Speaking of the media time of a sound, you can use the `getDuration()` and `getMediaTime()` methods to determine how much of a sound has been played. Both methods return an amount of time, in milliseconds: `getDuration()` tells you the total duration of a sound, whereas `getMediaTime()` tells you how much of a sound has been played.

When you're completely finished with the player for a wave sound, it's important to clean it up with a call to the `close()` method, like this:

```
gameoverPlayer.close();
```

That's really all it takes to successfully play a wave sound that is stored in a JAR file. This is the recommended approach for most mobile games because the sounds load reasonably quickly and with minimal latency.

Playing a Wave from a URL

In some scenarios you may need to play a wave sound over a network connection. For example, maybe your game involves playing some kind of dynamically generated sound that must be retrieved from a network server. In this scenario, you still create a player for the wave sound, but it acquires the wave from a URL as opposed to a JAR file. Following is an example of how this is accomplished:

```
try {
  Player gameoverPlayer = Manager.createPlayer(
    "http://yourserver/GameOver.wav");
  gameoverPlayer.prefetch();
  gameoverPlayer.start();
}
catch(IOException ioe) {
}
catch(MediaException e) {
}
```

This code is actually simpler than the JAR file approach to playing waves because you aren't required to construct an input stream for the wave file. Instead, you just specify the complete URL of the wave file when creating the player. After the player is created, playing the wave sound is no different than if you had loaded it from a JAR file.

Gamer's Garage

A wave sound loaded from a JAR file is available for playback much faster than a wave loaded over a network connection. For this reason, there may be some noticeable latency when you first attempt to play a wave sound that is loaded from a URL. Of course, this all depends on the size of the wave file and the speed of the network connection.

Feeling the Music with MIDI

Musical Instrument Digital Interface, or *MIDI*, started out in the early '80s as an attempt to establish a standard interface between musical instruments. The main use for MIDI back then was to enable a dedicated keyboard to control a synthesizer. Keyboard synthesizers consist of two main components: the keyboard and the synthesizer. The keyboard is responsible for keeping up with input information such as which musical note is being generated and how hard the key is being pressed on the keyboard. The synthesizer, on the other hand, is responsible for generating sounds based on the input information provided by the keyboard. So, the original goal of MIDI was to provide a standardized approach to controlling a synthesizer with a keyboard. MIDI eventually expanded to support an incredibly wide range of musical instruments and devices, but the keyboard/synthesizer relationship is significant to MIDI as it applies to computers.

Similar to wave sounds, MIDI music is digital. However, unlike waves, which are just approximations of analog sound waves, MIDI music consists of musical notes. In other words, a MIDI song consists of a series of carefully timed musical notes. This means that you can create a MIDI song much as you might write out a musical composition on paper. This task requires special software, but it is possible if you have the knowledge and skill to write music. Because MIDI music is composed of notes rather than wave data, the resulting output sound quality is entirely dependent on the MIDI output device used to play the music. In the case of mobile phones, the MIDI synthesizer is usually fairly limited as compared to desktop counterparts.

I've mentioned MIDI music several times throughout this discussion, but I haven't really clarified how it is stored or how you work with it. Similar to waves, MIDI music is stored in files, but MIDI files have the file extension .MID. Unlike waves, MIDI music files are typically fairly small because musical notes simply don't take up a whole lot of space. Like waves, you can play MIDI files with a media player such as Windows Media Player (see Figure 9.2). Unlike waves, creating MIDI music involves a fair amount of music knowledge and requires specialized software.

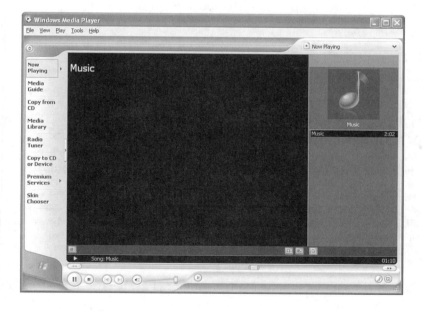

FIGURE 9.2
Windows Media Player can be used to play MIDI files, as well as wave files.

You will likely use a media player to test play MIDI files for use in your games. Or, if you're ambitious enough to create your own game music, you'll likely use a media player as a final means of testing a MIDI file before incorporating it into a game.

Playing MIDI Music in Mobile Games

Similar to wave sounds, MIDI music can easily be played in mobile games, thanks to the MIDP 2.0 Media API and the Player interface. In fact, the process of playing a piece of MIDI music is little different than that of playing wave sounds, as you find out in the next couple of sections.

Playing a MIDI Song from a JAR File

To play a MIDI song from a JAR file, you must first create an input stream based on the MIDI file that is stored in the JAR file. If this sounds familiar, it's because you had to do the same thing to play a wave sound from a JAR file. After you've created an input stream for the MIDI song, you use it to create a player, and then you're ready to roll. Following is the code required to create a player for a MIDI song that is stored in a JAR file and then play the tune.

Notice that a different MIME type is used when a MIDI song is played.

```
try {
  Player musicPlayer;
  InputStream is = getClass().getResourceAsStream("Music.mid");
  musicPlayer = Manager.createPlayer(is, "audio/midi");
  musicPlayer.prefetch();
  musicPlayer.start();
}
catch(IOException ioe) {
}
catch(MediaException e) {
}
```

About the only real trick in this code is the specification of the proper MIME type for the MIDI song when you create the player; the MIME type is audio/midi. Beyond that, you call the prefetch() method to make sure the tune is loaded as quickly as possible, and then the start() method to start it off playing.

Construction Cue

> The MIDP 2.0 Media API also supports the playback of MP3 music. To load and play an MP3 song, create an input stream and player just as you would for a wave sound or MIDI song, but specify the name of the MP3 file and use the MIME type audio/mpeg.

One detail I left out that is particularly useful for playing music is the loop count of the playback, which is how many times the tune is to be played; by default, the loop count is one. In many cases you will want the music in a game to loop over and over indefinitely, in which case it would be helpful to set a very high loop count. Following is a line of code that takes care of this:

```
musicPlayer.setLoopCount(-1);
```

Normally you pass the number of times you'd like a sound to loop into the `setLoopCount()` method, but in this case you're passing in a special value of `-1`. Passing a value of `-1` into the `setLoopCount()` method results in the sound being played indefinitely, or at least until the `stop()` method is called or the player is closed.

> If you want to control the number of times a sound is looped, it's important that you call the `setLoopCount()` method before calling the `start()` method.

Construction Cue

Following is the code required to close the player and clean up the MIDI song:

```
musicPlayer.close();
```

You may be starting to understand the flexibility of the `Player` interface in that it allows you to play MIDI songs just as easily as wave sounds, even though they are very different types of audio media.

Playing a MIDI Song from a URL

Any guesses as to how you might go about playing a MIDI song from a URL? Given that the code for the JAR file approach to playing a MIDI song mirrored that of playing a wave sound, you can probably guess that the network approach is also similar. And you would be correct! Following is the code to play a MIDI song over a network by specifying its URL:

```
try {
  Player musicPlayer = Manager.createPlayer("http://yourserver/Music.mid");
  musicPlayer.prefetch();
  musicPlayer.start();
}
catch(IOException ioe) {
}
catch(MediaException e) {
}
```

There aren't any surprises here; you simply specify the URL of the MIDI file when creating the player. Keep in mind that you may still want to tinker with the loop count when playing a MIDI song through this approach because many games rely on music that repeats over and over.

Building the Henway 2 Example Game

In Chapter 7, "Henway: Paying Tribute to Frogger," you designed and developed your first complete mobile game, Henway. Although the game was interesting from both a programming and game play perspective, it was a bit limiting in terms of its audio capabilities—it had none! The remainder of this chapter focuses on improving the Henway game to include digitized wave sound effects and MIDI music. You get to put all your new digitized audio knowledge to practical use.

The first step in adding sound capabilities to the Henway game is identifying what aspects of the game would benefit from sounds. It doesn't take too much in the way of brainstorming to realize a few obvious sound candidates: the chicken getting run over, the chicken making it safely across, and the game ending. You might also consider adding sound effects for each movement of the chicken, along with maybe having the cars honk their horns every now and then. However, this is one of those situations where you have to do some experimenting with real mobile phones to see where to draw the line in terms of too much sound interfering with game play. I don't mean that the sounds are a distraction—I mean that they may actually hinder the game's performance and cause it to stutter.

Construction Cue

If you encounter a situation where a sound would really be useful in a game but you're worried about it hindering the performance of the game, you can always use tones. There is no reason you can't mix tones with wave sounds—in fact, this can be a very good strategy for maintaining reasonable game performance but also including interesting sound effects.

To better understand this problem, you have to consider the fact that mobile phones have very limited memory and processing resources. Playing any digital sounds is fairly taxing when you consider that you're trying to get your games to run at as high a frame rate as possible. Therefore, you typically want to avoid sounds that have to be played rapidly or that otherwise aren't critical to game play. Knowing this, it's probably a good idea to avoid wave sound effects for chicken movements and random car horns.

This leaves us with the following list of sounds to be added to the Henway 2 game:

- ▶ **Celebration**—The chicken made it safely across.
- ▶ **Squish**—The chicken was run over.
- ▶ **Game Over**—The last chicken was lost and the game ended.
- ▶ **Music**—Background music played repeatedly during the game.

The first three sounds are wave sounds, whereas the last sound could be either a MIDI or MP3 song. Because MIDI songs are usually much smaller in size and less taxing on system resources than MP3 songs, I opted to go with a MIDI song for the Henway 2 background music.

Writing the Game Code

The first piece of new code in the Henway 2 example game is the code that creates the various sound players. Following are the four players required to represent each of the sounds in the game, which are declared as HCanvas member variables:

```
private Player   musicPlayer;
private Player   celebratePlayer;
private Player   squishPlayer;
private Player   gameoverPlayer;
```

As you can see, there is no difference in the players other than the variable names. The distinction between the MIDI player and the wave players isn't revealed until you actually create the players. And speaking of player creation, here's the code that does it, which resides in the Henway canvas start() method:

```
try {
  InputStream is = getClass().getResourceAsStream("Music.mid");
  musicPlayer = Manager.createPlayer(is, "audio/midi");
  musicPlayer.prefetch();
  is = getClass().getResourceAsStream("Celebrate.wav");
  celebratePlayer = Manager.createPlayer(is, "audio/X-wav");
  celebratePlayer.prefetch();
  is = getClass().getResourceAsStream("Squish.wav");
  squishPlayer = Manager.createPlayer(is, "audio/X-wav");
  squishPlayer.prefetch();
  is = getClass().getResourceAsStream("GameOver.wav");
  gameoverPlayer = Manager.createPlayer(is, "audio/X-wav");
  gameoverPlayer.prefetch();
}
catch (IOException ioe) {
}
catch (MediaException me) {
}
```

This code is more of a merger of the previous example code you've already seen than something completely new. More specifically, the Music.mid, Celebrate.wav, Squish.wav, and GameOver.wav sound files are used to create a MIDI player and three wave players from the MIDlet's JAR file. Notice that each player is prefetched just after being created so that all the sound resources are loaded and ready for playback.

The HCanvas start() method is also where the background music is initially
played, just after the creation of the players. Following is the code that starts
playing the background music:

```
try {
  musicPlayer.setLoopCount(-1);
  musicPlayer.start();
}
catch (MediaException me) {
}
```

The setLoopCount() method is called prior to the start() method with a value of
-1 to indicate that the music should be repeated indefinitely. After the start()
method is called, the music continues playing until it is interrupted with a call to
the stop() method or the music player is closed.

All the sound players are closed in the stop() method for the HCanvas class.
Following is the code that cleans up the players:

```
musicPlayer.close();
celebratePlayer.close();
gameoverPlayer.close();
squishPlayer.close();
```

At this point all the players are successfully created and ready for playback. In
fact, the music player is already started, but you haven't seen any of the code
that triggers the wave players. This code all resides in the update() method of the
HCanvas class, which is shown in Listing 9.1.

LISTING 9.1 The update() Method in the HCanvas Class Plays Sound
Effects and Music in the Henway 2 MIDlet

```
private void update() {
  // Check to see whether the game is being restarted
  if (gameOver) {
    int keyState = getKeyStates();
    if ((keyState & FIRE_PRESSED) != 0) {
      // Start a new game
        try {
        musicPlayer.setMediaTime(0);
        musicPlayer.start();
      }
      catch (MediaException me) {
      }
      chickenSprite.setPosition(2, 77);
      gameOver = false;
      score = 0;
      numLives = 3;
    }
```

*The music starts
playing at the
beginning when the
game is restarted.*

LISTING 9.1 Continued

```
    // The game is over, so don't update anything
    return;
}

// Process user input to move the chicken
if (++inputDelay > 2) {
  int keyState = getKeyStates();
  if ((keyState & LEFT_PRESSED) != 0) {
    chickenSprite.move(-6, 0);
    chickenSprite.nextFrame();
  }
  else if ((keyState & RIGHT_PRESSED) != 0) {
    chickenSprite.move(6, 0);
    chickenSprite.nextFrame();
  }
  if ((keyState & UP_PRESSED) != 0) {
    chickenSprite.move(0, -6);
    chickenSprite.nextFrame();
  }
  else if ((keyState & DOWN_PRESSED) != 0) {
    chickenSprite.move(0, 6);
    chickenSprite.nextFrame();
  }
  checkBounds(chickenSprite, false);

  // Reset the input delay
  inputDelay = 0;
}

// See whether the chicken made it across
if (chickenSprite.getX() > 154) {
  // Play a sound for making it safely across
  try {
    celebratePlayer.start();
  }
  catch (MediaException me) {
  }

  // Reset the chicken position and increment the score
  chickenSprite.setPosition(2, 77);
  score += 25;
}

// Update the car sprites
for (int i = 0; i < 4; i++) {
  // Move the car sprites
  carSprite[i].move(0, carYSpeed[i]);
  checkBounds(carSprite[i], true);

  // Check for a collision between the chicken and cars
  if (chickenSprite.collidesWith(carSprite[i], true)) {
    // Play a sound for losing a chicken
    try {
      squishPlayer.start();
    }
```

The celebration sound is played when the chicken makes it safely across the road.

The squish sound is played when the chicken gets run over by a car.

LISTING 9.1   Continued

```
catch (MediaException me) {
}

// Check for a game over
if (--numLives == 0) {
  // Stop the music and play a game over sound
  try {
    musicPlayer.stop();
    gameoverPlayer.start();
  }
  catch (MediaException me) {
  }

  gameOver = true;
} else {
  // Reset the chicken position
  chickenSprite.setPosition(2, 77);
}

// No need to continue updating the car sprites
break;
      }
    }
}
```

When the game ends, the music is stopped and the game over sound is played.

The first code in the update() method to pay attention to is the code near the beginning that checks for a game restart. If the game is being restarted, you know that it must have ended at some point, which means the background music would've been stopped. So part of starting a new game is starting up the background music again with a call to the start() method on the music player.

The next sound-related code in the update() method occurs roughly midway through the method in the section of code that checks to see whether the chicken made it safely across the road. If so, the celebration wave sound is played with a quick call to the start() method on the wave player. Similar code is used just a bit later in the update() method when the squish sound is played in response to the chicken getting hit by a car.

The last section of new code in the update() method appears near the bottom of the method, where a check is made to see whether the game is over. If so, the music is stopped and the game over sound is played.

Testing the Finished Product

The Henway 2 game is a lot of fun to test because the new sound effects and music add a significant impact to the feel of the game. Whether you test the game in the J2ME emulator or on an actual mobile phone, you'll hopefully realize how useful sound effects and music can be in jazzing up any mobile game. Take a look at Figure 9.3. Certainly the graphics convey that the chicken is getting smashed by the fast moving car, but you can't argue the wickedly humorous tone set by the new squishing sound.

As you play the game, make sure to pay close attention to any perceptible delay in the game play as sounds are played. As I mentioned earlier in the chapter, sounds can be taxing on mobile phones with limited memory and processing capabilities, so it's very important to carefully leverage their usage against game play performance. You should carefully test all your games on as many different phones as possible when you're considering adding sound effects and music.

FIGURE 9.3
The Henway 2 game carefully uses sounds to help add richness to important game events, such as the chicken getting run over by a car.

Summary

This chapter continued the discussion of sound from the previous chapter, and ultimately hit you with a lot of new game programming knowledge. More specifically, you found out how digitized sound works and how it fits into mobile games. You learned about digitized wave sounds, including how to access and play them from JAR files and over the network in mobile games. You also were introduced to MIDI and MP3 music, and how to incorporate them into your games. And finally, the chapter concluded by revisiting the Henway game from Chapter 7, and showing you how to add digitized sound effects and music to it.

Field Trip

For this field trip, you're going to need an electronic device that is capable of recording sounds. If you have one of those slick little digital audio recorders (some MP3 players have a record feature) you're in perfect shape, but if not then you can also use a tape recorder. The goal of this field trip is to go record real-world sounds for use in your games. So if you have a particular game in mind, then you may already have some sound needs. You'll probably find that recording sounds is surprisingly fun, and it conveniently dodges copyright issues because they are your own sounds that you have exclusive rights to use.

To get started, walk around your house or office and experiment with making different noises with everyday items. It's interesting how you can turn a clack or clang sound into gunfire in the context of a game. If you live near a busy street, try recording some automobile sounds; the Henway game from the previous chapter is a good example of how these sounds are useful. If you have a game in mind with a nature theme, try going to a park and recording natural sounds—animals moving, water rushing, leaves rustling, end so on. Even the snap of a twig can be made into an interesting sound effect in some games. The process of recording sounds in the real world is limited only by your creativity.

PART III

Virtual Worlds and Mobile Game Intelligence

CHAPTER 10

Creating Tiled Game Layers

Arcade Archive

A sequel to the arcade classic Defender, Stargate is worthy of "hall of fame" status in its own right. Released in 1981 by Williams, Stargate is a horizontally scrolling space shooter similar to Defender, but even more challenging. Some of the main enemies in Stargate are named after competitors of Williams: Yllabian (Bally) and Irata (Atari). A Flash version of Stargate is available online if you'd like to try it out for yourself: http://www.shockwave.com/sw/content/defender2. I still encourage you to play the real game if you can find an arcade version of it somewhere.

Have you ever played a game where the game world is much larger than what you see at any given moment on the screen? When the virtual game world is larger than what can be showed on the screen, some trickery has to be employed to keep track of how big the world is and how the game knows what part of it to display. In modern 3D games, this trickery can get very complicated, but in the realm of 2D games it isn't too terribly difficult. Fortunately, the MIDP 2.0 API provides a class that goes a long way toward making large virtual game worlds an easy task. The class is called TiledLayer, and it aids in the creation of tiled layers, which are like sprites except they are built out of multiple images, kind of like a puzzle. This chapter introduces you to tiled layers and shows you how to use them to map out virtual game worlds.

In this chapter, you'll learn

▶ Why tiled layers are a significant part of mobile game programming

▶ How to use special mapping software to ease the creation of tiled layers

> ► How to create maps, mazes, and other interesting game backgrounds with tiled layers
>
> ► That developing a scrolling mobile adventure simulator isn't too difficult

What Is a Tiled Layer?

You learned earlier in the book that a *layer* is a graphical component in a game, whereas a *sprite* is a specific kind of layer that uses an image or sequence of animated images as its visual representation. A *tiled layer* is similar to a sprite in that it is used as a visual component in a game, but instead of displaying a single image at a time, a tiled layer shows multiple images arranged next to each other. When you create a tiled layer, you specify several images, or tiles, that go into making the layer. You then specify how those tiles are arranged to form the complete tiled layer image. Figure 10.1 shows how multiple tile images go into creating a single tiled layer image.

FIGURE 10.1
Tiled images are arranged like puzzle pieces to build a larger tiled layer image.

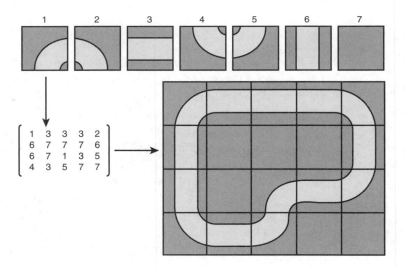

As the figure reveals, a small set of tiles can be carefully arranged to construct quite interesting tiled layers. In this example, just a handful of track pieces are used to build a complete race track tiled layer. It's not too difficult to envision how even a slightly larger set of tiles makes it possible to build extremely rich tiled layers that can serve as virtual world maps in games.

In taking a close look at Figure 10.1, you'll notice that the tiles are assigned unique numerical identifiers that start at zero and increase with each successive tile. These numbers are called *tile index numbers*, and are used to reference the tiles when you create a map for a tiled layer. In fact, the figure shows exactly how the tile indexes are used in a two-dimensional array to specify the layout of the tiled layer. Perhaps the most important revelation in this figure is how an enormous tiled layer can easily be created from a tiny set of tile images. This is a critically useful feature of tiled layers for mobile games when you consider the memory, storage, and communications limitations of mobile phones.

One requirement of tiled layers is that all the tile images must be the exact same size. This makes sense when you consider that they can be mixed and matched in any combination when the grid of tiles is arranged. Although the tiles themselves must be a consistent size, there is no limit on the dimensions of the tiled layer. For example, if you design tile images that are 32×32 in size, the overall tiled layer must be a multiple of 32 in both width and height, but it can be as large as you want. So if you wanted to make a rectangular tiled layer consisting of 24 tiles across and 16 tiles down, the resulting tiled layer would be 768×512 in size. This obviously won't fit on the screen of most mobile phones, so your game must be designed so that only a portion of the tiled layer is shown at any given time.

In the next chapter, "Managing Multiple Game Layers," you learn how to use a feature of the MIDP 2.0 API to manage multiple layers and establish a "viewing window" for viewing a specific region of a layer that is larger than the game screen. For now, you can still accomplish the same effect by drawing only a certain portion of a tiled layer in your game canvas' draw() method. This technique involves shifting the tiled layer with respect to the game screen so that only the area that lies within the screen is drawn. Figure 10.2 shows how the race track tiled layer from Figure 10.1 might be drawn within an actual game screen.

Given that all mobile games struggle in terms of having to deal with minimal available screen space, providing a view onto a larger tiled layer is an excellent way of effectively having a larger game play area than what can be viewed on the screen. Many PC and console video games use a similar technique, but in the case of mobile games it becomes even more useful because you are so very limited in terms of screen size.

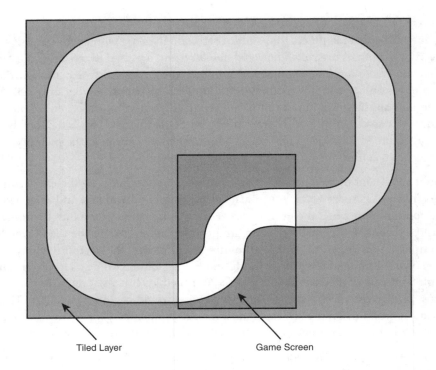

Tiled Layer   Game Screen

You may already be starting to realize the unique game design opportunities
afforded by tiled layers. World maps, race tracks, and cavernous mazes are but a
few of the types of things you can create as tiled layers. Perhaps even more interesting is the fact that the standard Sprite class supports tiled layers for collision
detection. So, for example, you can create a tiled layer maze where the walls
actually serve as barriers for any sprites that you drop into the game. You'll
explore this usage of tiled layers throughout the next few chapters, but for now
I want to explore how maps are created that form the basis of tiled layers.

Creating Maps for Tiled Layers

Tiled layers consist of a grid of individual tiles arranged so that they provide the
illusion of a single image but without all the unnecessary duplication of pixels.
Perhaps even more important, because tiled layers are arranged programmatically
instead of in an image editor, games can support different background maps and
levels if the arrangement of tiles in a tiled layer is altered. This provides an incredible amount of flexibility with a relatively low overhead.

Perhaps the trickiest part of using tiled layers is designing the actual maps that specify exactly how the tiles are arranged. Even the simplest of tiled layer maps usually requires that you draw them out on paper and number the tiles so that you can code the maps without complete and total mental overload. I have to admit to going through several sheets of paper while designing the tiled layer maps for the various examples and games you encounter throughout the remainder of the book. Unfortunately, late in the development stage I stumbled across map making software, which greatly simplifies the task of creating tiled maps.

I encountered two main software packages for creating maps, and both are equally useful for the development of tiled layer maps:

▶ Mappy   ▶ Tile Studio

The general idea behind both of these mapping applications is that you identify an image containing a set of tiles of a certain size, along with a map based on those tiles. What makes mapping software so much more efficient than pencil and paper is that you can experiment with different designs and see the finished result right there on the screen of your PC. When you consider that most mobile games see only a small portion of a tiled layer map at any given time, it is immensely helpful to be able to design the maps on a PC with a large monitor.

> Unfortunately, both Mappy and Tile Studio are available for the Windows platform only. The source code is available for Tile Studio, so you may be able to find a port for other platforms if you dig around on the web.

Gamer's
Garage

In terms of choosing mapping software, it's ultimately a personal preference. I didn't take the time to master either of the applications but I can say that with Mappy it was a bit easier to hit the ground running initially. On the other hand, Tile Studio appears to have some more advanced features if you should graduate to becoming a master map maker. For the purposes of this discussion, I opted to show you both applications at work. The next couple of sections explore the creation of a fairly complex tiled layer map on both Mappy and Tile Studio.

Using the Mappy Map Editor

The Mappy map editor is a fairly simple application that allows you to draw tiled maps for games visually. Along with being easy to learn, Mappy is nice because you can use it to generate the exact map code necessary to plug into your Java game code. You'll see what I'm talking about in a moment. For now, check out Figure 10.3, which shows a new map being created in Mappy.

Gamer's Garage

You can download Mappy for free from the following website: http://www.tilemap.co.uk/mappy.php.

FIGURE 10.3
Creating a new map in Mappy requires you to specify the tile size, map size, and number of colors.

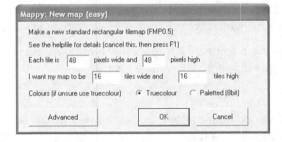

After specifying the tile size (in pixels) and the map size (in tiles), you're ready to import a tile image. After clicking Import from the File menu and selecting an image containing the tiles, you see the individual tiles on the right side of the screen along with a blank map on the left (Figure 10.4).

To begin creating a map, just click a tile on the right side of the screen to select it, and then click anywhere on the blank map to place the tile. You will realize very quickly how simple and intuitive mapping software makes the process of building game maps. I was extremely annoyed at myself for wasting time using a pencil and paper to design maps when I realized how much faster mapping software makes the task. Not only that, but applications such as Mappy enable you to see most if not all of a map on your screen at once, which is significant when you consider that a mobile phone screen is likely to provide only a small view onto the map when you actually begin testing a game.

Figure 10.5 shows a fairly large portion of a completed map as viewed in Mappy.

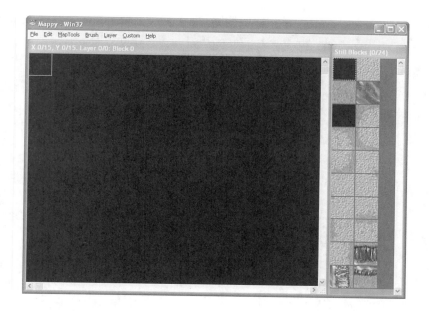

FIGURE 10.4
Tiles are loaded and ready for placement in this new map being created in Mappy.

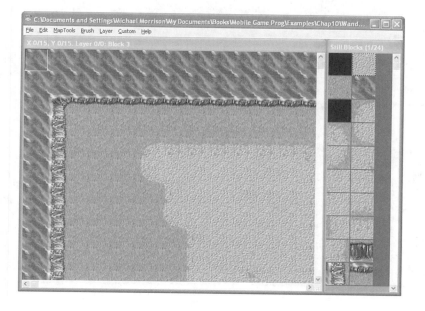

FIGURE 10.5
The upper-left portion of a completed map is visible in Mappy.

Of course, you can also scroll around the map window in Mappy while creating a map. Figure 10.6 shows another region of the map in Figure 10.5.

FIGURE 10.6
Scrolling around in Mappy enables you to work on different areas of a map.

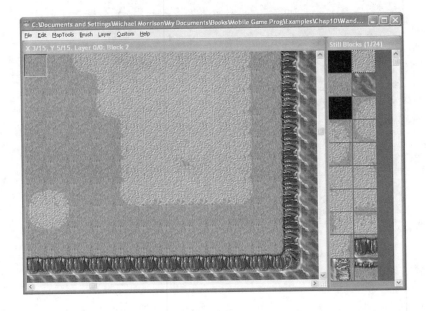

Gamer's Garage

CSV files are text files consisting of pieces of information separated by commas. You can create and open CSV files in Microsoft Excel or in any text editor.

FIGURE 10.7
Generating map data for your game code involves simply exporting the map from Mappy as a CSV file.

When you are satisfied that your map is complete, it's time to export it for use in your Java code. Although Mappy supports several approaches and data formats for exporting map code, I've found that exporting a CSV file is the best solution for mobile Java game maps. To export a map as a CSV file, select Export from the File menu, and make sure the settings in the Export dialog box match those in Figure 10.7.

Keep in mind that a CSV file is just a text file, so you can open it in any text editor and look at how your map was generated. Following is the CSV code generated by Mappy for the map shown in Figures 10.5 and 10.6:

```
3, 3, 3, 3, 3, 3, 3, 3, 3, 3, 3, 3, 3, 3, 3, 3,
3, 3, 3, 3, 3, 3, 3, 3, 3, 3, 3, 3, 3, 3, 3, 3,
3, 21, 19, 19, 19, 19, 19, 19, 19, 19, 19, 19, 19, 19, 22, 3,
3, 18, 2, 2, 2, 2, 2, 2, 2, 2, 2, 2, 2, 2, 20, 3,
3, 18, 2, 2, 2, 5, 15, 15, 15, 15, 15, 15, 6, 2, 20, 3,
3, 18, 2, 2, 2, 7, 10, 1, 1, 1, 1, 1, 16, 2, 20, 3,
3, 18, 2, 2, 2, 2, 14, 1, 1, 1, 1, 1, 16, 2, 20, 3,
3, 18, 2, 2, 2, 2, 7, 10, 1, 1, 1, 1, 16, 2, 20, 3,
3, 18, 2, 2, 2, 2, 2, 14, 1, 1, 1, 1, 16, 2, 20, 3,
3, 18, 2, 2, 2, 2, 2, 14, 1, 9, 10, 1, 16, 2, 20, 3,
3, 18, 2, 2, 2, 2, 2, 14, 1, 11, 12, 1, 16, 2, 20, 3,
3, 18, 2, 5, 6, 2, 2, 7, 13, 13, 13, 13, 8, 2, 20, 3,
3, 18, 2, 7, 8, 2, 2, 2, 2, 2, 2, 2, 2, 2, 20, 3,
3, 18, 2, 2, 2, 2, 2, 2, 2, 2, 2, 2, 2, 2, 20, 3,
3, 23, 17, 17, 17, 17, 17, 17, 17, 17, 17, 17, 17, 17, 24, 3,
3, 3, 3, 3, 3, 3, 3, 3, 3, 3, 3, 3, 3, 3, 3, 3
```

If you compare the tile indexes in the preceding code with the tiles shown in the preceding figures, you should be able to see how the generated map matches up with the map shown in the figures. If you have trouble connecting the dots, don't worry because we'll revisit this map a little later in the chapter when you build the Wanderer example MIDlet.

Using the Tile Studio Map Editor

The Tile Studio mapping application is similar to Mappy but more powerful. However, with the added power comes added complexity. Don't get me wrong— Tile Studio is a very useful program, and you may ultimately find it to be more useful than Mappy. But to quickly get started creating mobile game maps, I found Mappy to be a bit easier to use. For this reason, I don't want to spend too much time going over the intricacies of creating maps in Tile Studio. Instead, take a quick look at the screen shot in Figure 10.8, which shows the same map I created in Mappy being created in Tile Studio.

You can download Tile Studio for free from the following website: http://tilestudio.sourceforge.net/.

Gamer's
Garage

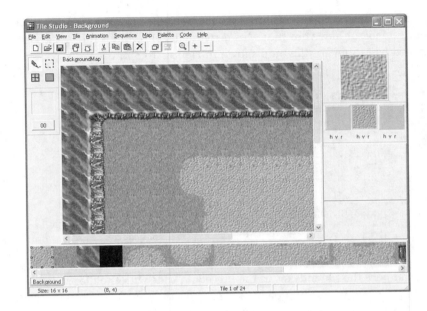

As Figure 10.8 reveals, Tile Studio allows you to select tiles (from the bottom of the screen in this case) and place them on a map area to build game maps. Tile Studio offers some more advanced features than Mappy, but you may or may not see them as being necessary for creating maps for your mobile games. I still encourage you to try out both applications and see which one suits your needs best. It's safe to say that mapping software dramatically speeds up and improves the process of creating mobile game maps.

Formatting Map Information for Games

Earlier in the discussion of the Mappy map creation application, I showed you the map code generated by Mappy as a CSV file. I didn't go into details about what the code meant, but you could probably ascertain that the numbers in the comma-separated list represented tile indexes for each cell of the map. There are actually several different ways you can code the cell data for maps. I've found the simplest and easiest-to-understand approach to be arranging the tile indexes in a one-dimensional array of integers. Although the array is a single list of numbers, you can separate them into rows and columns by arranging them carefully in your code.

The map code generated by the Mappy program is already formatted into rows, as you saw earlier, but the columns are a bit tougher to see because the numbers are not aligned. If you align the columns and place the list of tile indexes into an array of integers, you get the following Java map code:

```java
int[] layerMap = {
  3,  3,  3,  3,  3,  3,  3,  3,  3,  3,  3,  3,  3,  3,  3,  3,
  3,  3,  3,  3,  3,  3,  3,  3,  3,  3,  3,  3,  3,  3,  3,  3,
  3, 21, 19, 19, 19, 19, 19, 19, 19, 19, 19, 19, 19, 19, 22,  3,
  3, 18,  2,  2,  2,  2,  2,  2,  2,  2,  2,  2,  2,  2, 20,  3,
  3, 18,  2,  2,  2,  5, 15, 15, 15, 15, 15, 15,  6,  2, 20,  3,
  3, 18,  2,  2,  2,  7, 10,  1,  1,  1,  1,  1, 16,  2, 20,  3,
  3, 18,  2,  2,  2,  2, 14,  1,  1,  1,  1,  1, 16,  2, 20,  3,
  3, 18,  2,  2,  2,  7, 10,  1,  1,  1,  1, 16,  2, 20,  3,
  3, 18,  2,  2,  2,  2,  2, 14,  1,  1,  1,  1, 16,  2, 20,  3,
  3, 18,  2,  2,  2,  2,  2, 14,  1,  9, 10,  1, 16,  2, 20,  3,
  3, 18,  2,  5, 15,  6,  2, 14,  1, 11, 12,  1, 16,  2, 20,  3,
  3, 18,  2, 14,  1, 16,  2,  7, 13, 13, 13, 13,  8,  2, 20,  3,
  3, 18,  2,  7, 13,  8,  2,  2,  2,  2,  2,  2,  2,  2, 20,  3,
  3, 18,  2,  2,  2,  2,  2,  2,  2,  2,  2,  2,  2,  2, 20,  3,
  3, 23, 17, 17, 17, 17, 17, 17, 17, 17, 17, 17, 17, 17, 24,  3,
  3,  3,  3,  3,  3,  3,  3,  3,  3,  3,  3,  3,  3,  3,  3,  3
};
```

Now you have an array of tile indexes that is ready for use in creating a tiled layer map for a mobile game. Regardless of whether you use pencil and paper, Mappy, Tile Studio, or some other mapping software, the end result of your efforts should be an array similar to the preceding one that consists of rows and columns of tile indexes. If you're still having trouble understanding what this array means, check out the tiles shown in Figure 10.9.

FIGURE 10.9
The tile indexes in the image for a tiled layer are automatically numbered from left to right and top to bottom starting at 1.

Regardless of how many tiles are stored in the image for a tiled layer, they are always numbered starting at 1 with the upper leftmost tile. The tile indexes increase as you move from left to right and top to bottom in the tile list. If you now compare the tile indexes shown in Figure 10.9 with the formatted map code you just saw, it should be a bit easier to understand how it all comes together to create the complete map shown in Figure 10.10.

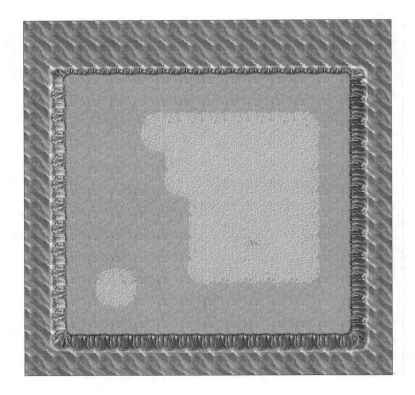

This figure should demystify the meaning of tile indexes and how they are used to construct a tiled layer map out of an array of integers in Java code; you'll revisit this map a bit later in the chapter when you construct the Wanderer example MIDlet. Now that you have a better idea of how maps work, you're ready to learn about the TiledLayer class and how it is used to actually create tiled layers.

Working with the TiledLayer **Class**

The MIDP 2.0 API supports tiled layers through the TiledLayer class, which makes it relatively easy to create and use tiled layers. Every tiled layer object has an associated image that specifies the set of tiles used to describe the tiled layer map. And speaking of maps, every tiled layer has a map containing tile indexes that reference the individual tiles in the layer image. Because the TiledLayer class is derived from the familiar Layer class, it can be manipulated in much the same way as sprites. In other words, you can change the position of a tiled layer, get its size and position, draw it, and control its visibility with a few simple method calls.

Creating a Tiled Layer

When you create a tiled layer, you specify its width and height in tiles, along with the image containing the tile set, and the width and height of the tiles; every tile must be the same size. This information is passed into the TiledLayer() constructor when you first create a tiled layer. Following is code that creates a tiled layer based on the race track shown earlier in the chapter in Figure 10.1.

```
TiledLayer backgroundLayer;
try {
  backgroundLayer = new TiledLayer(5, 4, Image.createImage("/RaceTrack.png"),
    100, 100);
}
catch (IOException e) {
  System.err.println("Failed loading images!");
}
```

The first two parameters in the TiledLayer() constructor specify the number of columns and number of rows in the tiled layer, respectively, which in this case are 5 and 4. The third parameter is an Image object, which is a hypothetical race track image based on the list of tiles shown in Figure 10.1. The remaining two parameters are the width and height of each individual tile; the race track tiles are perfectly square with a width and height of 100 pixels.

After creating a TiledLayer object, the next step is to establish its map by setting its individual cells to tile indexes. If you look back at Figure 10.1, you'll notice that each tile has a number associated with it. These numbers are the tile indexes for the tile set. Tile indexes always start at 1 and count up. Index 0 is a special tile index that represents the lack of a tile. In other words, cells in which you specify a tile index of 0 are transparent when the tiled layer is painted.

Before you set the map for a tiled layer, all the cells in the layer are set to a tile index of 0, which means the layer starts out being completely transparent.

Gamer's Garage

Using the track layout in Figure 10.1 as a guide, following is a layer map for the race track that is stored in a one-dimensional array of integers:

```
int[] layerMap = {
  1,  3,  3,  3,  2,
  6,  7,  7,  7,  6,
  6,  7,  1,  3,  5,
  4,  3,  5,  7,  7
};
```

All you must do to visualize this map is look at the tile index for each value in the array. To make this task a bit easier, you typically need to draw out a map on paper or use mapping software such as Mappy or Tile Studio, which were mentioned earlier in the chapter. The array in the previous code is actually a one-dimensional array, but it is coded so that you can see the map in terms of rows and columns of tile indexes.

Unfortunately, there is no method to pass an array of tile indexes to the TiledLayer class. Instead, you must set the tile index for each cell of a tiled layer by calling the setCell() method multiple times. Following is a for loop that accomplishes this task for the race track tiled layer:

```
for (int i = 0; i < layerMap.length; i++) {
  int column = i % 5;
  int row = (i - column) / 4;
  backgroundLayer.setCell(column, row, layerMap[i]);
}
```

The number 5 indicates the number of columns, whereas 4 indicates the number of rows.

This code iterates through each entry in the tile map, and then sets the appropriate cell in the tiled layer based on the specific column and row. This code can easily be modified to accommodate maps of different sizes if you change the number of columns (5) and number of rows (4) as referenced in the code on the second and third lines.

Moving and Drawing a Tiled Layer

You now know that creating a tiled layer with the TiledLayer class isn't difficult at all as soon as you figure out how to arrange the map containing tile indexes. The good news is that setting the position of tiled layers is also very simple, as the following code reveals:

```
backgroundLayer.setPosition(0, 0);
```

This code simply sets the position of the tiled layer to the origin of the game screen, which means the upper-left corner of the tiled layer appears at the upper-left corner of the game screen; assuming the game screen is smaller than the tiled layer, the lower-right portion of the tiled layer doesn't appear on the screen in this position. If you search through the MIDP API documentation for the setPosition() method, you'll notice that it isn't listed with the TiledLayer class. That's because this method is derived from the parent Layer class. Another method inherited from Layer is paint(), which is responsible for painting a tiled layer. Following is code to paint a tiled layer:

```
backgroundLayer.paint(g);
```

This code reveals how little effort is required to paint a tiled layer after it has been created and positioned properly.

Building the Wanderer Example Program

The remainder of this chapter is devoted to the development of an example called Wanderer, which is somewhat of an adventure simulator where you control a character around a scrolling map. Although the Wanderer example isn't technically a game, it could be transformed into an adventure game without too terribly much additional effort. The key to the Wanderer example is that it uses an oversized map that can be scrolled in any direction. Your character stays anchored in the middle of the game screen, and he has the appearance of movement because the map scrolls under him.

Not surprisingly, the map in the Wanderer example is created as a tiled layer. The example therefore makes use of two different layer objects: a background tiled layer map and a sprite representing the wandering person. You are already intimately familiar with the map used in the Wanderer example. Please refer back to Figures 10.9 and 10.10 and the associated map code for a refresher on the map used in the Wanderer example. This map shows a square piece of land bordered by water on all sides. The Wanderer MIDlet has to be careful to ensure that the person sprite is allowed to move only on the land areas of the map, and that movement over the cliffs and down into the water is restricted.

The majority of the work in creating the Wanderer example is simply setting up and managing the background tiled layer. In fact, because the tiled layer scrolls behind the stationary person sprite, you pretty much can leave the person sprite alone throughout the MIDlet, other than animating it so that the guy appears to be walking.

Writing the Program Code

The code for the Wanderer example program begins with the member variables that make it possible to implement a tiled layer background that can be scrolled to simulate movement. These member variables consist of a TiledLayer object and a Sprite object representing the person that is doing the wandering. Following are the declarations of these variables:

```
private TiledLayer backgroundLayer;
private Sprite     personSprite;
```

The backgroundLayer variable stores the tiled layer for the background in the MIDlet, whereas the personSprite variable keeps track of the wanderer person.

These two variables are initialized in the start() method of the WCanvas class, where the tiled layer and sprite are created. Following is the code that first creates the backgroundLayer object:

```
try {
  backgroundLayer = new TiledLayer(16, 16,
    Image.createImage("/Background.png"), 48, 48);
}
catch (IOException e) {
  System.err.println("Failed loading images!");
}
```

If you recall from earlier in the chapter, the TiledLayer() constructor requires you to specify the numbers of columns and rows in the tiled layer, along with an image containing the tiles and the width and height of each individual tile. This information is passed into the constructor in the preceding code, which reveals that the background tiled layer is 16 tiles wide by 16 tiles high, with each tile being 48×48 pixels in size. Additionally, the tiles are stored in the Background.png image, which you saw earlier in Figure 10.9.

The most important part of creating a tiled layer is specifying its layer map. You do this by creating an array, or map, consisting of tile indexes that specify the arrangement of tiles in the tiled layer map. Earlier in the chapter you saw how mapping software can aid in the creation of these maps, including generating map code. Following is a refresher of the array representing the background tiled layer map for the Wanderer example, which you saw a bit earlier in the chapter:

```
int[] layerMap = {
  3,  3,  3,  3,  3,  3,  3,  3,  3,  3,  3,  3,  3,  3,  3,  3,
  3,  3,  3,  3,  3,  3,  3,  3,  3,  3,  3,  3,  3,  3,  3,  3,
  3, 21, 19, 19, 19, 19, 19, 19, 19, 19, 19, 19, 19, 22,  3,
  3, 18,  2,  2,  2,  2,  2,  2,  2,  2,  2,  2,  2, 20,  3,
  3, 18,  2,  2,  2,  5, 15, 15, 15, 15, 15, 15,  6,  2, 20,  3,
  3, 18,  2,  2,  2,  7, 10,  1,  1,  1,  1,  1, 16,  2, 20,  3,
  3, 18,  2,  2,  2,  2, 14,  1,  1,  1,  1,  1, 16,  2, 20,  3,
  3, 18,  2,  2,  2,  7, 10,  1,  1,  1,  1, 16,  2, 20,  3,
  3, 18,  2,  2,  2,  2, 14,  1,  1,  1,  1, 16,  2, 20,  3,
  3, 18,  2,  2,  2,  2, 14,  1,  9, 10,  1, 16,  2, 20,  3,
  3, 18,  2,  5, 15,  6,  2, 14,  1, 11, 12,  1, 16,  2, 20,  3,
  3, 18,  2, 14,  1, 16,  2,  7, 13, 13, 13, 13,  8,  2, 20,  3,
  3, 18,  2,  7, 13,  8,  2,  2,  2,  2,  2,  2,  2,  2, 20,  3,
  3, 18,  2,  2,  2,  2,  2,  2,  2,  2,  2,  2,  2, 20,  3,
  3, 23, 17, 17, 17, 17, 17, 17, 17, 17, 17, 17, 17, 24,  3,
  3,  3,  3,  3,  3,  3,  3,  3,  3,  3,  3,  3,  3,  3,  3
};
```

This array should be somewhat familiar to you from the design of the background tiled layer in the previous section. Obviously, declaring the array alone isn't enough to establish the map for the tiled layer. You must use the setCell() method of the TiledLayer class to set each cell of the tiled layer individually. Fortunately, it isn't too hard to craft a for loop that handles this task with a minimal amount of code:

```
for (int i = 0; i < layerMap.length; i++) {
  int column = i % 16;
  int row = (i - column) / 16;
  backgroundLayer.setCell(column, row, layerMap[i]);
}
```

The map is 16 rows by 16 columns in size.

The most important aspect of this loop to pay attention to is the usage of the number 16 in the second and third lines of code. The 16 in the second line reflects the number of columns in the array, whereas the 16 in the third line reflects the number of rows. If you change the size of the map, and therefore the array, it is crucial that you adjust these numbers to reflect the new sizes. The nice thing about what is going on here is that you are setting the entire tiled layer map in only five lines of code.

Instead of iterating through a single array of tile indexes to set the map for a tiled layer, you could also specify the map as a two-dimensional array of rows and columns, and use two nested for loops. Both approaches are equally valid and probably similar in terms of efficiency; I just opted for the single-array approach here.

Construction Cue

With the background tiled layer successfully created and set with a map, all that is left to finish its initialization is to set its initial position. Keep in mind that the position of the background layer is specified with respect to the origin of the game screen, which is the upper-left corner of the game screen. So if you want to initially center the game screen with respect to the background, you must set the background layer at a negative position. If this sounds a bit confusing, check out Figure 10.11, which reveals why centering a background larger than the screen requires negative coordinates.

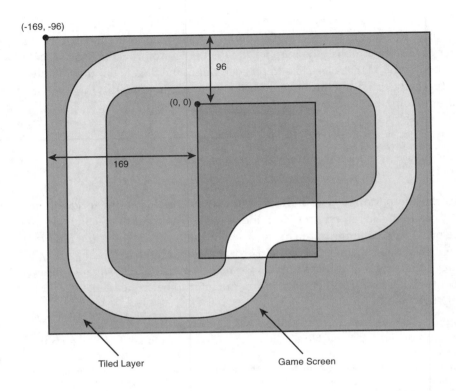

Following is the code that centers the background tiled layer so that the game screen reveals the middle of the virtual world:

```
backgroundLayer.setPosition((getWidth() - backgroundLayer.getWidth()) / 2,
  (getHeight() - backgroundLayer.getHeight()) / 2);
```

So where are the negative values for the background position? Because the width and height of the canvas are smaller than the width and height of the background layer, the position values will always be negative in the previous code. So the calculation works out without you having to explicitly set the position to negative values.

Okay, the background layer is now squared away so you can focus your attention on the person sprite. Following is the code that creates the person sprite, which is very straightforward given your previous experience with sprites:

```
try {
  personSprite = new Sprite(Image.createImage("/Person.png"), 20, 24);
  personSprite.setPosition((getWidth() - personSprite.getWidth()) / 2,
    (getHeight() - personSprite.getHeight()) / 2);
}
catch (IOException e) {
  System.err.println("Failed loading images!");
}
```

The person sprite is centered on the game screen.

The person sprite consists of two animation frames, but the 20×24 frame size is all the information required to reflect that there are multiple animation frames; the Sprite() constructor is smart enough to figure out that the actual Person.png image is 20×48 pixels to accommodate the two frames. After creating the sprite, the code goes on to center the sprite on the game screen with a quick calculation.

As you're familiar with from previous example MIDlets, the update() method is where you process key input and respond accordingly. In the case of the Wanderer example, the key input results in scrolling the background layer behind the person sprite, which remains stationary in the center of the game screen. Listing 10.1 contains the code for the update() method of the WCanvas class.

LISTING 10.1 The update() Method in the WCanvas Class Scrolls the Background Layer in Response to Key Presses in the Wanderer MIDlet

```
private void update() {
  // Process user input to move the background layer and animate the person
  if (++inputDelay > 2) {
    int keyState = getKeyStates();
    if ((keyState & LEFT_PRESSED) != 0) {
      backgroundLayer.move(12, 0);
      personSprite.nextFrame();
    }
    else if ((keyState & RIGHT_PRESSED) != 0) {
      backgroundLayer.move(-12, 0);
      personSprite.nextFrame();
    }
    if ((keyState & UP_PRESSED) != 0) {
      backgroundLayer.move(0, 12);
      personSprite.nextFrame();
    }
    else if ((keyState & DOWN_PRESSED) != 0) {
      backgroundLayer.move(0, -12);
      personSprite.nextFrame();
    }
    checkBackgroundBounds(backgroundLayer);

    // Reset the input delay
    inputDelay = 0;
  }
}
```

The background layer is moved in response to directional key presses.

The person sprite is animated to simulate walking with every directional key press.

This code ensures that the background layer isn't scrolled beyond its edges.

The update() method isn't too terribly tricky in terms of how it scrolls the background layer in response to key presses. What might surprise you is the fact that you must move the background layer in the opposite direction of that in which the user is attempting to move the person. This makes sense because the person sprite remains stationary in the middle of the screen, so to give the effect of the person moving to the left, the background must be moved to the right. The person sprite's animation frame is changed with each movement; because the sprite has only two animation frames, the end result is that they alternate back and forth with each movement.

Toward the end of the update() method, a call is made to the checkBackgroundBounds() method, which is responsible for keeping the background layer from being scrolled too far. This method is shown in Listing 10.2.

LISTING 10.2 The checkBackgroundBounds() Method Makes Sure that the Background Layer Isn't Scrolled Too Far

```
private void checkBackgroundBounds(TiledLayer background) {
  // Stop the background if necessary
  if (background.getX() > -15)
    background.setPosition(-15, background.getY());
  else if (background.getX() < -572)
    background.setPosition(-572, background.getY());
  if (background.getY() > -25)
    background.setPosition(background.getX(), -25);
  else if (background.getY() < -572)
    background.setPosition(background.getX(), -572);
}
```

The numbers in this code are carefully calculated to limit the background scrolling so that the person can't move beyond the grassy edges.

Although the main purpose of the checkBackgroundBounds() method is to make sure the background layer isn't scrolled beyond its edges, the movement of the background layer is actually restricted a bit further than that. You want to provide the illusion that the person sprite can't move beyond the grassy area of the background; otherwise, he would be able to walk over the cliff into the water, which would ruin the effect. The numbers you see hard-coded in the preceding code are used to provide exact limits for the background layer that allow the person sprite to walk just to the edge of the cliffs on the background.

The last code of interest in the Wanderer example MIDlet is the draw() method, which is responsible for drawing both the background tiled layer and person sprite. Listing 10.3 contains the code for this method.

LISTING 10.3 The draw() Method Draws the Background Tiled Layer and the Person Sprite

```
private void draw(Graphics g) {
  // Draw the background tiled layer
  backgroundLayer.paint(g);

  // Draw the person sprite
  personSprite.paint(g);

  // Flush the offscreen graphics buffer
  flushGraphics();
}
```

One line of code is all it takes to draw the tiled background layer.

Nothing too surprising in this code! The paint() method is called on both the backgroundLayer and personSprite objects to draw the background layer and person sprite.

Because the positioning of the background layer can be a little difficult to grasp at first, given that its coordinates can go from positive to negative, I have a little trick you can use to better understand what's going on. The trick involves displaying the background layer's position on the game screen so that you can see its exact position as you scroll around. To try out this trick, just place the following code near the end of the draw() method before the call to flushGraphics().

```
// Draw the current background layer position
String s = "X = " + backgroundLayer.getX() + ", Y = " + backgroundLayer.getY();
g.drawString(s, 0, 0, Graphics.TOP | Graphics.LEFT);
```

It's worth pointing out that you can use this same trick to display any game information that you want to keep up with. For example, you could display the speed or position of a sprite that is acting strangely.

FIGURE 10.12
When you first run the Wanderer MIDlet, your character appears in the middle of the virtual world.

FIGURE 10.13
In the Wanderer MIDlet the person remains stationary while the background tiled layer scrolls behind him.

Testing the Finished Product

With all the Wanderer code under your belt, it's time to take the example program for a spin. Or more accurately, it's time to take it for a scroll! Figure 10.12 shows the Wanderer example as it appears when you first start it.

Your character starts out in Wanderer centered on the game screen, and in the center of the virtual world (map). If you recall from the code in the game, the person in the example never moves from the center of the screen, which makes sense given that the background moves around behind him to simulate travel. As you maneuver the person with the directional keys in the J2ME emulator or on a real mobile phone, the background tiled layer scrolls to reveal other parts of the map. The end result is that the person appears to be traveling around the virtual world, as shown in Figure 10.13.

As with the real world, the virtual world map in the Wanderer example isn't without limits. The scrolling code in the example is careful to check for the edges of the map and not allow the scrolling to go past those edges. If you attempted to scroll past the map edges, you would get unexpected results such as repeated graphics. It's very important in all games that utilize tiled layers to provide code that either provides limits so that you can't scroll beyond the map edges or that gracefully wraps the map around to the other side in a seamless fashion. The Wanderer example uses the former approach, as is evident in Figure 10.14.

Okay, sure, there's a chance the universe is without limits, but all the maps humans have been able to create thus far certainly have limits. And maps for tiled layers are no different!

Although it isn't technically a game, you could certainly argue that the Wanderer example is one of the most interesting programs you've seen thus far in the book. A scrolling virtual world that you can roam around on is quite an accomplishment, and a huge step toward taking mobile games to another level.

FIGURE 10.14
The Wanderer MIDlet is smart enough to prevent you from scrolling past the edge of the tiled layer map.

Summary

Up until this chapter you probably thought of game graphics in terms of individual background and sprite images. It might have never crossed your mind that game graphics could be built out of small building blocks. You now have an intimate understanding of tiled layers, and how they make it possible to construct game graphics with a relatively small set of graphical blocks, or tiles. Not only are tiled layers beneficial from the perspective of making it easier to dynamically create game levels and alter backgrounds, but they are also extremely efficient because they rely on a limited set of small images. Given that efficiency is a critical part of every mobile game, you'll likely find yourself using tiled layers a great deal in your own games.

The next chapter continues your education on game layers by introducing you to the MIDP layer manager, which provides a means of gracefully controlling multiple layers in a game as a single unit. You've been managing layers yourself up until now, but the layer manager is here to make your life much easier!

Field Trip

I never thought I would recommend quilting in a book on how to create games, but believe it or not, there is a connection. Recently I saw a story on the news about how the widow of an American soldier cut her husband's clothes into squares and had a quilt made out of them. It was her unique way of remembering her husband, and avoiding throwing out his belongings. It occurred to me that the process of making a quilt is actually very similar to that of designing a tiled layer—you arrange small pieces to form a larger, more desirable pattern. If you or a friend or relative has a traditional handmade quilt, take some time to study it and take note of the unique patterns made by small pieces of material arranged simply. Then consider how very different the quilt could've looked if the pieces had been arranged in another pattern. That's the power of tiled layers!

CHAPTER 11

Managing Multiple Game Layers

Arcade Archive

As one of the most popular video game sequels in history, Donkey Kong Junior served as a reversal of sorts on the original storyline in the hit game Donkey Kong. Released in 1982 by Nintendo, Donkey Kong Junior puts you in control of a small gorilla in a diaper (Junior) whose job is to rescue his father (Donkey Kong) from the evil clutches of Mario. Donkey Kong Junior is unique among Nintendo games in that it is the only game where Mario is a bad guy. It is also the middle game in the Donkey Kong trilogy, with Donkey Kong and Donkey Kong 3 serving as the first and last installments, respectively.

Tiled layers open up lots of interesting possibilities for mobile games. As you start to use more tiled layers and sprites, which are also layers, it starts to get challenging keeping them under control. More specifically, it's somewhat of a pain keeping up with which layers appear on top of other layers and in what order to draw them. Fortunately, the MIDP API comes through with a special class that is designed solely for the management of layers in mobile games. I'm talking about the LayerManager class, which is very handy in automating some of the tasks associated with working with several layers in the context of games. Not only do you learn how to put the LayerManager class to good use in this chapter, but you also expand on the Wanderer example to make it significantly more interesting.

In this chapter, you'll learn

- ▶ About the challenges associated with managing multiple game layers

- ▶ How the standard LayerManager class helps ease the pain of layer management

▶ That two tiled layers can be used together to provide interesting game effects

▶ How to turn the Wanderer example program into a cool maze simulation

Dealing with Multiple Game Layers

By now you probably have a fairly good idea that mobile games based on the MIDP API are built out of layers. If you recall from earlier chapters, the general Layer class serves as the base class for both the Sprite and TiledLayer classes in the MIDP API. In the example MIDlets that you've encountered up to this point, multiple layers were used to represent various visual components, but they were always maintained independently. More specifically, each different layer had to be drawn individually with a call to its paint() method. Similarly, if you wanted one layer to appear on top of another layer, you had to make sure that you painted the layer after the other layer.

In addition to drawing and keeping track of layer depth on an individual basis, you also have had to use special case code to deal with layers that are larger than the game screen. For example, in the Wanderer example in Chapter 10, "Creating Tiled Game Layers," you had to move the background layer around to scroll it within the game screen and simulate movement. There is no problem with this approach, but when you start building more complex games, you may be dealing with several overlaid layers, not to mention a bunch of sprites. It could get messy attempting to move all the layers to just shift the view being displayed on the game screen.

You've probably figured out that I'm heading somewhere with this criticism of earlier example code. I criticize the earlier code you've seen only because it begins to get difficult to manage in more complex scenarios such as real mobile games. Fortunately, there is a solution to the problem of layer management in the form of a standard MIDP class called LayerManager. The LayerManager class provides a simple yet effective way of drawing, layering, and managing a view on multiple layers.

As part of managing a view on a set of layers, the LayerManager class is able to calculate a clipping region for layers, and therefore draw only the portions that are visible in the view window for the layer manager. Although you may assume that this view window is the same size as the game screen, this isn't always the case.

For example, the score, number of lives, and other game state information might appear along the top or bottom of the screen in a region separate from the "play area." In this scenario, you would shorten the height of the view window to allow space for the information area. Figure 11.1 shows how the view window of a layer manager provides a view on multiple game layers.

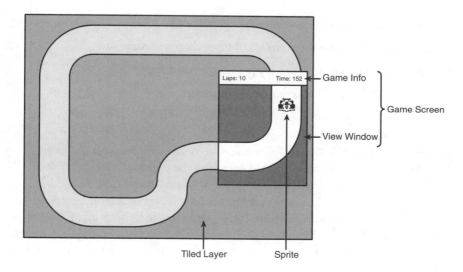

Laps: 10   Time: 152 ← Game Info
} Game Screen
← View Window
Tiled Layer   Sprite

FIGURE 11.1
The view window of a layer manager may deliberately be set smaller than the game screen to leave room for other game information.

The figure reveals how a tiled layer and a sprite are visible through the view window of a layer manager. Additionally, the view window doesn't take up all the game screen; a game information bar is displayed along the top of the game screen above the view window.

Working with the LayerManager Class

Although on the surface the concept of managing multiple layers in a mobile game may sound somewhat complex, the standard LayerManager class is actually fairly simple to use. This class comes into play after you've created the layers for your game, including both sprites and tiled layers. The idea is that you create your game layers and then append them to the layer manager, which is then responsible for drawing, layering, and keeping track of the view window on the layers.

A relatively small set of methods in the LayerManager class is used to work with layers in a layer manager:

- ▶ **append()**—Append a layer to the bottom of the layers being managed
- ▶ **insert()**—Insert a layer at a specific location within the layers being managed
- ▶ **remove()**—Remove a layer at a specified index
- ▶ **getSize()**—Retrieve the number of layers being managed
- ▶ **getLayerAt()**—Retrieve the layer at a specified index
- ▶ **paint()**—Paint all the layers being managed
- ▶ **setViewWindow()**—Set the position, width, and height of the view window

These methods reveal that each layer added to a layer manager is assigned a unique layer index. This layer index determines the depth of each layer with respect to the screen, with index 0 being closest to the screen and increasing indexes appearing deeper. In other words, the topmost layer being managed has an index of 0, while the largest index corresponds to the bottom layer. The layer manager automatically assigns and adjusts layer indexes as you append, insert, and remove layers, so in many cases you may not actually need to tinker with actual layer index values.

Although the LayerManager methods listed earlier are all useful in working with layer managers, you can accomplish an awful lot by using just a few of them. But before calling any methods you must first create a LayerManager object, like this:

```
LayerManager layers = new LayerManager();
```

After creating a LayerManager object, the next step you'll take in a real game is appending or inserting layers to the manager. Appending layers is a bit simpler because you don't have to specify a layer index, but it requires you to append the layers in the proper order. If you recall from the earlier mention of the append() method, it appends a layer to the bottom of the layers, which means you should append your topmost layers to the layer manager first. Following is an example of how you might append a couple of sprites and a background tiled layer to the newly created layer manager:

```
layers.append(sprite1);
layers.append(sprite2);
layers.append(backgroundLayer);
```

This code results in the background layer appearing behind the two sprites. Furthermore, if the two sprites should cross paths, sprite1 will be drawn on top of sprite2 because it sits on top of the layer pile.

The last step in creating a layer manager is establishing the view window. Following is code to set the view window at the upper-left corner of the entire layer manager area, and at the same size as the game screen, assuming this code is placed within the canvas class for your game:

```
layers.setViewWindow(0, 0, getWidth(), getHeight());
```

If you need to move the view window to reveal other regions of the layers, just call setViewWindow() again with a different set of coordinates in the first two parameters. That's really all it takes to manage layers with the LayerManager class.

Animating Tiled Layers

The previous chapter was so busy that I hated to overwhelm you with any more details associated with creating and working with tiled layers. So I deliberately avoided coverage of a nifty little tiled layer trick that allows you to animate individual tiles within a tiled layer. It works like this: In the tile map you identify animated tiles with a special negative value such as -1, -2, and so on. This value represents a particular animated tile, which can then be set to any of the tiles in the tile set at any point throughout a game.

As an example, let's say you wanted to animate some of the water tiles in the Wanderer example from the previous chapter so that the water looks a bit more realistic. You could designate some of the water tiles in the map for the tiled layer as -1 instead of 1; 1 was the tile index for the water tile. You would then add code somewhere in the update() method of the MIDlet to cycle all animated tiles with an index of -1. By "cycle" I mean changing the tile over time so that it appears to be moving. The neat thing about animated tiles is that you can use any tile in the tile set, so in the case of animated water you would just need to add some additional tiles to show the water splashing around.

Support for animated tiles comes in the TiledLayer class in the form of two methods:

▶ **createAnimatedTile()**—Create an animated tile

▶ **setAnimatedTile()**—Set the static tile for a specified animated tile index

To better understand how these methods work, we need to establish some termi-
nology. A *static tile* is a tile that appears in the tiled layer image, and has a tile
index of 1 or greater; a tile index of 0 is a special case that identifies an empty
cell in a tiled layer. An *animated tile* is a placeholder that enables you to show a
sequence of static tiles as an animation, and has a tile index of -1 or less. So, you
reference an animated tile through a negative tile index, but the actual tile being
displayed at any given moment as part of an animation is really just a static tile
with a positive tile index.

Take a look at the following simple tiled layer map to help put this stuff into
perspective:

```
 1,   1,  -1,   1,
-1,  -1,   1,   1,
 1,  -1,   1,  -1,
-1,   1,  -1,  -1
```

Before interpreting this map, let's establish that there are four static tiles showing
different water images that give the effect of water moving when shown in
sequence; these tiles have indexes of 1, 2, 3, and 4. Cells in the map with values of
1 are normal cells just like you're used to seeing, and they result in the first water
tile being displayed with no frills. Cells with values of -1 are animated cells, and
are therefore displayed as animated tiles. The animation of the tiles is just the display sequence of static tiles 1, 2, 3, and 4. This sequence isn't reflected in the map,
but you find out how it is applied to the animated tiles in just a moment.

In terms of code, you first create an animated tile prior to creating the map for a
tiled layer. Following is code to create the animated tile for the water example:

```
waterLayer.createAnimatedTile(1);
```

The parameter to this method is the initial static tile to be displayed for the animated tile. Although this tile will change because it is being animated, you have
to start with a valid static tile. The createAnimatedTile() method actually
returns the index of the newly created animated tile, but you don't really need to
store the value because you already know what it is. The first animated tile created for a map is automatically given the index -1, and the animated tile indexes
continue to count down by one as you create more.

You've now created the animated tile and established the map for the tiled layer.
At this point the tiled layer displays just as it would without any animation
because the animated tiles are initially set to the static tile with an index of 1. To
begin animating the tiles, all you must do is call the setAnimatedTile() method
with the new static tile index to be displayed, like this:

```
waterLayer.setAnimatedTile(-1, 2);
```

This code changes all the animated tiles with the animated tile index of -1 from the static tile 1 to the static tile 2. In practice, you would probably use a variable to store the value of the static tile being displayed so that you can increment it each time you update the animation. In this way, you can cycle the animated tiles through a sequence of static tiles by simply calling setAnimatedTile() repeatedly.

> If you really wanted to provide a realistic water effect, you could use several different animated tiles that are out of sync in terms of the static tiles that they show, which would give a more random appearance to the water.

Construction Cue

If you missed out on the main point in the details of the example, the killer power of animated tiles is that they provide you with the means to change an entire group of tiles with a single line of code. And if the animated water example sounded interesting, you'll be glad to know that the Wanderer 2 example program that you build in the next section uses this exact animated tile technique.

Building the Wanderer 2 Example Program

In the previous chapter you took your first foray into tiled layers by creating an example program called Wanderer. The Wanderer MIDlet enabled you to control a person around a map that is much larger than the screen on most mobile phones. Wanderer involved a single tiled layer that served more as a visual backdrop rather than a truly interactive part of the program. Layers become much more appealing when you design them so that they interact with sprites. For example, you could create a "barrier" layer containing walls that restrict the movement of sprites. This type of functionality is possible thanks to the Sprite class, which allows you to detect collisions not only between sprites and other sprites but also between sprites and tiled layers.

The remainder of this chapter focuses on modifying the Wanderer example program to make use of two tiled layers: a background layer and a barrier layer. The background layer is similar to the original background layer in Wanderer, but the barrier layer is entirely new and serves to establish a maze of walls for the player to navigate through. If you're familiar with old dungeon video games such as Gauntlet and the original Castle Wolfenstein, you may have an idea of how useful a "maze layer" can be in establishing levels in a game.

The Wanderer 2 example not only uses two tiled layers, but it also demonstrates how to take advantage of animated tiles within a tiled layer. In this case, the animated tiles are the water tiles that appear along the edges of the background layer in the original Wanderer example; in Wanderer 2 the water tiles are moved to the barrier layer.

The other significant restructuring of code between Wanderer and Wanderer 2 is the usage of the LayerManager class, which Wanderer 2 uses to manage the two layers and the person sprite. More importantly, the view window of the layer manager is used to alter the current view on the layers, as opposed to moving the layers around relative to the game screen.

To summarize, the following design changes distinguish the Wanderer 2 example from its counterpart in the previous chapter:

- A new barrier layer is added to go along with the slightly modified background layer. The barrier layer acts to restrict the movement of the person sprite.

- Animated tiles are used to give the water in the barrier layer a more realistic appearance.

- A layer manager is used to help manage and control the tiled layers and person sprite.

- As part of using the layer manager, the code to scroll the background is altered to move the position of the view window as opposed to moving the layers themselves. Because the person sprite should appear stationary with respect to the view window, it is moved along with the view window.

These steps should make sense in terms of making the Wanderer 2 example a bit more interesting than the previous version of the example. If you're having trouble visualizing the changes, you might want to revisit the Wanderer example in the previous chapter to remember how it works. Otherwise, the code for the Wanderer 2 example, which you see in a moment, should clear everything up.

Designing the Tiled Layer Maps

The Wanderer 2 example MIDlet relies on two tiled layers, and therefore two tiled layer maps. The two layers correspond to the background land, where the person can freely roam, and a barrier consisting of a water border and interior walls that serve as barriers to the person's movement. The barrier layer is designed to be drawn overlaid on the background layer so that they appear as one layer in the example.

The reason two layers are employed is so that you can distinguish between layer elements that obstruct the person and elements that don't; any graphics appearing on the barrier layer serve as obstructions.

The Background Map

You might think that the background map in Wanderer 2 would be identical to the similar version in the original Wanderer example, but there is an important difference. If you recall, in the original Wanderer example the person's movement was restricted so that it didn't appear to walk off the edge of the land into the water. This movement restriction involved simple observation of the person's location and limitation of its movement to a region within the background area. Because the barrier layer in Wanderer 2 can easily handle restricting the player's movement along the edges of the land, it is no longer necessary to limit the person's movement with specific code. And more important to the background layer, it means you don't even need to worry about placing real tiles around the edges of the layer where the edge barriers will be located.

To visualize what I'm talking about in regard to the background layer no longer needing edge tiles, take a look at Figure 11.2.

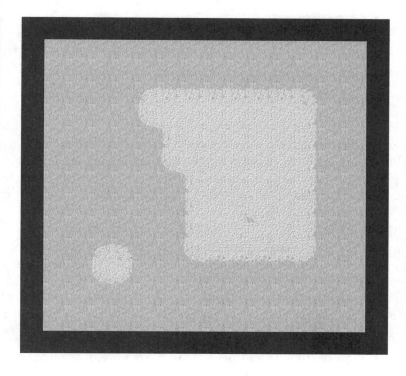

FIGURE 11.2
The new background tiled layer no longer requires edge tiles because they will be covered up by water tiles in the barrier layer.

The black border you see around the tiled layer image in the figure is a transparent area where no graphics appear. Similarly placed cells in the barrier layer contain water tiles that serve as barriers to the person's movement. In fact, part of the grassy edge of the background layer is obscured by the rocky cliffs on the barrier layer, as you will see in the next section.

For now you can focus your attention on the specific map code that makes the background layer a reality:

```
0,  0,  0,  0,  0,  0,  0,  0,  0,  0,  0,  0,  0,  0,  0,  0,
0,  0,  0,  0,  0,  0,  0,  0,  0,  0,  0,  0,  0,  0,  0,  0,
0,  2,  2,  2,  2,  2,  2,  2,  2,  2,  2,  2,  2,  2,  2,  0,
0,  2,  2,  2,  2,  2,  2,  2,  2,  2,  2,  2,  2,  2,  2,  0,
0,  2,  2,  2,  2,  5, 15, 15, 15, 15, 15, 15,  6,  2,  2,  0,
0,  2,  2,  2,  2,  7, 10,  1,  1,  1,  1,  1, 16,  2,  2,  0,
0,  2,  2,  2,  2,  2, 14,  1,  1,  1,  1,  1, 16,  2,  2,  0,
0,  2,  2,  2,  2,  2,  7, 10,  1,  1,  1,  1, 16,  2,  2,  0,
0,  2,  2,  2,  2,  2,  2, 14,  1,  1,  1,  1, 16,  2,  2,  0,
0,  2,  2,  2,  2,  2,  2, 14,  1,  9, 10,  1, 16,  2,  2,  0,
0,  2,  2,  5, 15,  6,  2, 14,  1, 11, 12,  1, 16,  2,  2,  0,
0,  2,  2, 14,  1, 16,  2,  7, 13, 13, 13, 13,  8,  2,  2,  0,
0,  2,  2,  7, 13,  8,  2,  2,  2,  2,  2,  2,  2,  2,  2,  0,
0,  2,  2,  2,  2,  2,  2,  2,  2,  2,  2,  2,  2,  2,  2,  0,
0,  2,  2,  2,  2,  2,  2,  2,  2,  2,  2,  2,  2,  2,  2,  0,
0,  0,  0,  0,  0,  0,  0,  0,  0,  0,  0,  0,  0,  0,  0,  0
```

FIGURE 11.3
The background tiled layer map is realized when the appropriate tiles are placed according to the map code.

Unfortunately, this code doesn't make much sense without referencing the tile image associated with the tiled layer. Figure 11.3 shows the tiles that are used to construct the background tiled layer map.

If you match up tile indexes with cells in the preceding map, you shouldn't have too much trouble visualizing the map shown in Figure 11.2. Keep in mind that all cells with a value of 0 in the map are empty cells, and therefore result in nothing being drawn when the tiled layer is drawn. The barrier tiled layer you see in the next section helps to clear up why the edges of the background layer are left empty.

The Barrier Map

The barrier tiled layer is designed to be drawn on top of the background layer, which means that graphics appearing on the barrier layer cover up graphics on the background layer. Furthermore, the Wanderer 2 MIDlet is designed so that all graphics on the barrier layer serve as obstructions for the person sprite. In other words, empty cells on the barrier map are areas where the person can walk freely, whereas all other cells are obstructions and prevent the person's movement.

Figure 11.4 shows the complete barrier layer with black areas denoting empty cells where the person is free to move about.

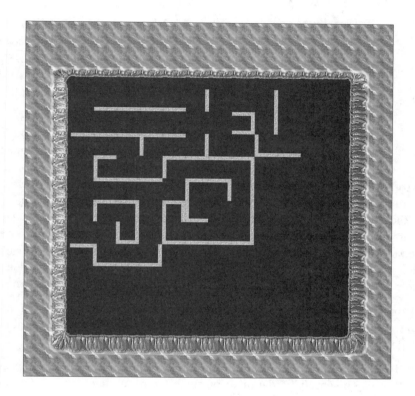

FIGURE 11.4
The barrier layer uses water, rocky edges, and maze pieces to present obstructions to the movement of the person sprite.

As you might have suspected, significant areas of the barrier layer are left empty so that the person has room to walk around. Even the maze tile pieces have a fair amount of transparency in them, which also translates to areas where the person can move. Following is the map code that results in the layer shown in Figure 11.4:

```
-1, -1,  1, -1, -1,  1, -1,  1, -1, -1,  1,  1, -1,  1, -1,  1,
-1, -1, -1,  1,  1, -1,  1, -1,  1,  1, -1,  1, -1, -1,  1, -1,
 1, 21, 19, 19, 19, 19, 19, 19, 19, 19, 19, 19, 19, 22,  1,
 1, 18,  0,  5,  5,  5,  5,  8,  0,  0,  8,  0,  0,  0, 20, -1,
 1, 18,  0,  0,  0,  0,  0,  0,  0, 16,  8,  0,  0,  0, 20,  1,
-1, 18,  7,  7,  7, 11,  7,  8,  0,  0, 10,  5,  0,  0, 20, -1,
 1, 18,  0, 11,  0,  0, 11,  7,  7, 12,  0,  0,  0,  0, 20, -1,
-1, 18,  0,  7,  7,  7,  0, 11, 12,  8,  0,  0,  0,  0, 20,  1,
 1, 18,  0, 11, 12,  0, 15, 10,  0,  8,  0,  0,  0,  0, 20,  1,
 1, 18,  0,  0, 13,  0, 10,  5,  5,  9,  0,  0,  0,  0, 20, -1,
-1, 18,  7, 10,  5,  9,  0,  0,  0,  0,  0,  0,  0,  0, 20,  1,
-1, 18,  0,  0,  0,  0,  0,  0,  0,  0,  0,  0,  0,  0, 20, -1,
 1, 18,  0,  0,  0,  0,  0,  0,  0,  0,  0,  0,  0,  0, 20,  1,
 1, 18,  0,  0,  0,  0,  0,  0,  0,  0,  0,  0,  0,  0, 20,  1,
-1, 23, 17, 17, 17, 17, 17, 17, 17, 17, 17, 17, 17, 24, -1,
-1, -1,  1, -1,  1, -1,  1,  1,  1, -1,  1, -1, -1,  1,  1, -1
```

FIGURE 11.5
The barrier tiled
layer map is real-
ized when tiles are
carefully arranged
according to the
map code.

This map code is tough to decipher without knowing what the tiles look like and their respective indexes. Figure 11.5 shows the tiles used to construct the barrier tiled layer according to the preceding map code.

Going back to the map code, it's hard to overlook the fact that there are some negative tile indexes in the code. If you recall from earlier in the chapter, negative tile indexes refer to animated tiles, which are tiles that can be made to cycle through several different tile images. In the case of the barrier layer, the cells with indexes of -1 are animated tiles that cycle through several different water images to simulate moving water. You'll notice in the barrier map code that some of the water is animated with a value of -1, whereas some of the water is static with a value of 1. This combination of animated and unanimated water helps to provide a little more realism because all the water isn't uniformly animating at the same time.

You learn the details of how the water is animated in the next section. Before you get to that, however, take a look at the background and barrier layers combined into one as they will appear in the Wanderer 2 example (see Figure 11.6).

Figure 11.6 should clear up any confusion you had regarding the empty spaces on the layers. The empty border areas on the background layer are hidden by water on the barrier layer, whereas the empty areas of the barrier layer appear as grassy and sandy areas in the background layer.

The layers are the meat of the Wanderer 2 example, and make the rest of the MIDlet code fairly straightforward, as the next section reveals.

Writing the Program Code

The Wanderer 2 example program relies on a few more member variables to manage the additional layer, the layer manager, the view window's location, and the animated water tile states. Following are the most important member variables in the Wanderer 2 example:

It's very important to keep track of the location of the layer manager's view window.

```
private LayerManager layers;
private int           xView, yView;
private TiledLayer    backgroundLayer;
private TiledLayer    barrierLayer;
private int           waterDelay, waterTile;
private Sprite        personSprite;
```

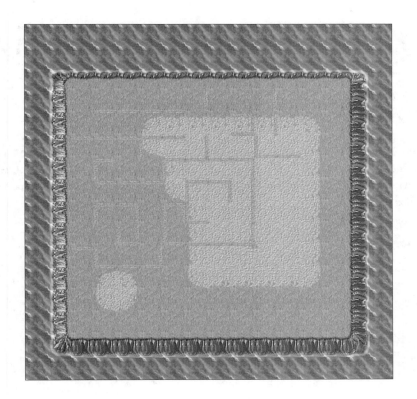

The first variable is the layer manager, which shouldn't be much of a surprise. The xView and yView variables store the location of the view window, which is the view onto the layers that the game screen is showing at any given time. If you recall from the earlier design of the MIDlet, the view window is moved to alter the view of the layers, as opposed to moving the layers themselves as in Wanderer.

The animated water tiles in the barrier layer require some help to work properly, and the waterDelay and waterTile variables provide this help. The waterDelay variable keeps up with a count that controls how fast the water is animated, whereas the waterTile variable stores the current water tile being displayed in the animation sequence.

The two tiled layers are created as TiledLayer objects, which is nothing to get excited about. Even so, the following code reveals how the layers are created with the exact same dimensions and tile sizes:

The background and barrier layers are created exactly the same size.

```
try {
  backgroundLayer = new TiledLayer(16, 16,
    Image.createImage("/Background.png"), 48, 48);
  barrierLayer = new TiledLayer(16, 16,
    Image.createImage("/Barrier.png"), 48, 48);
}
catch (IOException e) {
  System.err.println("Failed loading images!");
}
```

The background creation code appears in the start() method of the WCanvas class, along with the rest of the canvas initialization code. For example, the background layer map is represented by an array of integers, as the following code reveals:

The 0s in the code indicate empty cells that will be covered up by the barrier layer.

```
int[] backgroundMap = {
  0,  0,  0,  0,  0,  0,  0,  0,  0,  0,  0,  0,  0,  0,  0,  0,
  0,  0,  0,  0,  0,  0,  0,  0,  0,  0,  0,  0,  0,  0,  0,  0,
  0,  2,  2,  2,  2,  2,  2,  2,  2,  2,  2,  2,  2,  2,  2,  0,
  0,  2,  2,  2,  2,  2,  2,  2,  2,  2,  2,  2,  2,  2,  2,  0,
  0,  2,  2,  2,  2,  5, 15, 15, 15, 15, 15, 15,  6,  2,  2,  0,
  0,  2,  2,  2,  2,  7, 10,  1,  1,  1,  1,  1, 16,  2,  2,  0,
  0,  2,  2,  2,  2,  2, 14,  1,  1,  1,  1,  1, 16,  2,  2,  0,
  0,  2,  2,  2,  2,  2,  7, 10,  1,  1,  1,  1, 16,  2,  2,  0,
  0,  2,  2,  2,  2,  2,  2, 14,  1,  1,  1,  1, 16,  2,  2,  0,
  0,  2,  2,  2,  2,  2,  2, 14,  1,  9, 10,  1, 16,  2,  2,  0,
  0,  2,  2,  5, 15,  6,  2, 14,  1, 11, 12,  1, 16,  2,  2,  0,
  0,  2,  2, 14,  1, 16,  2,  7, 13, 13, 13, 13,  8,  2,  2,  0,
  0,  2,  2,  7, 13,  8,  2,  2,  2,  2,  2,  2,  2,  2,  2,  0,
  0,  2,  2,  2,  2,  2,  2,  2,  2,  2,  2,  2,  2,  2,  2,  0,
  0,  2,  2,  2,  2,  2,  2,  2,  2,  2,  2,  2,  2,  2,  2,  0,
  0,  0,  0,  0,  0,  0,  0,  0,  0,  0,  0,  0,  0,  0,  0,  0
};
```

This array should look very familiar, as it is virtually the same code you saw earlier when the design of the background layer was first presented. Following is the code required to initialize the background layer with the map data:

```
for (int i = 0; i < backgroundMap.length; i++) {
  int column = i % 16;
  int row = (i - column) / 16;
  backgroundLayer.setCell(column, row, backgroundMap[i]);
}
```

The most important aspect of this code is the values of 16 that are used to specify the numbers of columns and rows in the tiled layer.

The barrier layer is initialized in much the same way as the background layer. Following is the map code for the barrier layer, which also corresponds to the barrier map code that you saw earlier in the chapter:

```
barrierLayer.createAnimatedTile(1);
int[] barrierMap = {
 -1, -1,  1, -1, -1,  1, -1,  1, -1, -1,  1,  1, -1,  1, -1,  1,
 -1, -1, -1,  1,  1, -1,  1, -1,  1,  1, -1,  1, -1, -1,  1, -1,
  1, 21, 19, 19, 19, 19, 19, 19, 19, 19, 19, 19, 19, 22,  1,
  1, 18,  0,  5,  5,  5,  5,  8,  0,  0,  8,  0,  0,  0, 20, -1,
  1, 18,  0,  0,  0,  0,  0,  0, 16,  8,  0,  0,  0,  0, 20,  1,
 -1, 18,  7,  7,  7, 11,  7,  8,  0,  0, 10,  5,  0,  0, 20, -1,
  1, 18,  0, 11,  0,  0, 11,  7,  7, 12,  0,  0,  0,  0, 20, -1,
 -1, 18,  0,  7,  7,  7,  0, 11, 12,  8,  0,  0,  0,  0, 20,  1,
  1, 18,  0, 11, 12,  0, 15, 10,  0,  8,  0,  0,  0,  0, 20,  1,
  1, 18,  0,  0, 13,  0, 10,  5,  5,  9,  0,  0,  0,  0, 20, -1,
 -1, 18,  7, 10,  5,  9,  0,  0,  0,  0,  0,  0,  0,  0, 20,  1,
 -1, 18,  0,  0,  0,  0,  0,  0,  0,  0,  0,  0,  0,  0, 20, -1,
  1, 18,  0,  0,  0,  0,  0,  0,  0,  0,  0,  0,  0,  0, 20,  1,
  1, 18,  0,  0,  0,  0,  0,  0,  0,  0,  0,  0,  0,  0, 20,  1,
 -1, 23, 17, 17, 17, 17, 17, 17, 17, 17, 17, 17, 17, 24, -1,
 -1, -1,  1, -1,  1, -1,  1,  1,  1, -1,  1, -1, -1,  1,  1, -1
};
```

The -1s in the code indicate cells that hold animated water tiles.

This map is incorporated into the barrier layer with the following layer initialization code:

```
for (int i = 0; i < barrierMap.length; i++) {
  int column = i % 16;
  int row = (i - column) / 16;
  barrierLayer.setCell(column, row, barrierMap[i]);
}
```

With the layers created and initialized, you're ready to create the layer manager and get the layers added to it. Keep in mind that the layer manager is also responsible for managing the person sprite, as well as providing a view window on the sprite and both tiled layers. Following is the code that creates and initializes the layer manager and its related view window:

```
layers = new LayerManager();
layers.append(personSprite);
layers.append(barrierLayer);
layers.append(backgroundLayer);
xView = (backgroundLayer.getWidth() - getWidth()) / 2;
yView = (backgroundLayer.getHeight() - getHeight()) / 2;
layers.setViewWindow(xView, yView, getWidth(), getHeight());
personSprite.setPosition(xView + (getWidth() - personSprite.getWidth()) / 2,
  yView + (getHeight() - personSprite.getHeight()) / 2);
```

The order in which the layers are appended is extremely important because it determines their Z-order.

The layer manager's append() method is called to add each layer to the manager. It's important to note that layers are added from top to bottom, which means that the last layer added appears below previously added layers. This explains why the person sprite is appended first, followed by the barrier and background layers. The location and size of the view window is established next; the size is set to the size of the canvas and stored in the xView and yView variables, and the location is calculated to show the center of the tiled layers. The person sprite is then positioned to appear centered in the view window.

Earlier you found out that certain tiles within the barrier layer represent animated water. Two variables are required to animate the water in Wanderer 2. Following is how they are initialized:

```
waterDelay = 0;
waterTile = 1;
```

The `waterDelay` variable is simply a counter, so initializing it to 0 makes sense. `waterTile` is the initial tile to display when the MIDlet starts, which in this case is 1 (see Figure 11.5). The water animation variables come into play in the `update()` method, along with most of the other logic in the Wanderer 2 example. Listing 11.1 contains the code for the `update()` method.

LISTING 11.1   The `update()` Method in the `WCanvas` Class Moves the View Window in Response to Key Presses in the Wanderer 2 MIDlet

```
private void update() {
  // Process user input to move the background layer and animate the person
  if (++inputDelay > 2) {
    int keyState = getKeyStates();
    int xMove = 0, yMove = 0;
    if ((keyState & LEFT_PRESSED) != 0)
      xMove = -12;
    else if ((keyState & RIGHT_PRESSED) != 0)
      xMove = 12;
    if ((keyState & UP_PRESSED) != 0)
      yMove = -12;
    else if ((keyState & DOWN_PRESSED) != 0)
      yMove = 12;
    if (xMove != 0 || yMove != 0) {
      layers.setViewWindow(xView + xMove, yView + yMove, getWidth(),
        getHeight());
      personSprite.move(xMove, yMove);
      personSprite.nextFrame();
    }

    // Check for a collision with the person and the barrier tiled layer
    if (personSprite.collidesWith(barrierLayer, true)) {
      // Play a collision sound
      try {
        Manager.playTone(ToneControl.C4 + 12, 100, 100);
      }
      catch (Exception e) {
      }

      // Restore the original view window and person sprite positions
      layers.setViewWindow(xView, yView, getWidth(), getHeight());
      personSprite.move(-xMove, -yMove);
    }
    else {
      // If there is no collision, commit changes to the view window position
      xView += xMove;
      yView += yMove;
    }
```

If movement has occurred, reposition the view window, center the person sprite on the game screen, and animate the person sprite.

Play a sound if the person sprite bumps into the barrier layer.

LISTING 11.1   Continued

```
    // Update the animated water tiles
    if (++waterDelay > 2) {
      if (++waterTile > 4)
        waterTile = 1;
      barrierLayer.setAnimatedTile(-1, waterTile);
      waterDelay = 0;
    }

    // Reset the input delay
    inputDelay = 0;
  }
}
```

This code cycles through the animated water tiles.

The first chunk of code in the update() method tackles responding to user input so that the person appears to move around on the tiled layers. Unlike the previous Wanderer example, this version utilizes the view window of the layer manager to scroll around on the tiled layers. Temporary xMove and yMove variables are used to determine whether any movement on the view window is necessary, and if so the view window is moved accordingly. If that takes place, the person sprite is also repositioned to the center of the view window; otherwise, it would move around with the tiled layers and the walking effect would be blown!

The real magic of the Wanderer 2 example takes place in the middle of the update() method, where a collision is detected between the person sprite and the barrier tiled layer. This code is what makes the barrier layer actually act as a barrier. If a collision is detected, a tone is played to indicate that the person has bumped into a barrier. More importantly, the view window and person sprite positions are restored to their previous values prior to the collision. If there is no collision, the changes to the view window position are committed when they are stored in the xView and yView variables.

It's important to note that the update() method no longer makes a call to the checkBackgroundBounds() method, as was done in the original Wanderer MIDlet. This method is no longer required because the collision detection between the person sprite and the barrier tiled layer takes care of limiting the person's movement along the edges of the background layer.

Construction Cue

Near the end of the update() method you find the code that updates the animated water tiles. The waterDelay counter is set to update the animated tile every fourth cycle; the counter goes 0, 1, 2, update, and then it resets again. The water tile itself cycles from tile 1 to tile 4 repeatedly (see Figure 11.5). This code acts together to provide an animated water effect to all tiles that are set to -1 in the barrier layer map.

The last piece of code in the Wanderer 2 example worth examining is without a doubt the simplest of all the code in the MIDlet. Check out Listing 11.2 to see what I'm talking about.

LISTING 11.2   The draw() Method Draws the Layer Manager with a Single Line of Code

```
private void draw(Graphics g) {
  // Draw the layers
  layers.paint(g, 0, 0);

  // Flush the offscreen graphics buffer
  flushGraphics();
}
```

Drawing the sprites and layers consists solely of drawing the layer manager.

This listing contains the code for the Wanderer 2 draw() method, which is responsible for drawing all the graphics on the MIDlet's canvas. As you can see, the method makes only a single paint call, which is the call to the paint() method of the layer manager. Because the view window already establishes the area of the layer manager to be drawn, you simply pass in (0,0) as the coordinates for the layers to be drawn.

The changes to the code in the Wanderer 2 example from the previous version aren't really all that dramatic, but the resulting effect in the MIDlet is fairly significant, as you find out next.

Testing the Finished Product

The Wanderer 2 example MIDlet is just shy of being a legitimate mobile game—you control a character through a maze while exploring a landscape. All that's missing is a more challenging maze and some other sprites to interact with. Even with Wanderer 2 coming up a bit short as a mobile game, it's still a very interesting example MIDlet for the purposes of better understanding tiled layers and how to use them effectively.

Figure 11.7 shows the Wanderer 2 MIDlet upon first being run, where the game screen is centered on the tiled layers with the person sprite in the middle of the maze.

As you move the person through the maze, you'll notice that there is no way to discern that two different tiled layers are actually being used to create the landscape in the MIDlet. Eventually you'll make your way to an edge of the map, where you'll encounter animated water for the first time. Figure 11.8 shows the person near the edge of the map where some of the water tiles are animated.

Granted, the printed page doesn't really convey animation, but if you look closely at the figure you can see that some of the water tiles look slightly different than the others. Or better yet, just run the MIDlet for yourself and experience the animated water and tiled layers in the Wanderer 2 example on your own mobile phone or J2ME emulator.

Summary

You are now officially well on your way to becoming a serious mobile game developer. Although this chapter didn't cover all that much ground in terms of raw code, it did pull together what you've learned about sprites and tiled layers in previous chapters to give you more control over how they are managed in games. More specifically, you found out how to use the standard LayerManager class to interact with multiple game layers as a single group. You also modified the Wanderer example program from the previous chapter to take advantage of several layers, one of which serves as a maze of barriers that the user must navigate through.

You may be wondering how you're over halfway through the book with only one complete game to show for your efforts. The next chapter remedies this problem by guiding you through the development of one of the coolest games in the book, a scrolling pirate adventure game called High Seas.

FIGURE 11.7
The Wanderer 2 MIDlet shows a view of a person sprite that is maneuvered through a maze appearing on a background landscape.

FIGURE 11.8
Several of the water tiles around the edges of the background are animated to provide a more realistic effect.

Extreme Game Makeover

You probably noticed that I didn't use the entire area of the barrier layer in the Wanderer 2 example for maze walls. You could actually turn the Wanderer 2 example into a fairly interesting little maze game by expanding the size of the layers and making the entire barrier layer full of maze tiles. Follow these steps to beef up the "maziness" of the Wanderer 2 example:

1. First, decide on a new map size. Using pencil and paper or mapping software, design new background and barrier layer maps to fit the new map size.

2. Change the creation of the tiled layers in the start() method so that the number of rows and columns matches the new map size.

3. Plug the new background and barrier layer maps into the game code as integer arrays (also in the start() method).

4. When initializing the tiled layers, make sure that the for loops use the correct number of rows and columns to account for the new map size.

This is a relatively small number of code changes to reap such significant results. You might even figure out a creative way to generate a barrier layer map dynamically so that the maze varies each time the MIDlet runs.

CHAPTER 12

High Seas: A Game for the Pirate in You

Arcade Archive

As a take-off on the Tarzan theme, Jungle King hit arcades in 1982 thanks to game manufacturer Taito. The stakes are surprisingly high in this game, as your character swings from vine to vine to rescue a damsel in distress from jungle cannibals. Throughout different levels in the game, the main character must swing from vines, hurdle tumbling boulders, and carefully navigate a river full of hungry crocodiles with nothing more than a small knife. Taito was sued by the Edgar Rice Burrough's estate, which owns the rights to Tarzan. In response, Jungle King was later changed to Jungle Hunt, and the Tarzan character was changed to a jungle explorer wearing a safari outfit instead of a loin cloth. Not surprisingly, the Tarzan yell was also removed from the Jungle Hunt game.

Back in Chapter 7, "Henway: Paying Tribute to Frogger," you developed your first complete mobile game, High Seas. Although you've created some interesting example MIDlets since then, you haven't designed and built any other complete games. Your luck is about to change! This chapter leads you through the design and development of a complete mobile game called High Seas, which is a pirate game where you navigate a pirate ship attempting to rescue fellow mates who are lost at sea. High Seas literally makes use of everything you've learned throughout the book thus far, which makes it an excellent example game for you to both play and experiment with.

In this chapter, you'll learn

▶ That a mobile game based on pirates doesn't have to be about robbing and pillaging

▶ How to design a mobile game called High Seas that takes advantage of a large tiled game map

▶ How to manage interactions between a variety of different sprites in the context of a real game

▶ How to put together the code for the High Seas game

The Scoop on High Seas

The basic premise behind the High Seas game that you design and develop throughout this chapter is that the player controls a pirate ship that has lost several of its crew in a storm. The goal of the game is to rescue as many lost crew members as possible. Getting in your way are floating mines and pesky squid that are intent on making your rescue mission more difficult. Your ship in the game has a limited amount of energy that decreases each time you run into a mine or a squid. However, there are also floating barrels of supplies that you can pick up to regain lost energy. The game ends when your ship loses all its energy and sinks.

As you may be guessing, High Seas involves a map that is much larger than the game screen. The game map is scrolled as you navigate the ship so that you can explore different parts of the map. Similar to the Wanderer 2 example from the previous chapter, High Seas actually takes advantage of two tiled layers that together form the complete map for the game. More specifically, a water layer serves as the background and provides a nice visual backdrop for the game. On top of that layer is a land layer that includes a land border, large islands of land, and small mountain islands placed throughout the map that serve to obstruct the path of the pirate ship.

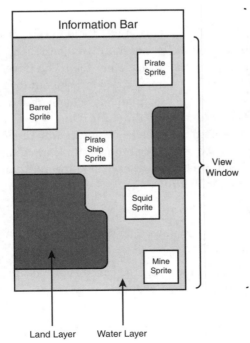

FIGURE 12.1
The High Seas game consists of an information bar, a view window on the game layers, two tiled background layers, and several sprites.

The High Seas game goes a step beyond Wanderer 2 in that it must display pertinent information related to the state of the game, such as the amount of energy remaining for the pirate ship, as well as the number of pirates you've rescued. This information is displayed in a game information bar that appears along the top of the game screen. The view window where the game action takes place starts just below this information area. Figure 12.1 shows the general layout of the game screen in High Seas.

Figure 12.1 provides a pretty good glimpse at how the game screen is laid out in High Seas. The information bar appears at the top of the screen above the view window, and provides important information such as the amount of remaining ship energy and the number of pirates that have been rescued. The view window is where all the action takes place. Two tiled layers are used to create the oceanic background complete with islands that serve as obstructions to the player's ship. And finally, several different kinds of sprites establish the actual play of the game: squids and mines cause damage to the player's ship, barrels restore energy to the ship, and pirates are rescued by the ship as a means of scoring.

There really isn't an end goal to the game such as completing a level or destroying an enemy. Somehow the chore of rescuing lost pirates just never ends—you must rescue as many as you can before you eventually fall prey to the roaming squids and drifting mines.

Designing the Game

The overview of the High Seas game has already given you a leg up on the game's design even if you don't realize it. For example, you already have an idea of how many sprites are required for the game. You know that there is one pirate ship that is controlled by the player, and at least one sprite for a lost pirate, barrel, mine, and squid. Although one each of these sprites would certainly work, it wouldn't provide enough interest (or danger) in terms of making the game fun to play. So, through trial and error more so than design sense, I opted for the following numbers of sprites: 2 pirates, 2 barrels, 3 mines, and 3 squids.

Notice that there are more "negative" sprites (mines and squids) than there are positive sprites (pirates and barrels). This tendency to include more negative than positive is necessary to ensure that the player will eventually lose the game and not continue playing forever, or until boredom sets in. And trust me, you'd rather have a game be too difficult than boring! Players can always learn and get better to overcome a difficult game, but there isn't much you can do to make a boring game more fun to play.

Many of the classic arcade games that have remained popular over the years are very difficult games to master. Joust and Defender are two games that come to mind as being fairly simple in design but very difficult from a game play perspective. Although you can certainly go overboard and make a game too difficult, most game players appreciate a good challenge.

Gamer's Garage

FIGURE 12.2
The pirate ship bitmap image shows four animation frames of a ship pointing in different directions.

FIGURE 12.3
The pirate image consists of four animation frames that make the pirate appear to float on the water.

FIGURE 12.4
The barrel image consists of four animation frames that make the barrel appear to bob in the water.

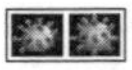

FIGURE 12.5
The mine image consists of two animation frames that make the mine appear to bob in the water.

FIGURE 12.6
The squid image consists of two animation frames that make the squid appear to flail its tentacles as it sweeps across the water.

Beyond the sprites, can you guess how many bitmap images the game needs? The game requires eight bitmap images, as the following list reveals:

- Information bar image
- Background image with water tiles
- Background image with land tiles
- Pirate ship sprite image (see Figure 12.2)
- Pirate sprite image (see Figure 12.3)
- Barrel sprite image (see Figure 12.4)
- Mine sprite image (see Figure 12.5)
- Squid sprite image (see Figure 12.6)

The first image (information bar) is probably the only one that comes as a surprise given the earlier game description. The information bar image is just a blank woodgrain image that makes the background for the game information a little more interesting. The two background images are tiles for the water and land backgrounds, respectively. You see these images in the context of the layer maps in the next two sections.

Gamer's Garage

The information bar is really the only part of the High Seas game that is tied to a specific mobile phone screen size (width). You could use a larger information bar image or possibly an image that tiles horizontally to make it possible to scale the entire game to larger screen sizes. Fortunately, a larger screen wouldn't change the dynamic of the game too much, other than allowing the player to see more of the map.

The remaining sprite images all use animation frames to some degree to make the sprites more visually interesting. For example, the pirate ship sprite uses four animation frames to aim the ship in the direction it is traveling, which adds a touch of realism. The pirate, barrel, and mine sprites all appear to bob in the water, as opposed to just sitting there with no motion, which wouldn't be very realistic. And finally, the squid sprite image shows the squid with its tentacles in different positions to give it more of an attacking appearance.

Now that you've gotten acquainted with most of the graphical objects involved in the game, let's consider other data that the game must maintain. First, it's fairly obvious that you need to keep track of how much energy the pirate ship has. You should also keep a running "score" of how many pirates have been rescued. A Boolean variable keeping track of whether the game is over is also required. To recap, the design of the High Seas game requires that the following pieces of information must be managed by the game:

- ▶ The amount of energy remaining for the pirate ship
- ▶ The score, which is the number of pirates rescued
- ▶ A Boolean game over variable

With this information in mind, you're now ready to move on and assemble the tiled layer maps for the High Seas game. Keep in mind that other member variables are certainly required to make the High Seas game work, such as sprites and sound players, but the previous list comprises the primary data that keeps track of the game's state at any given moment.

Putting Together the Water Map

As I explained earlier in the chapter, the High Seas game relies on two different tiled layers: a water layer and a land layer. The water layer is a "passive" layer, meaning that it is there purely as a backdrop and doesn't interact with any of the sprites in the game. Even so, the water layer does take advantage of animated tiles to make the water appear to have waves.

Similar to the background layer in the Wanderer 2 example from the previous chapter, the water layer doesn't require tiles around the edges to be defined, because the land layer provides a land border that covers up those tiles. For this reason, the edges of the water layer contain empty cells, as evident in Figure 12.7.

The black border you see around the tiled layer image in the figure is a transparent area where no graphics appear. Similarly placed cells in the land layer contain land tiles that serve as barriers to the pirate ship's movement. In fact, part of the watery edge of the water layer is obscured by the beach edge of the land layer, as you see in the next section.

Following is the map code that describes the water layer:

```
0, 0, 0, 0, 0, 0, 0, 0, 0, 0, 0, 0, 0, 0, 0, 0, 0, 0, 0, 0, 0, 0, 0,
0, 0, 0, 0, 0, 0, 0, 0, 0, 0, 0, 0, 0, 0, 0, 0, 0, 0, 0, 0, 0, 0, 0,
0, 0,-1, 1,-1, 1, 1,-1,-2, 1,-1, 1, 1,-1, 1, 1,-1, 1, 1,-1, 1,-2, 0, 0,
0, 0, 1, 1,-1, 1,-1, 1, 1,-1, 1, 1,-2, 1,-1, 1, 1,-2, 1, 1,-1, 1, 0, 0,
0, 0,-2,-1, 1,-1, 1,-2, 1, 1,-2, 1, 1,-1, 1,-2, 1, 1,-2, 1, 1,-1, 0, 0,
0, 0,-1, 1,-1, 1,-1, 1, 1,-1, 1, 1,-1, 1,-1, 1,-1,-1, 1, 1,-1, 1, 0, 0,
0, 0, 1,-1, 1,-1, 1, 1,-1, 1, 1,-1, 1,-2, 1,-1, 1, 1,-1, 1, 1, 1, 0, 0,
0, 0,-1, 1,-1, 1, 1,-1, 1, 1,-1, 1, 1,-1, 1, 1,-1, 1, 1,-1, 1,-1, 0, 0,
```

```
0, 0, 1,-1,-2, 1, 1, 1,-1, 1, 1,-2,-1, 1, 1,-2, 1, 1,-2, 1,-1,-2, 0, 0,
0, 0,-2, 1, 1, 1,-1,-2, 1,-1, 1,-1, 1, 1,-1, 1,-1, 1,-1, 1, 1, 1, 0, 0,
0, 0, 1, 1, 1,-1, 1, 1,-1, 1, 1, 1,-2,-1, 1, 1,-1, 1,-1, 1,-1,-1, 0, 0,
0, 0, 1,-1,-2, 1,-1,-2, 1,-2,-1, 1,-1, 1,-1,-1,-1, 1,-1, 1,-1, 1, 0, 0,
0, 0,-2, 1, 1, 1, 1, 1, 1, 1,-1,-1, 1,-1, 1, 1, 1,-2, 1, 1,-2,-1, 0, 0,
0, 0,-1, 1,-1,-1, 1,-1,-2,-1, 1, 1,-2, 1,-1, 1,-1, 1, 1,-1, 1, 1, 0, 0,
0, 0, 1,-2, 1, 1,-1, 1, 1, 1,-1,-1, 1,-1, 1, 1, 1, 1,-1, 1, 1,-1, 0, 0,
0, 0,-1, 1, 1,-2, 1,-2,-1, 1,-1, 1,-1, 1,-1,-2, 1,-1, 1,-2, 1, 0, 0,
0, 0,-2, 1,-1, 1,-1, 1, 1,-1, 1,-1, 1,-2,-1, 1,-1, 1,-1, 1, 1, 0, 0,
0, 0, 1, 1,-1, 1, 1,-1, 1, 1,-2, 1,-1, 1, 1, 1,-1, 1,-1, 1,-1,-1, 0, 0,
0, 0, 1,-1, 1,-2, 1,-2,-1, 1, 1,-1, 1,-1, 1,-1, 1,-1,-2,-1, 1, 1, 0, 0,
0, 0,-1, 1,-1, 1, 1,-1, 1,-2,-1, 1,-2,-1,-2, 1,-1,-2, 1,-1,-2, 1, 0, 0,
0, 0, 1, 1,-1, 1,-1, 1,-1, 1, 1,-1, 1,-1, 1,-1, 1,-1, 1, 1,-1, 0, 0,
0, 0,-2,-1, 1, 1,-2, 1,-1, 1,-1,-2, 1,-2,-1, 1,-2,-1, 1, 0, 0,
0, 0, 0, 0, 0, 0, 0, 0, 0, 0, 0, 0, 0, 0, 0, 0, 0, 0, 0, 0, 0, 0, 0, 0,
0, 0, 0, 0, 0, 0, 0, 0, 0, 0, 0, 0, 0, 0, 0, 0, 0, 0, 0, 0, 0, 0, 0, 0
```

Unless you have some kind of extraordinarily good imagination, this code doesn't make much sense without referencing the tile image associated with the tiled layer. Figure 12.8 shows the tiles that are used to construct the water tiled layer map. Of course, you do know from what you learned in the previous chapter that all the cells with negative tile indexes represent animated water tiles.

FIGURE 12.8
The water tiled layer map is realized when the appropriate water tiles are placed according to the map code.

The differences between the tiles in the water layer are very subtle, but keep in mind that the idea is to provide a subtle effect of the ocean water moving. Although Figure 12.7 appears to be just a huge map of the exact same static water tiles, the layer image in Figure 12.8 coupled with the map code reveal that the water layer is in fact much more dynamic.

Putting Together the Land Map

The land tiled layer is designed to be drawn on top of the water layer, which means that graphics appearing on the land layer will cover up graphics on the water layer. Additionally, the land layer serves as an "active" layer, which means that it interacts with the sprites in the game. More specifically, graphics on the land layer act as obstructions for the pirate ship and other sprites. In other words, empty cells on the land map are areas where the sprites can move around freely, whereas all other cells are obstructions and prevent movement.

Figure 12.9 shows the complete land layer with black areas denoting empty cells where the sprites are free to move about.

The land layer uses beach borders, large flat islands, and small mountain islands to present obstructions to the movement of the sprites in High Seas.

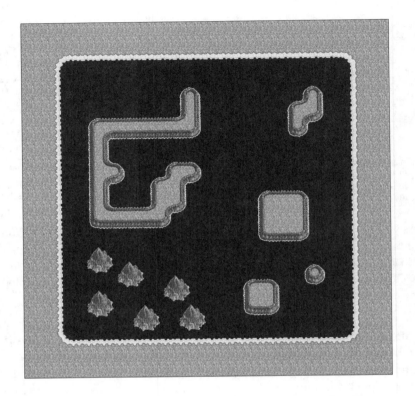

As the figure reveals, significant areas of the land layer are left empty so that the sprites have room to move around; these "open" areas are water. Following is the map code that results in the layer shown in Figure 12.9:

```
1, 1, 1, 1, 1, 1, 1, 1, 1, 1, 1, 1, 1, 1, 1, 1, 1, 1, 1, 1, 1, 1, 1, 1, 1,
1, 1, 1, 1, 1, 1, 1, 1, 1, 1, 1, 1, 1, 1, 1, 1, 1, 1, 1, 1, 1, 1, 1, 1, 1,
1, 1,32,25,25,25,25,25,25,25,25,25,25,25,25,25,25,25,25,25,25,25,26, 1, 1,
1, 1,31, 0, 0, 0, 0, 0, 0, 0, 0, 0, 0, 0, 0, 0, 0, 0, 0, 0, 0,27, 1, 1,
1, 1,31, 0, 0, 0, 0, 0, 0, 0, 6, 7, 0, 0, 0, 0, 0, 0, 6, 7, 0,27, 1, 1,
1, 1,31, 0, 0, 0, 0, 0, 0, 0,10,12, 0, 0, 0, 0, 0, 6,14,12, 0,27, 1, 1,
1, 1,31, 0, 6,11,11,11,11,11,14,12, 0, 0, 0, 0, 0,10,16, 8, 0,27, 1, 1,
1, 1,31, 0,10,16, 9, 9, 9, 9, 9, 8, 0, 0, 0, 0, 0, 5, 8, 0, 0,27, 1, 1,
1, 1,31, 0,10,12, 0, 0, 0, 0, 0, 0, 0, 0, 0, 0, 0, 0, 0, 0,27, 1, 1,
1, 1,31, 0,10,15, 7, 0, 0, 6,11, 7, 0, 0, 0, 0, 0, 0, 0, 0,27, 1, 1,
1, 1,31, 0,10,16, 8, 0, 6,14,16, 8, 0, 0, 0, 0, 0, 0, 0, 0,27, 1, 1,
1, 1,31, 0,10,12, 0, 0,10, 1,12, 0, 0, 0, 0, 6,11,11, 7, 0, 0,27, 1, 1,
1, 1,31, 0,10,15,11,11,14,16, 8, 0, 0, 0, 0,10, 1, 1,12, 0, 0,27, 1, 1,
1, 1,31, 0, 5, 9, 9, 9, 9, 8, 0, 0, 0, 0, 0,10, 1, 1,12, 0, 0,27, 1, 1,
1, 1,31, 0, 0, 0, 0, 0, 0, 0, 0, 0, 0, 0, 0, 5, 9, 9, 8, 0, 0,27, 1, 1,
1, 1,31, 0,17,18, 0, 0, 0, 0, 0, 0, 0, 0, 0, 0, 0, 0, 0, 0,27, 1, 1,
1, 1,31, 0,19,20,17,18, 0, 0, 0, 0, 0, 0, 0, 0, 6, 7, 0,27, 1, 1,
1, 1,31, 0, 0, 0,19,20, 0,17,18, 0, 0, 0, 6,11, 7, 0, 5, 8, 0,27, 1, 1,
```

```
1, 1,31, 0,17,18, 0, 0, 0,19,20, 0, 0, 0,10, 1,12, 0, 0, 0, 0,27, 1, 1,
1, 1,31, 0,19,20, 0,17,18, 0,17,18, 0, 0, 5, 9, 8, 0, 0, 0, 0,27, 1, 1,
1, 1,31, 0, 0, 0, 0,19,20, 0,19,20, 0, 0, 0, 0, 0, 0, 0, 0,27, 1, 1,
1, 1,30,29,29,29,29,29,29,29,29,29,29,29,29,29,29,29,29,29,28, 1, 1,
1, 1, 1, 1, 1, 1, 1, 1, 1, 1, 1, 1, 1, 1, 1, 1, 1, 1, 1, 1, 1, 1, 1,
1, 1, 1, 1, 1, 1, 1, 1, 1, 1, 1, 1, 1, 1, 1, 1, 1, 1, 1, 1, 1, 1, 1
```

Again, unless you're quite crafty at converting numbers to imagery, you'll probably find this map code tough to decipher unless you know what the land tiles look like and their respective indexes. Figure 12.10 shows the tiles used to construct the land tiled layer according to the preceding map code.

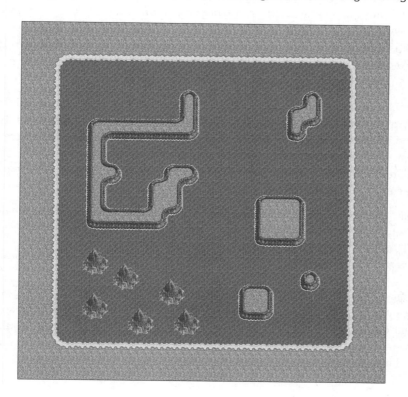

FIGURE 12.10
Realizing the land tiled layer map involves carefully arranging land tiles according to the map code.

Using Figure 12.10 as a guide, you should be able to see how the land image in Figure 12.9 is described by the preceding map code. Don't forget that all the black areas described in the map by 0s are empty cells where water from the water layer will show through. In fact, take a look at Figure 12.11 to see how the two layers stack up together to form the complete background of the High Seas game.

FIGURE 12.11
The High Seas game consists of two tiled layers that are overlaid to provide water in which the sprites can move as well as land obstructions.

This figure should clear up any confusion you had regarding the water and land layers. As you probably realize, these layers represent an enormous component of the High Seas game, and provide a great jumpstart to understanding the actual game code.

Developing the Game

With the tiled layers successfully designed and the sprite images nailed down, you're ready to begin putting together the code for the High Seas game. I have to warn you that I'm about to throw a lot of example code your way, but it's nothing you haven't already seen in one form or another in preceding examples. It's my hope that you'll find the end result to be worth the coding effort!

Creating a Drift Sprite

The first code required for the High Seas game is actually a new class that you will find useful in a lot of different games. In the design of the High Seas game you learned that several of the sprites in the game are required to drift or move slowly around the game screen in a more or less random pattern. Although you could certainly use the standard Sprite class to create these sprites, and then add drifting functionality to them in the update() method of the game's canvas class, it makes much more sense to subclass the Sprite class and create your own DriftSprite class.

The DriftSprite class has a fairly simple function in that it just moves around randomly at a certain speed. At slow speeds the object literally can appear as if it is drifting, whereas at higher speeds the object appears to be moving a little more on its own. Either way, this functionality serves our purposes well because the pirate, barrel, and mine sprites in the game need to appear to be drifting, whereas the squid sprite can appear to be moving a little faster because it has the ability to swim.

The DriftSprite class requires only two member variables to carry out the drifting feature:

```
private int        speed;
private TiledLayer barrier;
```

The speed variable is the speed of the sprite, which is measured in pixels per game cycle. You'll probably want to experiment with the speed of drifting sprites in your games, but generally speaking, a speed of 1 or 2 is good for sprites that you want to appear as if they are drifting, whereas higher values give the impression of a sprite moving more on its own will.

The `barrier` variable is a tiled layer that serves as a barrier for the sprite. This variable is necessary because the assumption is that most games will have a tiled layer that serves to somehow obstruct most sprites. This layer could be a maze, a landing pad, or simply the ground, but most games take advantage of such a barrier layer. The barrier layer associated with the drift sprite doesn't actually have anything to do with the drift feature, but it's necessary because you want to be able to detect the collision with the layer in the sprite's `update()` method.

Both member variables in the `DriftSprite` class are initialized in the `DriftSprite()` constructor, which is shown in Listing 12.1.

LISTING 12.1   The `DriftSprite()` Constructor Initializes the Speed and Barrier Layer Member Variables

```
public DriftSprite(Image image, int frameWidth, int frameHeight, int driftSpeed,
  TiledLayer barrierLayer) {
  super(image, frameWidth, frameHeight);

  // Initialize the random number generator
  rand = new Random();

  // Set the speed
  speed = driftSpeed;

  // Set the tiled layer barrier
  barrier = barrierLayer;
}
```

The `DriftSprite()` constructor calls the parent `Sprite()` constructor to take care of creating the core sprite, and then it initializes the member variables specific to the `DriftSprite` class.

The `update()` method is where the code for the `DriftSprite` class gets interesting. Listing 12.2 shows the code for this method.

LISTING 12.2   The `update()` Method in the `DriftSprite` Class Moves the Sprite in a Random Direction and Detects a Collision with the Barrier Layer

```
public void update() {
  // Temporarily save the position
  int xPos = getX();
  int yPos = getY();

  // Randomly move the sprite to simulate drift
  switch (Math.abs(rand.nextInt() % 4)) {
  // Drift left
  case 0:
    move(-speed, 0);
    break;
```

LISTING 12.2 Continued

```
// Drift right
case 1:
  move(speed, 0);
  break;
// Drift up
case 2:
  move(0, -speed);
  break;
// Drift down
case 3:
  move(0, speed);
  break;
}

// Check for a collision with the barrier
if ((barrier != null) && collidesWith(barrier, true)) {
  // Move the sprite back to its original position
  setPosition(xPos, yPos);
}

// Move to the next animation frame in the sequence
nextFrame();
}
```

If the newly updated position results in a collision with a barrier, then it is invalid and the old position needs to be restored.

The update() method starts out by saving the position of the sprite because it may be needed later if a collision is detected between the sprite and a barrier layer. The sprite is then moved randomly in one of four possible directions (left, right, up, or down) to give it a drifting effect.

The section of code near the bottom of the update() method checks for a collision between the sprite and the barrier layer, providing the barrier variable isn't set to null. This code is what makes it possible for you to establish barriers within a game that prevent sprites from moving. If a collision is detected between the drift sprite and the barrier, the sprite is restored to its original position prior to being updated.

Construction Cue

> It's very important to note that if the barrier layer is set to null, the drift sprite won't be constrained by a barrier in the update() method. In other words, you can create drift sprites that wander around freely by simply passing null as the barrier value to the DriftSprite() constructor. If you wanted to add a bird or flying enemy to the High Seas game, you would likely use this approach because the land wouldn't be a barrier for such a sprite.

The last piece of code in the update() method of the drift sprite is a call to the nextFrame() method, which simply advances the sprite's animation frame. Keep in mind that you can still create unanimated sprites with the DriftSprite class, in which case the call to the nextFrame() method results in nothing happening.

The handy new `DriftSprite` class is now ready to roll, so you can now turn your attention to the code specific to the High Seas game. Let's start out with the member variables.

Declaring the Member Variables

Not surprisingly, the code for the High Seas games begins in a customized canvas class, `HSCanvas`. The `HSCanvas` class is responsible for all the game logic in the High Seas game. Because the `HSCanvas` class is fairly big, we're going to cover it in bits and pieces; the entire source code for High Seas is available on the accompanying CD-ROM. Following are the most important member variables defined in the High Seas custom canvas class:

```
private LayerManager    layers;
private int             xView, yView;
private TiledLayer      waterLayer;
private TiledLayer      landLayer;
private int             waterDelay;
private int[]           waterTile = { 1, 3 };
private Image           infoBar;
private Sprite          playerSprite;
private DriftSprite[]   pirateSprite = new DriftSprite[2];
private DriftSprite[]   barrelSprite = new DriftSprite[2];
private DriftSprite[]   mineSprite = new DriftSprite[5];
private DriftSprite[]   squidSprite = new DriftSprite[5];
private Player          musicPlayer;
private Player          rescuePlayer;
private Player          minePlayer;
private Player          gameoverPlayer;
private boolean         gameOver;
private int             energy, piratesSaved;
```

Two different animated water tiles are used in the water layer.

The first few variables are used to store the layer manager, view window position, water layer, and land layer. The `waterDelay` and `waterTile` variables are responsible for taking care of the animated water effect in the water layer. Since there are actually two different animated water tiles, the `waterTile` variable is an array of two integer tile indexes.

The `infoBar` variable stores the bitmap image used to display the background for the player's energy and number of rescued pirates at the top of the screen. Several sprites are then created, including the player's pirate ship sprite, a couple of pirates and barrels, and three mines and squids. It's interesting to note that no other sprites are ever created throughout the game. You'll learn later in this chapter how the sprites are simply reused to give the illusion of there being more of them in the game.

The sounds effects and music in the game are handled next thanks to the various `Player` variables. And finally, the state of the game is reflected in the `gameOver`, `energy`, and `piratesSaved` variables.

Assembling the `start()` Method

The `start()` method in the High Seas game has a great deal of responsibility because it handles all the game-specific initialization tasks. For example, the following code creates the information bar image and the water and background tiled layers:

```
try {
  infoBar = Image.createImage("/InfoBar.png");
  waterLayer = new TiledLayer(24, 24, Image.createImage("/Water.png"), 32, 32);
  landLayer = new TiledLayer(24, 24, Image.createImage("/Land.png"), 32, 32);
}
catch (IOException e) {
  System.err.println("Failed loading images!");
}
```

If you recall, the water layer relies on a couple of animated tiles to provide the effect of moving water. Following is how these animated tiles are created in the `start()` method:

```
waterLayer.createAnimatedTile(1);
waterLayer.createAnimatedTile(3);
```

The two animated tiles are created with different starting tile indexes (1 and 3), which is important because it means a different tile image is shown for each type of animated tile as the animation progresses; if the same value were used for both of them, you wouldn't be able to tell the difference between them.

Earlier in the chapter you saw the design for the water layer, which results in an array of tile indexes named `waterMap` that describes the water map. The water map array is realized when the appropriate rows and columns of the actual water tiled layer are set. The following `for` loop takes care of setting the cells in the water layer:

```
for (int i = 0; i < waterMap.length; i++) {
  int column = i % 24;
  int row = (i - column) / 24;
  waterLayer.setCell(column, row, waterMap[i]);
}
```

To finish off the initialization of the water tiled layer, you must set an initial value for the `waterDelay` member variable, which is used as a counter to control the speed of the water animation:

```
waterDelay = 0;
```

Similar to the water layer, the land layer is described by a map of tile indexes named `landMap`, whose contents you saw earlier in the chapter. Also very similarly to the water layer, the following code is used to initialize the land layer with the map array:

```
for (int i = 0; i < landMap.length; i++) {
  int column = i % 24;
  int row = (i - column) / 24;
  landLayer.setCell(column, row, landMap[i]);
}
```

With the water and land layers successfully created, you can move on to the sprites in the game. If you recall, there is a pirate ship sprite controlled by the player, as well as two pirates, two barrels, three mines, and three squids. The player sprite (pirate ship) is of type `Sprite` because it doesn't need to do anything special, whereas all the others are of type `DriftSprite`, which is the new sprite class you created earlier in the chapter. Following is the code that creates all these sprites:

```
try {
  playerSprite = new Sprite(Image.createImage("/PlayerShip.png"), 43, 45);

  int sequence2[] = { 0, 0, 0, 1, 1, 1 };
  int sequence4[] = { 0, 0, 1, 1, 2, 2, 3, 3 };
  for (int i = 0; i < 2; i++) {
    pirateSprite[i] = new DriftSprite(Image.createImage("/Pirate.png"),
      29, 29, 2, landLayer);
    pirateSprite[i].setFrameSequence(sequence2);
    placeSprite(pirateSprite[i], landLayer);

    barrelSprite[i] = new DriftSprite(Image.createImage("/Barrel.png"),
      24, 22, 1, landLayer);
    barrelSprite[i].setFrameSequence(sequence4);
    placeSprite(barrelSprite[i], landLayer);
  }

  for (int i = 0; i < 5; i++) {
    mineSprite[i] = new DriftSprite(Image.createImage("/Mine.png"),
      27, 23, 1, landLayer);
    mineSprite[i].setFrameSequence(sequence2);
    placeSprite(mineSprite[i], landLayer);

    squidSprite[i] = new DriftSprite(Image.createImage("/Squid.png"),
      24, 35, 3, landLayer);
    squidSprite[i].setFrameSequence(sequence2);
    placeSprite(squidSprite[i], landLayer);
  }
}
catch (IOException e) {
  System.err.println("Failed loading images!");
}
```

The fourth and fifth parameters to the DriftSprite() constructor are the drift speed and barrier layer, respectively.

The placeSprite() method randomly places a sprite on the game map while ensuring that it isn't placed on top of a barrier.

The player sprite is created when the size of an animation frame is passed in for the sprite. The remaining sprites are created as drift sprites with varying speeds. For example, the pirate sprites have a speed of 2, whereas the barrel and mine sprites have a speed of 1. The idea is that the pirates are capable of swimming around a little, so they should be able to move faster than the barrels and mines, which are truly drifting. The same logic applies to the squid sprites, which can move even faster than the pirates at a speed of 3. It's important to note that the landLayer variable is provided as the barrier for all the drift sprites.

Construction Cue

> The speed of sprites is one of the most fun code changes to tinker with in mobile games. Because the squid sprites are not really intended to drift, try increasing their speed and noticing how it changes the game. Although they still move randomly, they become more dangerous enemies simply because of how quickly they jet around the game screen.

The tiled layers and game sprites all come together with the layer manager, which takes care of ordering and drawing them. Following is the code that adds the sprites and layers to the layer manager:

```
layers = new LayerManager();
layers.append(playerSprite);
for (int i = 0; i < 2; i++) {
  layers.append(pirateSprite[i]);
  layers.append(barrelSprite[i]);
}
for (int i = 0; i < 5; i++) {
  layers.append(mineSprite[i]);
  layers.append(squidSprite[i]);
}
layers.append(landLayer);
layers.append(waterLayer);
```

The water layer is added last so that it appears below the land layer and sprites.

Don't forget that the order in which you add sprites to the layer manager matters a great deal—the first sprites you add via the append() method appear on top of later sprites. That's why the tiled background layers are added to the layer manager last.

Sound effects and music play an important role in most games, and High Seas is no different in this regard. Following is the code that sets up the audio players for the game:

```
try {
  InputStream is = getClass().getResourceAsStream("Music.mid");
  musicPlayer = Manager.createPlayer(is, "audio/midi");
  musicPlayer.prefetch();
  musicPlayer.setLoopCount(-1);
  is = getClass().getResourceAsStream("Rescue.wav");
```

```
    rescuePlayer = Manager.createPlayer(is, "audio/X-wav");
    rescuePlayer.prefetch();
    is = getClass().getResourceAsStream("Mine.wav");
    minePlayer = Manager.createPlayer(is, "audio/X-wav");
    minePlayer.prefetch();
    is = getClass().getResourceAsStream("GameOver.wav");
    gameoverPlayer = Manager.createPlayer(is, "audio/X-wav");
    gameoverPlayer.prefetch();
}
catch (IOException ioe) {
}
catch (MediaException me) {
}
```

As you can see, there is a single MIDI audio player for the game music, as well as three other players for each of the three sound effects used throughout the game (a rescue sound, a mine collision sound, and a game over sound).

The last piece of business in the start() method is actually starting a new game via a call to the newGame() method:

```
newGame();
```

You find out exactly how the newGame() method works a little later in the chapter. For now, let's turn our attention to the update() method, which is the real work-horse method in most MIDlet games, including High Seas.

Piecing Together the update() Method

As you know, the update() method is called once every game cycle, and is responsible for updating sprites and layers, checking for collisions, and generally keeping the game running. In High Seas, the update() method starts off by checking to see whether the game is over, and if so, it starts a new game in response to the player pressing the "fire" key:

```
if (gameOver) {
  int keyState = getKeyStates();
  if ((keyState & FIRE_PRESSED) != 0)
    // Start a new game
    newGame();

  // The game is over, so don't update anything
  return;
}
```

Starting a new game involves a simple call to the newGame() method, which you learn about a little later in the chapter. Notice that the update() method immediately returns after calling newGame() because there is no reason to continue updating a newly started game in this particular game cycle.

Next on the agenda for the update() method is responding to key presses during a game. The following code handles the four directional keys, and moves the view window in the layer manager accordingly:

```
int keyState = getKeyStates();
int xMove = 0, yMove = 0;
if ((keyState & LEFT_PRESSED) != 0) {
  xMove = -4;
  playerSprite.setFrame(3);
}
else if ((keyState & RIGHT_PRESSED) != 0) {
  xMove = 4;
  playerSprite.setFrame(1);
}
if ((keyState & UP_PRESSED) != 0) {
  yMove = -4;
  playerSprite.setFrame(0);
}
else if ((keyState & DOWN_PRESSED) != 0) {
  yMove = 4;
  playerSprite.setFrame(2);
}
if (xMove != 0 || yMove != 0) {
  layers.setViewWindow(xView + xMove, yView + yMove, getWidth(),
    getHeight() - infoBar.getHeight());
  playerSprite.move(xMove, yMove);
}
```

You can make the player's pirate ship move faster by increasing this value, along with the other directional movement values.

Adjust only the view window and move the player sprite if a directional key was pressed.

If you recall from the design of the High Seas game, the player's pirate ship remains fixed in the middle of the screen while the other elements in the game scroll behind it. The key handling code takes care of the scrolling by setting the view window of the layer manager in response to directional key presses. The amount to move in each direction is first determined, and then the view window is moved by that amount with a call to setViewWindow(). The player sprite is then moved by the same amount to make sure that it remains centered on the game screen.

The DriftSprite class takes care of checking for collisions between the land layer and all the sprites in the game except for the player sprite. The following code in the update() method checks for a collision between the player sprite and the land layer:

```
if (playerSprite.collidesWith(landLayer, true)) {
  // Restore the original view window and player sprite positions
  layers.setViewWindow(xView, yView, getWidth(),
    getHeight() - infoBar.getHeight());
  playerSprite.move(-xMove, -yMove);
}
else {
  // If there is no collision, commit the changes to the view window position
  xView += xMove;
  yView += yMove;
}
```

If a collision has indeed occurred between the player sprite and the land layer, the view window is restored to its previous position, which was stored earlier in the xView and yView member variables. The player sprite itself is also moved back to its original position so that it remains centered on the screen. If no collision took place, then the new view window position is committed to the xView and yView member variables.

Updating the various sprites in the High Seas game is where most of the real work is done in the update() method. The following code handles updating the pirate and barrel sprites:

```
for (int i = 0; i < 2; i++) {
  // Update the pirate and barrel sprites
  pirateSprite[i].update();
  barrelSprite[i].update();

  // Check for a collision with the player and the pirate sprite
  if (playerSprite.collidesWith(pirateSprite[i], true)) {
    // Play a wave sound for rescuing a pirate
    try {
      rescuePlayer.start();
    }
    catch (MediaException me) {
    }

    // Increase the number of pirates saved
    piratesSaved++;

    // Randomly place the pirate in a new location
    placeSprite(pirateSprite[i], landLayer);
  }
  // Check for a collision with the player and the barrel sprite
  if (playerSprite.collidesWith(barrelSprite[i], true)) {
    // Play a tone sound for gaining energy from a barrel
    try {
      Manager.playTone(ToneControl.C4 + 12, 250, 100);
    }
    catch (MediaException me) {
    }

    // Increase the player's energy
    energy = Math.min(energy + 5, 45);

    // Randomly place the barrel in a new location
    placeSprite(barrelSprite[i], landLayer);
  }
}
```

Increase the pirate count because a pirate was rescued.

Reuse the pirate sprite by placing it in a new location.

Increase the player's energy because a barrel was picked up.

Reuse the barrel sprite by placing it in a new location.

After updating both sprites, this code checks for a collision between the player sprite and a pirate sprite. If a collision occurred, a rescue sound effect is played to indicate that the pirate was saved. The number of pirates stored in the piratesSaved variable is also incremented. The pirate sprite is then repositioned to a random location with a call to the placeSprite() method. From the perspective of the player, the pirate disappeared, but in reality it was just moved to another area of the game map. This is a sneaky way to remove a pirate and create a new one by simply repositioning an existing single sprite. Incidentally, you learn how the placeSprite() method works a little later in the chapter.

After a collision is handled between the player sprite and a pirate, a collision is detected between the player and a barrel. In this case, a tone is played instead of a wave sound effect. The player's energy is then increased, and the barrel is repositioned for the same reason the pirate was repositioned.

Construction Cue

> The maximum energy the player can have in the High Seas game is 45, which is why the code that increases the energy for a barrel collision establishes a maximum energy of 45. Without this code, the energy bar in the game could keep growing across the screen and obscure the number of saved pirates.

The mine and squid sprites are updated in the update() method in a very similar fashion as the pirate and barrel sprites. However, the code for them is broken out separately because there are three of each (mines and squids), as opposed to only two of each for the pirates and barrels. In other words, it takes two different for loops. Following is the code that updates the mine and squid sprites:

```
for (int i = 0; i < 5; i++) {
  // Update the mine and squid sprites
  mineSprite[i].update();
  squidSprite[i].update();

  // Check for a collision with the player and the mine sprite
  if (playerSprite.collidesWith(mineSprite[i], true)) {
    // Play a wave sound for hitting a mine
    try {
      minePlayer.start();
    }
    catch (MediaException me) {
    }

    // Decrease the player's energy
    energy -= 10;

    // Randomly place the mine in a new location
    placeSprite(mineSprite[i], landLayer);
  }
```

Decrease the player's energy because a mine was hit. [

Reuse the mine sprite by placing it in a new location. [

```
    // Check for a collision with the player and the squid sprite
    if (playerSprite.collidesWith(squidSprite[i], true)) {
      // Play a tone sound for hitting a squid
      try {
        Manager.playTone(ToneControl.C4, 250, 100);
      }
      catch (MediaException me) {
      }

      // Decrease the player's energy
      energy -= 5;
    }
}
```

Decrease the player's energy because a squid was hit; this can happen repeatedly because the squid isn't repositioned.

Both sprites are updated first, and then a collision is detected between the player and a mine, in which case a wave sound effect is played and the player's energy is decreased. The mine is also randomly repositioned through use of the same trick employed with the pirate and barrel sprites.

The collision with a squid sprite is handled somewhat similarly to how a mine collision is handled. A tone is played instead of a wave sound, but the player's energy is decreased similarly. However, the squid sprite is not repositioned, which means that colliding with a squid doesn't cause the squid to appear to die. This means that a squid continues to inflict damage on the player's ship for as long as it makes contact with the ship. This makes the squids more dangerous than mines even though they inflict half the amount of damage per collision.

Speaking of damage to the pirate ship's energy, when the energy falls below 0 the game ends. Following is the code that ends a game when the player runs out of energy:

```
if (energy <= 0) {
  // Stop the music
  try {
    musicPlayer.stop();
  }
  catch (MediaException me) {
  }

  // Play a wave sound for the player ship sinking
  try {
    gameoverPlayer.start();
  }
  catch (MediaException me) {
  }

  // Hide the player ship sprite
  playerSprite.setVisible(false);

  gameOver = true;
}
```

Hide the player's ship because the game has ended.

At the end of a game, the music is first stopped and a gurgling wave sound effect is played to make it sound as if the ship has sunk. The player sprite is then hidden with a call to setVisible(), which further reinforces the fact that the ship has sunk. Finally, the gameOver member variable is set to true to indicate that the game is over.

The last chunk of code in the update() method takes care of the water animation delay:

```
if (++waterDelay > 3) {
  if (++waterTile[0] > 3)
    waterTile[0] = 1;
  waterLayer.setAnimatedTile(-1, waterTile[0]);
  if (--waterTile[1] < 1)
    waterTile[1] = 3;
  waterLayer.setAnimatedTile(-2, waterTile[1]);
  waterDelay = 0;
}
```

In the case of the water animation, each of the two animated tiles is cycled to the next tile, provided that the water delay has elapsed. Notice that the animated water tiles cycle in reverse directions to ensure that they never look the same as they animate. This is important because they use the same set of tile images.

Drawing the Game Screen

Drawing the game screen in the High Seas is relatively straightforward thanks to the layer manager. Listing 12.3 contains the code for the draw() method in the HSCanvas class.

LISTING 12.3 The draw() Method in the HSCanvas Class Draws the Info Bar and the Game Layers, Along with the Game Over Message, if Necessary

```
private void draw(Graphics g) {
  // Draw the info bar with energy and pirate's saved
  g.drawImage(infoBar, 0, 0, Graphics.TOP | Graphics.LEFT);
  g.setColor(0, 0, 0); // black
  g.setFont(Font.getFont(Font.FACE_SYSTEM, Font.STYLE_PLAIN, Font.SIZE_MEDIUM));
  g.drawString("Energy:", 2, 1, Graphics.TOP | Graphics.LEFT);
  g.drawString("Pirates saved: " + piratesSaved, 88, 1,
    Graphics.TOP | Graphics.LEFT);
  g.setColor(32, 32, 255); // blue
  g.fillRect(40, 3, energy, 12);

  // Draw the layers
  layers.paint(g, 0, infoBar.getHeight());

  if (gameOver) {
```

Draw the remaining energy as a blue rectangle just to the right of the energy text.

LISTING 12.3   Continued

```
          // Draw the game over message and score
          g.setColor(255, 255, 255); // white
          g.setFont(Font.getFont(Font.FACE_SYSTEM, Font.STYLE_BOLD, Font.SIZE_LARGE));
          g.drawString("GAME OVER", 90, 40, Graphics.TOP | Graphics.HCENTER);
          g.setFont(Font.getFont(Font.FACE_SYSTEM, Font.STYLE_BOLD,
            Font.SIZE_MEDIUM));
          if (piratesSaved == 0)
            g.drawString("You didn't save any pirates.", 90, 70,
              Graphics.TOP | Graphics.HCENTER);
          else if (piratesSaved == 1)
            g.drawString("You saved only 1 pirate.", 90, 70,
              Graphics.TOP | Graphics.HCENTER);
          else
            g.drawString("You saved " + piratesSaved + " pirates.", 90, 70,
              Graphics.TOP | Graphics.HCENTER);
        }

        // Flush the offscreen graphics buffer
        flushGraphics();
}
```

Display the score with accurate text by checking to see how many pirates were saved.

The first block of code takes care of drawing the information bar, which consists of a bitmap image with an energy bar and the number of saved pirates overlaid on top of it. The energy bar is drawn with a call to `fillRect()`, and all the text is drawn with the `drawstring()` method.

The layers are drawn in the middle of the `draw()` method with a single line of code, followed by the game over message. If the game is over, the game over message is drawn, which consists of the words "GAME OVER," followed by a notification of how many pirates were saved, which serves as the score of the game.

Starting a New Game

I've mentioned the `newGame()` method a few times throughout the discussion of the High Seas game code. It's time to take a look at how it works. Listing 12.4 contains the code that allows the `newGame()` method to establish a new game.

LISTING 12.4   The `newGame()` Method in the `HSCanvas` Class Initializes the Game Variables, Repositions the Pirate Ship, and Starts the Music

```
private void newGame() {
  // Initialize the game variables
  gameOver = false;
  energy = 45;
  piratesSaved = 0;
```

It's very important to show the player's ship when a new game starts.

LISTING 12.4   Continued

```
// Show the player ship sprite
playerSprite.setVisible(true);

// Randomly place the player and adjust the view window
placeSprite(playerSprite, landLayer);
xView = playerSprite.getX() - ((getWidth() - playerSprite.getWidth()) / 2);
yView = playerSprite.getY() - ((getHeight() - playerSprite.getHeight()) / 2);
layers.setViewWindow(xView, yView, getWidth(),
  getHeight() - infoBar.getHeight());

// Start the music (at the beginning)
try {
  musicPlayer.setMediaTime(0);
  musicPlayer.start();
}
catch (MediaException me) {
}
}
```

The player's ship is randomly positioned at the start of each new game.

The newGame() method starts out by initializing the three main game variables—notice that the energy is set to its maximum possible value of 45. The player sprite is then made visible with a call to setVisible(); this is necessary because the sprite is hidden when a game ends. The player sprite is then randomly placed via a call to the placeSprite() method, and the view window is adjusted accordingly so that the player sprite appears in the middle of the game screen. The method concludes by restarting the game music at its beginning with calls to setMediaTime() and start() on the music player.

Safely Placing Sprites

I can understand if you're wearing down, but I promise this is the last leg of your marathon journey through the code of the High Seas game. Listing 12.5 contains the code for the placeSprite() method, which is responsible for placing a sprite at a random location on the game map.

LISTING 12.5   The placeSprite() Method in the HSCanvas Class Randomly Places a Sprite in a Location Where It Doesn't Collide with a Barrier

Take a shot at randomly placing the sprite to start out.

```
private void placeSprite(Sprite sprite, TiledLayer barrier) {
  // Initially try a random position
  sprite.setPosition(Math.abs(rand.nextInt() % barrier.getWidth()) -
    sprite.getWidth(), Math.abs(rand.nextInt() % barrier.getHeight()) -
    sprite.getHeight());
```

LISTING 12.5   Continued

```
// Reposition until there isn't a collision
while (sprite.collidesWith(barrier, true)) {
  sprite.setPosition(Math.abs(rand.nextInt() % barrier.getWidth()) -
    sprite.getWidth(), Math.abs(rand.nextInt() % barrier.getHeight()) -
    sprite.getHeight());
  }
}
```

See whether the sprite collides with the barrier layer, and continue repositioning it until there isn't a collision.

You might think that placing a sprite at a random location on the game map is just a matter of picking a few random numbers and being done with it. But keep in mind that there are areas on the map where it doesn't make sense to place a floating barrel or squid...such as on land! In other words, it's important that you not only place sprites randomly, but also place them intelligently. What this boils down to is making sure that when you place a sprite it doesn't end up in a location that collides with the land layer.

To randomly place a sprite at a "safe" location on the game map, you simply place it randomly and check for a collision with the land layer. If there is a collision, just try again. The place/test routine is in a loop so that it repeats over and over until a successful location is found. Technically, you could argue that this code is risky because there is no bail-out for the loop, but the game map is plenty big for a safe location to be found in a reasonable number of tries.

Testing the Game

Ah, finally, the long-awaited test phase for the High Seas game. You've been through enough code that I won't bother you with a bunch of pretest discussion. Figure 12.12 shows the game at startup.

Figure 12.12 reveals how every game is different thanks to the random placement of sprites. In this particular game, the pirate ship begins with a pirate in view ready to be rescued.

FIGURE 12.12
A lucky start to High Seas shows a pirate in view ready to be rescued.

FIGURE 12.13
Rescuing the first pirate results in the pirate disappearing and the number of saved pirates increasing by one.

Rescuing the pirate results in the sprite disappearing from view and the saved pirate count increasing by one in the information bar (see Figure 12.13).

Continuing along in the game, you'll sooner or later encounter other types of sprites such as floating mines and barrels, as shown in Figure 12.14.

Eventually your luck will run out and a squid or barrel will zap your last bit of energy and bring the game to an end. Figure 12.15 shows the "game over" message being displayed just after a pesky squid finishes off the pirate ship.

If you spend any time playing High Seas, you'll probably come to the conclusion that it isn't a very difficult game to master. The reality is that none of the sprites are intelligent enough to pose a realistic challenge to a human player. This problem is remedied in the next chapter when you learn how to incorporate artificial intelligence into your games.

FIGURE 12.14
Floating mines and barrels represent opposites in the game: One robs you of energy, whereas the other one restores it.

Summary

Any concerns you might have had over when you were going to get to construct another full-featured mobile game should have been put to rest in this chapter. Although the High Seas game could certainly be expanded and made more fun, I have to admit that I got a little carried away when developing the game. I never intended to throw so much game code at you at this point in the book, but theory goes only so far. Even if this chapter bowled you over a bit with the considerable quantity of code, the example game is compelling enough that you can really put it to use as a base for your own games. I'd rather stretch your skills a bit with a more involved game than present you with several cheesy little games with no substance.

FIGURE 12.15
Eventually, a squid overcomes the pirate ship and the game comes to an end with only three pirates having been saved.

The one drawback to the High Seas game is that it really isn't very challenging. Believe it or not, this was a deliberate design decision because in the next chapter you revisit High Seas and give the bad guys some intelligence. Not only that, but you introduce an entirely new bad guy that is quite fearsome!

Extreme Game Makeover

Perhaps the easiest and most dramatic change you can make to the High Seas game is to tinker with the tiled layers. For example, you might consider making the layers larger and rearranging the islands on the land layer into a more interesting layout. This involves fairly minor changes to the actual game logic. Just follow these steps to change the layer maps in the High Seas game code:

1. Find some additional tile images that will fit into the game, such as more interesting land pieces, shipwrecks, reefs, and so on. These pieces will just serve as barriers, but they will still add some more visual interest to the game.

2. Decide on a new, larger map size, and add new cells to both the land and water layers to make them the correct size, both in terms of rows and columns. Make sure to incorporate the new tiles into the maps. You can redesign the maps by hand or use mapping software (as mentioned in Chapter 10).

3. Change the initialization code for the land and water layers to factor in the new map dimensions.

These three changes add unique new visual barriers to the High Seas game, as well as making the map larger and more interesting. Of course, now that the map is larger, you may want to consider adding some more squid, mine, pirate, and barrel sprites, but that's up to you.

CHAPTER 13

Teaching Games to Think

Arcade Archive

Released by Sega in 1982, Pengo is quite likely the first video game to rely on a penguin as its main character. In the game you control a penguin that moves around in a maze of ice blocks constantly being pursued by "Sno-Bees," which are curious little blobby creatures. Pengo is somewhat of a cross between a strategy maze game and an action game. Because of its lighthearted and nonviolent (for the most part) graphics, Pengo is one of the few classic arcade games to cross the traditional male gender barrier. As an interesting aside, the background music in Pengo is a song titled "Popcorn," which was originally released by a musical group called Hot Butter.

One of the biggest challenges facing you as a mobile game developer is creating games that present a formidable challenge to the player. Some games can be made challenging if you simply overwhelm the player with enemies, whereas others require you to develop code that enables the game to think like a human player. This chapter focuses on understanding the fundamental theories of artificial intelligence and how they can be applied to games. You should leave this chapter with the basic knowledge required to begin implementing artificial intelligence strategies in your own games. More importantly, you will leave this chapter with a practical example of how to incorporate simple AI into a real mobile game.

In this chapter, you'll learn

- ▶ About the basics of artificial intelligence (AI)

- ▶ About the different types of AI used in games

- ▶ How to develop an AI strategy of your own

- ▶ How to create sprites that exhibit aggression and are capable of chasing each other

- ▶ How to put AI to work in a mobile game involving sprites that "intelligently" chase the human player

The Least You Need to Know About AI

If you saw the movies *A.I.* or *I, Robot*, then you have an idea as to what artificial intelligence is theoretically capable of offering. Good or bad, the promise of building computers that can think like humans is tremendously exciting. Artificial intelligence (AI) is defined as the techniques used to emulate the human thought process in a computer. This is admittedly a fairly general definition for AI, as it should be; AI is a very broad research area—with game-related AI being a relatively small subset of the whole of AI knowledge. The goal in this chapter is not to explore every facet of AI because that would easily fill more than one book, but rather to explore the fundamental concepts behind AI as it applies to games.

As you might have already guessed, human thought is no simple process to emulate, which explains why AI is such a broad area of research. Even though there are many different approaches to AI, they all basically boil down to attempting to make human decisions within the confines of a computer "brain." Most traditional AI systems use a variety of information-based algorithms to make decisions, just as people use a variety of previous experiences and mental rules to make a decision. In the past, the information-based AI algorithms were completely *deterministic*, which means that every decision could be traced back to a predictable flow of logic. Figure 13.1 shows an example of a purely logical human thought process. Obviously, human thinking doesn't work this way at all; if we were all this predictable, it would be quite a boring planet! Rational, but boring nonetheless.

FIGURE 13.1
A completely logical human thought process involves nothing more than strict reason.

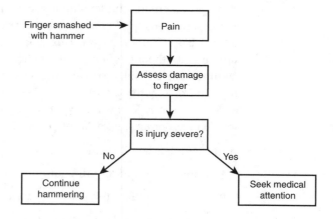

Eventually, AI researchers realized that the deterministic approach to AI wasn't sufficient to accurately model human thought. Their focus shifted from deterministic AI models to more realistic AI models that attempted to factor in the subtle complexities of human thought, such as best-guess decisions. In people, these types of decisions can result from a combination of past experience, personal bias, and/or the current state of emotion—in addition to the completely logical decision-making process. Figure 13.2 shows an example of this type of thought process. The point is that people don't always make scientifically predictable decisions based on analyzing their surroundings and arriving at a logical conclusion. The world would probably be a better place if we did act like this, but again, it would be awfully boring!

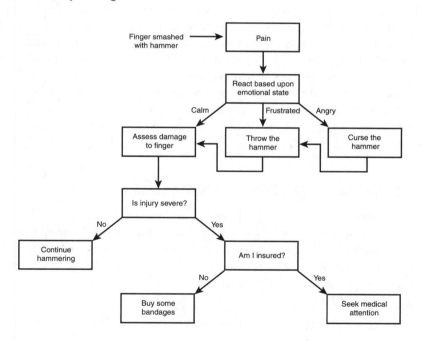

FIGURE 13.2
A more realistic human thought process adds emotion and a dash of irrationality with reason.

The logic flow in Figure 13.1 is an ideal scenario, in which each decision is made based on a totally objective logical evaluation of the situation. Figure 13.2 shows a more realistic scenario, which factors in the emotional state of the person, as well as a financial angle (the question of whether the person has insurance). Examining the second scenario from a completely logical angle, it makes no sense for the person to throw the hammer because that only slows down the task at hand.

However, this is a completely plausible and fairly common human response to pain and frustration. For an AI carpentry system to effectively model this situation, there would definitely have to be some hammer-throwing code somewhere!

This hypothetical thought example is meant to give you a tiny clue as to how many seemingly unrelated things go into forming a human thought. Likewise, it only makes sense that it would take an extremely complex AI system to effectively model human thought. Most of the time, this statement is true. However, the word "effectively" allows for a certain degree of interpretation, based on the context of the application requiring AI. For your purposes, "effective AI" means AI that makes mobile game objects more realistic and engaging.

AI research in recent years has been focused on tackling problems similar to the ones illustrated by the hypothetical carpentry example. One particularly interesting area is *fuzzy logic*, which attempts to make "best-guess" decisions rather than the concrete decisions of traditional AI systems. Another interesting AI research area in relation to games is genetic algorithms, which try to model evolved thought similarly to how scientists believe nature evolves through genetics. A game using genetic algorithms would theoretically have computer opponents that learn as the game progresses, providing the human player with a seemingly never-ending series of challenges.

Exploring Types of Game AI

There are many different types of AI systems and even more algorithms that carry out those systems. Even when you limit AI to the world of games, there is still a wide range of information and options from which to choose when it comes to adding AI to a mobile game of your own. Many different AI solutions are geared toward particular types of games—with a plethora of different possibilities that can be applied in different situations.

What I'm getting at is that there is no way to just present a bunch of AI algorithms and tell you which one goes with which particular type of game. Rather, it makes more sense to give you the theoretical background on a few of the most important types of AI, and then let you figure out how they might apply to your particular gaming needs. Having said all that, I've broken down game-related AI into three fundamental types:

▶ **Roaming AI**—Determines how a game object roams around a virtual game world

▶ **Behavioral AI**—Determines how aggressively a game object tracks and goes after another game object or objects

▶ **Strategic AI**—Determines the best move in a strategy game with a fixed set of well-defined rulesromaing

Please understand that these three types of AI are in no way meant to encompass all the AI approaches used in games; they are simply the most common types to recognize and use. Feel free to do your own research and expand on these if you find AI to be an interesting topic worthy of further study.

Roaming AI

Roaming AI refers to AI that models the movement of game objects—that is, the decisions game objects make that determine how they roam around a virtual game world. A good example of roaming AI is in shoot-em-up space games such as the classic arcade game Galaga, where aliens often tend to track and go after the player. Similarly, roaming AI is also used to implement aliens that fly around in a predetermined pattern. Basically, roaming AI is used whenever a computer-controlled object must make a decision to alter its current path—either to achieve a desired result in the game or simply to conform to a particular movement pattern. In the Galaga example, the desired result is for aliens to follow a pattern while also attempting to collide with and damage the player's ship. In other games, the desired result for a computer opponent might be to dodge the bullets being fired by a human player.

Implementing roaming AI is usually fairly simple; it typically involves altering an object's velocity or position (the alien) based on the position of another object (the player's ship). The roaming movement of the object can also be influenced by random or predetermined patterns. Three different types of roaming AI exist: chasing, evading, and patterned. The next few sections explore these types of roaming AI in more detail.

Chasing

Chasing is a type of roaming AI in which a game object tracks and goes after another game object or objects. Chasing is the approach used in many shoot-em-up games where an alien chases after the player's ship. It is implemented by altering the alien's velocity or position based on the current position of the player's ship.

Following is an example of a simple chasing algorithm involving an alien and a ship:

```
if (xAlien > xShip)
  xAlien--;
else if (xAlien < xShip)
  xAlien++;
if (yAlien > yShip)
  yAlien--;
else if (yAlien < yShip)
  yAlien++;
```

As you can see, the XY position (xAlien and yAlien) of the alien is altered based on where the ship is located (xShip and yShip). The only potential problem with this code is that it can work too well; the alien will hone in on the player with no hesitation, basically giving the player no chance to dodge it. This might be what you want, but more than likely, you want the alien to fly around a little while it chases the player. You probably also want the chasing to be somewhat imperfect, giving the player at least a chance of outmaneuvering the alien. In other words, you want the alien to have a *tendency* to chase the player without going in for an all-out blitz.

One method of smoothing out the chasing algorithm is to throw a little randomness into the equation, like this:

```
if ((Math.abs(rand.nextInt()) % 3) == 0) {
  if (xAlien > xShip)
    xAlien--;
  else if (xAlien < xShip)
    xAlien++;
}
if ((rand() % 3) == 0) {
  if (yAlien > yShip)
    yAlien--;
  else if (yAlien < yShip)
    yAlien++;
}
```

In this code, the alien has a one in three chance of tracking the player in each direction. Even with only a one in three chance, the alien will still tend to chase the player aggressively, while also allowing the player a fighting chance at getting out of the way. You might think that a one in three chance doesn't sound all that effective, but keep in mind that the alien alters its path only to chase the player. A smart player will probably figure this out and change directions frequently.

If you aren't too fired up about the random approach to leveling off the chase, you probably need to look into patterned movement. But you're getting a little ahead of yourself; let's take a look at evading first.

Evading

Evading is the logical counterpart to chasing; it is another type of roaming AI in which a game object specifically tries to get away from another object or objects. Evading is implemented in a similar manner to chasing, as the following code shows:

```
if (xAlien > xShip)
  xAlien++;
else if (xAlien < xShip)
  xAlien--;
if (yAlien > yShip)
  yAlien++;
else if (yAlien < yShip)
  yAlien--;
```

This code basically does the opposite of the code used by the chasing algorithm—with the only differences being the unary operators (++, --) used to change the alien's position so that it runs away, as opposed to chasing. Similar to chasing, evading can be softened with randomness or patterned movement. A good example of evading is the ghosts in the classic arcade game Pac-Man, who run away from the player when you eat a power pellet. Of course, the Pac-Man ghosts also take advantage of chasing when you aren't able to eat them, which is most of the time.

Another good example of using the evading algorithm would be for a computer-controlled version of the player's ship in a space game with a computer player. If you think about it, the player is using the evading algorithm to dodge the aliens; it's just implemented by key presses rather than in a piece of computer-controlled code. If you want to provide a demo mode in a game like this where the computer plays itself, you would use an evading algorithm to control the player's ship.

Patterned Roaming

Patterned movement refers to a type of roaming AI that uses a predefined set of movements for a game object. Good examples of patterned movement are the aliens in the classic Galaga arcade game, which perform all kinds of neat aerobatics on their way down the screen. Patterns can include circles, figure eights, zigzags, or even more complex movements. An even simpler example of patterned movement is the Space Invaders game, where a herd of aliens slowly and methodically inch across and down the screen.

In truth, the aliens in Galaga use a combined approach of both patterned and chasing movement; although they certainly follow specific patterns, the aliens still make sure to come after the player whenever possible. Additionally, as the player moves into higher levels, the roaming AI starts favoring chasing over patterned movement to make the game harder. This is a great use of combined roaming AI. This touches on the concept of behavioral AI, which you learn about in the next section.

Patterns are usually stored as an array of velocity or position offsets (or multipliers) that are applied to an object whenever patterned movement is required of it, like this:

```
int[][] zigZag = { {3, 2}, {-3, 2} };
xAlien += zigZag[patternStep][0];
yAlien += zigZag[patternStep][1];
```

This code shows how to implement a very simple vertical zigzag pattern. The integer array zigZag contains pairs of XY offsets used to apply the pattern to the alien. The patternStep variable is an integer representing the current step in the pattern. When this pattern is applied, the alien moves in a vertical direction at a speed of 2 pixels per game cycle, while zigzagging back and forth horizontally at a speed of 3 pixels per game cycle.

Behavioral AI

Although the types of roaming AI strategies are pretty useful in their own right, a practical gaming scenario often requires a mixture of all three. Behavioral AI is another fundamental type of gaming AI that often uses a mixture of roaming AI algorithms to give game objects specific behaviors. Using the trusted alien example again, what if you want the alien to chase sometimes, evade other times, follow a pattern still other times, and maybe even act totally randomly every once in a while? Another good reason for using behavioral AI is to alter the difficulty of a game. For example, you could favor a chasing algorithm more than random or patterned movement to make aliens more aggressive in higher levels of a space game.

To implement behavioral AI, you would need to establish a set of behaviors for the alien. Giving game objects behaviors isn't too difficult. It usually involves establishing a ranking system for each type of behavior present in the system, and then applying it to each object. For example, in the alien system, you would have the following behaviors: chase, evade, fly in a pattern, and fly randomly.

For each different type of alien, you would assign different percentages to the different behaviors, thereby giving them each different personalities. For example, an aggressive alien might have the following behavioral breakdown: chase 50% of the time, evade 10% of the time, fly in a pattern 30% of the time, and fly randomly 10% of the time. On the other hand, a more passive alien might act like this: chase 10% of the time, evade 50% of the time, fly in a pattern 20% of the time, and fly randomly 20% of the time.

This behavioral approach works amazingly well and yields surprising results considering how simple it is to implement. A typical implementation involves a `switch` statement or nested `if-else` statements to select a particular behavior. A sample implementation for the behavioral aggressive alien would look like this:

```
int behavior = Math.abs(rand.nextInt()) % 100;
if (behavior < 50)
  // chase
else if (behavior < 60)
  // evade
else if (behavior < 90)
  // fly in a pattern
else
  // fly randomly
```

As you can see, creating and assigning behaviors is open to a wide range of creativity. One of the best sources of ideas for creating game object behaviors is the primal responses common in the animal world (and unfortunately all too often in the human world, too). As a matter of fact, a simple fight-or-flight behavioral system can work wonders when applied intelligently to a variety of game objects. Basically, just use your imagination as a guide and create as many unique behaviors as you can dream up.

Strategic AI

The final fundamental type of game AI I want to mention is strategic AI, which is basically any AI designed to play a game with a fixed set of well-defined rules. For example, a computer-controlled chess player would use strategic AI to determine each move based on trying to improve the chances of winning the game. Strategic AI tends to vary considerably based on the nature of the game just because it is so tightly linked to the rules of the game. Even so, there are established and successful approaches to applying strategic AI to many general types of games, such as games played on a rectangular board with pieces. Checkers and chess immediately come to mind as fitting into this group, and likewise have a rich history of AI research devoted to them.

Gamer's Garage

Every few years the best human chess player matches up against the best computer chess program to see how chess AI is coming along. In 2003 the world's number one player Gary Kasparov faced off against the World Computer Champion Deep Junior in the "Man vs. Machine Chess Championship" in New York City. Although Kasparov was beaten by IBM's Deep Blue chess program in 1997, he put us humans back on respectable ground by battling to a draw against Deep Junior in 2003.

Strategic AI, especially for board games, typically involves some form of "look-ahead" approach to determine the best move to make. The look-ahead is usually used in conjunction with a fixed table of predetermined moves. For a look-ahead to make sense, however, there must be a method of looking at the board at any state and calculating a score. This is known as weighting, and is often the most difficult part of implementing strategic AI in a board game. As an example of how difficult weighting can be, watch a game of chess or checkers and try to figure out who is winning after every single move, even very early in the game. Then go a step further and think about trying to calculate a numeric score for each player at each point in the game. Obviously, near the end of the game, it gets easier, but early on it is very difficult to tell who is winning simply because so many different things can happen. Attempting to quantify the state of the game in a numeric score is even more difficult.

Nevertheless, there are ways to successfully calculate a weighted score for strategic games. Using a look-ahead approach with scoring, a strategic AI algorithm can test for every possible move for each player, including multiple moves into the future, and then determine which move is the best. This move is often referred to as the "least worst" move, rather than the best, because the goal typically is to make the move that helps the other player the least rather than the other way around. Of course, the end result is basically the same, but it is an interesting way to look at a game, nevertheless. Even though look-ahead approaches to implementing strategic AI are useful in many cases, they can require a fair amount of processing if very much depth is required (in other words, if the computer player needs to be very smart).

To better understand strategic AI, consider the case of a computer backgammon player. The computer player has to choose two or four moves from possibly several dozen, as well as decide whether to double or resign. A practical backgammon program might assign weights to different combinations of positions and calculate the value of each position reachable from the current position and dice roll.

A scoring system would then be used to evaluate the worth of each potential position, which gets back to the often difficult proposition of scoring, even in a game such as backgammon, with simple rules. Now apply this scenario to a war game with several dozen battle units—with every unit having unique characteristics, and the terrain and random factors complicating the issue still further. The optimal system of scoring simply cannot be determined in a reasonable amount of time, especially given the limited computing power of a mobile phone.

The solution in these cases is to settle for a "good enough" move, rather than the "best" move. One of the best ways to develop the algorithm for finding the "good enough" move is to set up the computer to play both sides in a game, using a lot of variation between the algorithms and weights playing each side. Then sit back and let the two computer players battle it out and see which one wins the most. This approach typically involves a lot of tinkering and trial-and-error with the AI code, but it can result in very good computer players, and it can be a lot of fun to watch.

Developing an AI Strategy

Now that you understand the basic concepts behind AI in games, you can start thinking about an AI strategy for your own specific games. When deciding how to implement AI in a game, you need to do some preliminary work to assess exactly what type and level of AI you think is warranted. You need to determine what level of computer response suits your needs, abilities, resources, and project time frame.

If your main concern is developing a game that keeps human players entertained and challenged, go with the simplest AI possible. Actually, try to go with the simplest AI regardless of your goals because you can always enhance it in phases. If you think your game needs a type of AI that doesn't quite fit into any I've described, do some research and see whether something out there is closer to what you need. Most importantly, budget plenty of time for implementing AI because 90% of the time it will take longer than you ever anticipated to get it all working at a level you are happy with.

What is the best way to get started? In small steps, of course. Many programmers like to write code as they design, and although that approach might work in some cases, I recommend at least some degree of preliminary design on paper. Furthermore, try to keep this design limited to a subset of the game's AI, such as a single computer opponent. Start with a small, simple map or grid and simple movement rules. Write the code to get a single opponent from point A to point B.

Then add complications piece by piece, building onto an evolving algorithm at each step. If you are careful to make each piece of the AI general and open enough to connect to other pieces, your final algorithms should be general enough to handle any conditions your game might encounter.

Getting back to more basic terms, a good way to gain AI experience is to write a computer opponent for a simple board game, such as tic-tac-toe or checkers. Detailed AI solutions exist for many popular games, so you should be able to find them if you search around a little on the web. Another good way to get some experience with AI is to modify an existing game in an attempt to make its computer-controlled characters a little smarter. For example, you could modify the Henway game so that the cars speed up and slow down deliberately to make it tougher on the chicken as she gets near each car. Or you could design a whole new sprite class that knows how to chase other sprites at varying levels of aggression…read on!

Teaching Sprites to Think…Sort Of

Earlier in the chapter I described a type of roaming AI known as chasing, where an object in a game is smart enough to chase another object, usually the one controlled by the human player. You're now ready to design and build a sprite that implements chasing so that you can improve the High Seas game from the previous chapter and make it a bit more challenging.

Designing the Chase Sprite

The basic premise behind a chase sprite is that you give it a target sprite, the chasee, and the chaser constantly moves in the direction of it. Just think of a game of tag where you constantly run after the person that is "it" and you get the idea behind a chase sprite. To understand how such a sprite might work, you have to think of a game of tag in somewhat nerdly terms. For example, give your current location an XY coordinate that is relative to some nearby location, such as the front porch of a house. You can use any unit of measurement you want—feet, yards, bicycle lengths…it doesn't matter. Now give the person you are chasing an XY coordinate based on his current position relative to the front porch.

With the position of the chaser and the position of the chasee in hand, you have all the information you need to form a plan of action. Just subtract the chasee's X position from your X position to determine which direction to move in the X direction; a negative value means you should move west, whereas a positive value requires you to move east. The same calculation must be done in the Y direction, with a negative value indicating a move north and a positive value indicating a move south.

Figure 13.3 shows how the positions of the people in this example result in a decision to move in a certain direction.

Figure 13.3 reveals how a simple calculation makes it possible to determine a movement direction for a chaser given the locations of the chaser and chasee. It is worth pointing out, however, that the chase approach shown in the figure has a problem that rears its ugly head when you actually try to code a sprite to chase in this manner. The problem is that the chaser is never idle. In other words, the chaser is always adjusting its chase direction even when it is generally on target with the chasee. This occurs because the chaser is likely to over-shoot the chasee slightly, resulting in a zigzagging

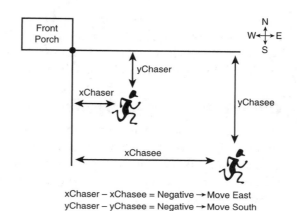

xChaser – xChasee = Negative → Move East
yChaser – yChasee = Negative → Move South

FIGURE 13.3
The direction in which a chaser moves can be determined through a simple calcula-tion of XY coordi-nates between the chaser and chasee.

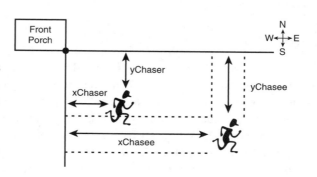

xChaser – xChasee = Negative ⟶ Move East
yChaser – yChasee = < Threshold → Don't Move

FIGURE 13.4
By establishing a chase threshold, you prevent the chaser from con-stantly changing directions unneces-sarily when it is already in line with the chasee.

attempt to exactly catch the chasee. The solution is to establish a chase threshold that gives the chaser a region in which it doesn't have to make any chase move-ments. Take a look at Figure 13.4 to see what I'm talking about.

The idea behind a chase threshold is to limit the movement of the chaser when it gets close enough to the chasee to touch it. You have to keep in mind that you're dealing with two different directions (X and Y), so even though the chaser might be close enough to "touch" the chasee in the X direction, it may actually be far away in the Y direction and therefore not actually near the chasee at all. However, the chase threshold would prevent the chaser from zig-zagging con-stantly in the X direction because it is within the chase threshold and therefore doesn't need to make any additional movements in the X direction.

If this discussion of the chase sprite sounds somewhat theoretical, then maybe the actual code for the sprite will help bring things into perspective. If nothing else, you will definitely learn to appreciate the usefulness of the chase sprite as you build the High Seas 2 example game later in the chapter.

Coding the Chase Sprite

You probably could've guessed that the ChaseSprite class is derived from the standard Sprite class—no big surprises there. The member variables for the ChaseSprite class provide the first glimpse into the inner workings of the class. Following are the most important member variables declared in the ChaseSprite class:

```
private int         speed;
private TiledLayer  barrier;
private boolean     directional;
private Sprite      chasee;
private int         aggression;  // 0 - 10
```

This is the sprite being chased.

The speed variable stores away the speed of the chase sprite, which is expressed in pixels per game cycle. Each time the sprite makes a move to chase the chasee sprite, it moves this many pixels. The barrier variable represents the tiled layer that serves as a barrier for the chase sprite's movement. It's important to note that you can set this variable as null if you don't want the chase sprite to be constrained by a barrier layer. As an example, if you created a castle maze game with various creatures roaming about, you would likely want ghosts to have no barriers so that they would appear to float through walls. Or in the case of the High Seas game, you might add a dragon or some other flying creature that is unencumbered by the land layer.

Getting back to the member variables of the ChaseSprite class, the directional variable keeps track of whether or not the sprite has a direction. A directional sprite has a noticeable front and back, which means that its animation frames are expected to contain the sprite facing in different directions, as opposed to a simple movement animation. Although it isn't a chase sprite, the player's pirate ship in the High Seas game is a good example of a directional sprite, whereas the squid is a good example of a sprite that has no direction; the squid just moves about without facing in any particular direction.

The chasee member variable is the sprite being chased, and is extremely important for the chase sprite to work properly. Finally, the aggression variable is
an integer in the range 0 to 10 that specifies how aggressive the chase sprite is.
A value of 0 represents the least aggressive chase sprite, which is no chasing at
all, whereas a value of 10 results in a sprite that is bent on hunting down the
chasee with virtually every move. This is a variable that you'll definitely want to
experiment with as you develop games with chase sprites.

The aggression of a chase sprite is a great attribute to increase as a game goes on
to make the game more challenging. You can tie the increased aggression to the
player completing levels in the game, reaching certain scoring thresholds, or just surviving for certain amounts of time.

Construction Cue

The member variables in the ChaseSprite class are initialized in the
ChaseSprite() constructor, which is shown in Listing 13.1.

LISTING 13.1   The ChaseSprite() Constructor Calls the Parent
Constructor and Initializes the Member Variables

```
public ChaseSprite(Image image, int frameWidth, int frameHeight, int chaseSpeed,
  TiledLayer barrierLayer, boolean hasDirection, Sprite chaseeSprite,
  int aggressionLevel) {
  super(image, frameWidth, frameHeight);

  // Initialize the random number generator
  rand = new Random();

  // Set the speed
  speed = chaseSpeed;

  // Set the tiled layer barrier
  barrier = barrierLayer;

  // Set whether or not the sprite is directional
  directional = hasDirection;

  // Set the chasee sprite
  chasee = chaseeSprite;

  // Set the aggression level
  aggression = aggressionLevel;
}
```

The higher the value, the more aggressive the sprite will be; this value is typically in the range of 0 to 10.

This code is very straightforward in that it mostly just assigns the new chase sprite parameters to the member variables you just learned about. It is important to notice the order of the chase parameters as they are passed into the constructor. It's also worth pointing out the call to the parent Sprite() constructor via the call to super()—the sprite image and frame width and height are passed into the parent constructor.

Beyond the new member variables, the entire functionality of the ChaseSprite is encased in a single method, update(). The update() method is called once every game cycle to update a chase sprite and give it a chance to move and update its animation frame. Listing 13.2 contains the code for the update() method in the ChaseSprite class.

LISTING 13.2   The update() Method in the ChaseSprite Class Handles All the Chores of Chasing the Chasee Sprite

```
public void update() {
  // Temporarily save the position
  int xPos = getX();
  int yPos = getY();
  int direction = 0;   // up = 0, right = 1, down = 2, left = 3

  // Chase or move randomly based on the aggression level
  if (Math.abs(rand.nextInt() % (aggression + 1)) > 0) {
    // Chase the chasee
    if (getX() > (chasee.getX() + chasee.getWidth() / 2)) {
      // Chase left
      move(-speed, 0);
      direction = 3;
    }
    else if ((getX() + getWidth() / 2) < chasee.getX()) {
      // Chase right
      move(speed, 0);
      direction = 1;
    }
    if (getY() > (chasee.getY() + chasee.getHeight() / 2)) {
      // Chase up
      move(0, -speed);
      direction = 0;
    }
    else if ((getY() + getHeight() / 2) < chasee.getY()) {
      // Chase down
      move(0, speed);
      direction = 2;
    }
  }
  else {
```

The chase occurs only if the chaser is not within the chase threshold.

LISTING 13.2 Continued

```java
    // Move in a random direction
    switch (Math.abs(rand.nextInt() % 4)) {
    // Move left
    case 0:
      move(-speed, 0);
      direction = 3;
      break;
    // Move right
    case 1:
      move(speed, 0);
      direction = 1;
      break;
    // Move up
    case 2:
      move(0, -speed);
      direction = 0;
      break;
    // Move down
    case 3:
      move(0, speed);
      direction = 2;
      break;
    }
  }

  // Check for a collision with the barrier
  if (barrier != null && collidesWith(barrier, true)) {
    // Move the sprite back to its original position
    setPosition(xPos, yPos);
  }

  // Move to the next animation frame based on directional or not
  if (directional)
    setFrame(direction);
  else
    nextFrame();
}
```

If no chasing is taking place, the sprite simply moves in a random direction.

If the sprite is a directional sprite, the animation frame is set to match the sprite's current direction; otherwise, the next animation frame is displayed.

I know; this is a fairly hefty method, but keep in mind that it represents virtually all the code in the ChaseSprite class. The update() method begins by temporarily saving the current position of the chase sprite. This is important because the method updates the position and direction next, but if there is a collision with a barrier you need to restore the old position to prevent movement. Notice that the direction of the sprite is expressed as an integer in the range of 0 to 3, where each number corresponds to a direction (up = 0, right = 1, down = 2, and left = 3).

The actual decision of whether the sprite is to chase is determined by the aggression variable. More specifically, a random number in the range 0 to aggression is obtained with a call to the rand.nextInt() method. If this number is anything other than 0, the sprite chases the chasee. What this means is that the larger the value of aggression, the better the odds that the sprite will chase. Following are some aggression values and how they impact the odds of the sprite chasing:

- ▶ Aggression of 0—no chasing at all
- ▶ Aggression of 1—chase 1 out of every 2 game cycles
- ▶ Aggression of 5—chase 5 out of every 6 game cycles
- ▶ Aggression of 10—chase 10 out of every 11 game cycles

As you can see, when you get past an aggression value of 5, the chase sprite becomes quite committed to the chase. For this reason, you are likely to use lower chase values for most chase sprites unless you really want to create a sprite that ruthlessly chases another sprite.

Getting back to the next block of code in the update() method, actually moving the sprite to carry out the chase is just a little tricky. If you recall from earlier in the design of the chase sprite, I mentioned how a chase threshold would help to keep the sprite from moving erratically as it honed in on the chasee. The chase movement code in the update() method is where the chase threshold is established. What's happening is that the code is checking to see whether the chase sprite is overlapping over half of the chasee sprite in the given direction; if so, no chase takes place. This means that the chase sprite chases in a given direction until it overlaps the chasee sprite by half its width. Keep in mind that in most cases the chase sprite won't truly be overlapping the chasee because we're talking about only one direction at a time; it's entirely possible for the sprites to be overlapping in one direction yet far away in the other.

If the earlier check of the aggression variable results in no chase, the chase sprite simply moves in a random direction much like the drift sprite from the previous chapter. After moving, the chase sprite checks for a collision with the barrier layer. It's important to note that this collision detection is made only if the barrier variable is not equal to null; this allows you to avoid the detection by simply setting the barrier variable to null. If a collision has indeed occurred, the original position that you saved earlier is restored for the chase sprite.

You could very easily combine the `ChaseSprite` and `DriftSprite` classes into one all-purpose sprite class that can chase or drift. In fact, the `ChaseSprite` class already has 90% of the functionality of the `DriftSprite` class. The only significant difference is the randomness that the `DriftSprite` class uses to determine which direction to drift. To keep things simple, I opted to keep the classes separate, but from a design perspective it wouldn't be a bad idea to merge them into one more general sprite class.

The last section of code in the `update()` method updates the animation frame based on whether or not the chase sprite is directional. If the sprite is directional, the animation frame is set based on which direction the sprite just moved. Otherwise, the `nextFrame()` method is called to simply move the animation to the next frame.

That wraps up the code for the `ChaseSprite` class. You're no doubt ready to see the sprite in action. The remainder of the chapter focuses on revamping the High Seas example game from the previous chapter to inject some simple AI into it via the `ChaseSprite` class.

Building the High Seas 2 Example Game

The High Seas game in the previous chapter is a pretty neat game, but I'm sure you realized that it is somewhat lacking in terms of presenting a challenge to the player. The bad guys in the game just don't try hard enough to pressure the player, which is because they move around randomly with no purpose. However, things are different now that you have a sprite class designed specifically to empower sprites with the ability to chase other sprites. It's time to up the difficulty level of the High Seas game by giving a few of the bad guys the capability to chase the player's pirate ship.

If you recall, the bad guys in the game consist of squids and floating mines. Because a mine is an inanimate object, it wouldn't make much sense to have it chase the pirate ship. And really, having only one type of chase sprite (squid) is kind of weak in my opinion, so adding another chaser is a good way to make the game more challenging. The chase sprite I have in mind is a large enemy pirate ship, which moves slower than the squids but is much more intent on chasing the player's pirate ship. Figure 13.5 shows the bitmap for the enemy pirate ship, which reveals it to be a directional sprite.

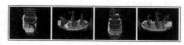

FIGURE 13.5
The enemy pirate ship bitmap image shows four animation frames of a large ship pointing in different directions.

Similar to the player's pirate ship, the enemy pirate ship's bitmap consists of four animation frames that each correspond to a particular direction of movement. Fortunately, you know that the ChaseSprite class easily takes into account directional sprites, so nothing special is required to plug the enemy ship into the High Seas 2 game.

Before digging into the code changes, let's recap what we're doing to make the High Seas 2 game tougher to play than the original version:

▶ Turn the squid sprites into chase sprites

▶ Add an enemy ship sprite that is also a chase sprite

If you think about how these different sprites would act in the real world, the squids would likely be quicker than a large ship, but the ship would undoubtedly be much more intelligent in terms of chasing the player. So the way to inject this real-world knowledge into the game is to make the squids fast but not too terribly aggressive, whereas the enemy ship will be slow but much more aggressive than the squids.

Enough theory—let's jump into the code so you can see how this stuff gets incorporated into the High Seas 2 game!

Writing the Program Code

The first changes required to the High Seas 2 game code occur in the member variable declarations. More specifically, you must change the squid sprites to be chase sprites, as well as add the new enemy ship sprite. Here's the code that takes care of these tasks:

```
private ChaseSprite[] squidSprite = new ChaseSprite[5];
private ChaseSprite    enemyShipSprite;
```

The ChaseSprite() constructor accepts some important parameters, including the sprite's speed, a barrier layer, whether or not it is directional, the chasee sprite, and the aggression.

In changing the squid sprites to use the ChaseSprite class, you must also alter their creation to provide the additional information required of the ChaseSprite() constructor. The following code is added to the start() method of the HSCanvas class:

```
for (int i = 0; i < 5; i++) {
  mineSprite[i] = new DriftSprite(Image.createImage("/Mine.png"), 27, 23, 1,
    landLayer);
  placeSprite(mineSprite[i], landLayer);

  squidSprite[i] = new ChaseSprite(Image.createImage("/Squid.png"), 24, 35, 3,
    landLayer, false, playerSprite, 3);
  placeSprite(squidSprite[i], landLayer);
}
```

The new chase sprite parameters start with the fourth parameter, which is the sprite's speed. In the case of the squids, the speed is set to 3, which is actually pretty fast considering the nature of the game. The barrier for the sprites is specified next, which in this case is landLayer, just like all the other sprites in the game. The next parameter is whether or not the sprites are directional, which for the squids is a definite no (false).

The next to last parameter to the ChaseSprite() constructor is the sprite to be chased, which obviously must be playerSprite. And finally, the last parameter is the aggression of the squid sprites, which is set to 3. This is one of those settings that you'll arrive at through some game testing—feel free to tweak it and try out different values to make the game easier or more difficult.

The enemy ship sprite is created in a manner very similar to the squid sprites, except in this case there is only one enemy ship:

```
enemyShipSprite = new ChaseSprite(Image.createImage("/EnemyShip.png"),
  86, 70, 1, landLayer, true, playerSprite, 10);
```

Starting again with the parameters specific to the chase sprite, the speed is set to 2, which is very slow. The landLayer tiled layer serves as the barrier for the sprite, whereas true indicates that the sprite is directional (remember Figure 13.5) and playerSprite is specified as the sprite being chased. The most interesting parameter is the last one, which specifies an aggression level of 10, the maximum. This ridiculous amount of aggression offsets the extremely slow speed of the enemy ship.

After creating the enemy ship, it's important to position it on the game screen. Because the ship is so big, the best placement of it is in the middle of the map where there is the most open water. The following code places the enemy ship in the middle of the map:

```
enemyShipSprite.setPosition(
  (landLayer.getWidth() - enemyShipSprite.getWidth()) / 2,
  (landLayer.getHeight() - enemyShipSprite.getHeight()) / 2);
```

The squid sprites and the enemy ship are added to the layer manager along with the other sprites in the game. This code is part of the initialization for the game, and therefore also appears in the start() method:

```
layers = new LayerManager();
layers.append(playerSprite);
layers.append(enemyShipSprite);
for (int i = 0; i < 2; i++) {
  layers.append(pirateSprite[i]);
  layers.append(barrelSprite[i]);
}
```

The new enemy ship is added to the layer manager just like the other sprites.

```
for (int i = 0; i < 5; i++) {
  layers.append(mineSprite[i]);
  layers.append(squidSprite[i]);
}
layers.append(landLayer);
layers.append(waterLayer);
```

Although the enemy ship is now successfully integrated into the game, you must still call its update() method within the update() method of the HSCanvas class. Fortunately, a single line of code is all it takes to pull this off:

```
enemyShipSprite.update();
```

The enemy ship is now getting updated along with the other sprites in the game, but you've yet to respond to a collision between the player's ship and the enemy ship. It's safe to say that the enemy ship should do a fair amount of damage to the player's ship in response to a collision. The following code, located in the update() method of the HSCanvas class, makes sure that this happens:

```
if (playerSprite.collidesWith(enemyShipSprite, true)) {
  // Play a wave sound for hitting the enemy ship
  try {
    minePlayer.start();
  }
  catch (MediaException me) {
  }

  // Decrease the player's energy
  energy -= 10;
}
```

Decrease the player's energy because the player's ship collided with the enemy ship.

The same sound as the player hitting a mine is played in response to colliding with the enemy ship. Additionally, the player's ship loses 10 energy units when it collides with the enemy ship. Although this may not sound too terribly bad, keep in mind that if you don't evade the enemy ship quickly, you can rack up multiple collisions and therefore lots of damage in a small amount of time.

I hope you've realized that the new code for the High Seas 2 game wasn't too daunting, thanks to the handy new ChaseSprite class. The only remaining work to be done is testing the game to see whether the squids and enemy ship actually go on the offensive. Testing games is a tough job, but someone has to do it!

Testing the Finished Product

Even though artificial intelligence is perhaps the toughest part of a game to get working properly, it can also be the most fun part of a game to test. There is just something uniquely rewarding about seeing a computer challenger in a game make informed decisions and react to human maneuvers. In the case of High Seas 2, the squid and enemy ship sprites are chaser sprites that know how to look at the position of the player's ship and go after it. Figure 13.6 shows the High Seas 2 game not too long after starting, where a squid has honed in on the ship and begun chasing it.

Even though the chaser sprites add some difficulty to the game, it doesn't take long for human players to figure out little tricks to keep them at bay, such as quickly moving around corners and hiding behind obstacles. Figure 13.7 shows how the player has evaded the first squid by simply maneuvering away from it, while another chasing squid is blocked by an island.

You can certainly view the scenario presented in Figure 13.7 as a weakness in the chaser sprites AI: A smarter chaser would know how to navigate around obstacles to find a way to the player's ship. Although this is true, you have to consider the fact that I've tried hard to present an AI example that isn't too terribly complex or processor intensive. Even so, I encourage you to experiment with beefing up the intelligence of the bad guys in the High Seas 2 game.

FIGURE 13.6
It doesn't take long for a squid to exhibit its aggression and begin chasing the player ship.

FIGURE 13.7
Through the island you can see another squid joining in the chase even though he isn't smart enough to realize the land is in the way.

FIGURE 13.8
Although not as quick as the squids, the large enemy ship is relentless in its pursuit of the player ship.

Who knows—you might figure out an interesting way to make them smarter without a bunch of complex code.

Figure 13.8 shows one last look at the High Seas 2 game where the large enemy ship is aggressively pursuing the player's ship.

If you recall from the game code, the enemy ship is extremely aggressive but not very fast. This provides a good balance in terms of difficulty because you can outrun the enemy ship fairly easily. However, if it ever gets you cornered, you're in big trouble. Additionally, if you run across some slightly less aggressive but much faster squids while trying to evade the enemy ship, you'll be in for even more trouble!

Construction Cue

A nifty feature that many games employ is to gradually increase the speed and aggression of bad guys as the game goes on. This increase in difficulty can be tied to levels in a game or maybe the score. In the case of High Seas, you might increase the speed of the enemy ship and the aggression of the squids as the number of rescued pirates increases; eventually, even a very good player will succumb to the increased difficulty. This is a good way to prevent a game from getting boring after a player starts to master it.

Summary

If I didn't make the point already, please understand that artificial intelligence is a topic that could span several books and still just scratch the surface. My goal in this chapter was to present you with the basics of AI as it applies to mobile action games. You learned about the three fundamental types of game AI (roaming, behavioral, and strategic), along with how they are used in typical gaming scenarios. As a game programmer with at least a passing interest in AI, your AI knowledge will likely grow a great deal as you encounter situations in which you can apply AI techniques.

After you get comfortable with implementing the basics, you can move on to more advanced AI solutions based on prior experience and research on the web. I hope this chapter at least provided you with a roadmap to begin your journey into the world of the computer mind.

This chapter marks the end of this part of the book. The next part tackles perhaps the most interesting and largely untapped potential of mobile games: networking. You learn how mobile phone networking works, and also develop a complete networked mobile game.

Extreme Game Makeover

By simply changing the graphics, you can turn the High Seas 2 example game into an entirely different game. For example, you could change all the background graphics to a desert theme where sand replaces water and desert mountains replace the islands. Each sprite in the game then must change to reflect a desert theme instead of a sea theme. For example, you might change the player's ship to a covered wagon that is traveling across the desert to simulate the wagon trains that traveled in America's early westward expansion. If you go with this theme, you could change the pirates to lost travelers who need help. The squids could become renegade outlaws, the large enemy pirate ship could be an entire gang of outlaws, the mines could be dynamite booby traps set by the outlaws, and the barrels could be boxes of supplies left by other travelers. And finally, you could add an entirely new bad guy in the form of a Thunderbird sprite, which is an enormous bird rumored to have terrorized the American West.

Following are the steps required to change the High Seas 2 example to a Western theme:

1. Replace all the game's graphics with Western desert–themed artwork instead of pirate and sea artwork.

2. If desired, redesign the layer maps to give the layout of the game a different feel.

3. Change the dynamite (mine) and supply box (barrel) sprites to use the `Sprite` class instead of the `DriftSprite` class because they no longer need to move (drift).

4. Add a new Thunderbird sprite that uses the `ChaseSprite` class. Make sure that the barrier layer is set to `null` for this sprite so that it can fly around at will without colliding with any layers.

Strangely enough, these changes are all that are required to completely make over the High Seas 2 game. Granted, there is a lot of graphic work to be done in changing the artwork, but it's surprising how little coding is required to make such a dramatic change to the game.

PART IV

Taking Advantage of the Wireless Network

CHAPTER 14

Mobile Game Networking Essentials

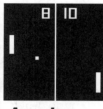

Arcade Archive

Yet another member of the illustrious class of 1982, Pole Position is one of the earliest racing games to gain widespread popularity. Although the game was developed by Namco, it was licensed by Atari for its American release. The game was manufactured in both stand-up and sit-down versions, with the sit-down version featuring separate gas and brake pedals; the stand-up version relies solely on a gas pedal. In what turned out to be an enormous licensing mistake, Bally/Midway chose the game Mappy over Pole Position when negotiating with Namco. Atari settled for what was left, Pole Position, and ended up with the hit game for 1983 and an enduring arcade classic.

In Chapter 13, "Teaching Games to Think," you learned the bare essentials of what it takes to enable a computer opponent to present a challenge to a human player. Although AI is very important and has countless uses in games, it's hard to discount the human factor in multiplayer games. This chapter focuses on mobile multiplayer games and why they are important in today's gaming landscape. Considering that mobile phones are express-ly designed as peer-to-peer communication devices, you have a great envi-ronment for mobile multiplayer games. Wireless network games bring with them their own unique set of problems and challenges that must be dealt with at the design level. This chapter exposes many of these problems and discusses various techniques for solving them. By the end of the chapter, you'll be ready to construct a mobile multiplayer game with J2ME.

In this chapter, you'll learn

▶ About the raw appeal of mobile multiplayer games

▶ About the fundamental types of mobile multiplayer games

▶ About wireless network game problems and solutions

- ► How to use the MIDP API to carry out wireless network communications
- ► How to build an example program that allows you to communicate wirelessly via Morse code

Multiplayer Game Basics

If you've been fortunate enough to play a multiplayer network game with your friends, you already know how much fun it can be. In many ways, outwitting a real person is much more fun than competing against a computer player. The reality of going head-to-head with another person can change the whole perspective of a game. I have yet to see a single-player game that evokes the same level of emotion and excitement as is generated from the human factor in multiplayer games.

There are endless possibilities for multiplayer games involving both cooperation and competition among human players. Regardless of the scenario, when real people are involved, a certain synthesis of ideas and reactions takes place that just isn't possible with computer players. It's then up to game designers like you and me to chart the course and dream up new ways for people to interact with each other through games. Now consider the uniqueness of being able to play a multiplayer game on a mobile phone over a wireless network connection from anywhere. This is what many of us have been waiting for in the "wireless revolution" we've been hearing so much about for the past few years.

Before you get into the design strategies for network games, it's important to understand the fundamental types of network games. The communication design can be affected dramatically by the way that game play progresses, which is determined by the type of game. Mobile network games can be generally broken down into two types: turn-based and event-based. Most games should easily fall into one of these two categories.

Turn-Based Games

Turn-based games are games in which each action in the game is based on a player's turn. The classic checkers, chess, and Connect 4 games are good examples of turn-based games because you are allowed to make a move only when it is your turn. Sure, you are free to think about your move during the other player's turn, but in the context of the game you can take action only during your turn.

Most turn-based games are board games or card games, or simple games played on paper such as Tic-Tac-Toe. Although they have a much slower pace than action games, turn-based games are very popular and well suited for networking.

Knowing that turn-based games revolve around whose turn it is, the network communication design is greatly simplified. Only one player can interact with the game at a time. Even though multiple players are technically playing the game, only one player is allowed to make a move at a time. The other players must wait their turns before they can do anything. In this way, the game can be designed so that all the players are in a wait state until it becomes their turn. In a two-player game such as Connect 4, the turns just move back and forth between the players.

Event-Based Games

Event-based games are games that are dictated by input events that can occur at any time. Event-based games are much more open-ended than turn-based games. In an event-based game, any player can interact with the game at any time, resulting in an input event. The flow of the game is dictated by the input events rather than turns. As a matter of fact, there is no concept of a "turn" in an event-based game. Event-based games include basically all games that don't revolve around turns; examples range from first-person shoot-em-ups such as the popular Halo and Doom series to strategy simulators such as Age of Empires. In the network modes of these games, any player can act independently of any other players, generating anywhere from no events to a massive flood of events.

If you haven't suspected, the communication design for event-based games is much more complex and difficult to implement than that for turn-based games. More importantly, event-based game communication typically requires a much wider bandwidth, because more information is usually being transmitted. It's probably safe to say that each different event-based game you create will have a unique solution because there are so many trade-offs to be made in regard to determining the best way to design the network communication logic. In a game such as Halo 2 or Doom 3, think about how many things are going on—and even more important, notice how quickly things are happening. Any change in the game from one player's perspective must be communicated to all the other players in some form.

Because bandwidth is a big consideration in event-based games, it is currently very challenging to develop event-based games on mobile phones. As mobile network speeds increase, this challenge will diminish, but developing efficient networking code is widely considered one of the most challenging aspects of game development, and even more so for mobile games.

Gamer's Garage

An event-based game never "allows" the players to do anything, as in turn-based games. The game just sits back and waits for the players to generate input events. Players can generate these events as often or as seldom as they want, fully independent of the other players. This is what enables you to patiently wait behind a corner while another player runs by haphazardly at full speed. Some people never learn!

Network Game Problems and Solutions

Now that you know which type of network games you are dealing with, let's look at some of the common problems you will encounter in a mobile network game design. The overriding concern to be dealt with in designing network games is maintaining synchronization. Synchronization refers to how multiple game instances running on different phones maintain the same game state information. Remember that each player is running a separate instance of the game, but the overall goal is to make each of these different instances function logically as one game. All the internal data structures modeling the game's state should match exactly on each player's system.

You can best understand this concept by looking at an example of what can happen when synchronization is lost. Suppose that two players are playing a network adventure game similar to one of the games in the popular Diablo series. As they are walking along together, they run across a demon. Player 1 is a little more assertive and starts fighting the demon. Player 2 is low on energy and decides to just sit in the shade and watch. When Player 1 finishes off the demon, Player 2 somehow must be notified, and not just as a matter of convenience; any change in the game that potentially can affect other players must be communicated to them.

Another common problem in regard to synchronization involves using random values in games. It is fairly common for games to place some objects randomly when a game starts, such as treasure or even monsters. Sometimes games use random events just to make things vary a little from game to game. In network games this creates big problems unless each game instance uses the exact same random values as all the other instances. It would totally blow the synchronization for each game to have things going on randomly with respect to each instance. The point here is that many seemingly insignificant things, such as generating random numbers, can cause major headaches in a network game environment.

Now that you understand the problems, let's move on to some solutions. There are many different approaches to designing network game communications, and they all must somehow address the problem of keeping each player's instance of the game synchronized with all others. You're going to focus on two basic types of network game synchronization strategies: state synchronization and input synchronization.

State Synchronization

State synchronization is a communication method by which each game instance communicates its current state to the other instances. The state synchronization method is very robust because there is no chance for information loss; everything regarding the current state of the game is sent to the other instances. In a two-player space battle game, for example, the position and speed of all the planets, asteroids, ships, and bullets would be sent as the current state of the game.

> Because of limited bandwidth on mobile phones, state synchronization represents the biggest challenge to developing networked mobile action games.

Gamer's Garage

Sounds good so far. But what about a more complex game, such as a role-playing adventure game with entire virtual worlds with which the players constantly are interacting? Sending the state of the entire game starts looking a little more difficult because of the vast amounts of information required to model the game state. And don't forget about the bandwidth limitation you learned about earlier, which keeps you from being able to send loads of information between mobile phones. Knowing this, it's easy to see that state synchronization is a fairly messy network communication solution. Although state synchronization is functionally a very solid network solution, technically it's not always feasible.

Input Synchronization

Input synchronization is a communication method in which each game communicates the input events of its player to the other game instances. Using input synchronization, each time a player generates input events, such as pressing keys, the game broadcasts these events to the other games. If you think about the space battle game example from before, rather than send the state of all the objects, the game just sends the key input events generated by the player. Each game then handles each remote (virtual) input from the other games in a similar manner as it handles its own local player's input.

There has to be a catch, right? Of course there's a catch! Input synchronization works fine as long as all the changes in the game are dictated solely by the players' inputs. Practically speaking, this rarely is the case except in very simple games. There are usually random effects in a game, such as placement of background objects. These random effects wreak havoc on games relying on input synchronization because they aren't affected by player input and therefore are never communicated between games.

If you happen to have a game in which the entire play flow is dictated by player input, input synchronization is for you. Otherwise, you'll have to come up with another solution. Can you think of any games that are dictated entirely by user input? Give up? It ends up that most turn-based games are driven completely by user input. So you usually can implement network support for turn-based games by using input synchronization.

Gamer's Garage

> The Connect 4 game that you design and develop in the next chapter is a good example of a turn-based game that relies solely on input synchronization.

A Hybrid Solution

Now that I've painted a pretty bleak picture of network game design, I'll let you in on a practical reality in mobile network game design: You usually will have to use some combination of the two methods mentioned. This hybrid solution would include elements of both state and input synchronization. Using the space battle game example one more time, you could send the user inputs back and forth using input synchronization, and then use state synchronization to send random events such as initial meteor positions. You still don't necessarily need to transmit the entire state of the game, just the aspects of the game state that can't be figured out by each instance on its own. In other words, random events need to be transmitted to each game instance.

If you run across a gaming scenario that doesn't fit well within any of these approaches, you might figure out a communication technique of your own to add to or replace one of these. Network gaming is a unique area of game programming that leaves room for very few general techniques. You usually have to come up with hybrid solutions that draw on what you've learned, combined with new ideas you dream up along the way.

Communicating over a Network with Sockets

Even though there are many network options, MIDP network game programming uses a particular type of network communication known as a *socket*. A socket is a software abstraction for an input or output medium of communication. More specifically, a socket is a communication channel enabling you to transfer data through a certain port. The MIDP API provides socket classes to make programming with sockets much easier. MIDP sockets are broken down into two types: stream sockets and datagram sockets.

Stream Sockets

A stream socket, or connected socket, is a socket over which data can be transmitted continuously. By continuously, I don't necessarily mean that data is being sent all the time, but that the socket itself is active and ready for communication all the time. Think of a stream socket as a dedicated network connection, in which a communication medium is always available for use. The benefit of using a stream socket is that information can be sent with less worry about when it will arrive at its destination. Because the communication link is always "live," data is generally transmitted immediately after you send it.

Datagram Sockets

The other type of socket supported by Java is the datagram socket. Unlike stream sockets, in which the communication is akin to a live network, a datagram socket is more akin to a dial-up Internet connection, in which the communication link isn't continuously active. A datagram socket is a socket over which data is bundled into packets and sent without requiring a "live" connection to the destination computer.

Because of the nature of the communication medium involved, datagram sockets aren't guaranteed to transmit information at a particular time, or even in any particular order. The reason datagram sockets perform this way is that they don't require an actual connection to another computer; the address of the target computer is just bundled with the information being sent. This bundle is then sent out over the network, leaving the sender to hope for the best. On the receiving end, the bundles of information can be received in any order and at any time. For this reason, datagrams also include a sequence number that specifies to which piece of the puzzle each bundle corresponds. The receiver waits to receive the entire sequence, and then puts them back together to form a complete information transfer.

You might be thinking that datagram sockets are less than ideal for network game programming, and in some cases this is true. However, not all games require the "live" connection afforded by stream sockets. And in the specific case of mobile games, datagram sockets are often a more realistic networking option because of the limited bandwidth of mobile phone networks.

This book focuses solely on using datagram sockets for network communication in mobile games. Mobile network game programming could easily take up an entire book of its own, so I opted to focus on the simplest form of mobile game networking, which uses datagrams.

Gamer's
Garage

Network Programming and J2ME

Network programming in MIDlets is carried out using a portion of the MIDP API known as the *Generic Connection Framework*, or GCF. The purpose of the GCF is to provide a level of abstraction for networking services, which helps in enabling different mobile devices to support only network protocols specific to their needs.

Although it is structured somewhat differently, the GCF is implemented as a functional subset of the J2SE API. The GCF describes one fundamental class named Connector that is used to establish all MIDlet network connections. Specific types of network connections are modeled by interfaces that are obtained through the Connector class. The Connector class and the connection interfaces are located in the javax.microedition.io package. Descriptions of a few of these interfaces follow:

▶ ContentConnection—A stream connection that provides access to web data

▶ DatagramConnection—A datagram connection suitable for handling packet-oriented communication

▶ StreamConnection—A two-way connection to a communications device

From the perspective of mobile game programming, you will typically use either the DatagramConnection or StreamConnection interfaces as the network connection types for games. You always use the Connector class to establish network connections, regardless of the connection type. All the methods in the Connector class are static, with the most important one being the open() method. The most commonly used version of the open() method follows:

```
static Connection open(String name) throws IOException
```

The parameter to this method is the connection string, which determines the type of connection being made. The connection string describes the connection by adhering to the following general form:

```
Scheme:Target[;Parameters]
```

The *Scheme* parameter is the name of the network protocol, such as http, ftp, or datagram. The *Target* parameter is typically the name of the network address for the connection, but can vary according to the specific protocol. The last parameter, *Parameters*, is a list of parameters associated with the connection. Some examples of different types of connection strings for various network connections are

▶ **HTTP**—"http://www.stalefishlabs.com/"

▶ **Socket**—"socket://www.stalefishlabs:1800"

- ▶ **Datagram**—`"datagram://:9000"`
- ▶ **File**—`"file:/Stats.txt"`

Keep in mind that although these examples are accurate in terms of describing possible connection strings, the only one of them that has guaranteed support in a given MIDP implementation is the first one. The MIDP specification requires an implementation only to support HTTP connections. If you happen to know that a given MIDP implementation supports a particular type of connection, then you can certainly take advantage of it. Otherwise, you will need to stick with HTTP connections, which admittedly aren't too useful in networked mobile games.

The open() method returns an object of type Connection, which is the base interface for all the other connection interfaces. To use a certain kind of connection interface, you cast the Connection interface returned by open() to the appropriate type. The following line of code illustrates how to use the DatagramConnection interface to open a datagram connection:

```
DatagramConnection dc = (DatagramConnection)Connector.open("datagram://:5555");
```

The number 5555 in this example code is the network port used by the datagram connection. This port number can be any value over 1024, but it's very important for the client and server code in a networked MIDlet to communicate through the same port number.

Construction Cue

The next few sections dig a little deeper into datagram connections, and how to send and receive data through them.

Creating Datagram Packets

Using datagrams to communicate over a mobile phone network involves packaging game data into discrete bundles of information called packets. When mobile games shuttle information back and forth through a datagram connection, they are actually sending and receiving packets. Datagram packets are designed to store an array of bytes, so any data that you package into a packet must be converted into a byte array. In fact, when you create a Datagram object you must specify how many bytes of data it is capable of holding. Following is an example of creating a Datagram object large enough to hold 64 bytes of data:

```
Datagram dg = dc.newDatagram(64);
```

What you may find interesting in this code is that you create a Datagram object by calling the newDatagram() method on a datagram connection. The parameter to the newDatagram() method is the size of the datagram, in bytes. This approach to creating a datagram packet is ideal for receiving game data sent over a network connection that gets stored in the datagram.

Another approach to creating a datagram packet is to create and fill the datagram with data in one step. This approach is better suited to sending game data, in which case you already have data that you want to place in the datagram. Many games use string messages to communicate, in which case each string must be first converted into a byte array before it is stored in a datagram, as the following code shows:

```
String message = "GameOver";
byte[] bytes = message.getBytes();
```

In this code, the string "GameOver" is converted into a byte array that is stored in the variable bytes. A different version of the newDatagram() method is then used to create a datagram packet containing the "GameOver" message:

```
Datagram dg = dc.newDatagram(bytes, bytes.length);
```

In this code, the byte array of game data is passed as the first parameter to the newDatagram() method, whereas the length of the data is passed as the second parameter. In some situations (a packet being sent from a server to a client), you need to use yet another version of the newDatagram() method, like this:

```
Datagram dg = dc.newDatagram(bytes, bytes.length, address);
```

This method includes a third parameter that contains the address of the target to receive the datagram packet. An address is required only when a server is communicating to a client, in which case the address can be obtained from a client datagram with a call to the getAddress() method on a datagram received from the client.

Gamer's Garage

You see a more complete example of creating datagrams for both the client and server side of a networked MIDlet later in the chapter when you build the Lighthouse example MIDlet.

Sending Datagram Packets

The DatagramConnection interface provides a single method for sending datagram packets. I'm referring to the send() method, which is extremely easy to use. In fact, a single line of code is all that is required to send a datagram packet:

```
dc.send(dg);
```

To help put this line of code in context, check out the following code, which shows how a Datagram object is created and sent over a datagram connection:

```
// Convert the string message to bytes
byte[] bytes = message.getBytes();

// Send the message
Datagram dg = null;
dg = dc.newDatagram(bytes, bytes.length);
dc.send(dg);
```

You've already seen all this code in pieces, but here you see it assembled together. This is really all that is required to package up game data into a datagram packet and send it over a wireless network connection.

Receiving Datagram Packets

Receiving a datagram packet is somewhat similar to sending a packet in that a single method of the DatagramConnection interface is used. The method is called receive(), and it accepts a single Datagram object as its only parameter, just like send(). Following is an example of calling the receive() method to receive a datagram packet:

```
dc.receive(dg);
```

Of course, the datagram packet in this case needs to have already been created and sized large enough to hold the incoming data. Following is a more complete example of creating a datagram packet and then using it to receive incoming game data:

```
// Try to receive a datagram packet
Datagram dg = dc.newDatagram(64);
dc.receive(dg);

// Make sure the datagram actually contains data
if (dg.getLength() > 0) {
  String data = new String(dg.getData(), 0, dg.getLength());
}
```

It's important to notice in this code that the resulting datagram length is checked via a call to getLength(). This check is important because it lets you know whether any data was actually received in the datagram packet. If there is indeed data, it is converted back to a string and stored in the data variable. It is then up to game-specific code to respond to the received data.

Building the Lighthouse Example

Many years before mobile phones and radio transmitters and receivers, a more primitive form of communication was used by seafarers. I'm talking about lighthouses, which are typically perched on the highest point of a shore, and include a light near the top that helps provide guidance and communication to ships at sea. Although today's lighthouses use modern communications technology such as radios, they still rely on a light for simple visual communication. Because mobile phones are themselves a modern form of personal communication, I thought a lighthouse theme might serve as a good example for a network MIDlet.

One way that lighthouses have been used for communications is through Morse code, which is a simple but highly effective method of communicating words and characters with sequences of "dots" and "dashes." A dot is a short visual or audible signal such as the flash of a light or a metallic click. A dash is defined as approximately three times the length of a dot, which equates to a light flash of longer duration or a longer resonating sound. You assemble sequences of dots and dashes to spell out words and sentences. Following are the alphanumeric codes that make up the International Morse Code standard:

A—. -	J—. - - -	S—. . .	1—. - - - -
B—- . . .	K—- . -	T—-	2—. . - - -
C—- . - .	L—. - . .	U—. . -	3—. . . - -
D—- . .	M—- -	V—. . . -	4—. . . . -
E—.	N—- .	W—. - -	5—. . . . .
F—. . - .	O—- .	X—- . . -	6—- . . . .
G—- - .	P—. - - .	Y—- . - -	7—- - . . .
H—. . . .	Q—- - . -	Z—- - . .	8—- - - . .
I—. .	R—. - .	0—- - - - -	9—- - - - .

Using these codes, you can assemble words and sentences; each letter has a brief pause between it and the next letter, whereas each sentence has a longer pause. Following is an example of the word "hello" coded in Morse:

. . . . . . - . . . - . . . - -

A popular Morse code "word" is SOS, which many people mistakenly believe stands for "Save Our Souls." SOS actually has no meaning as an acronym but it does serve as a very important distress signal. However, instead of being coded in Morse as the separated letters S O S, the letters are coded together with no pauses: . . . - - - . . . . ..

Getting back to the Lighthouse example MIDlet, the idea is to simulate a lighthouse on a mobile phone, and use Morse code to communicate with another mobile phone by flashing the lighthouse light. It works like this: Each phone displays an image of a lighthouse. You are looking at the other person's lighthouse, while that person is looking at your lighthouse. You use the left and right directional keys to signal dots and dashes over a wireless network connection, after which the lighthouse seen by the other person resolves the dots and dashes into light flashes.

An even simpler version of the Lighthouse MIDlet could rely on a single key to send both dots and dashes, in which case it would be up to the user to time them appropriately. This would more closely mimic a true telegraph, although it would make the example a bit less interesting.

The Lighthouse MIDlet is basically a high-tech simulation of a low-tech form of communication. From a mobile game programming perspective, it is very important in that it demonstrates how to establish a client-server connection between peer devices, and then send messages back and forth between them.

Designing the Client and Server

The Lighthouse MIDlet takes advantage of a client-server relationship between two mobile phones. The actual connection between the MIDlets is a datagram connection, which means that the messages sent between the phones are packaged as datagram packets. The client-server aspect of the Lighthouse design primarily has to do with which phone initiates the network connection. The following steps outline what takes place between client and server phones in the Lighthouse MIDlet:

1. The server phone opens a datagram connection and waits for the client.

2. The client phone opens a datagram connection with the server.

3. With a connection established, the client and server phones send and receive messages.

4. The client and server phones terminate the connection.

What is interesting about this client-server design is that one MIDlet must serve as both the client and the server, depending on the context. To handle this dual functionality, the user is allowed to declare whether it is the client or the server when the MIDlet first starts. From then on the MIDlet then operates in either client mode or server mode. Given that there are two operating modes for the Lighthouse MIDlet, it stands to reason that the network code for the MIDlet is divided between server code and client code.

Gamer's Garage

From a general game networking perspective, the Lighthouse MIDlet is more of a peer-to-peer example than a true client-server example. In true client-server games, there is usually a separate server program that runs on a network server. The MIDlets are then purely clients that connect to the server; the server manages the game flow between clients. The Lighthouse MIDlet is client-server only in a sense that one of the peers (the server) initially waits for a connection from the other peer (the client).

Writing the Program Code

The Lighthouse MIDlet can operate in two distinct modes: client mode or server mode. The mode is established by a user interface that appears when the MIDlet first starts, as you see a bit later in this section. Before you get to that, however, it's important to cover the network code that allows the MIDlet to send and receive Morse code messages over a wireless network connection.

The Lighthouse Client and Server

The client-server code in the Lighthouse MIDlet is a little easier to understand if you start with the server. The server functionality is contained within the LHServer class, which is responsible for waiting for a client datagram connection, and then responding with an acknowledgment. The LHServer class implements the Runnable interface, which means that it runs in its own thread:

```
public class LHServer implements Runnable {
```

This is important because it enables the thread to constantly monitor the network and receive messages from the client. In addition to communicating with the client over the network, the server must also be able to share information with the MIDlet's canvas, which displays the lighthouse visuals.

The member variables for the LHServer class start to reveal some of its functionality:

```
private LHCanvas           canvas;
private DatagramConnection dc;
private String             address;
private boolean            connected;
```

The canvas is stored as a member variable (canvas) of the LHServer class. The datagram connection is stored in the dc variable, which is a DatagramConnection object. The address variable keeps track of the client's address so that datagram packets can be sent to the client. And finally, the connected variable keeps up with whether or not a connection has been established with the client.

The constructor for the LHServer class requires an LHCanvas object as its only parameter, and then goes about initializing a couple of the member variables, as the following code shows:

```
public LHServer(LHCanvas c) {
  canvas = c;
  connected = false;
}
```

The start() method is also very simple, and takes care of getting the thread up and running:

```
public void start() {
  Thread t = new Thread(this);
  t.start();
}
```

The run() method is where the real work in the server takes place, as is evident in Listing 14.1.

LISTING 14.1   The run() Method in the LHServer Class Responds to Messages Received from the Client

```
public void run() {
  try {
    // Connect to the peer client
    canvas.setStatus("Waiting for peer client...");
    dc = null;
    while (dc == null)
      dc = (DatagramConnection)Connector.open("datagram://:5555");


    while (true) {
        // Try to receive a datagram packet
        Datagram dg = dc.newDatagram(32);
        dc.receive(dg);
        address = dg.getAddress();
```

The initial server status message indicates that the server is waiting on the client.

This port number must match the port number of the client connection.

The size of the datagram (32 bytes) must be large enough to hold the largest message, which isn't very large for the Lighthouse network data.

LISTING 14.1   Continued

```
                   // Make sure the datagram actually contains data
                   if (dg.getLength() > 0) {
                     String data = new String(dg.getData(), 0, dg.getLength());
                     if (data.equals("Client")) {
                       // Notify the user of a successful network connection
                       canvas.setStatus("Connected to peer client.");
                       connected = true;

                       // Try to reply with a connection message
                       sendMessage("Server");
                     }
                     else {
                       // Send along the network data
                       canvas.receiveMessage(data);
                     }
                   }
                 }
               }
               catch (IOException ioe) {
                 System.err.println("The network port is already taken.");
               }
               catch (Exception e) {
               }
            }
```

Respond to a client connection by setting the connected variable and replying to the client.

The message must contain Morse code data, so pass it along to the canvas for processing.

The run() begins by calling the setStatus() method in the LHCanvas class to set the status line of the canvas to "Waiting for peer client...". This is to let the user know that the server is waiting for the client to connect. After setting the status of the canvas, the run() method gets down to business by creating a datagram connection. The port number (5555) used for the connection is somewhat arbitrary; all that really matters is that the client and server are designed to use the same port number. It is also important that you specify datagram as the type of the connection.

After the datagram connection is established, the run() method enters an infinite loop that repeatedly tries to receive datagram packets from the client. A Datagram object is first created and then used as the storage medium for receiving a datagram. The datagram's address is stored so that the server can respond to the client if necessary.

If the datagram actually contains data, the actual bytes contained within the packet are converted into a string. The string is then checked to see whether it equals Client, which is a special message that indicates the client has connected with the server. If a successful connection has been made, the status is changed and a message is sent back to the client with the string Server, which lets the client know that the connection has successfully been made.

The datagram packet contains the string `Client` only when the connection is first being established. From then on, the packet contains a string that contains either the text `Dot` or `Dash`, depending on the message being sent by the client phone. This message is passed along to the `LHCanvas` object for processing via a call to the `receiveMessage()` method. You learn how this message works a little later when you dig into the Lighthouse canvas code.

The remaining method in the `LHServer` class is `sendMessage()` (see Listing 14.2), which handles sending a string message to the client.

LISTING 14.2 The `sendMessage()` Method in the `LHServer` Class Sends a String Message as a Datagram Packet to the Client

```
public void sendMessage(String message) {
  // Send the message
  try {
    // Convert the string message to bytes
    byte[] bytes = message.getBytes();

    // Send the message
    Datagram dg = null;
    dg = dc.newDatagram(bytes, bytes.length, address);
    dc.send(dg);
  }
  catch (Exception e) {
  }
}
```

The string message must first be converted to bytes.

Package the message as a datagram packet, and then send it to the client.

This code converts a string message into an array of bytes, and then sends it to the client as a datagram packet. Notice that the address that was stored away earlier in the `run()` method is now used to construct the `Datagram` object for sending the message. This address is required to send a datagram packet to a client. However, it is not required for sending data from the client to the server, as you see next.

The other side of the Lighthouse network code is the `LHClient` class, which is very similar to the `LHServer` class. Like `LHServer`, the `LHClient` class also implements the `Runnable` interface so that it runs in its own thread:

```
public class LHClient implements Runnable {
```

Following are the member variables used by the `LHClient` class:

```
private LHCanvas            canvas;
private DatagramConnection  dc;
private boolean             connected;
```

These member variables should be familiar to you because they are the same as those used in the LHServer class, minus the address variable. Following is the LHClient() constructor, which initializes a couple of the variables:

```
public LHClient(LHCanvas c) {
  canvas = c;
  connected = false;
}
```

The start() method in LHClient is identical to the one in LHServer, so let's move on to the client run() method. Listing 14.3 contains the code for the LHClient run() method.

LISTING 14.3 The run() Method in the LHClient Class Responds to Messages Received from the Server

```
public void run() {
  try {
    // Connect to the peer server
    canvas.setStatus("Connecting to peer server...");
    dc = null;
    while (dc == null)
      dc = (DatagramConnection)Connector.open("datagram://localhost:5555");

    while (true) {
      // Try to send a connection message
      if (!connected)
        sendMessage("Client");

      // Try to receive a datagram packet
      Datagram dg = dc.newDatagram(32);
      dc.receive(dg);

      // Make sure the datagram actually contains data
      if (dg.getLength() > 0) {
        String data = new String(dg.getData(), 0, dg.getLength());
        if (data.equals("Server")) {
          // Notify the user of a successful network connection
          canvas.setStatus("Connected to peer server.");
          connected = true;
        }
        else {
          // Send along the network data
          canvas.receiveMessage(data);
        }
      }
    }
  }
}
```

The client initially displays a status message indicating that the client is trying to connect to the server.

This port number must match the port number of the server connection.

If there is no connection, send a Client message to establish a connection with the server.

Respond to a server connection by setting the connected variable.

The message must contain Morse code data, so pass it along to the game canvas for processing.

LISTING 14.3   Continued

```
catch (ConnectionNotFoundException cnfe) {
  System.err.println("The network server is unavailable.");
}
catch (IOException ioe) {
}
}
```

The client run() method is very similar to the server version. In fact, the only significant differences are the status messages and the absence of the address variable when datagram packets are sent. Additionally, accounting for the URL is slightly different, this being the client end of the connection. Again, it's important to mention that the port number (5555) must match for the client and server.

The LHClient class also has a sendMessage() method that is very similar to the server version. Listing 14.4 contains the code for the client version.

LISTING 14.4   The sendMessage() Method in the LHClient Class Sends a String Message as a Datagram Packet to the Server

```
public void sendMessage(String message) {
  // Send the message
  try {
    // Convert the string message to bytes
    byte[] bytes = message.getBytes();

    // Send the message
    Datagram dg = null;
    dg = dc.newDatagram(bytes, bytes.length);      ⎤── Package the mes-
    dc.send(dg);                                    ⎦   sage as a datagram
  }                                                      packet, and then
  catch (Exception e) {                                  send it to the
  }                                                      server.
}
```

The only difference between the sendMessage() methods in the server and the client is that the client version doesn't use an address when sending a datagram packet to the server. This is a subtle but important difference.

The Lighthouse Canvas

With the server and client classes nailed down for the Lighthouse MIDlet, let's move on to the canvas class for the MIDlet. This class is named LHCanvas, and its job is to display the status line and appropriate lighthouse image based on network messages passed to the canvas. The LHCanvas class starts out with a few member variables:

```
private Image[]  background = new Image[2];
private LHClient client;
private LHServer server;
private boolean  isServer;
private String   status = "";
private int      mode;  // 0 = none, 1 = dot, 2 = dash
private int      morseTimer;
```

This variable reflects whether or not this instance of the MIDlet is the server.

The background variable contains the two lighthouse images: one showing the lighthouse dark and another showing it lit up. The client and server variables store LHClient and LHServer objects, respectively, and are responsible for carrying out the networking in the MIDlet. The isServer variable is very important because it knows under what network mode the MIDlet is operating at any given moment. More specifically, the isServer variable determines whether the MIDlet is acting as the server or client.

The status text is stored in the status member variable. The mode variable is used to control the display of the lighthouse images, as well as to coordinate their timing. Keep in mind that a dot in Morse code is one-third the duration of a dash, so the MIDlet must establish a timer to display the lit lighthouse image longer for dashes than for dots. The mode variable in conjunction with morseTimer is responsible for this timing.

The canvas member variables first enter the picture significantly in the start() method, which is shown in Listing 14.5.

LISTING 14.5 The start() Method in the LHCanvas Class Starts the Client/Server Network Service

```
public void start() {
  // Set the canvas as the current screen
  display.setCurrent(this);

  // Initialize the background images
  try {
    background[0] = Image.createImage("/LighthouseOff.png");
    background[1] = Image.createImage("/LighthouseOn.png");
  }
  catch (IOException e) {
    System.err.println("Failed loading images!");
  }

  // Initialize the mode and Morse code timer
  mode = 0;
  morseTimer = 0;
```

LISTING 14.5 Continued

```
// Start the networking service
if (isServer) {
  server = new LHServer(this);
  server.start();
}
else {
  client = new LHClient(this);
  client.start();
}

// Start the animation thread
sleeping = false;
Thread t = new Thread(this);
t.start();
}
```

From this point on, the MIDlet is permanently in server or client mode.

After initializing the background images, the start() method takes care of initializing the mode and mode timer. More specifically, the mode variable is set to 0, which corresponds to a dark lighthouse (no Morse code message), whereas the morseTimer is zeroed out even though it isn't used when no Morse code message is being displayed.

The most important code in the start() method takes care of creating a network server or client. An instance of the LHServer or LHClient class is created based on the value of the isServer variable. After a network object is created, the start() method is called on the object to get the network thread started.

The start() method gets the Lighthouse MIDlet initialized, but the update() method steps in to handle user input and allow you to send Morse code messages via the left and right directional keys. Listing 14.6 shows the code for the update() method.

LISTING 14.6 The update() Method in the LHCanvas Class Sends Morse Code Messages in Response to Key Presses

```
private void update() {
  // Process user input to issue dots and dashes
  int keyState = getKeyStates();
  if ((keyState & LEFT_PRESSED) != 0) {
    if (isServer)
      server.sendMessage("Dot");
    else
      client.sendMessage("Dot");
    status = "Dot";
  }
  else if ((keyState & RIGHT_PRESSED) != 0) {
```

Communicate the dot to the other phone.

LISTING 14.6   Continued

Communicate the dash to the other phone.

```
if (isServer)
    server.sendMessage("Dash");
else
    client.sendMessage("Dash");
status = "Dash";
}

// Update the Morse code timer
if (mode != 0) {
    morseTimer++;

    // Timeout a dot
    if (mode == 1 && morseTimer > 3)
        mode = 0;
    // Timeout a dash
    else if (mode == 2 && morseTimer > 9)
        mode = 0;
}
}
```

The update() method checks the status of the keys and responds specifically to the left and right directional keys. The left key corresponds to sending a Morse code dot, whereas the right key corresponds to a dash. To send a Morse code character in response to a key press, the update() method simply calls the sendMessage() method on the appropriate network object (client or server). The status line is then updated to reflect the message that was sent.

After checking the keys and sending a Morse code message, if necessary, the update() method moves on to updating the mode based on the Morse code timer. If the mode variable is set to 1, then a Morse code dot is displayed and the timer counts to 3 before returning the lit lighthouse image to the unlit version. A mode value of 2 indicates that a dash is being displayed, which requires a longer count to 9. And finally, a mode value of 0 indicates that the unlit lighthouse image is being displayed, and the timer has no effect.

The draw() method is where the lighthouse images finally enter the picture in the Lighthouse MIDlet (see Listing 14.7).

LISTING 14.7 The draw() Method in the LHCanvas Class Draws the Appropriate Lighthouse Background Based on the Mode

```
private void draw(Graphics g) {
  // Draw the background based on the mode
  if (mode == 0)
    g.drawImage(background[0], 0, 0, Graphics.TOP | Graphics.LEFT);
  else
    g.drawImage(background[1], 0, 0, Graphics.TOP | Graphics.LEFT);

  // Draw the status message
  g.setColor(255, 255, 255); // white
  g.setFont(Font.getFont(Font.FACE_SYSTEM, Font.STYLE_BOLD, Font.SIZE_MEDIUM));
  g.drawString(status, getWidth() / 2, 5, Graphics.TOP | Graphics.HCENTER);

  // Flush the offscreen graphics buffer
  flushGraphics();
}
```

Draw the lit or unlit lighthouse image based on the mode.

The status message line is drawn near the top of the screen.

The draw() method begins by checking the value of the mode member variable, which determines whether the lit or unlit lighthouse image is displayed. A mode value of 0 results in the unlit lighthouse image being displayed, whereas any other value (1 or 2) results in the lit lighthouse being shown. The remaining code in the draw() method displays the status message along the top edge of the screen.

Speaking of the status message, it is set externally via the setStatus() method, whose code follows:

```
public void setStatus(String s) {
  // Set the status message
  status = s;
}
```

The last method in the LHCanvas class is the receiveMessage() method, which accepts a Morse code message from a network service and sets the mode of the canvas accordingly. Listing 14.8 contains the code for this method.

LISTING 14.8 The receiveMessage() Method in the LHCanvas Class Receives a Morse Code Message That Has Been Sent over the Network

```
public void receiveMessage(String message) {
  // Set the mode
  if (message.equals("Dash"))
    mode = 2;
  else if (message.equals("Dot"))
    mode = 1;
  else
    mode = 0;
```

Change the mode in response to receiving a Morse code message.

LISTING 14.8   Continued

```
// Reset the Morse code timer
morseTimer = 0;

// Clear the status message
status = "";
}
```

There's no need to display any status text upon receiving a Morse code message.

The parameter to the `receiveMessage()` method is a string containing the message being sent. This message is always one of the following values: Dot or Dash. In the latter case, the mode is set to 2, whereas the former results in a mode of 1. If for some reason the message isn't one of these two values, the mode is set to 0. The Morse code timer is then reset so that the timing of the dot or dash works properly.

The Lighthouse MIDlet

The last functional piece of code of interest in the Lighthouse MIDlet is the MIDlet class itself, which has some code that makes it unique as compared to other MIDlets you've seen throughout the book thus far. Listing 14.9 contains the code for the `LighthouseMIDlet` class.

LISTING 14.9   The `LighthouseMIDlet` Class Establishes a User Interface for Selecting Client or Server Mode When It First Starts

This Form object is used to create the peer type selection user interface.

Present the user with a choice group containing two options: Server and Client.

```
public class LighthouseMIDlet extends MIDlet implements CommandListener {
  private Form          initForm;
  private ChoiceGroup   choices;
  private LHCanvas      gameCanvas;

  public void startApp() {
    // Create the Init form
    initForm = new Form("Connect 4");

    // Add the peer choice group
    String[] peerNames = { "Server", "Client" };
    choices = new ChoiceGroup("Please select peer type:", Choice.EXCLUSIVE,
      peerNames, null);
    initForm.append(choices);

    // Add the Exit and Play commands
    Command exitCommand = new Command("Exit", Command.EXIT, 0);
    initForm.addCommand(exitCommand);
    Command playCommand = new Command("Play", Command.OK, 0);
    initForm.addCommand(playCommand);
    initForm.setCommandListener(this);
```

LISTING 14.9   Continued

```
    // Set the form as the current screen
    Display.getDisplay(this).setCurrent(initForm);
}

public void pauseApp() {}

public void destroyApp(boolean unconditional) {
  gameCanvas.stop();
}

public void commandAction(Command c, Displayable s) {
  if (c.getCommandType() == Command.EXIT) {
    destroyApp(true);
    notifyDestroyed();
  }
  else if (c.getCommandType() == Command.OK) {
    // Find out which type of peer connection is being used
    String name = choices.getString(choices.getSelectedIndex());

    // Create the game canvas
    if (gameCanvas == null) {
      gameCanvas = new LHCanvas(Display.getDisplay(this), name);
      Command exitCommand = new Command("Exit", Command.EXIT, 0);
      gameCanvas.addCommand(exitCommand);
      gameCanvas.setCommandListener(this);
    }

    // Start up the gameCanvas
    gameCanvas.start();
  }
}
}
```

When the Play command is executed, display the Lighthouse canvas and pass it the peer type (server or client).

The interesting thing about the LighthouseMIDlet class is that it provides a user interface in addition to the main canvas that allows you to select client or server mode. The MIDP Form class is used to construct this interface as a form. Forms allow you to use standard graphical user interface components such as buttons and choice groups. In the case of the Lighthouse MIDlet, a choice group with two choices ("Server" or "Client") is perfect for the input that needs to be obtained from the user.

The choice group is created as an object of type ChoiceGroup, which is initialized with the string array peerNames. The newly created choice group is appended to the form so that it becomes a part of the form. Two commands are then added to the form: Exit and Play. The Exit command allows you to exit the MIDlet rather than make a selection, whereas the Play command accepts the choice and allows the MIDlet to continue. The Play command is mapped to the Command.OK constant, which results in an LHCanvas object getting created. This is the main canvas that you just developed.

FIGURE 14.1
The Lighthouse MIDlet begins by prompting the user to select either client or server mode.

It's important to notice that the peer selection ("Server" or "Client") is passed as the second parameter into the LHCanvas class. This is how the canvas finds out whether it should operate in client or server mode, which ultimately sets the isServer variable in the LHCanvas object.

Testing the Finished Product

The Lighthouse example MIDlet is probably the trickiest example program you've tested thus far in the book simply because it requires either two mobile phones or two instances of the J2ME emulator. Although I certainly recommend testing with two real phones, the J2ME emulator provides a good way to test networked MIDlets side by side with virtual phones. To test the Lighthouse MIDlet, just run two instances of the MIDlet in the J2ME emulator. Make sure to select "Server" as the peer type in one of the MIDlets, and "Client" in the other. Figure 14.1 shows the peer type being selected in the server Lighthouse MIDlet.

FIGURE 14.2
The "server mode" Lighthouse MIDlet waits for a client connection.

After selecting server mode, the user is presented with a status message stating that the server is ready and waiting for a client connection (see Figure 14.2).

On the other side of the network equation, the client Lighthouse MIDlet is launched in client mode. When the connection is made between client and server, the status lines of both MIDlets change to reflect that a connection has been successfully established.

Figure 14.3 shows the client MIDlet after a successful network connection has been made.

With a network connection made, the users on both sides of the networked Lighthouse program can begin sending and receiving Morse code messages by pressing the left (dot) and right (dash) arrow keys. Figure 14.4 shows the client MIDlet upon sending a dot message via the left arrow key.

As the figure shows, the word "Dot" is displayed in the status line of the client MIDlet to indicate that the message was sent. On the server side, the dot message appears as a quick flash of the lighthouse light, as shown in Figure 14.5.

Morse code communication continues in this manner until the two parties finish their conversation. Although you will probably find it easier to just communicate with another person by talking on mobile phones, the Lighthouse example MIDlet provides an important demonstration of how an alternative form of communication can be carried out over a wireless network. More importantly, it lays the groundwork for carrying out mobile game–specific network communication, which is covered in detail in the next chapter.

FIGURE 14.3
The "client mode" Lighthouse MIDlet displays a successful connection in its status line.

FIGURE 14.4
The player on the client side of the Lighthouse MIDlet sends a Morse code dot.

FIGURE 14.5
The lighthouse on the server side of the Lighthouse MIDlet lights up briefly to show the dot message sent by the client.

Summary

This chapter broke away from the confines of programming for a single user and moved into the world of wireless network programming for mobile phones. You learned that the MIDP API makes network programming surprisingly easy by providing standard classes that hide most of the nastiness typically associated with network programming. You began the chapter with some multiplayer game and networking fundamentals, progressing onward to learn all about how the MIDP API makes it possible to carry out wireless network communication. The chapter finished up by guiding you through the creation of a MIDlet that uses mobile networking to allow two people to communicate via Morse code and flashing lighthouse images.

The next chapter continues with the wireless networking discussion by leading you through the design and development of a networked two-player mobile Connect 4 game.

Field Trip

The Lighthouse example in this chapter provides a great excuse for learning Morse code. Granted, you may never find yourself in a situation where Morse code is required, but it's not a bad form of communication to know how to use. If nothing else, I know I could've used Morse code in school to communicate with friends by tapping on our desks. Morse code benefits from being an extremely stealthy "language" because it enables people to communicate easily in complete silence with a discrete flashing light, or to tap a sound in situations where speech isn't an option. The point of all this is to encourage you to take some time and start learning Morse code. If nothing else, the Lighthouse MIDlet will be more fun to tinker with.

CHAPTER 15

Connect 4: A Classic Game Goes Wireless

Arcade Archive

I can still clearly remember the first time I saw Dragon's Lair in an arcade. Seeing an arcade game with "cartoon quality" graphics was nothing short of mind-blowing at the time. Dragon's Lair was created by Cinematronics and released in 1983 to much fanfare because of its incredible graphics and storyline. What gamers eventually learned is that Dragon's Lair was more of an animated choose-your-own-adventure game than a true video game; in fact, it is an animated laserdisc game. I'm not taking anything away from the game, but "playing" it is more about choosing options as the story progresses rather than truly controlling a character. Dragon's Lair still represents a significant milestone in the evolution of video game graphics, and it's evident in the fact that the animation in the game took six years to complete.

In the previous chapter, you learned how to carry out wireless network communications in a MIDlet through a simplistic client/server model. This chapter carries the network topic a step further by guiding you through the design and development of a complete turn-based mobile game that supports multiple players. More specifically, you develop a mobile version of the classic Connect 4 game, where you drop pieces down vertical columns on a game "board" in an attempt to line up four in a row before your opponent.

In this chapter, you'll learn

▶ The basics of how to play Connect 4

▶ How to design a networked mobile version of Connect 4

▶ How to build a mobile Connect 4 game that utilizes datagram network communications

▶ That testing networked mobile games can be a tricky task

The Scoop on Connect 4

In case you've never played the classic Connect 4 game, let's briefly go over the basic rules. It is a simple game that is similar to tic-tac-toe in that the goal is to complete a continuous row, column, or diagonal series of four game pieces. The game is played on a rectangular "board" that contains a 7×6 array of positions. You use round pieces, similar to checker pieces, to represent each move. Figure 15.1 shows what a Connect 4 board looks like.

FIGURE 15.1
The Connect 4 game "board" consists of a 7×6 array of spaces.

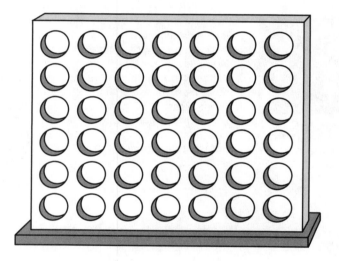

The main catch to Connect 4 is that the board stands upright, with each column being slotted. So a move consists of selecting a column to drop your piece in, and then gravity takes care of the rest. This means that instead of explicitly choosing the vertical position of each move, you only can stack up the pieces vertically. This fact impacts the strategy greatly. Figure 15.2 shows a Connect 4 game after several moves, and reveals how the game pieces stack up to form columns.

The game is won when one of the players manages to connect a horizontal, vertical, or diagonal series of four pieces. There is the chance for a tie, as in tic-tac-toe, but it is less likely, simply because of the number of ways in which the game can be won. Figure 15.3 shows a victory in Connect 4, which in this case involves a series of four game pieces arranged in a horizontal row.

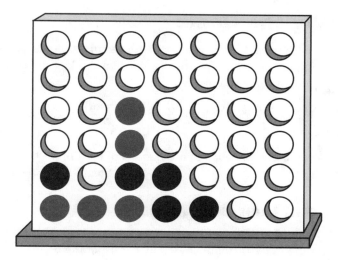

FIGURE 15.2
The columns in the Connect 4 game "board" are filled with round game pieces as the game progresses.

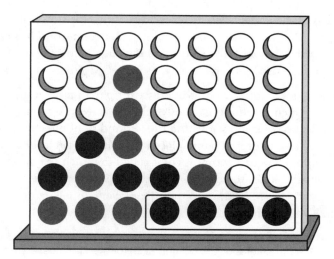

FIGURE 15.3
The Connect 4 game ends when a player manages to "connect" four game pieces in a horizontal, vertical, or diagonal series.

It is technically possible to always win at Connect 4 if you are the player to make the first move, regardless of the other player's strategy.

Gamer's Garage

Designing the Game

The design of the Connect 4 game is a little easier to digest if you break it down into separate components. More specifically, you can think of the game design as consisting of the following elements:

- Graphics and user interface
- Networking
- Game logic

The next few sections explore each of these facets of the Connect 4 game design in greater detail.

Graphics and User Interface

As with most games, the design of the Connect 4 game begins with the game graphics. The graphics for the game basically consist of the board and pieces. In addition to that, it is helpful to have some status information regarding the multiplayer aspects of the game, such as whose turn it is. This status line can also be used to indicate whether or not a successful network connection has been established. At any given moment, the status line indicates just the state of the game, with a message such as "Waiting for player's move" or "Your turn."

To help provide a more intuitive user interface for playing the game, it would be helpful to show which column is currently selected when it is your turn. To make a move, you select a column by pressing the left and right directional keys, followed by the Fire key, to drop a game piece in a column. The column selector for Connect 4 is a graphical arrow that is color-coded to match the appropriate player (red is the server, blue is the client). The column selector arrow is displayed over the currently selected column so that the player can tell exactly into which column a piece will be dropped.

Gamer's Garage

In reality, the different colors for the column selector aren't necessary because the game players see the game from their own perspectives only. However, for the purposes of testing the game, it is extremely useful to be able to quickly distinguish between the client and server by color.

To recap, the Connect 4 game requires four graphic elements:

- Board
- Pieces
- Status line
- Arrow selector

Seeing that you've already developed a couple of complete action games with multiple animated sprites that interact with each other, the graphics for the Connect 4 game are extremely simple. So let's move on to the logic required to actually carry out a game of Connect 4.

Game Logic

The most challenging obstacle in the design of the Connect 4 game is successfully detecting a winner. This might at first seem trivial; just look for a series of four pieces in a row, column, or diagonal, right? That's right for you or me, but teaching the computer how to look at the board and figure this out isn't quite so simple. Think about how you might go about explaining in Java code how to assess a game of Connect 4 at any moment and determine whether there is a winner.

One possible approach is to keep up with every possible combination of piece positions that constitutes a victory. These combinations could be stored in a table and then used as a basis to determine how close each player is to winning the game. Although this approach sounds fairly cumbersome, it's actually not too hard to implement. This "brute force" approach is in fact what you're going to use in the Connect 4 game code a little later in the chapter. Granted, there might be more elegant ways to solve this problem, but a table of winning combinations is actually fairly simple and quite efficient in terms of processing overhead.

Networking

As you've no doubt realized, Connect 4 is a turn-based game, which means that it is ideally suited to the use of datagram packets. As it turns out, the Connect 4 game can be built on the same design used in the Lighthouse example MIDlet from Chapter 14, "Mobile Game Networking Essentials." Rather than send Morse code "dot" and "dash" messages between mobile phones, you just send the column for each move in the game. The only issue that makes the Connect 4 game trickier than the Lighthouse example is that of managing player turns. In other words, you can't allow the free-form communication that was allowed in the Lighthouse example.

Similar to the Lighthouse example, the Connect 4 MIDlet operates under two basic network modes: client and server. The network mode is set when you first run the game, and it is always assumed that a client must connect to a server to play the game. After the client-server connection is made, the game proceeds a turn at a time with the two mobile phones passing messages back and forth to indicate game moves. The key is to make sure that the client and server instances of the Connect 4 MIDlet stay synchronized. This is accomplished with careful monitoring of whose turn it is, and turns that are changed only when a move has been successfully communicated to the other player.

Following are the series of network-related steps involved in a typical game of Connect 4:

1. The server phone opens a datagram connection and waits for the client.

2. The client phone opens a datagram connection with the server.

3. With a connection established, the game begins by giving the client the first move; the server waits. In future games, the loser starts first.

4. The client makes a move and notifies the server of the column selected.

5. The turn moves to the server, who then makes a move.

6. Moves are exchanged until one of the players eventually wins or there is a tie.

7. Either of the players initiates a restart and the game starts over.

8. The client and server phones terminate the connection.

As you can see, in terms of networking, the Connect 4 game is really just a more interesting version of the Lighthouse example program. The only significant difference is the management of player turns and the exchange of column information instead of Morse code dots and dashes. The actual networking code for the two MIDlets is surprisingly similar, as you soon find out.

Developing the Game

Similar to the design of the Connect 4 game, which was broken down into three functional pieces, the code for the game can be divided along similar lines. The next few sections explore the various code pieces of the Connect 4 puzzle one component at a time.

The Connect 4 Client and Server

The majority of the networking code in the Connect 4 game is divided between two classes, C4Client and C4Server. Not surprisingly, these two classes represent the client and server that pass messages back and forth between mobile phones in a networked two-player game of Connect 4. Both of these classes implement the Runnable interface, which means that each has its own thread of execution. Because the server is typically launched first in a real game of Connect 4, let's start with the code for the C4Server class.

Following are the member variables declared in the C4Server class:

```
private C4Canvas           canvas;
private DatagramConnection dc;
private String             address;
private boolean            connected;
```

The server must be able to communicate information about game state changes to the game canvas, which actually manages the game. For this reason, it is important for the C4Server class to store the game canvas in the canvas variable. The dc variable keeps track of the datagram connection, which is critical for managing a communication link with the game client. The address variable stores away the client's address, which is necessary to send datagram packets to the client. And finally, the connected variable serves the purpose of keeping up with whether or not a connection has been established.

The constructor for the C4Server class requires a C4Canvas object as its only parameter, as the following code reveals:

```
public C4Server(C4Canvas c) {
  canvas = c;
  connected = false;
}
```

The C4Server() constructor is surprisingly simple, and does nothing more than initialize two of its member variables. The start() method, which is inherited from the Runnable interface, isn't much more interesting:

```
public void start() {
  Thread t = new Thread(this);
  t.start();
}
```

Nothing too shocking here—just standard thread launching code. Perhaps the only method more boring than start() in the C4Server code is the stop() method, which literally does nothing at all:

```
public void stop() {
}
```

The C4Server code doesn't really get interesting until the run() method, which is shown in Listing 15.1.

LISTING 15.1   The run() Method in the C4Server Class Serves as the Heart of the Connect 4 Game Server

The initial server status message indicates that the server game is waiting on the client. [

This port number [must match the port number of the client connection.

The size of the [datagram (32 bytes) must be large enough to hold the largest message, which isn't very large for Connect 4.

Respond to a client connection by starting the game and replying to the client.

The message must [contain move data, so pass it along to the game canvas for processing.

```java
public void run() {
  try {
    // Connect to the peer client
    canvas.setStatus("Waiting for peer client...");
    dc = null;
    while (dc == null)
      dc = (DatagramConnection)Connector.open("datagram://:5555");


    while (true) {
      // Try to receive a datagram packet
      Datagram dg = dc.newDatagram(32);
      dc.receive(dg);
      address = dg.getAddress();


      // Make sure the datagram actually contains data
      if (dg.getLength() > 0) {
        String data = new String(dg.getData(), 0, dg.getLength());
        if (data.equals("Client")) {
          // Notify the user of a successful network connection
          canvas.setStatus("Connected to peer client.");
          canvas.newGame();
          connected = true;

          // Try to reply with a connection message
          sendMessage("Server");
        }
        else {
          // Send along the network game data
          canvas.receiveMessage(data);
        }
      }
    }
  }
  catch (IOException ioe) {
    System.err.println("The network port is already taken.");
  }
  catch (Exception e) {
  }
}
```

The run() method starts out with an important line of code that sets the status of the canvas to "Waiting for peer client...". The setStatus() method in the C4Canvas class sets the message that is displayed in the status line along the top of the game screen. Any time you set the status, you are directly sharing a piece of information with the user. In this case, the information being shared is that the server is awaiting a client connection. After setting the status of the canvas, the run() method creates a datagram connection.

The remainder of the run() method is an infinite loop that repeatedly tries to receive datagram packets and react to them. If a packet is received, its address is stored away and its length is checked to make sure it isn't empty. The value of the message is then checked to see whether it is equal to the string Client, which is a special message that is sent when the client first connects to the server. If a successful connection has been established, the status is changed and a new game is started. A message is also sent back to the client with the string Server to indicate that the connection was established.

If the datagram packet that is received is not equal to Client, then you know it must be a piece of game data. The game data is actually the column in which a piece is to be dropped for the other player. However, it isn't the server's job to interpret this data—all it must do is send the data along to the canvas via the canvas' receiveMessage() method.

The only other method in the C4Server class is the sendMessage() method (see Listing 15.2), which is responsible for sending a string message to the client.

LISTING 15.2 The sendMessage() Method in the C4Server Class Sends a String Message as a Datagram Packet to the Client

```
public void sendMessage(String message) {
  // Send the message
  try {
    // Convert the string message to bytes
    byte[] bytes = message.getBytes();

    // Send the message
    Datagram dg = null;
    dg = dc.newDatagram(bytes, bytes.length, address);
    dc.send(dg);
  }
  catch (Exception e) {
  }
}
```

The string message must first be converted to bytes.

Package the message as a datagram packet, and then send it to the client.

The sendMessage() method packages up a string message into an array of bytes and sends it to the client as a datagram packet. There aren't really any surprises in this code; it is very similar to the message sending code used in the Lighthouse server from Chapter 14.

The other half of the Connect 4 network equation is the C4Client class, which is actually quite similar to the C4Server class. Following are the member variables used by the C4Client class:

```
private C4Canvas           canvas;
private DatagramConnection dc;
private boolean            connected;
```

These member variables mirror those declared in the C4Server class, except that the client doesn't require an address. The C4Client() constructor is also similar to the C4Server() constructor, as the following code reveals:

```
public C4Client(C4Canvas c) {
  canvas = c;
  connected = false;
}
```

In fact, this code is identical to the code for the server except for the name of the constructor. Not only is this code the same, but so is the code for the client start() and stop() methods, which follow:

```
public void start() {
  Thread t = new Thread(this);
  t.start();
}

public void stop() {
}
```

Okay, so the client and server code are looking a lot alike so far, but things start to stray in the run() method for the C4Client class, which is shown in Listing 15.3.

The client initially displays a status message indicating that the client is trying to connect to the server.

This port number must match the port number of the server connection.

If there is no connection, send a Client message to establish a connection with the server.

LISTING 15.3   The run() Method in the C4Client Class Serves as the Heart of the Connect 4 Game Client

```
public void run() {
  try {
    // Connect to the peer server
    canvas.setStatus("Connecting to peer server...");
    dc = null;
    while (dc == null)
      dc = (DatagramConnection)Connector.open("datagram://localhost:5555");

    while (true) {


      // Try to send a connection message
      if (!connected)
        sendMessage("Client");

      // Try to receive a datagram packet
      Datagram dg = dc.newDatagram(32);
      dc.receive(dg);
```

LISTING 15.3 Continued

```
    // Make sure the datagram actually contains data
    if (dg.getLength() > 0) {
      String data = new String(dg.getData(), 0, dg.getLength());
      if (data.equals("Server")) {
        // Notify the user of a successful network connection
        canvas.setStatus("Connected to peer server.");
        canvas.newGame();
        connected = true;
      }
      else {
        // Send along the network game data
        canvas.receiveMessage(data);
      }
    }
  }
}
catch (ConnectionNotFoundException cnfe) {
  System.err.println("The network server is unavailable.");
}
catch (IOException ioe) {
}
}
```

Respond to a server connection by starting the game.

The message must contain move data, so pass it along to the game canvas for processing.

Actually, this code looks somewhat familiar, come to think of it. The run() method for the client is similarly structured as the server's run() method, but a few things are handled differently. First off, the status text is different because the client begins by attempting to connect to a server, as opposed to waiting for a client connection. A datagram connection is still created just after the status is set, but in this case the URL is slightly different to account for this being the client end of the connection. It is very important to point out that the port numbers must match for the client and server.

After entering the infinite loop for the client, a message (Client) is immediately sent to the server to notify it that the client is connected. The client then goes into "receive mode," much as the server does. More specifically, the client settles in to processing network messages, which are either the special Server message or game state messages that indicate the other player's moves. If the special Server message is received, the client changes the status of the canvas and starts a new game. Otherwise, the message is passed along to the canvas for game-specific processing.

The C4Client class also has a sendMessage() method that is shockingly similar to the server equivalent. Before you go thinking I'm reproducing code with reckless abandon, take a close look at Listing 15.4.

LISTING 15.4 The sendMessage() Method in the C4Client Class Sends a String Message as a Datagram Packet to the Server

```
public void sendMessage(String message) {
  // Send the message
  try {
    // Convert the string message to bytes
    byte[] bytes = message.getBytes();

    // Send the message
    Datagram dg = null;
    dg = dc.newDatagram(bytes, bytes.length);
    dc.send(dg);
  }
  catch (Exception e) {
  }
}
```

Package the message as a datagram packet, and then send it to the server.

A really close look reveals that the client version of sendMessage() doesn't use an address when sending a datagram packet to the server. Admittedly, this is a subtle difference, but it's important nonetheless.

You now have the network client and server in place for the Connect 4 game, so it's time to dig into the canvas class.

The Connect 4 Game Canvas

The Connect 4 game canvas is encapsulated in the C4Canvas class, which is responsible for a great deal of the game's functionality. Following are the member variables declared in the C4Canvas class:

The C4State class encapsulates the majority of the Connect 4 game logic, including the state of pieces on the game board.

This variable reflects whether or not this instance of the game is the server.

```
private Image[]   piece = new Image[2];
private Sprite    arrowSprite;
private Player    legalPlayer;
private Player    illegalPlayer;
private Player    winPlayer;
private Player    losePlayer;
private C4State    gameState;
private C4Client   client;
private C4Server   server;
private boolean    isServer;
private String     status = "";
private boolean    gameOver;
private boolean    myMove;
private int        curSlot;
```

The piece variable stores the two game pieces used in the game, which are color coded (red and blue) for each player. The arrowSprite variable is the arrow sprite that is shown over the columns of the game board to indicate into which column a piece should be dropped. The Player variables are all wave audio players that are used to provide audio cues for game events such as legal and illegal moves, as well as wins and losses.

Gamer's Garage

An illegal move in the Connect 4 game is attempting to drop a piece in a column that is already full.

The gameState variable is extremely important, and deserves considerably more explanation than the other member variables. You learn much more about it later in the section titled "The Connect 4 Game State," but for now it's important to understand that it represents the state of the actual Connect 4 game at any given moment, including the locations of the game pieces, the "score" for each player, and a table of winning combinations that is used to determine a winner.

The client and server variables represent the game's client and server networking components. It's important to understand that only one of these variables is used in any given instance of the Connect 4 game. In other words, when a game is run as a server, the server variable is used exclusively for network communications, whereas the client variable enters the picture for a client game. The isServer variable keeps track of whether or not a game is running in server mode.

Of the remaining member variables, the status variable stores the text for the game's status line, whereas the gameOver variable indicates whether the game is over or not. The myMove variable is extremely important in keeping track of whether it is the player's move or the player is waiting for a move over the network. And finally, the curSlot variable stores the currently selected slot on the game board, which is where the arrow indicator is drawn.

You can see these member variables start to enter the picture in the Connect 4 game in the start() method, which is shown in Listing 15.5.

LISTING 15.5   The start() Method in the C4Canvas Class Starts the Connect 4 Game by Initializing Game Variables and the Client/Server Network Service

```
public void start() {
  // Set the canvas as the current screen
  display.setCurrent(this);

  // Initialize the piece images
  try {
    piece[0] = Image.createImage("/RedPiece.png");
    piece[1] = Image.createImage("/BluePiece.png");
  }
  catch (IOException e) {
    System.err.println("Failed loading images!");
  }
```

LISTING 15.5   Continued

The arrow sprite has two animation frames (a red one and a blue one) that are displayed based on whether the game is in client or server mode.

```
// Initialize the arrow sprite
try {
  // Create the arrow sprite
  arrowSprite = new Sprite(Image.createImage("/Arrow.png"), 18, 16);
  arrowSprite.setFrame(isServer ? 0 : 1);
}
catch (IOException e) {
  System.err.println("Failed loading images!");
}

// Initialize the wave players
try {
  InputStream is = getClass().getResourceAsStream("Legal.wav");
  legalPlayer = Manager.createPlayer(is, "audio/X-wav");
  legalPlayer.prefetch();
  is = getClass().getResourceAsStream("Illegal.wav");
  illegalPlayer = Manager.createPlayer(is, "audio/X-wav");
  illegalPlayer.prefetch();
  is = getClass().getResourceAsStream("Win.wav");
  winPlayer = Manager.createPlayer(is, "audio/X-wav");
  winPlayer.prefetch();
  is = getClass().getResourceAsStream("Lose.wav");
  losePlayer = Manager.createPlayer(is, "audio/X-wav");
  losePlayer.prefetch();
}
catch (IOException ioe) {
}
catch (MediaException me) {
}

// Initialize the game variables
gameOver = true;
myMove = !isServer;  // client always goes first
curSlot = 0;
gameState = new C4State();

// Start the networking service
if (isServer) {
  server = new C4Server(this);
  server.start();
}
else {
  client = new C4Client(this);
  client.start();
}

// Start the animation thread
sleeping = false;
Thread t = new Thread(this);
t.start();
}
```

From this point on, the game is permanently in server or client mode.

The start() method takes care of several important initialization tasks, such as initializing the game piece images and the arrow sprite. The arrow sprite actually contains two different frame images (red and blue), so the frame of the sprite is set according to whether or not the game is in client or server mode. The wave players are then initialized, followed by the four main game variables (gameOver, myMove, curSlot, and gameState). The appropriate networking service (client or server) is then started based on the value of the isServer variable. This variable is initially set in the C4Canvas() constructor, which is passed in the peer type (Client or Server) as a string when the canvas is created.

Although the start() method is certainly important for initialization purposes, the update() method (see Listing 15.6) is where user input is handled and converted into game actions that are shared over the network.

LISTING 15.6 The update() Method in the C4Canvas Class Responds to Keys and Sends Messages Regarding Game Moves

```
private void update() {
  // Check to see whether the game is being restarted
  if (gameOver) {
    int keyState = getKeyStates();
    if ((keyState & FIRE_PRESSED) != 0) {
      // Start a new game
      newGame();

      // Send a new game message to the other player
      if (isServer)
        server.sendMessage("NewGame");
      else
        client.sendMessage("NewGame");
    }

    // The game is over, so don't update anything
    return;
  }

  // Handle the left/right directional keys and the fire key
  if (!gameOver && myMove) {
    // Process user input to move the arrow and drop piece
    int keyState = getKeyStates();
    if ((keyState & LEFT_PRESSED) != 0) {
      if (--curSlot < 0)
        curSlot = 0;
    }
    else if ((keyState & RIGHT_PRESSED) != 0) {
      if (++curSlot > 6)
        curSlot = 6;
    }
    else if ((keyState & FIRE_PRESSED) != 0) {
      if (makeMove(isServer ? 0 : 1, curSlot)) {
        myMove = false;
```

Notify the other player of a new game being started.

Move the current slot selector to the left.

Move the current slot selector to the right.

The current player's move is over.

LISTING 15.6   Continued

Communicate the move to the other player.

```
    // Send the move message to the other player
    if (isServer)
      server.sendMessage(Integer.toString(curSlot));
    else
      client.sendMessage(Integer.toString(curSlot));
  }
}
```

Reposition the arrow selector based on the currently selected slot.

```
  // Update the arrow position
  arrowSprite.setPosition(
    getWidth() * (curSlot + 1) / 8 - arrowSprite.getWidth() / 2, 21);
  }
}
```

The update() method begins by checking to see whether the game is over, and if so, whether the game is being restarted. Notice that restarting a game involves both calling the newGame() method as well as passing a NewGame message to the other game instance over the network. If a new game isn't being started, the left and right directional keys are checked, as well as the Fire key. Notice that none of the input keys are responded to unless the game is still in progress and it is the current player's move.

The left and right directional keys simply result in the curSlot variable being modified to point to a different slot (column) of the game board. The code for the Fire key is much more interesting in that it actually carries out a game move with a call to makeMove(), after which it sends a message over the network to convey the move. You learn more about the makeMove() method in just a moment. Independently of the Fire key, the arrow sprite is updated near the end of the update() method to reflect any changes in the curSlot variable.

Listing 15.7 contains the code for the draw() method, which is responsible for drawing the Connect 4 game graphics.

LISTING 15.7   The draw() **Method in the** C4Canvas **Class Draws the Connect 4 Game Graphics**

```
private void draw(Graphics g) {
  // Fill the background
  g.setColor(128, 128, 128); // gray
  g.fillRect(0, 0, getWidth(), getHeight());

  // Draw the status message
  g.setColor(0, 0, 0); // black
  g.setFont(Font.getFont(Font.FACE_SYSTEM, Font.STYLE_BOLD, Font.SIZE_MEDIUM));
  g.drawString(status, getWidth() / 2, 2, Graphics.TOP | Graphics.HCENTER);
```

The status message line is drawn near the top of the game screen.

LISTING 15.7 Continued

```
if (!gameOver && myMove) {
  // Draw the arrow sprite
  arrowSprite.paint(g);
}

// Draw the pieces
for (int i = 0; i < 7; i++)
  for (int j = 0; j < 6; j++)
  switch(gameState.board[i][j]) {
  case 0:
    g.drawImage(piece[0],
      (getWidth() * (i + 1)) / 8 - (piece[0].getWidth() / 2),
      ((getHeight() - 33) * (6 - j)) / 7 - (piece[0].getHeight() / 2) + 33,
      Graphics.TOP | Graphics.LEFT);
    break;

  case 1:
    g.drawImage(piece[1],
      (getWidth() * (i + 1)) / 8 - (piece[0].getWidth() / 2),
      ((getHeight() - 33) * (6 - j)) / 7 - (piece[1].getHeight() / 2) + 33,
      Graphics.TOP | Graphics.LEFT);
    break;

  default:
    g.setColor(255, 255, 255); // white
    g.fillArc((getWidth() * (i + 1)) / 8 - (piece[0].getWidth() / 2),
      ((getHeight() - 33) * (6 - j)) / 7 - (piece[0].getHeight() / 2) + 33,
      piece[0].getWidth(), piece[0].getHeight(), 0, 360);
    break;
  }

// Flush the offscreen graphics buffer
flushGraphics();
}
```

Draw the arrow sprite only if the game is in progress and it is the local player's move.

Draw the server player's pieces.

Draw the client player's pieces.

Draw the empty spaces.

The draw() method begins by filling the background of the game screen with a solid gray color. The status line text is then drawn along the top of the screen to indicate the current status of the game. If the game is in progress and it is the player's move, the arrow sprite is drawn just below the status line. The bulk of the draw() method is then left to focus on drawing the game pieces and empty spaces on the game board. A value of 0 for a game piece on the board corresponds to the server player, which is a red piece, whereas a value of 1 corresponds to the client player (blue piece). Any other value indicates an empty space on the board, which is drawn simply as a white circle.

The newGame() method is called to start a new game, so its job is to initialize the game variables and update the status message to signal a new game. Listing 15.8 contains the code for the newGame() method.

LISTING 15.8   The `newGame()` Method in the `C4Canvas` Class Starts a New Game of Connect 4

```
public void newGame() {
  // Initialize the game variables
  gameOver = false;
  curSlot = 0;
  gameState = new C4State();

  // Update the status message
  status = myMove ? "Your turn." : "Waiting for player's move...";
}
```

This code is fairly predictable in that it sets the gameOver variable to false, initializes the curSlot variable to 0 for the first slot, and renews the gameState variable to clear the board. The status message is then updated to reflect the turn.

A method you've seen used a few times thus far is the receiveMessage() method (see Listing 15.9), which is responsible for receiving a network message and doing something useful with it.

LISTING 15.9   The `receiveMessage()` Method in the `C4Canvas` Class Receives a Network Message and Responds by Starting a New Game or Carrying Out a Move

```
public void receiveMessage(String message) {
  if (gameOver) {
    // Check for a new game message
    if (message.equals("NewGame"))
      newGame();
  }
  else {
    if (!myMove) {
      // Attempt to receive a numeric move
      try {
        // Carry out the other player's move
        int slot = Integer.parseInt(message);
        if (slot >= 0 && slot <= 6) {
          if (makeMove(isServer ? 1 : 0, slot))
            myMove = true;
        }
      }
      catch (NumberFormatException nfe) {
      }
    }
  }
}
```

If the NewGame message is received, start a new game.

Make sure the message contains a valid slot number (0 to 6), and then carry out the move.

This method is called by the client and server components of the Connect 4 game to indicate that a network message has been received from the other player.

The network message always consists of one of two possible pieces of information: a NewGame notification or a slot (column) on the game board that indicates a move. If a NewGame notification is received, a new game is started. If a move is received in the message, the integer slot is extracted from the text message and passed into the makeMove() method to carry out the other player's move.

Speaking of the makeMove() method, it represents the last method of interest in the C4Canvas class. Listing 15.10 contains the code for the makeMove() method, which contains much of the game logic for Connect 4.

LISTING 15.10 The makeMove() Method in the C4Canvas Class Carries Out a Connect 4 Game Move

```
private boolean makeMove(int player, int slot) {
  // Drop the piece
  if (gameState.dropPiece(player, slot) == -1) {
    // Play a wave sound for an illegal move
    try {
      illegalPlayer.start();
    }
    catch (MediaException me) {
    }

    return false;
  }

  // Play a wave sound for a legal move
  try {
    legalPlayer.start();
  }
  catch (MediaException me) {
  }

  // See whether the game is over
  if (gameState.isWinner(player)) {
    if ((isServer && (player == 0)) || (!isServer && (player == 1))) {
      // Play a wave sound for winning the game
      try {
        winPlayer.start();
      }
      catch (MediaException me) {
      }

      status = "You won!";
    }
    else {
      // Play a wave sound for losing the game
      try {
        losePlayer.start();
      }
      catch (MediaException me) {
      }
```

Attempt to drop the piece in the specified slot, and return false if it isn't successful.

See whether the local player won the game.

The local player lost.

LISTING 15.10   Continued

See whether the game has ended in a tie. ⌐

```
            status = "You lost!";
        }

        gameOver = true;
    }
    else if (gameState.isTie()) {
        // Play a wave sound for tying the game
        try {
            losePlayer.start();
        }
        catch (MediaException me) {
        }

        status = "The game ended in a tie!";
        gameOver = true;
    }
    else {
        // Update the status message
        status = myMove ? "Waiting for other player..." : "Your turn.";
    }

    return true;
}
```

I know, the makeMove() method is fairly hefty, but it's not too complicated when you examine it carefully. First off, it's important to notice that the two parameters to the method are the player and the slot for the move—this is the slot into which the game piece is being dropped. The method starts off by calling the dropPiece() method on the gameState variable to attempt to carry out the move. I say "attempt" because it is possible that the move won't be allowed if the slot is already full of pieces. In this case, the method returns false to indicate that the move was not carried out.

If the move is legal, the makeMove() method continues by playing a wave sound and then checking to see whether the move results in the game ending. The isWinner() method is first called on the game state object to see whether the player who made the move has won the game. If so, the player is then checked to see whether it is the local player or the network player, which determines whether a win sound or loss sound is played. The status message is then updated and the gameOver variable is set to true to end the game.

A Connect 4 game can end in a tie when the entire board fills up with pieces and none of them form a four-piece series. The isTie() method in the C4State class is all that is required to check for a tie game. The makeMove() method calls isTie() to check for a tie and end the game if necessary.

The Connect 4 Game State

The last piece of the Connect 4 puzzle is the class that represents the actual Connect 4 game details, such as the positions of the pieces on the game board. The C4State class models the current state of a Connect 4 game and contains the following member variables:

```
private static boolean[][][] map;
private int[][]              score = new int[2][winPlaces];
public static final int      winPlaces = 69, maxPieces = 42, Empty = 2;
private int                  numPieces;
public int[][]               board = new int[7][6];
```

To help make the C4State class easier to digest, let's start with the winPlaces, maxPieces, and Empty member variables, which are all static final integers; this simply means that they are all constant. The following equation is used to calculate winPlaces, which specifies the number of possible winning combinations on the board:

```
winPlaces = 4*w*h - 3*w*n - 3*h*n + 3*w + 3*h - 4*n + 2*n*n;
```

This is a general equation that can be applied to any ConnectX-type game. In the equation, w and h represent the width and height of the game board, and n represents the number of pieces that must be in a series to constitute a victory. Because Connect 4 uses a 7×6 game board with a four-piece series constituting a win, you can simply precalculate winPlaces and get a value of 69, which is exactly what it is set to in C4State.

The maxPieces member specifies the maximum number of pieces that can be placed on the board. The following equation is used to calculate it:

```
maxPieces = w*h;
```

This calculation is pretty straightforward. The result is used to detect whether there is a tie; a tie occurs when nobody has won and the number of pieces in the game equals maxPieces.

The other constant member, Empty, represents an empty space on the board. Each space on the board can contain a player number (0 or 1) or the Empty constant, which is set to 2.

Moving back to the top of the member variable list, the map member variable is a three-dimensional array of Booleans that holds the lookup table of winning combinations. To better understand how the map is laid out, first think of it as a two-dimensional array with the same dimensions as the board for the game; in other words, think of it as a 7×6 two-dimensional array. Now, add a third dimension by attaching an array of winning positions onto each two-dimensional array entry.

Each different winning combination in the game is given a unique position within this array (the winning position array is winPlaces in length). Each location in this array is set to true or false, based on whether the winning series intersects the associated board position.

Let's go over a quick example to make sure you understand how the map works. Take a look at the upper-left space on the game board back in Figure 15.1; let's call this position 0,0 on the board. Now, think about which different winning series of pieces would include this position. Give up? Check out Figure 15.4.

FIGURE 15.4
There are three possible winning series for position 0,0 on the Connect 4 game board.

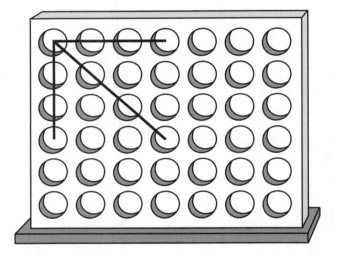

As you can see, position 0,0 on the board has three different winning scenarios. Therefore, the winning position array for position 0,0 would have these three entries set to true, and all the others would be set to false. If the winning moves shown in Figure 15.4 were at positions 11–13 in the winning series array, you would initialize position 0,0 in the map like this:

```
...
map[0][0][9] = false;
map[0][0][10] = false;
map[0][0][11] = true;
map[0][0][12] = true;
map[0][0][13] = true;
map[0][0][14] = false;
map[0][0][15] = false;
...
```

After the entire map is constructed, you can use it to look up winning combinations and determine how close each player is to winning.

The board member variable is simply a 7×6 two-dimensional array of integers that represents the state of the game. Each integer entry can be set to either 0 or 1 (for a player occupying that position on the board) or Empty.

The score member variable contains a two-dimensional array of integers representing the "score" for the players. The main array in score contains a sub-array for each player that is winPlaces in length. These sub-arrays contain information describing how close the player is to completing a winning series. It works like this: Each sub-array entry corresponds to a potential winning series and contains a count of how many of the player's pieces occupy the series. If a series is no longer a winning possibility for the player, its entry in the array is set to 0. Otherwise, the entry is set to 2 raised to the power of p, where p is the number of the player's pieces occupying the series. So if one of these entries is set to 16 (2 to the power of 4), that player has won.

> It's not terribly important for you to understand every detail of how the C4State code calculates a score and determines a winner. The main point of this example is to demonstrate a functioning mobile network game. The tricky "scoring" code is a necessary part of determining a winner in the Connect 4 game, but it isn't critical in understanding the networking aspect of the game.

Construction Cue

Rounding out the member variables for C4State is numPieces, which is just a count of how many pieces have been played in the game. numPieces is really used only in determining whether the game is a tie; in the event of a tie, numPieces is equal to maxPieces.

That covers the member variables for the C4State class. You might have realized by now that by understanding the member variables and what they model, you already understand a great deal about the inner workings of the game state. Let's move on to the methods in C4State.

The constructor for C4State takes on the role of initializing the map, board, and score arrays, and is shown in Listing 15.11.

LISTING 15.11 The C4State() Constructor Initializes the Connect 4 Map and Game Board

```
public C4State() {
  // Initialize the map
  int i, j, k, count = 0;
  if (map == null) {
    map = new boolean[7][6][winPlaces];
    for (i = 0; i < 7; i++)
      for (j = 0; j < 6; j++)
        for (k = 0; k < winPlaces; k++)
          map[i][j][k] = false;
```

LISTING 15.11   Continued

```
// Set the horizontal win positions
for (i = 0; i < 6; i++)
  for (j = 0; j < 4; j++) {
    for (k = 0; k < 4; k++)
      map[j + k][i][count] = true;
    count++;
  }

// Set the vertical win positions
for (i = 0; i < 7; i++)
  for (j = 0; j < 3; j++) {
    for (k = 0; k < 4; k++)
      map[i][j + k][count] = true;
    count++;
  }

// Set the forward diagonal win positions
for (i = 0; i < 3; i++)
  for (j = 0; j < 4; j++) {
    for (k = 0; k < 4; k++)
      map[j + k][i + k][count] = true;
    count++;
  }

// Set the backward diagonal win positions
for (i = 0; i < 3; i++)
  for (j = 6; j >= 3; j--) {
    for (k = 0; k < 4; k++)
      map[j - k][i + k][count] = true;
    count++;
  }
}

// Initialize the board
for (i = 0; i < 7; i++)
  for (j = 0; j < 6; j++)
    board[i][j] = Empty;

// Initialize the scores
for (i = 0; i < 2; i++)
  for (j = 0; j < winPlaces; j++)
    score[i][j] = 1;

numPieces = 0;
}
```

The game board starts out with all the spaces empty.

Although the C4State() constructor contains a decent amount of code, it is mainly just initializing the game state arrays with predictable settings.

The isWinner() method in C4State (see Listing 15.12) checks to see whether a player has won the game.

LISTING 15.12 The `isWinner()` Method in the `C4State` Class Checks to See Whether a Player Has Won the Game

```
public boolean isWinner(int player) {
  // See whether the player has won
  for (int i = 0; i < winPlaces: i++)
    if (score[player][i] == 16)
      return true;
  return false;
}
```

A value of 16 in the score array indicates a winner.

The `isWinner()` method looks for a winner by checking to see whether any member in the score array is equal to 16 (2 to the power of 4). This indicates victory because it means that four pieces occupy the series.

The `isTie()` method checks for a tie by simply seeing whether `numPieces` equals `maxPieces`, which indicates that the board is full. The source code for `isTie()` is shown in Listing 15.13.

LISTING 15.13 The `isTie()` Method in the `C4State` Class Checks to See Whether the Game Has Ended in a Tie

```
public boolean isTie() {
  // See whether there is a tie
  return (numPieces == maxPieces);
}
```

The `dropPiece()` method handles dropping a new piece into a slot of the game board, as you can see from the code in Listing 15.14.

LISTING 15.14 The `dropPiece()` Method in the `C4State` Class Drops a Piece in a Specified Slot on the Game Board

```
public int dropPiece(int player, int xPos) {
  // See if the slot has room for the piece
  int yPos = 0;
  while ((board[xPos][yPos] != Empty) && (++yPos < 6))
    ;

  // The slot is full
  if (yPos == 6)
    return -1;

  // The slot has room, so drop the piece
  board[xPos][yPos] = player;
  numPieces++;
  updateScore(player, xPos, yPos);
  return yPos;
}
```

The slot is full of pieces, so return an error value (-1).

The dropPiece() method takes a player and an X position (slot or column) as its only parameters. It first checks to make sure there is room in the specified column to drop a new piece. Incidentally, you might have noticed from this code that the board is stored upside down in the board member variable. Having the board inverted simplifies the process of adding a new piece. If the move is valid, the entry in the board array is set to identify the player, and numPieces is incremented. Then the score is updated to reflect the move with a call to updateScore().

The updateScore() method handles updating the score for a player after a move, as shown in Listing 15.15.

LISTING 15.15   The updateScore() Method in the C4State Class Updates the Score for a Specified Piece on the Game Board

```
private void updateScore(int player, int x, int y) {
  // Update the score for the specified piece
  for (int i = 0; i < winPlaces; i++)
    if (map[x][y][i]) {
      score[player][i] <<= 1;
      score[1 - player][i] = 0;
    }
}
```

The updateScore() method sets the appropriate entries in the score array to reflect the move; the move is specified in the x and y parameters.

This wraps up the code for both the C4State class and the Connect 4 game as a whole. If some of the Connect 4 game state logic bowled you over, don't worry too much. The goal of this example game isn't so much to teach you the gory details of calculating a Connect 4 game winner as it is demonstrating how to build a wireless networked mobile game.

Construction Cue

Attempting to play both sides of a multiplayer network game can get confusing, but fortunately the Connect 4 game is a turn-based game, so you have time to plan each move. In a real-time action game it is much more difficult to test networked multiplayer functionality without actually relying on additional human players.

Testing the Game

I've mentioned a few times throughout the book that testing games is often the most fun part of the development process, and this is usually the case.

However, in the case of networked multiplayer games the testing phase can also be the most challenging. There just isn't an easy way to simulate two players participating in a game together. Fortunately, the J2ME emulator does allow you to launch multiple instances and communicate between them as if they were different devices communicating over a real network.

Similar to the Lighthouse example MIDlet from the previous chapter, the Connect 4 MIDlet first presents a simple user interface that enables the user to select whether the game should be run in client or server mode. Figure 15.5 shows this selection process taking place in the Connect 4 MIDlet.

After selecting server mode, the player is presented with a status message. The message indicates that the server is ready and waiting for a client connection (see Figure 15.6).

On the other side of the network equation, another Connect 4 MIDlet is launched in client mode. When the connection is made between client and server, the status lines of both MIDlets change to reflect that the game is now underway. Figure 15.7 shows the server game waiting for the client player's first move.

FIGURE 15.5
The Connect 4 MIDlet begins by prompting the user to select either client or server mode.

FIGURE 15.6
The server Connect 4 game waits for a client connection.

FIGURE 15.7
After detecting the client connection, the server game waits for the other player's first move.

Game play continues with moves swapping back and forth between the client and server players. Figure 15.8 shows the client game with several moves already having been made.

Eventually, one of the players will win or the game will end in a tie when all the spaces on the game board are filled. Figure 15.9 shows the client player winning the game.

To start a new game, either player just presses the Fire key. The player who lost the game gets to go first when a new game starts, which is a nice touch to the game because there is a slight advantage to going first.

Summary

Wireless networking and multiplayer game programming are actually fairly advanced topics, but it wouldn't be fair to not show you at least one fully functional networked mobile game in this book. So this chapter guided you through the design and development of a complete networked multiplayer game called Connect 4. Although the game is fairly simplistic in terms of its networking requirements, it is still nonetheless a valuable example game onto which you can build more interesting networked mobile games of your own.

FIGURE 15.8
The player on the client side of the Connect 4 game contemplates a move.

The next chapter takes a break from the barrage of code you saw in this chapter, and addresses mobile game testing, debugging, and deployment.

Field Trip

To help you better understand the significance of turn-based games such as Connect 4, take some time to play a few real turn-based games with a friend or family member. It doesn't matter if it's Connect 4, chess, or checkers. Just taking the time to play a traditional game and observing the game flow can help you become a better and more intuitive mobile game designer.

FIGURE 15.9
The client player wins the game.

CHAPTER 16

Debugging and Deploying Mobile Games

Arcade Archive

Released by Taito in 1983, Elevator Action used a unique blend of elevators, escalators, and espionage to create a great spy game for its era. Your character in the game is Agent 17, codenamed Otto, and your job is to grab secret documents starting at the top of a 30-floor building and escape in a getaway car in the basement. One of the neat game play strategies in the game is the ability to crush bad guys with the elevator while you're in it. Another nice touch to the game is how you can shoot out the lights and drop them on bad guys. However, the bad guys become more difficult to see in the dark, so there is a tradeoff to this strategy. Small touches like this are what make Elevator Action one of the classics.

Although I hate to broach such a thorny subject, it simply wouldn't be fair to teach you about mobile game programming without covering the often dreaded issue of debugging. This chapter lets you in on the fact that bugs are a natural part of mobile game programming; as humans, we simply are error prone. So you should embrace debugging as a necessary part of the development process and accept the fact that even your precious code will have bugs. I do what I can throughout the chapter to help you develop skills that keep bugs to a minimum, but the rest is up to you.

This chapter also addresses mobile game deployment, which is an extremely important topic because it involves getting your games out to game players. Although the concept of delivering software over a wireless network connection to a mobile device may sound somewhat mysterious, there really isn't anything tricky about it.

In this chapter, you'll learn

- ▶ The basics of game debugging
- ▶ How to prevent and detect mobile game bugs

▶ How to prepare a mobile game for deployment over a wireless network

▶ How to simulate over-the-air provisioning of mobile games with the KToolbar tool

Game Debugging Basics

Before getting into a serious discussion regarding mobile game debugging, let's take a moment to define exactly what a bug is. A bug is simply a coding error that results in some unwanted action taking place in your game. This unwanted action can vary from a score not being updated correctly to the user's phone going down in flames. Although the latter case is admittedly a little exaggerated, you should take bugs very seriously because they speak volumes about the quality (or lack of quality) of your games.

The concept of bugs has been an accepted part of programming for a long time now. Although all programmers strive for perfection, few are ever able to attain it. Even those that do reach that nerd nirvana typically encounter significant numbers of bugs along the way. The difference is that these programmers anticipate bugs rather than imagine that their code is immune to bugs. Therefore, the first rule in regard to debugging is to assume that bugs are in your code and that it is your responsibility to hunt them down and fix them to the best of your ability.

The issue of finding and fixing bugs is especially important in games, because game players are often very fickle. If a game does something screwy like trashing a player's score, the player will probably get frustrated and toss your game. This makes it all the more important to be vigilant in finding bugs before you release your game. Sure, you can always distribute a patch to fix a bug in a release version, but it typically leaves game players with a less than high opinion of your development ethic.

Before getting into specific debugging strategies, let's go over a few debugging basics. If you are already familiar with debugging in Java or in another language, feel free to jump to the next section. The following are three fundamental debugging techniques that you will find indispensable when finding and fixing bugs in your mobile games:

▶ Single-stepping code   ▶ Using breakpoints

▶ Watching variables

The next few sections explore these debugging techniques in a little more detail.

Single-Stepping Code

A very common debugger feature is the capability of single-stepping through code. Single-stepping is the process of executing your code one line at a time (in single steps). The significance of single-stepping as a debugging technique is that it provides you with a way to see exactly what code is being executed, as well as trace the flow of execution through your program. Typically, single-stepping in itself isn't entirely useful; you usually combine it with another technique known as *watching* to see what happens to variables as you step through code.

A debugger is a software tool specifically designed to help you find bugs by letting you analyze your code as it is running. The Java 2 SDK ships with a debugger called jdb, which you learn about a little later in the "Choosing a Debugger" section.

Gamer's Garage

Watching Variables

Watching is a technique that involves specifying certain variables in your code as *watch variables*. A watch variable is a variable whose contents you can see while code is executing in a debugger. Of course, in the context of a program running at normal speed, watch variables don't help much. But if you watch variables as you single-step through code, you can gain lots of insight into what is happening. Very often, you will find that the values of variables are changing unexpectedly or being set to values that don't make sense in the context of what you thought the code was doing. This type of insight into the inner workings of your code can lead you directly to bugs. Single-stepping combined with watch variables provides a standard approach to finding bugs with a debugger.

Using Breakpoints

Another fundamental debugging technique is that of using breakpoints. A breakpoint is a line of code that halts a program's execution. To understand the usefulness of breakpoints, imagine that you are interested in a line of code in the middle of a program. To get to that line of code in the debugger, you would have to single-step for hours. Or you could set a breakpoint on that line and let the debugger run the program like normal. The program then runs in the debugger until it hits the breakpoint, in which case the program halts and leaves you sitting on the specified line of code. At this point, you can watch variables and even single-step through the code if you want. You also have the option of setting multiple breakpoints at key locations in your code, which is very useful when dealing with complex execution flow problems.

Game Debugging Strategies

Although debugging tools have come a long way since the early days of programming, the ultimate responsibility of eliminating bugs still rests squarely on your shoulders. Think of debuggers and standard debugging techniques simply as a means of helping you find bugs, but not as your sole line of bug defense. It takes a diversified arsenal of knowledge, programming practices, debugging tools, and even some luck to truly rid your mobile games of bugs.

Debugging can almost be likened to a hunt: You know there is something out there, and you must go find it. For this reason, you need to approach debugging with a very definite strategy. Debugging strategies can be broken into two fundamental groupings: bug prevention and bug detection. Let's take a look at both and see how they can be used together to help make your games bug free.

Bug Prevention

Bug prevention is the process of eliminating the occurrence of bugs before they have a chance to surface. Bug prevention might sound completely logical, and that's because it is. However, surprising numbers of programmers don't employ enough bug prevention strategies in their code, and they end up paying for it in the end. Keep in mind the simple fact that bug detection is a far more time-consuming and brain-aching task than bug prevention. I'm all for bug prevention as a primary way to eliminate bugs.

Think of bug prevention versus bug detection as roughly parallel to getting an immunization shot versus treating a disease after you've contracted it. Certainly the short-term pain of getting the shot is much easier to deal with than the long-term treatment associated with a full-blown disease. This metaphor is dangerously on the money when it comes to debugging, because bugs can often act like code diseases; just when you think you've got a bug whipped, it rears its ugly head in a new way that you never anticipated.

Getting Explicit with Parentheses and Precedence

One area prone to bugs is that of operator precedence. I've been busted plenty of times myself for thinking that I remembered the precedence of operators correctly when I didn't. Take a look at the following code:

```
int a = 37, b = 26;
int n = a % 3 + b / 7 ^ 8;
```

If you are a whiz at remembering things and you can immediately say without a shadow of a doubt what this expression is equal to, then good for you. For the rest of us, this is a pretty risky piece of code because it can yield a variety of different results depending on the precedence of the operators. Actually, it only yields one result, based on the correct order of operator precedence set forth by the Java language. But it's easy for programmers to mix up the precedence and write code that they think is doing one thing when it is doing something else.

What's the solution? The solution is to use parentheses even when you don't technically need them, just to be safe about the precedence. The following is the same code with extra parentheses added to make the precedence more clear:

```
int a = 37, b = 26;
int n = ((a % 3) + (b / 7)) ^ 8;
```

Avoiding Hidden Member Variables

Another potentially tricky bug that is common in object-oriented game programming is the hidden member variable. A hidden member variable is a variable that has become "hidden" because of a derived class implementing a new variable of the same name. Take a look at Listing 16.1, which contains two classes: Weapon and Bazooka.

LISTING 16.1   The Weapon and Bazooka Classes

```
class Weapon {
  int power;
  int numShots;

  public Weapon() {
    power = 5;
    numShots = 10;
  }

  public void fire() {
    numShots--;
  }
}

class Bazooka : extends Weapon {
  int numShots;

  public Bazooka() {
    super();
  }

  public blastEm() {
    power--;
    numShots -= 2;
  }
}
```

The numShots variable in the Weapon class is decremented.

This numShots variable hides the numShots variable in the parent Weapon class.

The numShots variable in the Bazooka class is decremented, whereas the hidden numShots variable in Weapon remains unchanged.

The Weapon class defines two member variables: power and numShots. The Bazooka class is derived from Weapon and also implements a numShots member variable, which effectively hides the original numShots inherited from Weapon. The problem with this code is that when the Weapon constructor is called by Bazooka (via the call to super()), the hidden numShots variable defined in Weapon is initialized, not the one in Bazooka. Later, when the blastEm() method is called in Bazooka, the visible (derived) numShots variable is used, which has been initialized by default to zero. As you can probably imagine, more complex classes with this problem can end up causing some seriously tricky and hard-to-trace bugs, especially in game code.

The solution to the problem is to simply make sure that you never hide variables. That doesn't mean that there aren't a few isolated circumstances in which you might want to use variable hiding on purpose; just keep in mind the risks involved in doing so.

Making the Most of Exception Handling

One useful preventive debugging mechanism in Java is exception handling, which is a technique focused on detecting and responding to unexpected events at runtime. An exception is something (usually bad) that occurs in your program that you weren't expecting.

To handle exceptions in your game code, you enclose potentially troublesome code within a try clause. A try clause is a special Java construct that tells the runtime system that a section of code could cause trouble. You then add another piece of code (a handler) in a corresponding catch clause that responds to errors caused by the code in the try clause. The error event itself is the exception, and the code in the catch clause is known as an exception handler.

Following is some exception handling code that you've seen used throughout the book in a few places:

```
try {
  // Do something that is capable of causing an exception
}
catch (Exception e) {
  System.err.println(e);
}
```

In this code, the exception being handled is of type Exception, which is the most general of all exceptions. In some cases you may want to take action in response to an exception, as opposed to just printing information about the exception to the standard error "device." You may even opt to do nothing in response to some exceptions, as you've seen done throughout the book in some of the example MIDlets.

Java supports standard input and output devices, the latter of which can be used to display debugging information. System.err is the standard error "device," which is handy for printing messages that are displayed in a special error window or on the command line from which the J2ME emulator is run. The System.err.println() method prints a string to the standard error device.

Construction Cue

This discussion of exception handling really only scratches the surface of handling runtime errors (exceptions). I strongly encourage you to learn more about exception handling and how to effectively use it. Fortunately, a lot of information has been published about exception handling in Java, so you shouldn't have much trouble finding useful references.

Bug Detection

Even if you rigorously employ bug avoidance techniques, you will still have to contend with a certain number of bugs. It's just a fact of life that programmers make mistakes, and the sheer complexity of many mobile game programming projects often causes problems that elude us. Just embrace the notion that you're imperfect and focus your attention on tracking down the mistakes. The point is that in addition to applying bug prevention techniques as much as possible, you must learn how to track down the inevitable bugs that will surface when you start testing your game. Let's look at a few techniques for hunting down bugs.

Taking Advantage of Standard Output

The age-old technique for tracking down bugs is to print information to standard output. This approach probably sounds pretty archaic, and in many ways it is, but if you want a quick and dirty look into what's going on in your game, it's often your best bet.

Employing the standard output technique is as simple as inserting calls to System.out.println() at appropriate locations in your code. You can use standard output for anything from looking at the value of variables to determining whether a method is being called; just sprinkle those println() calls wherever you need them! The primary caveat to this approach is that you should be careful when placing the println() call in an update loop, such as the update() method, which controls the animation in MIDlet games. In this case, the println() call might slow the game to a crawl simply because of the overhead involved in printing text to the standard output device at such a rapid pace.

> Standard output is very similar to the standard error device. In fact, in many cases they are one and the same. However, it is generally a good idea to print error messages to the standard error device, and save standard output for general debugging information.

Tracing the Call Stack

An indispensable tool in tracking down hard-to-find bugs is the *method call stack*. The method call stack is a list of the methods called to arrive at the currently executing code. By examining the call stack, you can see exactly which methods were called to get to the current piece of code in question. This information often sheds light on a problem regarding a method being called inadvertently.

You can view the call stack by calling the printStackTrace() method, which is a member of the Throwable class. Because printStackTrace() is a method in Throwable, you must have a Throwable object to look at the call stack. It just so happens that all exceptions are derived from Throwable, so any time you have an exception, you can view the call stack. Check out the following code:

```
try {
  int nums[] = new int[5];
  for (int i = 0; i < 10; i++)
    nums[i] = 6670;
}
catch (ArrayIndexOutOfBoundsException e) {
  System.out.println("**Exception** : " + e.getMessage());
  e.printStackTrace();
}
```

Print the call stack.

In this code, the array nums is indexed out of bounds in the for loop, generating an ArrayIndexOutOfBoundsException. The exception is logged to standard output in the catch clause, along with a call to printStackTrace().

Choosing a Debugger

An important regarding how you finally decide to debug your game is that of choosing a debugger. A debugger is an invaluable tool in ridding your game of bugs, and it can directly determine how much time you spend debugging. Therefore, you should make sure to invest your resources wisely and choose a debugger that fits your development style.

There are several third-party integrated development environments that include built-in visual debuggers for Java. These are very nice and usually include lots of cool features beyond the ones you just learned about; definitelylook into getting a full-featured debugger if at all possible.

Just keep in mind that choosing a debugger that fits your needs is important in determining how successfully you can rid your code of bugs. Fortunately, nearly all debuggers perform the basic debugging functions of single-stepping, supporting watch variables, and using breakpoints.

For the record, I'm both stubborn and "old-school," which aren't two good traits to combine. I'm telling you this because I developed all the code for this book using nothing more than the System.out.println() method for all of my debugging. If you find my code to be riddled with bugs, at least I have a good excuse! But seriously, the point is that you don't have to use elaborate tools as long as you're committed to writing robust code and doing a lot of testing.

Construction Cue

The Java 2 SDK comes standard with a debugger (jdb) that performs basic debugging functions such as those you learned about earlier. It is a command-line debugger, which means that it has no fancy graphics or point-and-click features but it does get the job done. If you aren't ready to commit to a third-party tool, by all means try out jdb. After you get comfortable with jdb, you might find that it serves your purposes well enough.

Before you can use jdb, you need to compile your code so that it includes debugging information. The Java compiler switch for doing this is -g, which causes the compiler to generate debugging tables containing information about line numbers and variables.

Using the jdb debugger is a topic best left to the introductory books on Java. However, there is a nice online tutorial for using jdb to debug Java code on Sun's Java website, which is located at http://java.sun.com/learning/.

Gamer's Garage

Deploying Mobile Games

Unlike traditional PC and console games, which are usually distributed on a CD-ROM, mobile games are typically downloaded and installed directly over a wireless network. This primarily has to do with the fact that most mobile phones don't support removable media such as CD-ROMs, but they do all have network connectivity. Knowing that your games will be installed over a network connection, you can probably guess that there are some installation issues that need to be addressed before you can make your mobile games available to the general public.

There are actually two options when it comes to downloading and installing mobile games:

▶ **Local installation**—The MIDlet is transferred from your local computer to your mobile phone over a direct connection such as a USB cable.

▶ **Remote installation**—The MIDlet is downloaded and installed over a wireless network connection.

The first scenario is what you may have already been using to test the example games in this book on your own mobile phone. This option is entirely device dependent, meaning that you have to rely on whatever direct connection is supported by your phone. You also end up using your phone's own Application Management Software, or AMS, to successfully install the mobile game MIDlet through a direct connection.

Gamer's Garage

You will likely need a special cable to perform a "local install" of your own mobile games to a mobile phone for testing. Most phones use a USB or serial cable for establishing a direction connection, although you may find Infrared (IR) or Bluetooth to be a viable wireless option for some phones. Of course, you will need Bluetooth support on your PC to carry out a direct Bluetooth connection; you can buy a USB Bluetooth adapter that simply plugs into a USB port on your PC.

The second approach still involves your phone's AMS, but it retrieves the game from a remote network connection. In this scenario, you typically visit a website that has a link to the mobile game's JAD file. Upon downloading the JAD file, which includes information about the game such as the size of the JAR file, you can then continue on by downloading the JAR file itself. The remainder of the installation then proceeds through the AMS as if you had transferred the game through a direct connection.

So, to summarize, the critical difference between the two mobile game installation options is how a game's JAR file is acquired. It is either transferred directly over a local connection or downloaded remotely from a web server. Because the first approach is almost entirely dependent on your phone's own unique AMS, I'll focus on the second approach, which is in fact much more important for distributing your mobile games to end users.

Understanding Over-the-Air Provisioning

The process of downloading and installing a mobile game over a wireless network connection is known as *over-the-air provisioning*, or OTA provisioning for short.

OTA provisioning is a fairly new concept in application delivery that is entirely unique to wireless mobile devices. The general idea is to allow users to get information about a mobile application before committing to downloading and installing it. Additionally, OTA provisioning relies on existing, stable technologies for delivering MIDlet files. More specifically, mobile games are accessed via web page hyperlinks, and then downloaded from web servers.

To offer a mobile game for download and installation via OTA provisioning, you must make it available on a web server. More specifically, the following files are typically used when a mobile game is made available for OTA provisioning:

▶ A JAD file

▶ A JAR file

▶ An HTML or WML web page with a link to the JAD/JAR file

As you already know, a JAD file is a small text file that contains a description of a MIDlet or suite of MIDlets. The JAR file in this case is the game itself, as it has been packaged for distribution. You are already accustomed to packaging mobile games into JAR files and creating JAD files to test them in the J2ME emulator. The only missing ingredient is the HTML or WML web page that provides a link to the JAD or JAR file.

Construction Cue

In case you don't remember, the JAR file for a mobile game contains all the compiled class files, a manifest file (similar to the JAD file), and all the resources for the game (images, wave sounds, and so on).

It is possible to serve up a mobile game via OTA provisioning using nothing more than a web page that links directly to the game's JAR file. However, this isn't a very user-friendly approach because it requires the user to download the entire game before learning any details about it. The purpose of a JAD file is to provide somewhat of a preview of what the user is getting. I don't mean a preview in terms of how the game plays or anything like that—I simply mean the version of the game, the size of the JAR file, and so on.

Gamer's Garage

Don't forget that most mobile phone users are charged for how much data they receive over their wireless data network. This is why JAD files play such an important role in OTA provisioning: They enable a user to get information about a game with a minimal transfer of data.

In reality, although you can certainly serve your own mobile games directly from your own websites, it helps immensely to partner with a game "syndication" company or a wireless carrier. This can be the entire difference in your game getting noticed by a wide audience or falling completely off the radar. Partnering with a wireless carrier is a fairly difficult prospect for a new game developer, but there are several wireless game and application syndication sites that are worth considering. JAMDAT Mobile (http://www.jamdat.com/) and MFORMA (http://www.mforma.com/) are two good options that focus solely on games, whereas Handango (http://www.handango.com/) delivers both wireless games and other applications.

Preparing Your Game for Deployment

You've already grown accustomed to packaging MIDlet games into JAR files and creating a JAD file to go with it. But you haven't learned how to create a web page that is capable of providing a link to a downloadable game online. Two options are available for creating such a web page: HTML and WML. As you probably know, HTML (HyperText Markup Language) is the standard language used to create the vast majority of web pages out there. However, many mobile phones use a smaller, scaled-down version of HTML known as WML (Wireless Markup Language). WML is ideal for mobile phones because it limits web pages to a much simpler user interface that is easier to view on small screens.

Construction Cue

After packaging a MIDlet into a JAR file, there is an optional step where you can digitally sign a MIDlet for security purposes. Signed MIDlets are considered more secure than unsigned MIDlets because their publisher (you) has been validated and the end user can rest assured that no one other than the publisher has tampered with the MIDlet. It is a good idea to sign your mobile game MIDlets before making them available to the general public. Unfortunately, MIDlet signing is a bit beyond the scope of this book. I encourage you to refer to the User's Guide with the J2ME Wireless Toolkit to learn more about security and signed MIDlets.

The decision to use HTML or WML in creating a delivery web page for your games ultimately depends on the specific mobile phones you are targeting. Fortunately, it is very easy to hedge your bets and create pages in both languages. The key element required in a delivery web page regardless of the language of choice is an anchor tag that provides a link to the game's JAD/JAR file. Following is how this line of code is structured:

```
<a href="http://localhost:2728/HighSeas2/bin/HighSeas2.jad">HighSeas2.jad</a>
```

Even if you aren't too familiar with HTML/WML, it's not too hard to read between the lines in this code and see that a URL is being provided that is linked to the text `HighSeas2.jad`. In this particular example, the URL is to a local file, as is evident by `localhost` in the URL. In a web page that is serving up a game on a true web server, the code would look more like this:

```
<a href="http://www.stalefishlabs/games/HighSeas2.jad">HighSeas2.jad</a>
```

This code shows how a more traditional URL is provided as a link for the High Seas 2 JAD file.

The hyperlink for the game that is marked up with the `<a>` tag is coded the same in both HTML and WML web pages. Listing 16.2 contains the HTML version of the High Seas 2 delivery web page, whereas Listing 16.3 contains the WML version.

LISTING 16.2   The `HighSeas2.html` HTML Web Page Includes a Link That Delivers the High Seas 2 JAD File

```
<html>
<head>
<title>HighSeas2</title>
</head>
<body>
<a href="http://localhost:2728/HighSeas2/bin/HighSeas2.jad">HighSeas2.jad</a>
</body>
</html>
```

LISTING 16.3   The `HighSeas2.wml` WML Web Page Includes a Link That Delivers the High Seas 2 JAD File

```
<wml>
<card id="High Seas 2" title="High Seas 2 MIDlet">
<a href="http://localhost:2728/HighSeas2/bin/HighSeas2.jad">HighSeas2.jad</a>
</card>
</wml>
```

It isn't terribly important that you understand the code surrounding the hypertext link to the JAD file in each of these code listings. Just know that the URL in the links must point to the absolute location of the JAD file on the web server.

With a suitable web page now ready to provide users with access to your mobile game, there is one other important step you must take to make the game available for successful wireless download. Within the JAD file for the MIDlet, there is a reference to the JAR file that looks something like this:

```
MIDlet-Jar-URL: HighSeas.jar
```

You must change this JAR file reference to be the exact absolute URL for the JAR file as it resides on the web server. Assuming the JAR file is in the same location as the JAD file in Listings 16.2 and 16.3, the following change does the trick:

```
MIDlet-Jar-URL: http://localhost:2728/HighSeas2/bin/HighSeas2.jar
```

Again, this URL points to an actual web address and not a local address in a MIDlet that is deployed on a real web server.

You've almost successfully made your mobile game MIDlet ready for prime time. If you've already tried to download and install the MIDlet over the air from a web page and found that it didn't work, it's because you're still missing a tweak on your web server settings. Let's find out how to fix that!

Tweaking Your Web Server

For a web browser to successfully serve up JAD and JAR files, it must recognize both types of files according to their official MIME types. A MIME type is a recognized file type that helps applications figure out what to do with files. HTML, GIF, JPEG, and other popular web file formats all have recognizable MIME types. Because JAD and JAR files are fairly new in the big picture of browsers and the web, your web server likely doesn't currently recognize them by MIME type. For this reason, you'll need to configure your web server to recognize the following MIME types:

- ▶ JAD files—`text/vnd.sun.j2me.app-descriptor`
- ▶ JAR files—`application/java-archive`

The specifics of how to carry out this configuration change on a web server are unique to your web server software. If you administer your own web server, just refer to the documentation. If someone else administers your web server, ask how to go about registering these two new MIME types.

Testing OTA Provisioning with KToolbar

Although testing OTA provisioning of your mobile game with a real web server and a real mobile phone is ultimately your goal before releasing the game to the general public, there is a way to simulate the provisioning process. The KToolbar application that ships with the J2ME Wireless Toolkit allows you to run a MIDlet in "OTA mode," which simply means that the MIDlet is downloaded and installed from a local file as if it was being delivered remotely via OTA provisioning. This is an incredibly useful feature for testing mobile game installation without having to rely on a real web server and phone.

To run a MIDlet in OTA mode, follow these steps:

1. Copy the game folder (HighSeas, for example) to the apps folder within the J2ME Wireless Toolkit install folder.

2. From the KToolbar menu, click Project; then Run via OTA.

3. Follow the steps in the emulator to install and run the MIDlet.

The first step is necessary so that the game is accessible as a project from within KToolbar. The second step then launches the J2ME emulator in OTA mode, which simulates the game being delivered over a wireless network connection. The last step involves interacting with the emulator's AMS, which is ultimately responsible for allowing you to carry out the installation of the game.

After an initial splash screen, the emulator displays an option enabling you to install a mobile application. Selecting this option results in the display of a text entry form where you can enter the URL of the MIDlet delivery web page, as shown in Figure 16.1. What's nice in this case is that the delivery web page is generated for you automatically, as is the URL.

Accepting the URL for the delivery web page results in the emulator downloading the page for the MIDlet and then searching it for links. Figure 16.2 shows the web page being downloaded into the emulator.

FIGURE 16.1
The J2ME emulator starts out in OTA mode by displaying the URL for the High Seas 2 MIDlet's delivery web page.

FIGURE 16.2
The J2ME emulator is busy downloading the delivery web page so that it can access the MIDlet's JAD/JAR link(s).

FIGURE 16.3
The MIDlet's JAD file is shown so that you can select it for viewing.

After finding a JAD file for the High Seas 2 MIDlet, the J2ME emulator displays the file for you to select (see Figure 16.3).

After you select the High Seas 2 JAD file and proceed onward, the emulator downloads the JAD file and retrieves MIDlet information from it. Figure 16.4 shows a Confirmation screen for the High Seas 2 installation that enables you to see information about the MIDlet before finalizing its installation. Notice that the JAR file size (95K), MIDlet version, and software vendor are all displayed on this screen.

If you select Install to move forward with the High Seas 2 installation, you will be presented with a download screen similar to the one shown in Figure 16.5.

Upon successfully downloading the MIDlet to the emulator, you will finally see the MIDlet added to the list of installed applications, as shown in Figure 16.6.

FIGURE 16.4
The emulator's Confirmation screen allows you to view information about the MIDlet prior to download-ing and installing it.

The figure reveals that you can now launch the MIDlet and play the game. You might also notice that an Update option is visible on the emulator menu. Updating a MIDlet is similar to installing a MIDlet, except that the update takes place only if there is a newer version of the MIDlet available. If you recall, the version number is list-ed right there in the JAD file, so it's possible to look for a new version of a MIDlet simply by checking the JAD file quickly. This makes it easy for you to offer updated games that users can download easily.

Summary

This chapter took you down two different but equally important paths that lead to delivering a quality game to eager mobile game players. The first topic was game debugging, where you learned not only the importance of diagnosing and putting an end to bugs in games, but also some valuable tips on how to help prevent bugs before they can even appear. You then moved on to mobile game deployment, which involves making a game available for download and installation over a wireless network. Although there are a few steps required to prepare a game for wireless deployment, you found out that it's nothing complicated or particularly challenging. You also found out how the J2ME Wireless Toolkit makes it possible to simulate a wireless mobile game installation without a real web server or mobile phone.

This chapter marks the end of this part of the book, but there is still plenty to come. The next part of the book focuses on sprucing up your mobile games. We provide optimization tips and tricks, a way to keep persistent high scores, and a complete space shoot-em-up game that you design and build from scratch.

FIGURE 16.5
The emulator's download screen shows you the progress of the MIDlet download.

FIGURE 16.6
The successfully installed MIDlet is shown in the emulator's application list, ready to be run.

Field Trip

It's time to put some of your hard work to practical use. Whether it's your own game that you've already begun developing, or one of the example games you've seen throughout this book, find a game to offer up for OTA provisioning. Follow the steps presented throughout this chapter, and make the game available for download from a real web page. Now travel as far away from your desktop computer as possible, even if it means taking a small vacation. Just make sure to take your mobile phone with you. Now connect to the web page from your phone over a wireless connection and download and install the game. This field trip is revealing because it shows the power and flexibility of mobile game delivery.

PART V

Sprucing Up Your Games

CHAPTER 17

Optimizing Mobile Java Games

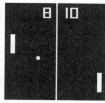

Arcade Archive

In 1983, Bally Midway released what is undoubtedly the most well-known spy racing game to date, Spy Hunter. Your character in the game is a secret agent along the lines of James Bond, who is behind the wheel of a car or boat equipped with all kinds of cool weapons. The game is a top-view vertically scrolling driving game, but shooting up the bad guys is just as much work as driving around them. The name of the main car in the game is G-6155, which is a tribute to the game's designer, George Gomez—the numbers are his birthday. The early prototype of the game used the James Bond theme song, but the music was switched to the Peter Gunn theme song in the final game when rights couldn't be secured for the Bond theme.

You know that mobile phones are constrained in terms of how much memory and processing power they have at their disposal. These devices have certainly come a long way in the past few years, but it is still unfair to compare the capabilities of a mobile phone to PCs or console game systems. For this reason, you must design and code mobile games with the limited capabilities of mobile phones in mind. Fortunately, the MIDP API goes a long way toward helping you create efficient MIDlet games because the API itself is optimized for mobile devices. However, this does not mean there aren't things you can do to optimize your games for maximum performance. The optimization strategies you learn in this chapter include MIDP-specific optimizations as well as general Java and game coding optimizations that apply to mobile game development.

In this chapter, you'll learn

- ▶ The fundamentals of mobile game optimization
- ▶ Different techniques for optimizing mobile games

▶ Coding tricks for optimizing mobile Java game code

▶ How to use a profiler to isolate and target game code for optimization

▶ How to track memory usage of your mobile game code

Understanding Mobile Game Optimization

The vast majority of mobile phones have significantly less computing power than their desktop, console, and even handheld computer counterparts. This normally wouldn't be of much concern because such devices have traditionally been used only to perform relatively mundane tasks. However, this book is about developing games for mobile phones, and games have long been known for pushing the envelope in terms of processor and memory requirements. It is no small challenge to develop compelling games on hardware as limited as mobile phones have to offer. Optimization is one of the key strategies a mobile game developer has in trying to overcome this challenge.

For better or for worse, the Java programming language is extremely flexible. You can create bloated, inefficient code even in an efficient environment such as the one offered by J2ME. Additionally, even if your code is reasonably efficient, the design of your mobile game could be inefficient and result in poor performance. For example, it could be that you are processing far more data than is ideal within the constraints of a mobile phone, or maybe your game AI performs complex computational tasks that are not suited to a device with such limited processing power. Anyone can get carried away and attempt to incorporate into mobile games the depth of features found in PC or console games, which is usually not a good idea.

The moral of the story here is that you should do everything in your power to create *optimized MIDlets*, which are MIDlets that are designed to be extremely efficient, resulting in a minimal strain on device resources. Obviously, there are limitations to how much you can optimize a MIDlet. Realistically, mobile network connections are usually relatively slow, so it is to be expected that MIDlets that are heavily dependent on networking are not going to be as responsive as non-networked MIDlets. Does this mean you shouldn't develop networked mobile games? If the previous section of the book is any indication, the answer is obviously no. However, you should attempt to minimize the amount of data being transferred over a mobile network connection to help reduce the effects of relatively limited bandwidth.

There are several facets to MIDlet optimization, some of which are considerably more important to mobile game development than others. The following are the three main aspects of a MIDlet that you should assess when optimizing your games:

- Maintainability
- Portability
- Size
- Speed

The next few sections explore each of these types of optimization in more detail.

Optimizing for Maintainability

The least important type of mobile game optimization is maintainability optimization, which involves taking steps to help make your code more manageable in the future. This type of optimization is usually geared toward the structure and organization of code, rather than modifications of the algorithms used in the code. In general, maintainability optimization involves studying a game and making changes to help other programmers understand and modify its code in the future.

In many ways, maintainability optimization works against the other two types of optimization because it stresses the understanding and organization of code in a MIDlet over the size or performance of the code. For this reason, maintainability optimization doesn't rank very high on the list of important optimizations used by mobile game developers. It is still important to organize your code, enforce some structure, and by all means document the code well, but don't let maintainability optimization become an overriding concern. Players of your games will never know how elegant or well documented your code is, so make sure that your games are playable before you spend too much time optimizing for maintainability.

Even though I've downplayed the importance of optimizing mobile games for maintainability, I am in no way suggesting that you take a cavalier attitude toward organizing and documenting your code. Keep in mind that if you create a successful game, you'll likely want to be able to create sequels and spin-offs to capitalize on its success. The cleaner and better documented your code is, the easier it will be for you to create additional games from an existing code base.

Gamer's Garage

Optimizing for Portability

Similar to optimizing a mobile game for maintainability, optimizing a game for portability has more to do with easing development hassles than it does improving the performance of a game. By portability, I'm referring to the process of releasing a game for different mobile phones. As you probably know, hardware varies considerably from one mobile phone to another, and can therefore dramatically impact how a game runs. Even more important, perhaps, is the considerable variance in mobile phone screen sizes, which often necessitate redesigns of game graphics.

To successfully optimize a mobile game for portability, you must clearly identify the main distinctions between the mobile phones that you are targeting. For example, you might determine that the processors among several phones are fairly similar, but the screen sizes and available memory vary considerably. In this event, you would want to focus your portability optimizations on making the graphics easily scalable, as well as possibly building in options to limit parts of the game on the phones with less memory.

Construction Cue

One way to make the graphics for a game more portable is to use graphics primitives (lines, rectangles, ellipses, and so on) instead of bitmap images. Graphics primitives are easily scaled, whereas bitmap images typically have to be scaled with an image editor to preserve image quality. Graphics primitives work particularly well if you're attempting to emulate classic vector arcade games such as Battlezone and Asteroids.

The ultimate goal of portability optimization is to avoid having to rewrite significant portions of a game to port it to different mobile phones. With only a small amount of foresight and planning, you should be able to develop portable games that require only isolated code and graphics changes to run on a wide range of mobile phones.

Construction Cue

You learned in Chapter 3, "Constructing a Mobile Game Skeleton," how to determine the screen size and number of colors supported by a particular mobile phone. With this information, you may be able to design mobile games that respond to device capabilities on the fly and adjust themselves accordingly. This may not be realistic for all games, but it works particularly well with games that rely on graphics primitives and bitmap images that don't require scaling. The Connect4 game in Chapter 15, "Connect 4: A Classic Game Goes Wireless," is a good example of a game that scales well to different mobile phones without requiring any modifications.

Optimizing for Size

Another type of mobile game optimization is size optimization, which primarily involves making changes to code that result in smaller executable class files. Size optimization is important to mobile games because it determines a game's memory requirements. The cornerstone of size optimization is code reuse, which comes in the form of inheritance for Java classes. Fortunately, good object-oriented design strategies naturally favor size optimization, so you will rarely need to go out of your way to perform this type of optimization, at least when it comes to game code. For example, it is just good design practice to place code that is reused a few times within a method. In this way, some degree of size optimization naturally takes place during the initial code development for a game.

A more important facet of mobile game size optimization deals with the resources required by games, such as images, sound effects, and music. Compared to compiled Java bytecode, game resources can get very large if you aren't careful. You need to be extremely vigilant when tightening up the image and sound requirements for your mobile games. This can mean using smaller images, fewer images, and lower-quality sounds, to name a few possibilities. You also should carefully monitor the size of any other data that a mobile game requires, such as data that is read from a network or stored for later use.

You can really gain some quick size savings in your mobile games by crunching wave sounds down to the lowest possible sound quality you can stand. For example, all the wave sounds in the examples throughout this book are recorded as 8kHz 8-bit mono sounds.

Construction Cue

Optimizing for Speed

Speed optimization is arguably the most important optimization approach for mobile games because it does the most to determine how well they perform. Speed optimization involves speeding up the execution of game code by fine-tuning the code. Considering the performance problems inherent in Java, not to mention the relatively slow processors employed by mobile phones, speed optimization plays a critical role in MIDlet development of any kind, but it is especially important for MIDlet games. The Java compiler has the last word on how executable Java bytecode is generated, so most speed optimizations must be performed with the compiler in mind.

Much of this chapter focuses on issues of speed optimization and how to get the best performance from your MIDlet code. At times, you will sacrifice the other areas of optimization for the sake of speed. In most cases, this sacrifice is entirely acceptable, even expected, because the organization of the code and size of the executable classes won't matter much if a mobile game is too slow to be any fun. However, you still must strike a balance between optimizing for speed and optimizing for size. A fast MIDlet game that is too big to fit within the memory constraints of a mobile phone and too slow to download over a wireless connection clearly isn't beneficial. Fortunately, size and speed optimizations sometimes go hand in hand because simpler algorithms can often be faster and smaller than complex algorithms.

Gamer's Garage

As a benchmark, you want for your games to be able to run at a minimum of 15fps or 20fps without any noticeable stutters or hiccups in the animation. To refresh yourself on animation and frame rates, refer back to Chapter 5, "Using Sprite Animation."

General Mobile Game Optimization Tips

Before getting into the specifics of how to tweak Java game code to squeeze every ounce of performance from it, it is worth taking a moment to cover some general MIDlet optimization strategies that you should consider as you begin designing and developing game MIDlets of your own. These strategies focus more on size optimization because the majority of size optimizations take place through the careful design of efficient MIDlets, as opposed to tricky algorithmic code changes. Don't worry—there is plenty of coding trickery in store for you later in the chapter!

Reducing Memory Usage

It's no secret that mobile phones have very little memory as compared to most other computing environments. In many ways, the memory limitations of mobile phones are more constraining than the limited processing power of the devices. It is therefore extremely important to try to reduce the memory usage of mobile games whenever possible. Fortunately, you can employ several practical development practices to reduce the amount of memory required of a game MIDlet:

- ▶ Avoid using objects whenever possible.

- ▶ When you do use objects, try to recycle them.

- ▶ Explicitly clean up objects when you're finished with them.

The next few sections explore these MIDlet memory-reduction techniques in more detail.

Avoiding Objects Whenever Possible

This might seem like a strange suggestion, but it is a good idea to avoid the use of objects in game MIDlets whenever possible. Objects must be allocated from run-time memory, as opposed to primitive data types, which are allocated directly on the stack. Primitive data types, which are also known as *scalars*, include standard Java language types such as `int`, `long`, `boolean`, and `char`. Of course, the CLDC and MIDP APIs are full of classes, and MIDlets themselves are objects, so there are obvious limitations as to how much you can reduce the usage of objects in MIDlets. However, the reduction in object usage has more to do with MIDlet data, which in many cases can be stored in primitive data types as opposed to full-blown objects.

If you study the CLDC and MIDP APIs, you will find that many of the familiar classes used as helper classes throughout the J2SE API are missing. For example, the `Rectangle` class is used throughout the J2SE API as a means of housing the four integers (X, Y, width, and height) that describe a rectangular shape. This class is missing in the MIDP API, and in places where the `Rectangle` class would have been used you use the four integers directly. The memory requirements of the four primitive integers are less than the memory requirements of an object with memory that must be allocated and managed. Therefore, you will notice throughout the CLDC and MIDP APIs that objects are used only when it clearly makes functional sense to use an object. Otherwise, primitive data types are used.

You should follow the lead of the CLDC and MIDP APIs when it comes to your own mobile game data. Don't jump to encapsulate data in a class unless there is a significant reason to do so. Otherwise, you'll be much better off to stick with primitive data types, which are much more efficient than objects.

When You Do Use Objects, Recycle Them

Clearly there is no way to avoid the use of objects entirely in your mobile games. Objects play an extremely important role in all Java programming, and MIDlets are no different in this regard. One way to minimize the memory impact of objects is to recycle them whenever possible. Object recycling is reusing an existing object rather than creating a new one. Of course, this works only in situations where you need to use an object of the same type repeatedly, but you would be surprised at how often this technique can be pulled off in a typical MIDlet.

Construction Cue

> A good example of object recycling is reusing a `Sprite` object as opposed to destroying it and creating a new one; repositioning a sprite can often give the illusion of one sprite being destroyed and another one being created. This approach was used extensively in the High Seas game from Chapters 12, "High Seas: A Game for the Pirate in You" and 13, "Teaching Games to Think."

Object recycling avoids an unnecessary memory allocation. As an example, if you create an object and then quit using it, the Java garbage collector will eventually free the memory allocated for it. If you then need another object of the same type and you create a new one, the memory for the object is allocated all over again. Instead, you could reinitialize the original object rather than create a new one, thereby recycling the object.

Cleaning Up After Yourself

Speaking of recycling and garbage collection, one last optimization tip related to objects involves the manner in which objects are freed from memory. In traditional J2SE or J2EE programming, you create objects at will, and rely on Java's garbage collector to detect when an object is no longer being used and clean it up. J2ME works the same way, but the garbage collector is not exactly the most efficient means of freeing up memory. The garbage collector runs as a low-priority background thread that detects and frees unused objects every so often. An object isn't deemed "unused" until it goes out of scope or is set to `null`.

One way to help the garbage collector is to explicitly set unused objects to `null` so that the garbage collector can go ahead and free the memory for them as soon as possible. All objects eventually get freed from memory, but this little trick helps the garbage collector to clean up objects from memory a little faster.

Minimizing Network Data

You know that mobile phones rely on wireless networking connections that provide relatively slow transfer speeds. Because networked mobile games must communicate over this connection, serious limitations exist as to how much data can be sent and received without causing delays. The last thing a mobile game player wants is to have to wait for a phone to download time-critical information such as another player's movement in a maze shoot-em-up. The solution is to minimize the size of data shuttled across the network in networked games. This might sound obvious, but PC and console game developers don't have to deal so much with the extremely limited bandwidth of wireless phone networks, so minimizing the size of network data isn't quite as crucial to them.

Eliminating Unnecessary Graphics

You might think of all the graphics in your games as being absolutely essential, but in reality this may not be the case. For example, if you have any graphics that are rotated and mirrored in your game, then you are likely wasting precious memory and storage space. This is because the Sprite class allows you to apply a transformation to any sprite image to yield a rotated (in 90° increments) and/or mirrored variation. By taking advantage of sprite transformations, you can potentially reduce the size of your game graphics by 75%.

FIGURE 17.1
The pirate ship sprite in the High Seas example game consists of four directional animation frames.

Consider, for example, the High Seas example game from Chapters 12 and 13. In this game, the pirate ship sprite image consists of four animation frames (see Figure 17.1), which show the ship aiming north, east, south, and west. These directions correspond to 90° rotations, which means that you could eliminate three of the frames and generate them by transforming a single frame by the appropriate angle (90, 180, or 270), as shown in Figure 17.2.

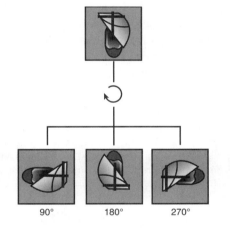

90°   180°   270°

FIGURE 17.2
All but one of the pirate ship animation frames can be eliminated and dynamically generated with sprite transformations.

Gamer's Garage

Using a sprite transformation could negatively impact the realism of some game graphics. For example, the pirate ship in the High Seas game shows the front and back of the sail, along with a shadow cast by the ship that comes from a constant direction. Although this detail is subtle, it is lost when you rotate a single pirate ship image (see Figure 17.2), which causes the ship to look less realistic.

The main drawback to using sprite transformations is that you're sacrificing speed for size. More specifically, it requires a little more overhead to transform a sprite image, as opposed to simply drawing a prepared image. However, in many cases this overhead isn't noticeable, so the size savings is worthwhile.

Java Code Optimization Tricks

Thus far I've discussed mobile game optimization in fairly general terms, without giving any concrete examples of how to tweak game code to get the most out of it. In the next few sections I present some detailed coding techniques you can use to squeeze additional performance out of your MIDlet games. Most of these techniques focus on speeding up game code, as opposed to reducing the size of it, but that's okay because the tweaks will probably be made in isolated places.

This is an important point because you really shouldn't focus on optimizing every bit of your code for speed. Some isolated sections of code are probably called much more often than others. Knowing this, you should focus your optimization efforts on the code that is called the most. Keep in mind that it isn't realistic to think that you'll be able to optimize every piece of problem (slow) code in a game; the goal is to make big dents in the areas that can be optimized without an enormous amount of effort. Later, in the section titled, "Profiling Your Mobile Game Code," you find out how to isolate problem areas of your code so that you can apply optimizations wisely.

Construction Cue

> Do not worry too terribly much about optimizing any code in a mobile game for size or speed until you get the game working. Optimized code can often involve tricky algorithms that are difficult to debug. Therefore, you should always start with working code when it comes time to perform code optimization tricks.

Compiling Without Debug Information

Perhaps the simplest optimization you can make to your mobile games involves no programming at all. I'm referring to the elimination of debug information that is included in your class files by default when you use the Java compiler (javac). By default, the Java compiler includes extra debugging information in every compiled class file that aids debuggers in identifying and analyzing code. After you finish debugging a game, it is very important to turn off debugging information in the Java compiler with the -g:none switch. Following is a simple example of how this switch is used:

```
javac -g:none MyMIDlet.java
```

Fortunately, all the example games and programs included on the CD-ROM for this book are already built with debugging information turned off. In fact, this means that you'll need to remove the -g:none switch if you plan on debugging any of the examples.

Eliminating Unnecessary Evaluations

The next Java optimization technique is purely a coding issue, and has to do with unnecessary evaluations. Such evaluations are problematic because all they do is eat up precious processor time. Following is an example of some code that unnecessarily performs an evaluation that acts effectively as a constant:

```
for (int i = 0; i < size(); i++)
  a = (b + c) / i;
```

The addition of b + c, although itself a pretty efficient piece of code, is better off being calculated before the loop, like this:

```
int tmp = b + c;
for (int i = 0; i < size(); i++)
  a = tmp / i;
```

This simple change could have fairly dramatic effects, depending on how many times the loop is iterated. There is one other optimization you might have missed. Notice that size() is a method call, which might bring to mind the performance costs involved in calling a method versus simply checking a variable. You might not realize it, but size() is being called every time through the loop as part of the conditional loop expression. The same technique used to eliminate the unnecessary addition operation can be used to fix this problem. Check out the resulting code:

```
int s = size();
int tmp = b + c;
for (int i = 0; i < s; i++)
  a = tmp / i;
```

Eliminating Common Subexpressions

While we are on the subject of optimizing expressions, consider another expression problem that robs your code of performance: common subexpressions. You can use a costly subexpression repeatedly in your game code without realizing the consequences. In the heat of programming, it's easy to reuse common subexpressions instead of storing them in a temporary variable, like this:

```
b = Math.abs(a) * c;
d = e / (Math.abs(a) + b);
```

The multiple calls to Math.abs() are costly compared to calling it once and storing the result in a temporary variable, like this:

```
int tmp = Math.abs(a);
b = tmp * c;
d = e / (tmp + b);
```

Taking Advantage of Local Variables

You might not realize it, but it takes longer for Java code to access member variables than it does to access local variables. The reason for this deals with how the two different types of variables are accessed in memory. The practical implication is that you should use local variables rather than member variables whenever performance is critical. For example, if you have a loop that accesses a member variable repeatedly, then you might consider storing the value of the member variable in a local variable just before the start of the loop, and then accessing the local variable within the loop. Following is an example of code that accesses a member variable in a loop:

```
for (int i = 0; i < 1000; i++)
  a = obj.b * i;
```

As you can see, the b member variable of the obj object is accessed 1,000 times within the loop. A quick optimization of this code involves setting the obj.b to a local variable, and then accessing that variable in the loop, like this:

```
int localb = obj.b;
for (int i = 0; i < 1000; i++)
  a = localb * i;
```

Expanding Loops

A popular "brute force" speed optimization trick is known as *loop expansion*, and involves expanding a loop to get rid of the overhead involved in maintaining the loop. You might wonder exactly what overhead this refers to. Even a simple counting loop has the overhead of performing a comparison and an increment each time through. This might not seem like much, but every little bit of performance can matter in games.

Loop expansion involves replacing a loop with the brute-force equivalent. To better understand it, check out the following piece of code:

```
for (int i = 0; i < 1000; i++)
  a[i] = 25;
```

This probably looks like some efficient code, and in fact it is. But if you want to go the extra distance and perform a loop expansion on it, here's one approach:

```
int i = 0;
for (int j = 0; j < 100; j++) {
  a[i++] = 25;
  a[i++] = 25;
  a[i++] = 25;
  a[i++] = 25;
  a[i++] = 25;
  a[i++] = 25;
  a[i++] = 25;
  a[i++] = 25;
  a[i++] = 25;
  a[i++] = 25;
}
```

In this code, you've reduced the loop overhead by an order of magnitude (from 1,000 to 100), but you've introduced some new overhead by having to increment the new index variable (i) inside the loop. Overall, this code does outperform the original code, but don't expect any miracles. Loop expansion can be effective at times, but I don't recommend placing it too high on your list of optimization tricks. Again, it applies only to the most extreme games that are scratching and clawing for every millisecond of improved performance.

Code Shrinking and Obfuscation

Although you, the developer, hold the most power in your hands in terms of reducing the amount of code in your mobile games, there is also an automated approach to reducing code size after your game is ready for prime time. I'm referring to code shrinkers and obfuscators, which are special tools that shrink the size of the code for a Java program as well as rename the identifiers within the code to make it difficult to reverse-engineer. Even the most ruthlessly optimized code will likely still contain a few unused packages, classes, methods, and member variables—that's where a code shrinker comes into play. A code obfuscator isn't so much about efficiency as it is about protecting your code from would-be copycats.

Most code shrinkers and obfuscators are paired together as a single tool. As an example, the open source tool ProGuard serves as both a code shrinker and obfuscator, and can be freely downloaded at http://proguard.sourceforge.net/. Tools such as ProGuard strip out comments and unused code, along with renaming identifiers with shorter, more cryptic names. The end result is class files that are 20% to 50% smaller and more secure, at least in terms of people attempting to steal your code.

Profiling Your Mobile Game Code

An old adage of game programming states that 90% of a game's execution time is spent running 10% of the game's code. What this means is that a fairly small portion of a game's code is actually responsible for most of the processing taking place. This is actually good news because it enables you to focus your optimization efforts on 10% of the game code. Any time you can hone in your optimization efforts to a smaller section of a program, the more likely you'll be to make strides toward making the program more efficient.

The principal challenge for most game developers entering the optimization stage of development is not so much coming up with inventive optimization tricks, but rather finding out what portion of the code constitutes that elusive 10%. Isolating the minority of the game code that has the overriding effect on a game's performance is the single most important facet of game code optimization. Fortunately, there is a tool you can use to help make this task somewhat automatic.

A profiler is a tool that analyzes a program while it is running, and reports on how much time and how many CPU cycles are spent in each part of the program. You can study the data generated by a profiler to determine where most of the time-consuming work is taking place in your games. This information can then serve as a guide for you to focus your optimization efforts, including the tips and tricks you learned about earlier in the chapter.

The J2ME Wireless Toolkit ships with a Java profiler that is relatively easy to use. To get started, open the Preferences application for the J2ME Wireless Toolkit from the standard installation of the toolkit. Click the Monitor tab in the Preferences application, and you'll see a window similar to the one shown in Figure 17.3.

The only difference between the window you see on your computer and the one in the figure is that the Enable Profiling check box probably isn't checked on your end. Check this box to enable profiling for MIDlets. After you click OK, the Java profiler is ready to roll the next time you run a MIDlet game using the J2ME emulator.

The next step is to go ahead and run a game in the emulator, such as the Henway game from Chapter 7, "Henway: Paying Tribute to Frogger." You won't realize the profiler is doing anything until you exit the emulator, after which the profiler application will automatically launch and show you the profiler results for the game. Figure 17.4 shows the profiler results for the Henway game on my computer.

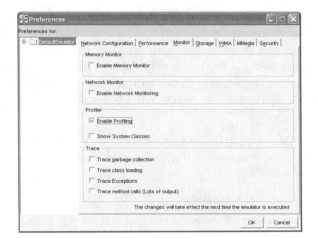

FIGURE 17.3
The Monitor tab of the Preferences application allows you to turn on profiling for the J2ME emulator.

Make sure that you don't run your game code through a code obfuscator prior to using the profiler tool. If you do, the method names reported by the profiler won't make sense.

Construction Cue

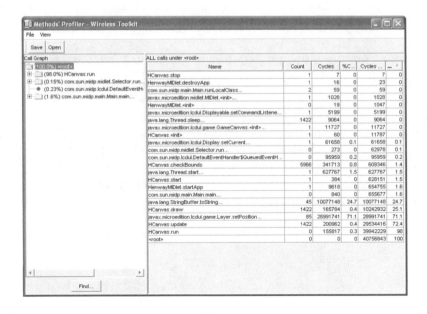

FIGURE 17.4
The J2ME Wireless Toolkit's profiler provides detailed information about where time and processor energy is spent in your game code.

Name	Count	Cycles	%C...	Cycles ...	...
HCanvas.stop	1	7	0	7	0
HenwayMIDlet.destroyApp	1	16	0	23	0
com.sun.midp.main.Main.runLocalClass...	2	59	0	59	0
javax.microedition.midlet.MIDlet.<init>...	1	1028	0	1028	0
HenwayMIDlet.<init>	0	19	0	1047	0
javax.microedition.lcdui.Displayable.setCommandListene...	1	5199	0	5199	0
java.lang.Thread.sleep...	1422	9064	0	9064	0
javax.microedition.lcdui.game.GameCanvas.<init>...	1	11727	0	11727	0
HCanvas.<init>	1	60	0	11787	0
javax.microedition.lcdui.Display.setCurrent...	1	61658	0.1	61658	0.1
com.sun.midp.midlet.Selector.run...	0	273	0	62978	0.1
com.sun.midp.lcdui.DefaultEventHandler$QueuedEventH...	0	95959	0.2	95959	0.2
HCanvas.checkBounds	5966	341713	0.8	609346	1.4
java.lang.Thread.start...	1	627767	1.5	627767	1.5
HCanvas.start	1	384	0	628151	1.5
HenwayMIDlet.startApp	1	9618	0	654755	1.6
com.sun.midp.main.Main.main...	0	840	0	655677	1.6
java.lang.StringBuffer.toString...	45	10077148	24.7	10077148	24.7
HCanvas.draw	1422	165784	0.4	10242932	25.1
javax.microedition.lcdui.game.Layer.setPosition...	85	28991741	71.1	28991741	71.1
HCanvas.update	1422	200962	0.4	29534416	72.4
HCanvas.run	0	155817	0.3	39942229	98
<root>	0	0	0	40756843	100

The job of the Java profiler is to clue you in on where the processor time is being spent in your Java programs. It does this by listing method calls within your MIDlet, along with how much time is spent in each. The method call list, or call graph, is organized as a hierarchical tree in the left pane of the profiler, where child nodes of the tree show method calls within methods. This allows you to drill down into the tree and isolate the exact methods where most of the time is being spent.

The headings in the right tab of the profiler window (see Figure 17.4) are important in figuring out how to understand the profiler data. Following are what the profiler headings mean:

- **Name**—The method's full name
- **Count**—The number of times the method was called
- **Cycles**—The execution time of the method by itself (in CPU cycles)
- **%Cycles**—The percentage of total execution time spent in the method by itself
- **Cycles with Children**—The execution time of the method and any child methods that it calls (in CPU cycles)
- **%Cycles with Children**—The percentage of total execution time spent in the method and any child methods that it calls

You can click on any of the headings to sort according to that particular criterion.

To begin understanding how to use the profiler, take a look at the list of methods in the left pane (again, refer to Figure 17.4). If you add up the percentages of each method, they will always total 100%, which makes sense given that the profiler is showing you a method breakdown of total processor usage. Clicking the plus sign (+) next to a method enables you to drill down and find out how that percentage is further divided among child method calls. In Figure 17.4, the profiler reveals that the HCanvas.run() method hogs 98% of the processor time. Figure 17.5 shows this method expanded to show child method calls.

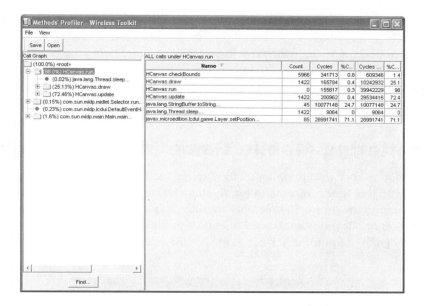

Ah, now things are getting more interesting—Figure 17.5 reveals how the 98% of processor time devoted to `HCanvas.run()` is divided among child methods. More specifically, `HCanvas.draw()` accounts for about 25%, whereas `HCanvas.update()` eats up over 72% of the overall MIDlet processor time. Although this probably isn't a shocker, the profiler has already revealed that nearly three fourths of the processor overhead for the Henway game is accounted for in the `HCanvas.update()` method. This is the kind of information that allows you to tightly focus your code optimization efforts.

> The Java profiler isn't intended to simulate Java code as it runs on specific mobile phones, so it is entirely possible that some phones behave differently than others. In other words, an optimization that works wonders in the emulator may not pay off so greatly on a real mobile phone. For this reason, it is very important to test any optimizations on target devices in addition to the emulator.

Construction Cue

Keep in mind that in most cases the profiler leads you directly to the update and draw code for your games, as you might expect. Even so, you should be able to drill down and figure out which specific method calls are doing the most damage in terms of processor expense. Then you can carry out isolated optimizations based on techniques covered earlier in the chapter in an attempt to make significant performance improvements with relatively small code modifications.

Monitoring Mobile Game Memory Usage

In addition to code profiling, the J2ME Wireless Toolkit also includes a memory monitoring tool that can come in handy in assessing how much memory your mobile games are using. The memory monitor is enabled via the same Preferences application that is used to enable profiling. Figure 17.6 shows the Enable Memory Monitor check box set to enable memory monitoring.

FIGURE 17.6
The Monitor tab of the Preferences application also enables you to turn on memory monitoring for the J2ME emulator.

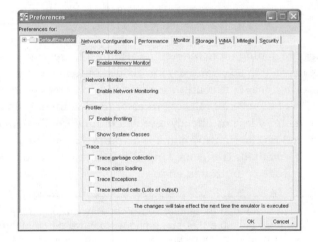

Unlike profiling, which involves analyzing how a MIDlet ran after the fact, memory monitoring is done live while a MIDlet is running. When you enable memory monitoring and run a MIDlet in the J2ME emulator, a memory monitor window launches along with the emulator. Figure 17.7 shows the memory monitor, which begins by showing a trace of memory usage for the MIDlet.

FIGURE 17.7
The memory monitor begins by showing you a memory trace that indicates a mobile game MIDlet's current memory usage.

The memory monitor initially shows the Graph tab, which contains a memory trace for the MIDlet being run. The graph reflects the current amount of memory being used by the MIDlet; refer to the status bar along the bottom of the memory monitor window to see the exact memory amounts and object count. It is interesting to watch the ebb and flow of memory as you play a game in the emulator alongside the memory monitor. You can even simulate memory garbage collections by clicking the Run GC button near the top of the memory monitor window.

The other tab in the memory monitor is the Objects tab, which displays memory information on an object-by-object basis. Figure 17.8 shows the object memory details for the Henway game.

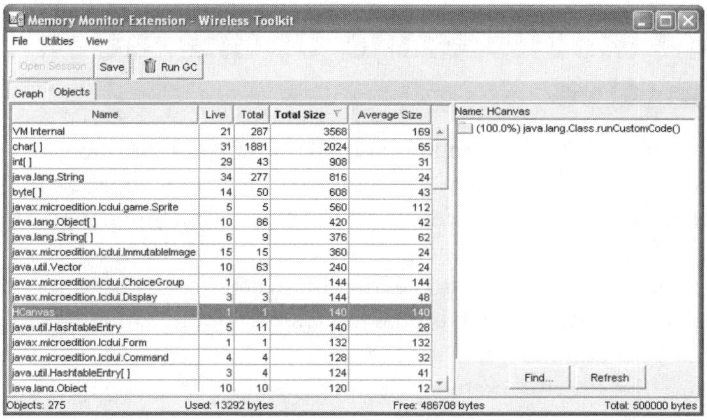

FIGURE 17.8
The Objects tab in the memory monitor provides a detailed look at all the objects in memory for a mobile game.

The left pane of the Objects tab consists of a list of all the objects in memory for a mobile game MIDlet, in this case the Henway game. Following are the meanings of the columns in the left pane object list:

- ▶ **Name**—The object's full name
- ▶ **Live**—The number of active objects in memory
- ▶ **Total**—The total number of objects in memory (live and dead)
- ▶ **Total size**—The total memory taken up by the objects (in bytes)
- ▶ **Average size**—The average size of an individual object (in bytes)

You can use this memory information to determine how many of a particular object are in memory at any given time, along with how much memory the objects are using. Keep in mind that object creation and destruction is a particularly time-consuming chore for mobile games, so you should attempt to reuse objects as much as possible. You can compare the number of live and total objects to see how many objects are being left around in memory between garbage collections. In an ideal world, the live and total numbers would always be equal, which means that no dead objects are left hanging around in memory.

Construction Cue

Although the memory monitor can be very useful in charting the memory requirements of a mobile game MIDlet, it is not a simulation of an actual mobile phone—the memory management on real mobile devices may differ from the J2ME emulator. Even so, the memory monitor is a useful tool for getting a general idea for a mobile game's memory usage.

Putting Mobile Game Optimization into Perspective

Now that you have an understanding of mobile game optimization, not to mention a few techniques for optimizing MIDlet game code, it's time to assess the overall significance of mobile game optimization. To the extent that you design MIDlet games that are relatively efficient and not memory hogs, it is very important to consider the optimization strategies discussed earlier in this chapter. However, I don't recommend focusing too terribly much on the latter speed optimization techniques unless you find that your game is really running too slowly. In other words, it's always good to reduce the size and memory requirements of a MIDlet game, but don't unnecessarily complicate the code to improve speed unless it is truly needed.

One last issue relating to mobile game optimization is a bit of a confession. If you study the sample code for this book you won't find much in the way of specific code optimizations. The reality is that code optimizations often add complexity, and the focus of this book is to teach you how mobile game code works. So, please don't think I'm lazy or hypocritical when you find that much of the code in this book isn't optimized. An area where I do focus on optimization is on the overall design of the examples. You'll find all the examples throughout this book to be relatively straightforward and simplistic in their requirements, which is the best optimization of all.

Summary

This chapter departed from the heavy coding of the past few chapters by tackling an interesting topic related to mobile games: optimization. There are several facets to MIDlet game optimization that impact both design and coding, but there is no doubt that optimization at some level is an important concern for every game developer. This chapter began by introducing the basics of optimization as it applies to mobile games. You then learned some general strategies for optimizing your games primarily so that they are smaller and use less memory. From there you moved on to learn some specific Java coding techniques that enable you to squeeze every bit of performance out of MIDlet game code. Finally, the chapter concluded by introducing you to code profiling and memory monitoring, which play important roles in aiding the optimization process.

The next chapter takes a sharp turn back into heavy-duty mobile game programming by leading you through the design and development of another complete mobile game. The game is called Space Out, and it's somewhat of a goof on the classic Space Invaders vertical shoot-em-up.

Extreme Game Makeover

I mentioned near the end of the chapter how I deliberately didn't focus a lot of energy on optimizing the example code throughout the book. It's not that the example code isn't efficient; it's just that I didn't go the extra mile to attempt to squeeze every ounce of performance out of it. One noticeable size optimization that can easily be made involves the High Seas game, which relies on a directional pirate ship sprite with four animation frames.

This chapter explained how you could reduce the ship's animation frames to one frame by using sprite transformations to dynamically generate the other frames. Following are the steps required to reduce the pirate ship's images by 75%:

1. Edit the pirate ship image so that only the first frame remains.

2. In the game canvas' `update()` method, rather than set the animation frame for the sprite in response to directional key presses, set a transformation instead.

Wow, that was simple! In fact, it's so simple that you might be tempted to carry out the same size optimization on the large enemy pirate ship as well. However, the enemy ship's animation frame is set within the `DriftSprite` class, so you'd have to redesign `DriftSprite` to optimize the enemy ship, and this takes a little more effort.

CHAPTER 18

Space Out: Paying Tribute to Space Invaders

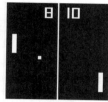

Arcade Archive

Released by Capcom in 1985, Ghosts 'n Goblins put somewhat of a Halloween face on what would become a surprisingly popular game given its difficulty of game play. I personally have a lot of experience with this game because it was the favorite of my late friend and game programming mentor, Randy Weems, who eventually bought his own stand-up arcade Ghosts 'n Goblins game. In the game you play a chivalrous knight named Arthur, who is on a mission to save Princess Guinevere from evil zombies, bats, demons, and ghosts. The game includes several subtle game play tricks and techniques, one of which is that if you shoot a tombstone 15 times, a demon will be summoned that turns you into a frog for a few seconds.

This chapter embarks yet again on the development of another complete mobile game. The game is called Space Out, and it represents a culmination of everything you've learned about mobile game programming throughout the book. The Space Out game is a vertical space shoot-em-up that is in some ways a tribute to the arcade classic Space Invaders. The aliens in Space Out are certainly different than those in Space Invaders, and they move with much more speed and random motion. Regardless of whether you're a big Space Invaders fan, I think you'll find Space Out to be a fun and entertaining mobile game, both from a programming and a playability perspective.

In this chapter, you'll learn

▶ About the basic premise behind the Space Out game

▶ How to design the Space Out game

▶ How to develop a custom sprite class for moving sprites

▶ About the nuts and bolts of programming the Space Out game

▶ That testing is still the most fun part of developing a new game

The Scoop on Space Out

One of the most classic genres of video games has always been the vertical space shoot-em-up. Space Invaders started it all back in 1978, but many games followed and added their own unique contributions to the genre. One of the most enduring vertical space shooters is Galaga, where a relentless sequence of invading aliens fly down from the top of the game screen and attack your ship, which is free to move horizontally across the bottom of the screen. The Space Out game that you develop in this chapter is loosely based on both Space Invaders and Galaga, although the theme for the game is a little more whimsical.

In Space Out, you are the driver of a small green car on a trek across the desert. Whether you believe in UFOs, it's hard to argue that quite a few sightings seem to have occurred in remote desert settings such as Roswell, New Mexico. For this reason, your traveler in the game can't seem to get away from a constant onslaught of alien visitors from above. Unfortunately, the aliens in Space Out are bent on putting an end to your traveler's trip. The cast of alien characters in the Space Out game are somewhat comical, and add a degree of whimsy to the game. Following are the three kinds of aliens that appear throughout the game:

- ▶ Blobbo the Galactic Ooze
- ▶ Jellybiafra (Jelly for short)
- ▶ Timmy the Space Worm

Granted, these probably aren't very realistic aliens when it comes to what you might imagine truly encountering in an extraterrestrial sighting, but this game isn't about reality. Each of the aliens has its own movement pattern and style of attack, and they each fire different missiles. The idea here isn't to simulate a realistic alien invasion, but to have some fun with outlandish characters in the context of a vertical shoot-em-up. To keep the comical theme going, your ill-fated desert traveler fires Twinkies snack cakes up at the aliens as bullets; like I said, this game isn't about realism.

Gamer's Garage

> The characters and concept for the Space Out game were created by Rebecca Rose, a computer artist and game designer.

Designing the Game

Now that you understand the basic idea behind the game, let's focus on a few details regarding the design of the game. The player's car can move horizontally across the game screen, which means that its position is confined to the X axis.

The player can shoot up vertically—with his Twinkies missiles terminating at the top of the screen.

The aliens in Space Out can move around in any direction and at different velocities. The Blobbo and Jelly aliens bounce off the edges of the screen. Timmy, though, is allowed to wrap around and appear on the other side because he has a tendency to fly horizontally across the screen, whereas the others move around a little more randomly. All the aliens fire missiles down toward the player's car—with the missiles terminating when they strike the car or the ground. The aliens are immune from their own missiles, so they can't hit each other. This is a good thing for the aliens because they aren't very careful in terms of how they aim.

Space Out has no discrete levels and no real goal other than surviving. However, the difficulty level of the game does gradually increase as the player progresses through the game. The difficulty of the game is based on the score, and increases as aliens are added at a faster pace. Eventually the player will have his hands full trying to contend with a never-ending army of aliens. That's the whole fun of shoot-em-ups!

To help you get a feel for how the Space Out game is laid out, take a look at Figure 18.1.

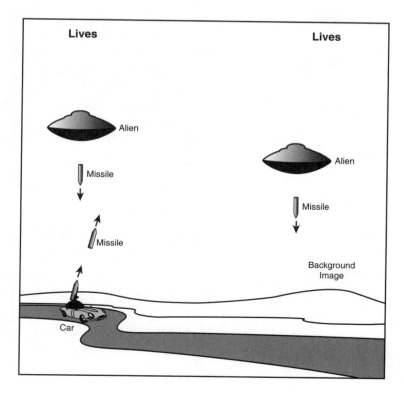

FIGURE 18.1
The Space Out game consists of a desert sky background image, a car, aliens, and missiles that are fired between the car and aliens.

The figure shows the desert background image, which consists of a desert along the bottom and a starry sky everywhere else. The car sprite moves around on top of the desert area of the background image. The aliens appear in the sky and move around trying to hit the car by firing various missiles. Of course, the car also fires missiles back at the aliens. The score for the game is displayed in the upper-right corner of the game screen, and the number of remaining lives (cars) is displayed in the upper-left corner.

FIGURE 18.2
The car bitmap image consists of a green car facing to the right.

FIGURE 18.3
The Blobbo alien bitmap image consists of five animation frames that make the alien appear to shrink and grow.

FIGURE 18.4
The Jelly alien bitmap image consists of three animation frames that make the alien appear to move its tentacles.

FIGURE 18.5
The Timmy alien bitmap image consists of three animation frames that make the alien appear to bob as it flies.

FIGURE 18.6
The missile bitmap image consists of several animation frames, each of which corresponds to a different type of missile.

FIGURE 18.7
The explosion bitmap image is animated to simulate an explosion.

FIGURE 18.8
The small car bitmap image is used to display the number of remaining lives.

Now that you understand the basics of the game, it's important to examine the sprites that it requires. Following is a list of the sprites that go into the Space Out game:

► Car sprite

► Alien sprites

► Missile sprites (from the aliens and the car)

► Explosion sprite

The only type of sprite in this list that I haven't mentioned is the explosion sprite, which is used to show an alien being destroyed by a missile, as well as the car being destroyed by an alien missile. In addition to the sprites, the Space Out game requires several bitmaps. Following are the bitmap images required of the game:

► Background desert image

► Car image (see Figure 18.2)

► Blobbo alien image (see Figure 18.3)

► Jelly alien image (see Figure 18.4)

► Timmy alien image (see Figure 18.5)

► Missile image, containing different missiles fired by the car and each of the three aliens (see Figure 18.6)

► Animated explosion image (see Figure 18.7)

► Small car image (see Figure 18.8)

These images flow directly from the design of the game that you've covered thus far, so there shouldn't be any big surprises here. Perhaps the main thing to point out is that the aliens all rely on animated images (refer to Figures 18.3 through 18.5) to provide them with a more interesting appearance as they move around on the game screen. The other traditional animated image in the game is the explosion image (refer to Figure 18.7), which goes with the explosion sprite.

The Space Out game also makes use of a nontraditional animated image in the missile image (see Figure 18.6). This image contains multiple animation frames, but each frame corresponds to a completely different type of missile, as opposed to a sequence of frames that is animated. In other words, the animation frames in the missile image are never displayed in sequence like the other animated sprites in the game. Instead, one of the frames is displayed exclusively for a particular type of missile. The four missile types seen in the animation frames correspond to the player and the three aliens.

Other important elements of the Space Out game design are the score, which needs to be maintained throughout the game, as well as the number of remaining lives (cars); the game ends when all four of your cars have been destroyed. The game's difficulty level is stored away in a variable and gradually increases as the player racks up points and progresses through the game. Another important piece of information is the familiar Boolean variable that keeps track of whether the game is over.

To recap, the design of the Space Out game has led us to the following pieces of information that must be managed by the game:

▶ The number of lives (cars) remaining

▶ The score

▶ A Boolean game over variable

This information reflects the core game data that must be maintained throughout the game. Keep in mind that the game sprites also serve as an important part of the game state. With this in mind, you're now ready to dig into the actual code for Space Out. Similar to the High Seas game from Chapter 12, "High Seas: A Game for the Pirate in You," Space Out is one of the biggest code development efforts of the book, but the payoff is well worth it! You'll see.

Developing the Game

The construction of the Space Out game is similar to that of the other mobile games you've developed throughout the book. The next few sections guide you through the development of the game's code and resources.

Creating a Moving Sprite

The first development work for the Space Out game involves a new sprite class that is used extensively throughout the game to represent moving sprites. This MovingSprite class is similar in some ways to the DriftSprite class from Chapter 12, except that MovingSprite takes into consideration both X and Y speed components, as well as bounds actions that are associated with reaching the edge of the game screen.

It is common for any moving sprite to eventually reach an edge of the game screen, in which case there are several possible ways to deal with the situation. In a game such as Pong or Breakout, a sprite reaching the edge of the screen might bounce. On the other hand, in a game such as Asteroids, the sprite would wrap around to the other side of the screen. Still other games might simply stop a sprite when it reaches a screen edge, or maybe even destroy (hide) the sprite. All these potential "bounds actions" are made possible via the MovingSprite class. Following is a recap of what they are:

> ▶ **Hide**—Hide a sprite when it reaches an edge of the game screen.

> ▶ **Wrap**—Wrap a sprite to the other side of the game screen when it reaches an edge of the screen.

> ▶ **Bounce**—Reverse a sprite's direction so that it bounces when it reaches an edge of the game screen.

> ▶ **Stop**—Stop a sprite when it reaches an edge of the game screen.

These bounds actions translate into member constants of the MovingSprite class. Following are the member variables for the MovingSprite class, along with the bounds action constants:

These constants identify different possible bounds actions for moving sprites:

```
private int          xSpeed, ySpeed;
private int          action;
private Canvas       canvas;
public static final int BA_HIDE = 1;
public static final int BA_WRAP = 2;
public static final int BA_BOUNCE = 3;
public static final int BA_STOP = 4;
```

The xSpeed and ySpeed variables store the X and Y components of the sprite's speed, which are measured in pixels per game cycle. The action variable keeps track of the bounds action for the sprite, which is one of the four bounds action constants. So every moving sprite must be set to hide, wrap, bounce, or stop when it reaches an edge of the game screen.

The edge of the game screen is determined by the canvas variable, which stores the canvas on which the sprite is drawn. The purpose of this variable is to provide the rectangular boundary that limits the sprite's movement. In other words, the dimensions of the canvas variable serve as the dimensions for the area in which the sprite can move—moving beyond these dimensions results in a bounds action being triggered.

The member variables in the MovingSprite class are initialized in the MovingSprite() constructors, which are shown in Listing 18.1.

LISTING 18.1   The MovingSprite() **Constructors Create Both Nonanimated and Animated Moving Sprites**

```
public MovingSprite(Image image, int xMoveSpeed, int yMoveSpeed,
  int boundsAction, Canvas parentCanvas) {
  super(image);                                                  ──── Call the parent
                                                                      nonanimated
  // Set the XY speed                                                 Sprite()
  xSpeed = xMoveSpeed;                                                constructor.
  ySpeed = yMoveSpeed;

  // Set the bounds action
  action = boundsAction;

  // Set the parent canvas
  canvas = parentCanvas;
}

public MovingSprite(Image image, int frameWidth, int frameHeight,
  int xMoveSpeed, int yMoveSpeed, int boundsAction, Canvas parentCanvas) {
  super(image, frameWidth, frameHeight);                         ──── Call the parent
                                                                      animated Sprite()
  // Set the XY speed                                                 constructor.
  xSpeed = xMoveSpeed;
  ySpeed = yMoveSpeed;

  // Set the bounds action
  action = boundsAction;

  // Set the parent canvas
  canvas = parentCanvas;
}
```

The MovingSprite() class utilizes two constructors so that you can easily create both nonanimated and animated moving sprites. Both constructors call the parent Sprite() constructor to take care of creating the core sprite, and then they initialize the member variables specific to the MovingSprite class.

Unlike the DriftSprite class from Chapter 12, the update() method in the MovingSprite class is surprisingly tame:

```
public void update() {
  // Move the sprite based on its speed
  move(xSpeed, ySpeed);

  // Check for a collision with the screen boundary
  checkBounds();
}
```

The update() method first moves the sprite based on its current speed, as stored in the xSpeed and ySpeed variables. The method then finishes up by checking to see whether the sprite went beyond its bounds. This is accomplished with a call to the checkBounds() method, which is shown in Listing 18.2.

LISTING 18.2 The checkBounds() Method in the SOCanvas **Class Checks for a Collision with a Screen Edge, and Reacts with a Bounds Action**

Hide the sprite if it hits the edge of the game screen.

Wrap the sprite to the other side of the game screen if it hits the edge of the screen.

Make the sprite bounce if it hits the edge of the game screen.

```
private void checkBounds() {
  // Hide the sprite if necessary
  if (action == BA_HIDE) {
    if (getX() < 0 || getX() > (canvas.getWidth() - getWidth()) ||
      getY() < 0 || getY() > (canvas.getHeight() - getHeight()))
      setVisible(false);
  }
  // Wrap the sprite if necessary
  else if (action == BA_WRAP) {
    // Wrap the sprite around the edges of the screen
    if (getX() < -getWidth())
      setPosition(canvas.getWidth(), getY());
    else if (getX() > canvas.getWidth())
      setPosition(-getWidth(), getY());
    if (getY() < -getHeight())
      setPosition(getX(), canvas.getHeight());
    else if (getY() > canvas.getHeight())
      setPosition(getX(), -getHeight());
  }
  // Bounce the sprite if necessary
  else if (action == BA_BOUNCE) {
    // Bounce the sprite at the edges of the screen
    if (getX() < 0 || getX() > (canvas.getWidth() - getWidth()))
      xSpeed = -xSpeed;
    if (getY() < 0 || getY() > (canvas.getHeight() - getHeight()))
      ySpeed = -ySpeed;
  }
  // Stop the sprite if necessary
```

LISTING 18.2 Continued

```
else {
  if (getX() < 0)
    setPosition(0, getY());
  else if (getX() > (canvas.getWidth() - getWidth()))
    setPosition(canvas.getWidth() - getWidth(), getY());
  if (getY() < 0)
    setPosition(getX(), 0);
  else if (getY() > (canvas.getHeight() - getHeight()))
    setPosition(getX(), canvas.getHeight() - getHeight());
}
}
```

Stop the sprite if it hits the edge of the game screen.

The checkBounds() method is the workhorse method in the MovingSprite class, and its job is to carry out a bounds action if the sprite has reached an edge of its boundary. The method first checks to see whether the BA_HIDE bounds action is set, in which case the sprite is hidden if it has reached a boundary. The BA_WRAP bounds action is checked next, and the end result changes the sprite's position to the other side of the game screen if it has reached a boundary. The BA_BOUNCE bounds action causes the sprite's speed to be reversed if a boundary is encountered, which has the effect of causing the sprite to bounce in the opposite direction. And finally, the last conditional block of code in the checkBounds() method simply stops the sprite if it reaches a boundary.

There are a few other helper methods in the MovingSprite class that you haven't learned about yet. Following are these methods, which provide access to the X and Y speed variables:

```
public int getXSpeed() {
  return xSpeed;
}

public int getYSpeed() {
  return ySpeed;
}

public void setXSpeed(int xMoveSpeed) {
  xSpeed = xMoveSpeed;
}

public void setYSpeed(int yMoveSpeed) {
  ySpeed = yMoveSpeed;
}
```

These methods are simple accessor methods that allow you to read and write a moving sprite's X and Y speed properties.

The handy new MovingSprite class is now ready to roll, so you can now turn your attention to the code specific to the Space Out game. Let's start out with the member variables.

Declaring the Member Variables

The key member variables for the Space Out game are located in a customized game canvas class, SOCanvas. The SOCanvas class is responsible for all the game logic in the Space Out game. Because the SOCanvas class is fairly big, I've broken it down into bits and pieces; the entire source code for Space Out is available on the accompanying CD-ROM. Following are the most important member variables defined in the Space Out custom canvas class:

```
private LayerManager    layers;
private Image           background;
private Image           smallCar;
private MovingSprite     playerSprite;
private MovingSprite[]  blobboSprite = new MovingSprite[3];
private MovingSprite[]  jellySprite = new MovingSprite[3];
private MovingSprite[]  timmySprite = new MovingSprite[3];
private MovingSprite[]  missileSprite = new MovingSprite[10];
private Sprite[]        explosionSprite = new Sprite[3];
private Player          musicPlayer;
private Player          explosionPlayer;
private Player          gameoverPlayer;
private boolean         gameOver;
private int             score, carsLeft;
```

The explosion sprites don't move, so they are created as normal Sprite objects, not moving sprites.

The first few variables are used to store the layer manager, the background and small car images, and the various sprites in the game. The background image is the desert sky background, whereas the smallCar image is used to show how many cars (lives) you have remaining in the game. The sprite member variables are interesting because they reveal an important design issue in the Space Out game: Sprites aren't created and destroyed while the game is being played.

Rather than dynamically create and destroy sprites throughout the game, as you would maybe expect it to do, the Space Out game instead creates a fixed number of sprites when the game first starts. Sprites are then hidden to give the effect of them being destroyed. For example, when an alien sprite is hit and killed by a missile sprite, both sprites are hidden, not destroyed. As the sprite member variables reveal, there is a maximum of three Blobbo aliens, three Jelly aliens, three Timmy aliens, ten missiles, and three explosions visible in the game at any given time.

The sound effects and music in the game are handled next thanks to the various Player variables. And finally, the state of the game is reflected in the gameOver, score, and carsLeft variables.

Assembling the start() Method

The start() method in the Space Out game has a great deal of responsibility because it handles all the game-specific initialization tasks. For example, the following code creates the starry night background image and the small car image:

```
try {
  background = Image.createImage("/StarryNight.png");
  smallCar = Image.createImage("/SmallCar.png");
}
catch (IOException e) {
  System.err.println("Failed loading images!");
}
```

With these two images loaded and ready, you can move on to the sprites in the game. If you recall, there is a car sprite controlled by the player, as well as several alien, missile, and explosion sprites. All these sprites except the explosions are instances of the new MovingSprite class; the explosions are normal Sprite objects because they don't need to move. Following is the code that creates all these sprites:

```
try {
  // Create the player car sprite
  playerSprite = new MovingSprite(Image.createImage("/Car.png"), 0, 0,
    MovingSprite.BA_STOP, this);
```

The player sprite stops when it encounters the edge of the game screen.

```
  int sequence5[] = { 0, 0, 1, 1, 2, 2, 2, 2, 2, 2, 3, 3, 4, 4, 3, 3, 2, 2, 1, 1
};
  int sequence3[] = { 0, 0, 0, 1, 1, 1, 2, 2, 2, 1, 1, 1 };
  for (int i = 0; i < 3; i++) {
    // Create the Blobbo alien sprites
    blobboSprite[i] = new MovingSprite(Image.createImage("/Blobbo.png"), 20, 21,
3, 2,
```

These sequences help to slow down the frame animations for the sprites so that they don't animate too fast.

```
    MovingSprite.BA_BOUNCE, this);
    blobboSprite[i].setFrameSequence(sequence5);
    blobboSprite[i].setVisible(false);
```

The Blobbo alien sprites bounce when they encounter the edge of the game screen.

```
    // Create the Jelly alien sprites
    jellySprite[i] = new MovingSprite(Image.createImage("/Jelly.png"), 21, 21, 1,
4,
```

```
    MovingSprite.BA_BOUNCE, this);
    jellySprite[i].setFrameSequence(sequence3);
    jellySprite[i].setVisible(false);
```

The Jelly alien sprites bounce when they encounter the edge of the game screen.

```
    // Create the Timmy alien sprites
    timmySprite[i] = new MovingSprite(Image.createImage("/Timmy.png"), 21, 11, 5,
0,
```

```
    MovingSprite.BA_WRAP, this);
    timmySprite[i].setFrameSequence(sequence3);
    timmySprite[i].setVisible(false);
```

The Timmy alien sprites wrap around when they encounter the edge of the game screen.

```
      // Create the explosion sprites
      explosionSprite[i] = new Sprite(Image.createImage("/Explosion.png"), 21, 21);
      explosionSprite[i].setVisible(false);
    }

    // Create the missile sprites
    for (int i = 0; i < 10; i++) {
      missileSprite[i] = new MovingSprite(Image.createImage("/Missiles.png"),
        11, 11, 0, 0, MovingSprite.BA_HIDE, this);
      missileSprite[i].setVisible(false);
    }
  }
catch (IOException e) {
  System.err.println("Failed loading images!");
}
```

All the sprites in the game are initially hidden until needed.

The player sprite is created as a moving sprite with a bounds action that causes it to stop when it reaches the game screen boundary. The remaining sprites are also created as moving sprites, but with differing speeds and bounds actions. For example, the Jelly alien sprites have an X speed of 1 and a Y speed of 4, whereas the Timmy alien sprites have an X speed of 5 and a Y speed of 0. The Blobbo and Jelly sprites are created to bounce off the game screen edges, the Timmy sprites wrap around to the other side of the screen, and the missile sprites are hidden upon reaching a screen edge. Finally, the explosion sprites take advantage of frame animation but they don't move. All the sprites except the player car sprite are initially created so that they are hidden from view.

The sprites all come together when they are added to the layer manager, which takes care of ordering and drawing them. Following is the code that adds the sprites to the layer manager:

```
layers = new LayerManager();
layers.append(playerSprite);
for (int i = 0; i < 3; i++) {
  layers.append(blobboSprite[i]);
  layers.append(jellySprite[i]);
  layers.append(timmySprite[i]);
  layers.append(explosionSprite[i]);
}
for (int i = 0; i < 10; i++) {
  layers.append(missileSprite[i]);
}
```

Although it isn't as critical in the Space Out game as it is in some other games, don't forget that the order in which you add sprites to the layer manager determines their Z-order—the first sprites you add via the append() method appear on top of later sprites. This isn't a crucial issue in Space Out because in the context of the game it doesn't really matter which sprites appear in front of each other.

Sound effects and music play an important role in the Space Out game, which probably doesn't come as a big surprise. Following is the code that sets up the audio players for the game:

```
try {
  InputStream is = getClass().getResourceAsStream("Music.mid");
  musicPlayer = Manager.createPlayer(is, "audio/midi");
  musicPlayer.prefetch();
  musicPlayer.setLoopCount(-1);
  is = getClass().getResourceAsStream("Explosion.wav");
  explosionPlayer = Manager.createPlayer(is, "audio/X-wav");
  explosionPlayer.prefetch();
  is = getClass().getResourceAsStream("GameOver.wav");
  gameoverPlayer = Manager.createPlayer(is, "audio/X-wav");
  gameoverPlayer.prefetch();
}
catch (IOException ioe) {
}
catch (MediaException me) {
}
```

This code reveals that there is a single MIDI audio player for the game music, as well as a couple of other players for the sound effects used throughout the game (an explosion sound and a game over sound).

The last piece of business in the start() method is actually starting a new game via a call to the newGame() method:

```
newGame();
```

You learn about the inner workings of the newGame() method a little later in the chapter. For now, let's turn our attention to the update() method, which serves as the heart of most MIDlet games, including Space Out.

Piecing Together the update() Method

The update() method is called once every Space Out game cycle, and is responsible for checking for user input, updating sprites, checking for collisions, randomly adding new aliens, and generally keeping the game running. The update() method starts off by checking to see whether the game is over, and if so, it starts a new game in response to the player pressing the "fire" key:

```
if (gameOver) {
  int keyState = getKeyStates();
  if ((keyState & FIRE_PRESSED) != 0)
    // Start a new game
    newGame();
```

```
  // The game is over, so don't update anything
  return;
}
```

Starting a new game simply involves a call to the `newGame()` method, which you learn about later in the chapter. Notice that the `update()` method immediately returns after calling `newGame()` because there is no reason to continue updating a newly started game in this particular game cycle. In fact, the `update()` method returns even if the Fire key wasn't pressed because no updating needs to take place as long as the game is over.

If the game isn't over, the `update()` method continues along by responding to key presses. The following code handles the left and right directional keys to move the car back and forth, as well as the Fire key to fire missiles at the aliens:

```
int keyState = getKeyStates();
if ((keyState & LEFT_PRESSED) != 0) {
  playerSprite.setXSpeed(-2);
}
else if ((keyState & RIGHT_PRESSED) != 0) {
  playerSprite.setXSpeed(4);
}
if ((keyState & FIRE_PRESSED) != 0) {
  // Play a fire sound
  try {
    Manager.playTone(ToneControl.C4 + 12, 10, 100);
  }
  catch (Exception e) {
  }

  addMissile(playerSprite);
}
playerSprite.update();
```

The player car sprite moves faster to the right than to the left because it is in reverse when moving left; this adds a nice little touch of realism to the game.

If you recall from the design of the Space Out game (see Figure 18.1), the player's car appears near the bottom of the screen and can move horizontally back and forth. The key handling code sets the X speed of the car sprite to provide this movement in response to left and right directional key presses. It's important to note that the speed in the left direction is slower than the speed in the right direction. The reason for this speed difference has to do with the fact that the car is aimed toward the right, which means that it is moving in reverse when it goes left. As a touch of realism, the car moves slower when it is going in reverse.

Gamer's Garage

In addition to adding a touch of realism to the Space Out game, having the player's car move slower to the left than it moves to the right adds a bit of trickiness to mastering the game. More specifically, it's tougher to dodge missiles when moving in reverse (left).

The key handling code responds to a Fire key press by playing a simple tone sound and calling the addMissile() method. You learn how this method works later in the chapter, but for now it's important to notice that the player sprite is passed into the method. The idea behind the addMissile() method is that it fires a missile for the sprite that is passed as its only parameter. So you can call the addMissile() method and pass the player sprite or any of the alien sprites, and it will fire the appropriate missile in the correct direction (up or down).

Updating the various sprites in the Space Out game is where most of the real work is done in the update() method. The following code handles updating the alien and explosion sprites:

```
for (int i = 0; i < 3; i++) {
  if (blobboSprite[i].isVisible()) {
    blobboSprite[i].update();
    blobboSprite[i].nextFrame();
  }
  if (jellySprite[i].isVisible()) {
    jellySprite[i].update();
    jellySprite[i].nextFrame();
  }
  if (timmySprite[i].isVisible()) {
    timmySprite[i].update();
    timmySprite[i].nextFrame();
  }
  if (explosionSprite[i].isVisible()) {
    if (explosionSprite[i].getFrame() < 3)
      explosionSprite[i].nextFrame();
    else
      explosionSprite[i].setVisible(false);
  }
}
```

Only visible sprites are updated.

This code causes the explosion to cycle through its frame animation one time and then disappear.

This code is relatively straightforward in that the aliens and explosions are updated and moved to their next animation frames. It's very important to realize that only visible sprites are updated. Perhaps equally important is the fact that explosion sprites are hidden after their animation sequence finishes.

To make the game more efficient and not create and destroy a bunch of objects dynamically, all the sprites are created initially when the game starts, and are then shown and hidden to simulate creation and destruction. At any given moment throughout the game, only visible sprites are considered "alive." This is therefore why only visible sprites are updated in the update() method.

Construction Cue

The next section of code in the update() method is fairly large because it embodies the majority of the actual game logic in the Space Out game.

The code to which I'm referring is the missile update code, which is important because the game logic is driven by what happens when a missile collides with the player sprite or an alien sprite. Following is the missile update code:

```
for (int i = 0; i < 10; i++) {
  if (missileSprite[i].isVisible()) {
    // Is the missile a player missile?
    if (missileSprite[i].getFrame() == 0) {
      for (int j = 0; j < 3; j++) {
        // Did the missile hit a Blobbo alien?
        if (blobboSprite[j].isVisible())
          if (missileSprite[i].collidesWith(blobboSprite[j], false)) {
            // Play a destruction sound
            try {
              Manager.playTone(ToneControl.C4 - 6, 100, 100);
            }
            catch (Exception e) {
            }

            // Create an explosion
            addExplosion(blobboSprite[j]);

            // Hide the sprites and update the score
            blobboSprite[j].setVisible(false);
            missileSprite[i].setVisible(false);
            score += 10;
            break;
          }
        // Did the missile hit a Jelly alien?
        if (jellySprite[j].isVisible())
          if (missileSprite[i].collidesWith(jellySprite[j], false)) {
            // Play a destruction sound
            try {
              Manager.playTone(ToneControl.C4 - 6, 100, 100);
            }
            catch (Exception e) {
            }

            // Create an explosion
            addExplosion(jellySprite[j]);

            // Hide the sprites and update the score
            jellySprite[j].setVisible(false);
            missileSprite[i].setVisible(false);
            score += 15;
            break;
          }
        // Did the missile hit a Timmy alien?
        if (timmySprite[j].isVisible())
          if (missileSprite[i].collidesWith(timmySprite[j], false)) {
            // Play a destruction sound
            try {
              Manager.playTone(ToneControl.C4 - 6, 100, 100);
            }
            catch (Exception e) {
            }
```

The missile sprite's frame index is used to determine what kind of missile it is.

When a player missile hits an alien sprite, both sprites are hidden.

```
        // Create an explosion
        addExplosion(timmySprite[j]);

        // Hide the sprites and update the score
        timmySprite[j].setVisible(false);
        missileSprite[i].setVisible(false);
        score += 20;
        break;
      }
    }
  }
// The missile is an alien missile
else {
  // Did the missile hit the player car sprite
  if (missileSprite[i].collidesWith(playerSprite, false)) {
    // Play a wave sound for the car getting destroyed
    try {
      explosionPlayer.start();
    }
    catch (MediaException me) {
    }

    // Create an explosion
    addExplosion(playerSprite);

    // Reset the player car sprite
    playerSprite.setPosition(0,
      getHeight() - playerSprite.getHeight() - 10);
    playerSprite.setXSpeed(4);
    playerSprite.setYSpeed(0);

    // Hide the missile sprite
    missileSprite[i].setVisible(false);

    // See whether the game is over
    if (carsLeft-- == 0) {
      // Stop the music
      try {
        musicPlayer.stop();
      }
      catch (MediaException me) {
      }

      // Play a wave sound for the game ending
      try {
        gameoverPlayer.start();
      }
      catch (MediaException me) {
      }

      // Hide the player car
      playerSprite.setVisible(false);

      gameOver = true;
      return;
    }
  }
}
```

Because the Timmy aliens fly faster than the others, more points are awarded for shooting them.

If an alien missile hits the player car sprite, a wave explosion sound is played.

The player car sprite is repositioned to give the effect of starting with a new car.

```
      missileSprite[i].update();
    }
  }
}
```

While iterating through the missile sprites, the missile update code first checks to see whether the missile is a player missile or an alien missile. This is a very important piece of information because it determines how the missile interacts with other sprites. More specifically, player missiles can hit only aliens, whereas alien missiles can hit only the player.

Construction Cue

To keep the alien sprites from destroying each other, the missile sprites are designed so that aliens are immune to their own missiles. This is why the missile update code first checks to see what kind of missile is being updated before checking for a collision. Additionally, this design helps minimize the number of collision detections performed, which goes a long way toward making the game code more efficient.

If you study the code closely, you'll find that when a player missile hits an alien, the following steps take place:

1. A brief tone sound is played.

2. An explosion sprite is created.

3. The alien and missile sprites are hidden.

4. The score is increased.

If the missile is an alien missile, an entirely different set of steps is carried out:

1. A wave sound effect is played.

2. An explosion sprite is created.

3. The car sprite is repositioned on the left side of the screen with a default speed so that it appears to be a new car.

4. The missile sprite is hidden.

5. A game over check is carried out.

If the carsLeft variable reveals that the player has run out of cars, the game comes to an end. The music is stopped, a game over wave is played, and the car sprite is hidden from view. Most importantly, the gameOver member variable is set to true.

> As another attempt to keep the Space Out game as efficient as possible, the `collidesWith()` method is called with a second parameter of `false` in all the collision detection code. If you recall from earlier in the book, this parameter determines whether the collision detection is performed on a pixel-by-pixel basis. In the case of Space Out, pixel-level collision detection isn't absolutely necessary, and not using it is a significant performance enhancer.

Construction Cue

The next block of code in the hefty Space Out `update()` method handles randomly adding new alien sprites to the game. The speed at which new aliens are added to the game determines how difficult the game plays. Therefore, you can slowly increase the game's difficulty level by adding aliens more rapidly as the game goes on. This is accomplished by using the score to determine the "randomness" of the alien addition. Check out the following code:

```
if (score < 250) {
  if (rand.nextInt() % 40 == 0)
    addAlien();
}
else if (score < 500) {
  if (rand.nextInt() % 20 == 0)
    addAlien();
}
else if (score < 1000) {
  if (rand.nextInt() % 10 == 0)
    addAlien();
}
else {
  if (rand.nextInt() % 5 == 0)
    addAlien();
}
```

This is the easiest difficulty level in the game, which results when the score is less than 250 points.

This is the highest difficulty level in the game, which results when the score passes 1,000 points.

If the score is less than 250, there is a 1-in-40 chance of adding a new alien in each game cycle. This corresponds to the easiest difficulty level of the game. The difficulty level ramps up until the score crosses 1,000 points, when the odds of adding a new alien increase to a 1-in-5 chance every game cycle. When you think about how fast the game cycles are flying by, these are actually very good odds, and result in aliens being added to the game quite rapidly.

The last chunk of code in the `update()` method is the code that randomly fires alien missiles:

```
if (rand.nextInt() % 4 == 0) {
  switch (Math.abs(rand.nextInt() % 3)) {
  // Fire a missile from a Blobbo alien
  case 0:
    for (int i = 0; i < 3; i++)
      if (blobboSprite[i].isVisible()) {
        addMissile(blobboSprite[i]);
        break;
      }
    break;
```

```
      // Fire a missile from a Jelly alien
      case 1:
        for (int i = 0; i < 3; i++)
          if (jellySprite[i].isVisible()) {
            addMissile(jellySprite[i]);
            break;
          }
        break;
      // Fire a missile from a Timmy alien
      case 2:
        for (int i = 0; i < 3; i++)
          if (timmySprite[i].isVisible()) {
            addMissile(timmySprite[i]);
            break;
          }
        break;
    }
  }
```

The code first randomly determines whether an alien should fire a missile. The 1-in-4 odds of an alien firing a missile were arrived at through trial and error, and basically just seeing what appeared to be a reasonable amount of alien missile fire. If the code determines that a missile is to be fired, the type of alien to fire the missile is chosen. A visible alien of the given type is then found, and the addMissile() method is called to fire the missile. Notice that the alien sprite is passed into the addMissile() method to indicate the sprite that is doing the firing.

Construction Cue

Just as the frequency of aliens being added to the game is increased to make the game more difficult, you could do the same thing with the frequency of alien missile fire. Just use the score as a basis for increasing the odds of an alien firing a missile.

Drawing the Game Screen

Drawing the game screen in Space Out will look easy compared to the code required to update the game. Listing 18.3 contains the code for the draw() method in the SOCanvas class.

LISTING 18.3   The draw() Method in the SOCanvas Class Draws the Background and Game Layers, Along with the Game Over Message if Necessary

```
private void draw(Graphics g) {
  // Draw the starry night background
  g.drawImage(background, 0, 0, Graphics.TOP | Graphics.LEFT);

  // Draw the layers
  layers.paint(g, 0, 0);
```

LISTING 18.3 Continued

```
  // Draw the remaining cars and the score
  for (int i = 0; i < carsLeft; i++)
    g.drawImage(smallCar, 2 + (i * 20), 2, Graphics.TOP | Graphics.LEFT);
  g.setColor(255, 255, 255); // white
  g.setFont(Font.getFont(Font.FACE_SYSTEM, Font.STYLE_PLAIN,
    Font.SIZE_MEDIUM));
  g.drawString(Integer.toString(score), 175, 2, Graphics.TOP |
    Graphics.RIGHT);

  if (gameOver) {
    // Draw the game over message and score
    g.setColor(255, 255, 255); // white
    g.setFont(Font.getFont(Font.FACE_SYSTEM, Font.STYLE_BOLD,
      Font.SIZE_LARGE));
    g.drawString("GAME OVER", 90, 40, Graphics.TOP | Graphics.HCENTER);
    g.setFont(Font.getFont(Font.FACE_SYSTEM, Font.STYLE_BOLD,
      Font.SIZE_MEDIUM));
    g.drawString("Final Score : " + score, 90, 70, Graphics.TOP |
      Graphics.HCENTER);
  }

  // Flush the offscreen graphics buffer
  flushGraphics();
}
```

This code draws the number of remaining lives (cars).

The first block of code takes care of drawing the background image, which is a starry desert background. The layers are then drawn with a single line of code, followed by the number of remaining cars and the score. If the game is over, the game over message is drawn, which consists of the words "GAME OVER" followed by the final game score.

Starting a New Game

I've mentioned the newGame() method a few times throughout the discussion of the Space Out game code. Listing 18.4 contains the code that allows the newGame() method to establish a new game of Space Out.

LISTING 18.4 The newGame() Method in the SOCanvas Class Initializes the Game Variables and Sprites and Starts the Music

```
private void newGame() {
  // Initialize the game variables
  gameOver = false;
  score = 0;
  carsLeft = 3;
```

LISTING 18.4   Continued

Position the car sprite vertically in the center of the desert.

```
// Initialize the player car sprite
playerSprite.setPosition(0, getHeight() - playerSprite.getHeight() - 10);
playerSprite.setXSpeed(4);
playerSprite.setYSpeed(0);
playerSprite.setVisible(true);
```

No aliens are visible when the game first starts.

```
// Initialize the alien and explosion sprites
for (int i = 0; i < 3; i++) {
  blobboSprite[i].setVisible(false);
  jellySprite[i].setVisible(false);
  timmySprite[i].setVisible(false);
  explosionSprite[i].setVisible(false);
}

// Initialize the missile sprites
for (int i = 0; i < 10; i++) {
  missileSprite[i].setVisible(false);
}

// Start the music (at the beginning)
try {
  musicPlayer.setMediaTime(0);
  musicPlayer.start();
}
catch (MediaException me) {
}
}
```

The newGame() method starts out by initializing the three main game variables: gameOver, score, and carsLeft. The player sprite is then repositioned and made visible; this is necessary because the sprite is hidden when a game ends. All the alien, explosion, and missile sprites are hidden, which effectively resets the sprites in the game. The newGame() method concludes by restarting the game music at its beginning with calls to setMediaTime() and start() on the music player.

Adding Aliens, Missiles, and Explosions

The remaining code in the Space Out game involves the details of adding aliens, missiles, and explosions. This code is divided among three methods, the first of which is addAlien(). Listing 18.5 contains the code for the addAlien() method, which is responsible for adding an alien sprite to the game.

LISTING 18.5   The addAlien() Method in the SOCanvas Class Adds an Alien to the Space Out Game in a Random Location

```
private void addAlien() {
  switch (Math.abs(rand.nextInt() % 3)) {
  // Add a Blobbo alien
  case 0:
```

LISTING 18.5   Continued

```
    for (int i = 0; i < 3; i++)
      if (!blobboSprite[i].isVisible()) {
        placeSprite(blobboSprite[i]);
        blobboSprite[i].setVisible(true);
        break;
      }
    break;
  // Add a Jelly alien
  case 1:
    for (int i = 0; i < 3; i++)
      if (!jellySprite[i].isVisible()) {
        placeSprite(jellySprite[i]);
        jellySprite[i].setVisible(true);
        break;
      }
    break;
  // Add a Timmy alien
  case 2:
    for (int i = 0; i < 3; i++)
      if (!timmySprite[i].isVisible()) {
        placeSprite(timmySprite[i]);
        timmySprite[i].setVisible(true);
        break;
      }
    break;
  }
}
```

Check to find a Blobbo alien sprite that isn't already visible, and then place it and show it.

If all three Jelly sprites are already visible, a new one won't be added.

The placeSprite() method is called by addAlien(), and its job is to calculate a random position on the game screen and place the specified sprite in the position. The calculation helps to ensure that the sprite isn't positioned too far down the game screen, which keeps it from popping up on top of the player's car sprite. The sprite also isn't placed close to the edges of the game screen, which is important so that a boundary isn't reached as soon as the sprite is placed. The code for the placeSprite() method can be found on the accompanying CD-ROM as part of the complete Space Out example code.

Construction Cue

This method randomly selects an alien type, and then adds a sprite of that alien type to the game. The following steps are followed to add a new alien:

1. Find a suitable alien sprite that isn't already visible.
2. Place the sprite at a random location on the game screen.
3. Show the sprite.

Similar to adding alien sprites, the addMissile() method adds missile sprites. However, this method is a bit different from addAlien() in that it uses a sprite passed as its only parameter to determine what kind of missile to add. Listing 18.6 contains the code for the addMissile() method.

LISTING 18.6   The addMissile() Method in the SOCanvas Class Adds a Missile So That It Appears to Be Fired from a Specified Sprite

```
private void addMissile(MovingSprite sprite) {
  for (int i = 0; i < 10; i++)
    if (!missileSprite[i].isVisible()) {
      switch (Math.abs(sprite.getXSpeed())) {
      // Fire a Blobbo missile
      case 3:
        missileSprite[i].setFrame(1);
        missileSprite[i].setPosition(sprite.getX() + 5, sprite.getY() + 21);
        missileSprite[i].setXSpeed(sprite.getXSpeed() / 2);
        missileSprite[i].setYSpeed(5);
        break;
      // Fire a Jelly missile
      case 1:
        missileSprite[i].setFrame(2);
        missileSprite[i].setPosition(sprite.getX() + 5, sprite.getY() + 21);
        missileSprite[i].setXSpeed(0);
        missileSprite[i].setYSpeed(4);
        break;
      // Fire a Timmy missile
      case 5:
        missileSprite[i].setFrame(3);
        missileSprite[i].setPosition(sprite.getX() + 5, sprite.getY() + 11);
        missileSprite[i].setXSpeed(sprite.getXSpeed() / 2);
        missileSprite[i].setYSpeed(3);
        break;
      // Fire a player missile
      case 2:
      case 4:
        missileSprite[i].setFrame(0);
        missileSprite[i].setPosition(sprite.getX() + 6, sprite.getY() - 11);
        missileSprite[i].setXSpeed(0);
        missileSprite[i].setYSpeed(-4);
        break;
      }

      // Show the missile
      missileSprite[i].setVisible(true);

      break;
    }
}
```

Because the player car and aliens all have unique X speeds, you can use the X speed as a trick to determine what kind of missile to fire.

Each animation frame of the missile sprite image corresponds to a different type of missile.

The addMissile() method accepts the player sprite or an alien sprite as its only parameter, and adds a missile sprite so that it appears to be fired from that sprite.

The key trick in this method is how it figures out what kind of missile to fire. You need a quick and reliable way to figure out whether the specified sprite is the player sprite, a Blobbo sprite, a Jelly sprite, or a Timmy sprite. The trick is to look at the sprite's X speed; this works because these sprites are designed to have unique X speeds. Therefore, the switch statement is structured to use the sprites' X speed as the determining factor for establishing the type of missile to be added.

Actually adding a missile involves the following simple steps:

1. Find a suitable missile sprite that isn't already visible.

2. Set the animation frame to the appropriate missile type.

3. Place the missile at a location near the sprite that is firing it.

4. Set the speed of the missile based on its type.

5. Show the missile.

At long last, we come to the last method in the Space Out game, which should look familiar now that you've worked through the addAlien() and addMissile() methods. Listing 18.7 contains the code for the addExplosion() method.

LISTING 18.7   The addExplosion() **Method in the** SOCanvas **Class Adds an Explosion so that the Specified Sprite Appears to Be Destroyed**

```
private void addExplosion(MovingSprite sprite) {
  for (int i = 0; i < 3; i++)
    if (!explosionSprite[i].isVisible()) {
      // Add an explosion where the moving sprite is located
      explosionSprite[i].setFrame(0);
      explosionSprite[i].setPosition(sprite.getX(), sprite.getY());
      explosionSprite[i].setVisible(true);
      break;
    }
}
```

Make sure the explosion starts animating at its first animation frame.

This method adds an explosion sprite based on the specified player or alien sprite. Following are the steps involved in adding an explosion sprite:

1. Find a suitable explosion sprite that isn't already visible.

2. Set the animation frame to 0 so that the explosion animation starts at the beginning.

3. Place the explosion centered on the sprite that is exploding.

4. Show the explosion.

FIGURE 18.9
The Space Out game gets started with an alien firing a missile at the car below.

FIGURE 18.10
An explosion appears when you successfully shoot an alien.

The addExplosion() method wraps up the code for the Space Out game. I realize this has been a Herculean coding effort, but the next section reveals the significant payoff!

Testing the Game

I've already said numerous times that testing a game is the most fun part, and yet again you've arrived at the testing phase of a completely new game. Similar to the High Seas game, the Space Out game requires a fair amount of testing simply because a lot of different interactions are taking place among the various sprites in the game. The great thing is that you test a game simply by playing it. Figure 18.9 shows the Space Out game at the beginning with an alien firing a missile at the car below, and the car returning fire.

You can move the car with your left and right directional arrow keys, and fire back at the alien with the mobile phone's Fire key (Return key on your keyboard if you're using the emulator). Shooting an alien results in an explosion appearing, as shown in Figure 18.10.

Eventually, you'll venture into dangerous territory and get shot by an alien, which results in an explosion appearing in the car's last position, as shown in Figure 18.11.

You only have four cars to lose, and the number of remaining cars is shown in the upper-left corner of the game screen; the score appears in the upper-right corner. When you lose all the cars, the game ends, as shown in Figure 18.12.

To start a new game, just press the Fire button. I hope you find the finished Space Out game to be interesting enough to justify the hard work it took to figure out how it works.

Summary

Regardless of whether you are a fan of shoot-em-up space games, I hope you realize the significance of the Space Out game that you designed and built in this chapter. In addition to adding yet another fully functioning game to your accomplishments, the Space Out game is important because it represents the most complete game in the book. Not only that, but the Space Out game is a great game for experimenting with your own ideas, simply because it is the kind of game that can be expanded upon in so many different ways. Before you get too crazy modifying the Space Out game, however, sit tight because I have a modification of my own to throw at you.

The next chapter guides you through the addition of a high score feature to the Space Out game. Although mobile phones don't have hard drives (yet!), J2ME provides a way to persistently store data such as high scores that you'd like to keep from one game session to another.

FIGURE 18.11
An explosion also appears when the car gets shot by an alien.

FIGURE 18.12
When you lose all your cars, the game ends and the game over message is displayed.

Extreme Game Makeover

The Space Out game is such a complete game that I hate to see you get too extreme with its makeover. So instead of completely ripping apart the game and applying a different theme, I'd like to focus on ways to improve the play of the game. First off, you can never have enough bad guys in a game, so adding a few new aliens is first on the list of Space Out improvements. In addition to new flying aliens, you could also add a new ground alien that walks across the desert floor trying to eat the player's car. Because the player can't fire sideways, he or she must simply evade the ground alien by driving in the other direction until the alien eventually leaves. The other change worth considering for the Space Out game is power-ups, which are game play enhancements that you obtain by picking up objects that randomly appear on the screen. The best way to incorporate power-ups into Space Out is to have them drop from the sky and give the player new abilities such as a temporary shield and multiple missiles per shot. Here are the general steps required to add these new features to Space Out:

1. Create images for the new alien sprites.

2. Modify the addAlien() method to randomly add the new alien sprites. Be sure to set the speed appropriately for the particular types of alien sprites; for example, the alien that moves across the ground must have a Y velocity of 0.

3. Modify the update() method so that it detects collisions between a player missile and the new alien sprites, and hides the sprites upon a collision.

4. Create a new addPowerup() method that is similar in structure to addAlien() except that it adds a power-up sprite rather than an alien sprite.

5. Modify the update() method so that it randomly calls the addPowerup() method to create a power-up sprite.

6. Add Boolean member variables to reflect whether or not power-up enhancements are active (temporary shield, multifire, and so on), and then modify the update() method to accommodate these new features.

7. Modify the update() method to detect a collision with the player sprite (car) and a power-up, and react accordingly by altering the value of the power-up variables.

Although I'll admit that I've been getting less specific with the code changes required of game makeovers as the book has progressed, you are more than capable of carrying out this makeover of the Space Out game. The idea is for you to begin to understand what it takes to turn a conceptual aspect of a game into coding elements that make the feature possible. You'll likely find that brainstorming creative improvements to an existing game is easier and more immediately rewarding than attempting to build a new game from scratch.

CHAPTER 19

Keeping Track of High Scores

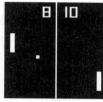

Arcade Archive

Released by Sega in 1982, Zaxxon was one of the first video games to take advantage of an isometric "three-quarters" perspective. It's difficult to imagine in present terms, but Zaxxon's isometric graphics were incredibly advanced for its time. Not only that, but the game actually allows you to fly your "attack shuttle" in three-dimensional space; an altimeter on the left edge of the game screen plays an important role in the strategy of the game as you must constantly adjust the shuttle's altitude to fire on different targets. Zaxxon is one of the more addictively difficult games to be released in the early 1980s, and is an enduring classic to this day.

Unless you grew up during the heyday of arcade games in the 1980s, you might not have an appreciation for the sense of nerd accomplishment associated with a top spot on a game's high score list. The high score list in arcade games serves as a public acknowledgement of who has the time, skills, and quarters to be the best of the best. If you think I'm dramatizing this a bit, keep in mind that a major plot device within an episode of *Seinfeld* involved George Castanza attempting to move a Frogger game across a busy street while connecting it to a temporary battery supply to keep his high score from being lost. Even if you don't have a large nerd ego, it can be rewarding to know that you placed within the upper ranks of those who have played a game before you. Granted, this sense of accomplishment might be diminished slightly when the high score list is limited to your mobile phone, but the idea is still the same. This chapter shows you how to develop a high score list that is saved to the persistent memory of a mobile phone so that high scores are retained between games.

In this chapter, you'll learn

▶ Why it's important to keep track of high scores

▶ How to represent high score data in a game

▶ How to store and retrieve high score data with the J2ME Record Management System (RMS)

▶ How to add a high score list to the Space Out game

The Importance of Logging Your Achievements

In years past, the best video game players were known only by their three initials, which appeared in the high score lists of arcade games. The high score list in a classic arcade game was quite important to many early gamers because it was the only way to show off their gaming achievements.

It's kind of sad, really, that high score lists aren't as popular as they once were, but we can't lament advances in technology. On the other hand, it doesn't mean that high scores are entirely a thing of the past. For example, many popular games, such as the Tony Hawk Pro Skater and Underground series, still rely on a score to indicate how well a player performed. So the idea of using a numeric score to measure your video game playing prowess is still valid. What has changed is that the shift away from arcade games has made it less of an issue to keep track of high scores. However, I still like the idea of a high score list—even if it's only shared between friends. If nothing else, it's fun to challenge yourself to beat a personal best as your skills get sharper in a particular game.

This chapter focuses on adding a high score list to the Space Out game that was designed and developed in the previous chapter. A high score list presents a new challenge to you as a mobile game programmer because you must store away the scores so that they can be retrieved even when a game program is closed. But wait a minute—mobile phones don't have disk drives. How can you possibly save high score data from one game to the next? The answer lies in the *Java Record Management System,* or RMS, which enables you to persistently store away data in the memory of a mobile device.

Before you get into the nuts and bolts of the Java RMS, let's take a brief detour and take a look at how to model high score data. In other words, you first need to determine what you're going to keep up with and how. For right now, all you need to know is that the RMS allows you to store data in a special container known as a *record store.*

Getting to Know the Java RMS

As you know, disk drives aren't a standard feature of mobile phones—at least not yet. For this reason, you have to look at other options when it comes to storing information persistently so that it can be accessed later. Fortunately, there are areas of memory in mobile phones that provide persistent storage, so you can effectively think of them as mini disk drives. Unlike disk drives, however, which operate on the basis of files, the fundamental storage concept in J2ME is a record store.

Gamer's Garage

It is ultimately up to a particular mobile device to decide how it persistently stores data in an RMS record store. Current mobile phones typically use device memory, but future phones could easily rely on micro hard drives or some other media to handle the data storage. The good news is that from a programming perspective, you don't need to worry with how data is being stored at the hardware level.

Understanding Records and Record Stores

A *record store* is a simplified database that consists of records. A *record* is a single piece of data with a unique numeric identifier (ID) associated with it. You can think of a record store as a simple table of data with two columns, as shown in Figure 19.1.

ID	Data
1	975
2	850
3	410
4	395
5	240

FIGURE 19.1
A record store consists of records that each have a unique ID and a piece of data.

Each record store in RMS is associated with a MIDlet suite, and has a text name that identifies it. So, for example, a high score record store for the Space Out game might have the name HiScores, and it would be accessible to only the Space Out MIDlet. If you were to distribute other games with the Space Out game in a MIDlet suite, all the games would have access to the high scores record store.

Gamer's Garage

A MIDlet suite is defined by a JAR file. To create a MIDlet suite, you just package multiple MIDlets together into a JAR file, and provide a Java descriptor (JAD) file for each of them. All the example games and programs throughout this book are packaged individually in JAR files.

The actual data stored within a record in a record store is always an array of bytes. Regardless of whether you are storing strings of text or integer numbers, they are read from and written to a record as an array of bytes.

Later in the chapter you learn that it isn't difficult to convert back and forth between common Java data types and byte arrays. More specifically, you find out how to convert an array of integers to an array of bytes, and back.

Exploring the RecordStore Class

The MIDP API supports the RMS through a package named javax.microedition.rms. Within this package are a class and several interfaces that support the creation and manipulation of record stores. The class that makes it all possible is called RecordStore, and it provides a programmatic interface to a single record store. The RecordStore class makes the task of reading and writing records to a record store a very straightforward task.

The process of using the RecordStore class typically involves the following series of steps:

1. Open/create a record store.
2. Read/write data from/to the record store.
3. Close the record store.

You might want to carry out additional tasks, such as deleting individual records or even deleting an entire record store, but this series of steps provides a general sequence for record management.

Following are some of the more important methods in the RecordStore class that are used to interact with records:

- ▶ openRecordStore()—Opens a record store for reading/writing
- ▶ getNumRecords()—Gets the number of records in a record store
- ▶ getRecordSize()—Gets the size of the data for a specified individual record
- ▶ getRecord()—Gets the data for a specified individual record
- ▶ addRecord()—Adds a record of data to a record store
- ▶ deleteRecord()—Deletes a specified individual record
- ▶ deleteRecordStore()—Deletes an entire record store
- ▶ closeRecordStore()—Closes a record store

As you can see, these methods provide a means of carrying out most common record management tasks. More methods certainly are available in the RecordStore class, but these are sufficient to carry out the persistent storage of high score lists for mobile games.

To get started with a record store, you first need to establish a variable to hold a RecordStore object. The following code is sufficient for this:

```
RecordStore rs = null;
```

Creating the actual RecordStore object involves calling the static openRecordStore() method, like this:

```
try {
  rs = RecordStore.openRecordStore("HiScores", false);
}
catch (Exception e) {
  System.err.println("Failed opening record store!");
}
```

The first parameter to this method is the name of the record store, which in this case identifies the record store as containing high scores for a game. The second parameter indicates whether or not a new record store should be created if one does not exist under the specified name. A value of true means that a new record store will be created and opened, whereas false means that the opening will succeed only if a record store indeed exists. This is why the RecordStore variable was initialized to null—so that you can check to see whether it was actually opened successfully.

With the record store open, you're ready to begin reading and/or writing records of data. If you recall from earlier, a record consists of a unique numeric ID and an array of bytes. Let's take a look at how you might write a record of data by using the addRecord() method of the RecordStore class:

```
try {
  rs.addRecord(recordData, 0, recordData.length);
}
catch (Exception e) {
  System.err.println("Failed writing to record store!");
}
```

In this code, the variable recordData is assumed to be a byte array containing record data. The addRecord() method accepts three parameters: a byte array of data, the offset where the data starts within the array, and the number of bytes of data to write. If you want to write an entire array of bytes, just pass 0 as the second parameter and the length of the array as the third parameter, as the example shows.

Reading data from a record store is a little trickier than writing simply because you have to contend with not knowing how much data is stored in a record. The steps for reading a record of data can be summarized as follows:

1. Iterate through the records in the record store.

2. Get the size of the current record.

3. Reallocate the record holder to accommodate the actual record size, if necessary.

4. Read the record into the record holder.

I could just show you how to read a single record, but in many cases you'll want to read the entire contents of a record store. The previous series of steps highlights this approach by iterating through a record store based on the number of records contained within. The following code shows exactly how these steps are carried out in code:

There is nothing magical about a default record size of 8 bytes—it's just a guess as to what an average record size might be.

```
try {
    int     len;
    byte[] recordData = new byte[8];

    for (int i = 1; i <= rs.getNumRecords(); i++) {
        // Re-allocate record holder if necessary
        if (rs.getRecordSize(i) > recordData.length)
            recordData = new byte[rs.getRecordSize(i)];

        // Read the record into the array
        len = rs.getRecord(i, recordData, 0);
```

If the actual record data is longer than 8 bytes, this code makes sure to reallocate the record holder to fit the larger size.

This is where you would place game-specific code to convert and store the byte data to a meaningful data format, such as an integer high score.

```
        // Do something with the record data
        ...
    }
}
catch (Exception e) {
    System.err.println("Failed reading from record store!");
}
```

This code shows how to iterate through an entire record store and read a record at a time. It's important to notice how the recordData record holder is reallocated, if necessary, to account for larger than expected record data. This is unlikely to take place when reading high scores because the scores will likely all be close to the same size, but it's still not a bad safeguard.

There are some situations where you may need to delete an entire record store. Fortunately, the static deleteRecordStore() method in the RecordStore class allows you to carry out this task in a single step. All you have to do is provide the string name of the record store, as the following code reveals:

```
try {
    RecordStore.deleteRecordStore("HiScores");
}
```

```
catch (Exception e) {
  System.err.println("Failed deleting record store!");
}
```

The deleteRecordStore() method is useful in situations where you don't mind completely blitzing a record store and writing a whole new one. This technique is used later in the chapter when you find out how to add a high score feature to the Space Out game. Instead of tediously sifting through a record store and replacing high score entries, the high score code in Space Out 2 just clears out the entire high score record store and writes a new one. More on that a bit later in the chapter!

In the meantime, the closeRecordStore() method is the last method in the RecordStore class of particular interest to mobile games. This method is required to close a record store when you're finished reading and writing to it:

```
try {
  rs.closeRecordStore();
}
catch (Exception e) {
  System.err.println("Failed closing record store!");
}
```

Although there is much more to record stores and the MIDP API support for RMS than I've mentioned here, this is a book about mobile games, so you need to know only enough to add interesting features to your mobile games. With this in mind, the remainder of the chapter focuses on adding a persistent high score list to the Space Out game from the previous chapter.

Preparing High Score Data for Storage

I would love to tell you that I'm going to show you how to create a classic arcade game high score feature in which you get to enter your name or initials, and then see them displayed for all to see. Unfortunately, the seemingly simple task of allowing a player to enter his name or initials is fairly complex from a game programming perspective. Or more accurately, it requires a significant enough side-step from the topic at hand that I don't want to burden you with the details. So, you're instead going to focus on a high score list that simply keeps up with the top five scores for a game, without any personalization associated with the scores. Although this approach to keeping track of a high score list doesn't give credit for each score, it's still a useful means of keeping up with the top scores for a game.

Because we're dealing with mobile phones, which are highly personal devices, odds are you'll be competing with yourself for a spot on the high score list most of the time. This makes the issue of attempting to identify each score owner by name or initials even less of an issue.

Because you aren't going to worry with storing the name of the person for each score, you have to contend only with storing away five numbers. If you recall from the previous chapter, scores in the Space Out game tend to stay within four digits, which means that an int data type is sufficient to store each score in a high score list. However, you know that record data in a record store is always stored as an array of bytes, not integers. You therefore need a means of converting high scores back and forth between integers and byte arrays.

Let's address the integer-to-byte conversion from the perspective of writing a single high score record. The idea is to take a single integer value and convert it to an array of bytes. Following is a single line of code that carries out this task:

```
byte[] recordData = Integer.toString(hiScore).getBytes();
```

In this example, the high score is stored in the variable named hiScore, which is first converted to a string via the static Integer.toString() method. The string is then converted to an array of bytes with a call to getBytes(). This single line of code is all that it takes to convert an integer high score to an array of bytes that is suitable for being written to a record store. Figure 19.2 recaps the conversion process from a byte array to an integer.

FIGURE 19.2
To store an integer high score in a record store, the score must go through a conversion process.

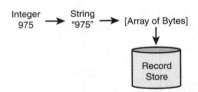

Reading high score data into a meaningful format is essentially the reverse of the conversion required to write a high score. You start with a byte array, and using a string as an intermediate type, you convert the byte array to a single integer value. Here's the code that carries out the conversion:

```
hiScore = (Integer.parseInt(new String(recordData, 0, len)));
```

The String() constructor used in this code requires an array of bytes along with an offset and the number of bytes to be converted. The len variable that indicates the number of bytes is obtained as the return value of the getRecord() method that read the record data. The string is then passed into the static Integer.parseInt() method to finish off the conversion into an integer. Figure 19.3 shows the reverse conversion process involved in reading an integer high score from a record store.

When you aren't reading and writing high scores, they are treated as normal integers. In other words, the trickiness associated with converting high score data enters the picture only when high scores are written or read. The only other time you need to convert a high score value is when you draw the high scores to the game screen, in which case you have to convert an integer to a string for the drawString() method.

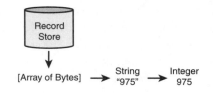

FIGURE 19.3
Reading an integer high score from a record store involves a conversion process that is the reverse of that shown in Figure 19.2.

Keep in mind that the previous line of code that reads a high score from a record store involves reading only a single score. In reality, a mobile game will likely read multiple high scores from a record store. So you will end up structuring the record reading code so that the record store is looped through and each record is read one at a time. In this way, you can easily read several high scores from a record store with relatively little code.

Building the Space Out 2 Example Game

The Space Out game you built in the previous chapter is a perfect candidate for a high score list. The remainder of this chapter is focused on adding a persistent high score list to the game. Not only that, but the new version of the game, Space Out 2, displays the high score list as part of a splash screen that shows the name of the game as a bitmap image.

Designing the Game Enhancements

The splash screen for a video game appears when the game first starts, as well as in between games. Splash screens can be very fancy or very simple, and can include information such as the title of the game, game artwork, copyright information, game instructions, and high scores. In the case of Space Out 2, you're going to create a splash screen that consists of a bitmap title for the game and a high score list. Figure 19.4 shows the splash bitmap for Space Out 2.

FIGURE 19.4
The splash screen bitmap image consists of a Space Out title.

In your own games it's a good idea to include copyright information in your splash screens just to make sure that it's clear who owns the rights to the games.

Construction Cue

The simplicity of the Space Out 2 splash screen has a lot to do with the fact that this is a mobile game that runs within limited screen space. You could certainly cram more information into the screen, but sometimes less is more. Besides, you need to leave room for a list of high scores below the game title.

Writing the Game Code

The Space Out 2 game keeps track of the top five high scores for the game, which are persistently stored in a record store. Although a record store is used for persistent storage of high scores, they are stored in a simple integer array throughout the game. Following are the two new member variables required in the Space Out 2 game to store the splash bitmap image and high score array:

```
private Image   splash;
private int[]   hiScores = new int[5];
```

Construction Cue

There isn't really anything stopping you from using a larger high score list in Space Out 2 if you want. Just keep in mind that displaying a larger list will take up more screen space.

The high score addition to the Space Out 2 game first enters the picture in the start() method, which as you know is responsible for getting the game up and running. This method is an ideal place to read the high score list from the high score record store. Following is the single line of new code in the start() method that reads the high scores from a record store:

```
readHiScores();
```

The readHiScores() method is responsible for opening a record store and reading the high scores one at a time into the hiScores integer array. Listing 19.1 contains the code for the readHiScores() method.

LISTING 19.1 The readHiScores() **Method Reads the High Score List from a Persistent Record Store**

The record store is named "HiScores".

```
private void readHiScores()
{
  // Open the hi scores record store
  RecordStore rs = null;
  try {
    rs = RecordStore.openRecordStore("HiScores", false);
  }
  catch (Exception e) {
  }
```

LISTING 19.1 Continued

```
if (rs != null) {
  // Read the hi score records
  try {
    int     len;
    byte[] recordData = new byte[8];

    for (int i = 1; i <= rs.getNumRecords(); i++) {          Iterate through all
      // Re-allocate record holder if necessary               the records in the
      if (rs.getRecordSize(i) > recordData.length)            record store.
        recordData = new byte[rs.getRecordSize(i)];

      // Read the score and store it in the hi score array
      len = rs.getRecord(i, recordData, 0);
      hiScores[i - 1] = (Integer.parseInt(new String(recordData, 0, len)));    Convert the byte
    }                                                                          array to an integer
  }                                                                            high score and
  catch (Exception e) {                                                        store it in the high
    System.err.println("Failed reading hi scores!");                          score array.
  }

  // Close the record store
  try {
    rs.closeRecordStore();
  }
  catch (Exception e) {
    System.err.println("Failed closing hi score record store!");
  }
}
else {
  // The record store doesn't exist, so initialize the scores to 0
  for (int i = 0; i < 5; i++)
    hiScores[i] = 0;
}
}
```

The readHiScores() method begins by attempting to open the record store named "HiScores". The second parameter to the method (false) indicates that a new record store should not be created in the event that the named record store isn't found. If the record store is successfully opened, the readHiScores() method continues by iterating through the records and reading them one by one into the hiScores integer array. After reading the high scores, the record store is closed. Notice that in the event that the record store doesn't exist, the hiScores integer array is initialized to scores of 0. This last scenario takes place the very first time you run the Space Out 2 game.

Another minor but very important change in the start() method for Space Out 2 has to do with initially starting the game in "game over" mode. In the original version of Space Out, the game immediately begins when you run the MIDlet.

In Space Out 2, the splash screen with the high score list is displayed when the MIDlet is first run. In other words, the Space Out 2 game starts out in "game over" mode. To accomplish this, you no longer call newGame() from the start() method. Instead, you just set the gameOver variable to true, like this:

```
gameOver = true;
```

Just as the high scores are read in the start() method, they are also written in the stop() method, like this:

```
writeHiScores();
```

The writeHiScores() method takes care of writing out the integer hiScores array to the high score record store. Listing 19.2 contains the code for this method.

LISTING 19.2   The writeHiScores() **Method Writes the High Score List to a Persistent Record Store**

```
private void writeHiScores()
{
  // Delete the previous hi scores record store
  try {
    RecordStore.deleteRecordStore("HiScores");
  }
  catch (Exception e) {
  }

  // Create the new hi scores record store
  RecordStore rs = null;
  try {
    rs = RecordStore.openRecordStore("HiScores", true);
  }
  catch (Exception e) {
    System.err.println("Failed creating hi score record store!");
  }

  // Write the scores
  for (int i = 0; i < 5; i++) {

    // Format each score for writing
    byte[] recordData = Integer.toString(hiScores[i]).getBytes();

    try {
      // Write the score as a record
      rs.addRecord(recordData, 0, recordData.length);
    }
    catch (Exception e) {
      System.err.println("Failed writing hi scores!");
    }
  }
}
```

First delete the record store so that you can add new high scores to an empty list.

The value of true in the second parameter indicates that the record store should be created if it doesn't already exist.

Convert the integer high score to a byte array so that it can be written as a record.

LISTING 19.2   Continued

```
// Close the record store
try {
  rs.closeRecordStore();
}
catch (Exception e) {
  System.err.println("Failed closing hi score record store!");
}
}
```

The writeHiScores()method takes a unique approach to writing the high scores. Rather than attempting to find and replace a specific high score record within the record store with a new score, the method deletes the entire record store and writes a new one. Although this approach may sound a bit dramatic, it simplifies the code considerably by enabling you to simply write out all the high score records. This explains why the writeHiScores() method begins by deleting the high score record store.

After deleting the record store, the writeHiScores() method opens a new record store, making sure to pass true as the second parameter to openRecordStore() this time to ensure that a new record store is created. The hiScores array is then iterated through, and each high score record is written to the newly created record store. When all the high scores are written, the record store is closed with a simple call to closeRecordStore().

The code is now in place to read the high score records when the game begins, and then write them when the game ends. But I haven't mentioned how the high scores get updated as the game is played. This code appears in the update() method where the game comes to an end. More specifically, the following "game over" code in the update() method now calls the updateHiScores() method to update the high score list with the new score, if necessary.

```
if (carsLeft-- == 0) {
  // Stop the music
  try {
    musicPlayer.stop();
  }
  catch (MediaException me) {
  }

  // Play a wave sound for the game ending
  try {
    gameoverPlayer.start();
  }
  catch (MediaException me) {
  }
```

```
// Hide the player car
playerSprite.setVisible(false);

// Update the high score list
updateHiScores();

gameOver = true;
return;
}
```

This call to the updateHiScores() method is all that is required to update the high scores.

The updateHiScores() method is a helper method that takes care of the chore of checking to see whether a score is high enough to make it into the high score list. If so, it is added to the list, thereby displacing a previous high score. Listing 19.3 shows the code for the updateHiScores() method.

LISTING 19.3 The updateHiScores() **Method Updates the High Score List with the Latest Game Score**

```
private void updateHiScores() {
  // See whether the current score made the hi score list
  int i;
  for (i = 0; i < 5; i++)
    if (score > hiScores[i])
      break;

  // Insert the current score into the hi score list
  if (i < 5) {
    for (int j = 4; j > i; j--) {
      hiScores[j] = hiScores[j - 1];
    }
    hiScores[i] = score;
  }
}
```

If the score is greater than the current high score, break out of the loop so you can insert the score.

This loop shifts the lower scores down to make room for the new score.

The updateHiScores() method first checks to see whether the current score is high enough to make the high score list. If it is, the score is inserted into the high score list, and any scores lower than it are moved down the list. No more than five high scores are ever kept in the high score list, so scores are regularly dropped as newer high scores make their way onto the list. Keep in mind that the scores in the high score list are temporarily kept in memory until the game exits; none of the high scores are committed to persistent storage until the stop() method is called upon exiting the game.

The last change required to add high score support to the Space Out game is the draw() method, which must now draw both the high score list as well as the splash screen image. Listing 19.4 shows how the draw() method pulls off this feat.

LISTING 19.4 The draw() Method Draws the Splash Screen Image and
High Score List When the Game Is Over

```
private void draw(Graphics g) {
  // Draw the starry night background
  g.drawImage(background, 0, 0, Graphics.TOP | Graphics.LEFT);

  // Draw the layers
  layers.paint(g, 0, 0);

  if (gameOver) {
    // Draw the splash screen image and score
    g.drawImage(splash, 90, 10, Graphics.TOP | Graphics.HCENTER);
    g.setColor(255, 255, 255); // white
    g.setFont(Font.getFont(Font.FACE_SYSTEM, Font.STYLE_BOLD,
      Font.SIZE_LARGE));
    for (int i = 0; i < 5; i++)
      g.drawString(Integer.toString(hiScores[i]), 90, 90 + (i * 15),
        Graphics.TOP | Graphics.HCENTER);
  }
  else {
  // Draw the remaining cars and the score
    for (int i = 0; i < carsLeft; i++)
      g.drawImage(smallCar, 2 + (i * 20), 2, Graphics.TOP | Graphics.LEFT);
    g.setColor(255, 255, 255); // white
    g.setFont(Font.getFont(Font.FACE_SYSTEM, Font.STYLE_PLAIN,
      Font.SIZE_MEDIUM));
    g.drawString(Integer.toString(score), 175, 2, Graphics.TOP |
      Graphics.RIGHT);
  }

  // Flush the offscreen graphics buffer
  flushGraphics();
}
```

The draw() method in Space Out 2 is organized a little differently than its previous
version, with an if statement that draws different information based on whether
the game is over or not. If the game is over, the draw() method draws the splash
screen image followed by the five high scores stored in the hiScores array. If the
game is not over, the remaining number of cars and the score are displayed,
which is probably what you expected to be drawn. The layers are drawn regardless of the game status because it is visually appealing to see the desert sky background behind the title image and high scores.

FIGURE 19.5
Before the Space Out 2 game is played for the first time, the splash screen consists of a high score list full of zero scores.

FIGURE 19.6
The high score list is read from a record store, which causes it to persist between games.

Testing the Finished Product

Similar to its predecessor, the Space Out 2 game is quite simple to test. In fact, it's also a fun test to perform because you need to play the game a few times and build up some scores on the high score list. Figure 19.5 shows the splash screen, including the high score list, when the game is running for the first time, which means that the list is filled with scores of 0.

Keep in mind that in this figure the game still tried to read the high scores from a record store, but the record store didn't exist, so the scores were zeroed out. After you play a few games, the list will start looking better as it fills out with new high scores. Whenever you exit the game, the high score list gets stored persistently to the mobile phone's memory. When the game is restarted, the scores from the high score record store are read to restore the high score list. Figure 19.6 shows a high score list that has just been loaded from a record store.

The high score list really is a useful enhancement to the Space Out game because it allows you to keep track of the best games you've played, potentially over a long time.

Please don't judge my game-playing skills too harshly based on the high scores shown in Figure 19.6. Although you can certainly sometimes master a game while testing it, I wouldn't consider myself a Space Out master. I'm quite certain that with a little practice my high scores can be obliterated by better game players!

Summary

Although high score lists aren't as popular these days as they were back when arcades were all the rage, you can't entirely discount them. It's still cool to keep track of your gaming achievements and establish benchmarks to beat. High score lists are a great way to remember the best games you've played, and also serve as a way for competitive gamers to share a high score with friends. High score lists certainly aren't necessary in all mobile games, but you should consider adding them to games where it makes sense. The Space Out game is a good example of a game that benefits from keeping track of high scores.

This chapter concludes the book, but I hope it is only the beginning of your venture into mobile game design and development. You're probably ready to get busy using the knowledge and code gained from this book to embark on your own mobile game development projects. I wish you the best of luck in your game programming adventures. Feel free to stop by my website and share your game ideas on the Forum for this book—http://www.michaelmorrison.com/.

Field Trip

This could very well be the toughest field trip of the book. Like George Castanza in the classic Frogger episode of *Seinfeld*, you need to use your mastery of video games to leave a mark on an arcade game's high score list. It doesn't matter what game it is, but go to your local arcade and play a game until you're able to obtain a score high enough to make the list. Not only will this give you bragging rights to point out your accomplishment to friends and family members, but it will help add some real world impact to the high score list you added to the Space Out 2 game in this chapter. Who knows—it may even inspire you to enhance Space Out 2 so that it allows players to enter their initials when they achieve a high score.

PART VI

Appendixes

Java Game API Reference

Java is not just a programming language; it is also a library of classes and interfaces that provides a wide range of features for developers. Even the MIDP API, which is the subset of the Java API designed for mobile phone programming, has a surprisingly wide range of interesting features given its constrained size. Within the MIDP API is a package with classes devoted solely to the development of mobile games. This package is called javax.microedition.lcdui.game, and it was added in version 2.0 of the MIDP API to meet the increasing demands of mobile game developers.

The classes offered in the javax.microedition.lcdui.game package are loosely referred to as the "mobile game API," and are important because they support features that MIDP 1.0 developers had to create on their own. In other words, you don't have to reinvent the wheel to create games with the MIDP 2.0 API. Perhaps the most significant feature in the mobile game API is built-in support for double-buffered graphics, which makes it relatively easy to develop games with smooth graphical animation. Other features in the mobile game API include sprite animation, tiled layers, and collision detection, to name a few.

The mobile game API in MIDP 2.0 comprises five classes:

- ▶ GameCanvas
- ▶ Layer
- ▶ LayerManager
- ▶ Sprite
- ▶ TiledLayer

The remainder of this appendix serves as a quick reference for the mobile game API, including brief descriptions of these MIDP 2.0 classes that directly support mobile game programming.

The GameCanvas Class

The GameCanvas class is derived from the standard Canvas class, and provides a game-specific canvas that supports double-buffered graphics. You can think of the GameCanvas class as providing the game screen for your mobile games. Although it may sound like a strange feature to provide through the game screen, the GameCanvas class provides key handling support for games. It's true that other J2ME classes can be used to process key input, but the key handling support in the GameCanvas class is much more efficient, and therefore better suited to the highly responsive input demands of mobile games.

Member Constants

The following integer member constants are defined in the GameCanvas class, and are used to identify keys on a mobile phone:

- LEFT_PRESSED—Left directional key
- RIGHT_PRESSED—Right directional key
- UP_PRESSED—Up directional key
- DOWN_PRESSED—Down directional key
- FIRE_PRESSED—Primary Fire button key
- GAME_A_PRESSED—Game A button key (optional)
- GAME_B_PRESSED—Game B button key (optional)
- GAME_C_PRESSED—Game C button key (optional)
- GAME_D_PRESSED—Game D button key (optional)

These key constants are used in conjunction with the getKeyStates() method, which is covered in the upcoming "Methods" section for the GameCanvas class. All the key constants are bit masks, which means that you use them on a single return value from the getKeyStates() method to determine whether each key is pressed.

As the list reveals, the LEFT_PRESSED, RIGHT_PRESSED, UP_PRESSED, DOWN_PRESSED, and FIRE_PRESSED keys are the only keys guaranteed to be supported on all mobile phones; the four remaining game button keys are optional.

Constructor

The GameCanvas class has only one constructor, and it accepts a single parameter that determines whether the default key handling mechanism used in J2ME is to be allowed:

```
GameCanvas(boolean suppressKeyEvents)
```

The GameCanvas class provides its own high-efficiency key handling method, getKeyStates(), which means that most games don't utilize the default J2ME approach to responding to key presses. For this reason, most games pass true into the GameCanvas constructor to disable default key handling. The end result is that the getKeyStates() method will be more efficient because it isn't competing with an alternative key handling mechanism. If your game happens to use a mixed approach to handling keys, then you should pass false into the constructor to enable default key handling.

Methods

The following methods are supported in the GameCanvas class:

- ▶ Graphics getGraphics()—Gets a Graphics object for drawing on the game canvas

- ▶ void flushGraphics()—Flushes the offscreen buffer so that it is drawn to the actual game screen

- ▶ void flushGraphics(int x, int y, int width, int height)—Flushes the specified region of the offscreen buffer so that it is drawn to the actual game screen

- ▶ int getKeyStates()—Gets the state of the game keys (the key constants are used as bit masks to determine the state of each key)

- ▶ void paint(Graphics g)—Draws the game canvas

Supporting double-buffered graphics in a mobile game is as simple as drawing to the Graphics object returned by getGraphics(), and then flushing the graphics to the screen with a call to flushGraphics() when you're finished.

The Layer **Class**

The Layer class represents a generic graphical object in a mobile game, and serves as the base class for the Sprite and TiledLayer classes. Although you don't ever directly create Layer objects, you do regularly use methods of the Layer class when working with sprites and tiled layers.

Methods

The following methods are supported in the Layer class:

- ▶ int getX()—Gets the X position of the layer's upper-left corner relative to the coordinate system of the object that is drawing the layer (canvas or layer manager)
- ▶ int getY()—Gets the Y position of the layer's upper-left corner relative to the coordinate system of the object that is drawing the layer (canvas or layer manager)
- ▶ int getWidth()—Gets the layer's width (in pixels)
- ▶ int getHeight()—Gets the layer's height (in pixels)
- ▶ void setPosition(int x, int y)—Sets the XY position of the layer's upper-left corner relative to the coordinate system of the object that is drawing the layer (canvas or layer manager)
- ▶ void move(int dx, int dy)—Changes the XY position of the layer by a specified horizontal and vertical offset (in pixels)
- ▶ boolean isVisible()—Gets the layer's visibility
- ▶ void setVisible(boolean visible)—Sets the layer's visibility
- ▶ abstract void paint(Graphics g)—Draws the layer if it is visible

These methods provide access to common layer properties such as the XY position, width, height, and visibility of a layer. Keep in mind that all these methods are supported in the Sprite and TiledLayer classes because they are both derived from Layer.

The Sprite **Class**

The Sprite class models a two-dimensional sprite that is capable of moving and having its appearance animated at the same time. A sprite moves by having its XY position altered, whereas its appearance is changed via a set of animation frames that are part of the sprite's image. Each animation frame is sized the same, and the frames are arranged next to each other in the sprite's image. By default, a sprite has an animation sequence where the animation frames are in the same order that they appear in the image. However, you can set the animation sequence to anything you want to get unique animation effects for a sprite.

Sprites can also be transformed, which means you can rotate and/or mirror them to get additional appearances and minimize the number of images required. One other interesting sprite feature is the reference pixel, which is an XY coordinate within a sprite that can be used as the basis for referencing the sprite, as opposed to the upper-left corner of the sprite, which is the default. Drawing operations and transformations take place with respect to the reference pixel, which can make it easier to rotate or otherwise manipulate a sprite with respect to a meaningful part of the sprite, rather than just use the upper-left corner.

Member Constants

The following integer member constants are defined in the Sprite class, and are used to identify transformations that can be applied to a sprite:

- ▶ TRANS_NONE—The sprite is not transformed in any way.
- ▶ TRANS_ROT90—The sprite is rotated clockwise by 90°.
- ▶ TRANS_ROT180—The sprite is rotated clockwise by 180°.
- ▶ TRANS_ROT270—The sprite is rotated clockwise by 270°.
- ▶ TRANS_MIRROR—The sprite is flipped along its vertical axis.
- ▶ TRANS_MIRROR_ROT90—The sprite is flipped along its vertical axis and then rotated clockwise by 90°.
- ▶ TRANS_MIRROR_ROT180—The sprite is flipped along its vertical axis and then rotated clockwise by 180°.
- ▶ TRANS_MIRROR_ROT270—The sprite is flipped along its vertical axis and then rotated clockwise by 270°.

These transformation constants are applied via the setTransform() method, and enable you to carry out various rotation and mirror effects on a sprite.

Constructors

The following constructors are supported in the Sprite class as a means of creating sprites:

▶ Sprite(Image image)—Creates a nonanimated sprite based on the specified image

▶ Sprite(Image image, int frameWidth, int frameHeight)—Creates an animated sprite based on the specified image, which contains the animation frames (the size and number of frames are determined by the specified frame width and height)

▶ Sprite(Sprite s)—Creates a sprite from another sprite

The first two constructors enable you to create nonanimated and animated sprites, respectively, whereas the last constructor is used to simply make a copy of a sprite.

Methods

The following methods are supported in the Sprite class:

▶ void setFrameSequence(int[] sequence)—Sets the animation frame sequence for the sprite

▶ void nextFrame()—Sets the current sprite frame to the next frame in the animation frame sequence

▶ void prevFrame()—Sets the current sprite frame to the previous frame in the animation frame sequence

▶ int getFrame()—Gets the current sprite frame index in the frame sequence

▶ void setFrame(int sequenceIndex)—Sets the current sprite frame in the animation frame sequence to the specified frame index

▶ int getFrameSequenceLength()—Gets the number of frames in the animation frame sequence

▶ int getRawFrameCount()—Gets the number of raw animation frames for the sprite, as determined by the sprite image

▶ void setImage(Image img, int frameWidth, int frameHeight)—Sets the image for the sprite to the specified image

▶ boolean collidesWith(Image image, int x, int y, boolean pixelLevel)—Checks for a collision between the sprite and the specified image at the specified XY position (the last parameter determines whether the collision detection should be pixel by pixel or based simply on rectangle collision)

▶ boolean collidesWith(Sprite s, boolean pixelLevel)—Checks for a collision between the sprite and the specified sprite (the second parameter determines whether the collision detection should be pixel by pixel or based simply on rectangle collision)

▶ boolean collidesWith(TiledLayer t, boolean pixelLevel)—Checks for a collision between the sprite and the specified tiled layer (the second parameter determines whether the collision detection should be pixel by pixel or based simply on rectangle collision)

▶ void defineCollisionRectangle(int x, int y, int width, int height)—Establishes a bounding rectangle for the sprite for the purpose of rectangle collision detection (this rectangle is often smaller than the actual sprite size to account for sprites that aren't rectangular in shape)

▶ void defineReferencePixel(int x, int y)—Establishes a reference pixel for the sprite, which is used in lieu of the sprite's upper-left corner for positioning and transforming the sprite

▶ int getRefPixelX()—Gets the X position of the sprite's reference pixel relative to the coordinate system of the object that is drawing the sprite (canvas or layer manager)

▶ int getRefPixelY()—Gets the Y position of the sprite's reference pixel relative to the coordinate system of the object that is drawing the sprite (canvas or layer manager)

▶ void setRefPixelPosition(int x, int y)—Sets the XY position of the layer's reference pixel relative to the coordinate system of the object that is drawing the layer (canvas or layer manager)

▶ void setTransform(int transform)—Sets the transform for the sprite (the transform constants are used to specify which transform to apply)

▶ void paint(Graphics g)—Draws the sprite if it is visible

These methods support a wide range of sprite features such as establishing and manipulating an animation sequence, handling collision detection, working with a reference pixel, and carrying out transformations.

The TiledLayer Class

The TiledLayer class represents a layer comprising multiple tiles that are arranged in a pattern to appear as one single graphical object. You can think of a tiled layer as a puzzle consisting solely of rectangular pieces that are all exactly the same size. Tiled layers are very useful for creating game backgrounds and maps, especially those that are larger than the game screen. The primary benefits of the TiledLayer class are image efficiency because you typically reuse tiles repeatedly, as well as flexibility in creating backgrounds because you can generate backgrounds dynamically by rearranging tiles.

Similar to the animation frames that are stored in a single animated sprite image, the tiles for a tiled layer are stored in a single image that is associated with a tiled layer. The TiledLayer class even supports animation, although it works a bit differently than the frame animation in Sprite class.

Constructor

The TiledLayer class has only one constructor, and it accepts several parameters that determine the map size and tile size for the tiled layer:

TiledLayer(int columns, int rows, Image image, int tileWidth, int tileHeight)

The first two parameters to this constructor establish the size of the tiled layer, as measured in tiles. The third parameter is the image that contains the tiles, whereas the last two parameters specify the width and height of the individual tiles that make up the tiled layer.

Methods

The following methods are supported in the TiledLayer class:

- ▶ void fillCells(int col, int row, int numCols, int numRows, int tileIndex)—Fills a rectangular group of cells with the specified tile index

- ▶ int createAnimatedTile(int staticTileIndex)—Creates a new animated tile that is initially set to the specified static tile index (the animated tile index is returned, which is always negative)

- ▶ `int getCell(int col, int row)`—Gets the tile index at the specified cell

- ▶ `int getCellWidth()`—Gets the width of a cell (in pixels)

- ▶ `int getCellHeight()`—Gets the height of a cell (in pixels)

- ▶ `void setCell(int col, int row, int tileIndex)`—Sets the tile index of the specified cell

- ▶ `int getColumns()`—Gets the number of columns in the tiled layer map

- ▶ `int getRows()`—Gets the number of rows in the tiled layer map

- ▶ `void setStaticTileSet(Image image, int tileWidth, int tileHeight)`— Sets the image for the tiled layer, which contains the static tiles

- ▶ `int getAnimatedTile(int animatedTileIndex)`—Gets the static tile currently associated with the specified animated tile index

- ▶ `void setAnimatedTile(int animatedTileIndex, int staticTileIndex)`— Sets the specified static tile index as the current tile for the specified animated tile index

- ▶ `void paint(Graphics g)`—Draws the tiled layer

These methods provide a surprisingly rich set of features for creating and managing tiled layers. Not only can you easily establish the map for a tiled layer, but you also can create animated tiles, set individual cells within a tiled layer map, and even change out the tile image at any time.

The LayerManager Class

The LayerManager class serves as somewhat of a container for layers, and provides a handy means of organizing and managing sprites and tiled layers. Along with helping you control the depth (Z-order) of layers, the LayerManager class also allows you to draw a group of layers with a single call to the layer manager's paint() method. The most important feature of the LayerManager class, however, is its support for a view window, which provides a limited view on a group of layers. The view window of a layer manager is what allows you to provide the game player with a limited view on a much larger game world.

Constructor

The `LayerManager` class has only one constructor, and it doesn't accept any parameters:

```
LayerManager()
```

Creating a layer manager requires nothing more than invoking this default constructor. The details of adding and managing layers are handled by methods that are called on a layer manager after it is created.

Methods

The following methods are supported in the `LayerManager` class:

- ▶ void append(Layer l)—Appends a layer to the bottom of the layer manager
- ▶ void insert(Layer l, int index)—Inserts a layer at the specified index within the layer manager
- ▶ void remove(Layer l)—Removes the specified layer from the layer manager
- ▶ int getSize()—Gets the number of layers managed by the layer manager
- ▶ Layer getLayerAt(int index)—Gets the layer at the specified index in the layer manager
- ▶ void setViewWindow(int x, int y, int width, int height)—Sets the view window of the layer manager
- ▶ void paint(Graphics g, int x, int y)—Draws the layer manager at the specified XY position as seen through its view window (the upper-left corner of the view window is drawn at the XY position of the game screen)

These methods provide a fair amount of control over the layers that are under the control of a layer manager. You can append and insert layers to achieve the appropriate Z-order for them, as well as remove layers whenever necessary. Setting the view window and drawing a group of layers is also very straightforward.

Mobile Game Programming Resources

Perhaps the most important aspect of continued success in mobile game programming is keeping up with the latest trends and technologies. Fortunately, there are plenty of online resources for keeping your game programming skills up to date. This appendix points you to some of the more useful resources, which I encourage you to make use of as often as possible. Although it's important to hone your game programming skills by hacking away at code, it's equally important to read articles, partici-pate in online forums, and generally try to learn from others.

Micro Dev Net

Micro Dev Net is one of my favorite mobile game programming websites, thanks primarily to its excellent articles. You'll find a wide range of excel-lent articles specific to developing mobile games with J2ME, not to men-tion information about Java-powered devices, mobile games you can download, and a MIDP discussion forum. Definitely check out Micro Dev Net at http://www.microjava.com/.

J2ME Gamer

Although not as large or as commercial as Micro Dev Net, J2ME Gamer is another website worth visiting to learn more about mobile game devel-opment. J2ME Gamer is organized more as a community for mobile game developers, which means there is a lot of knowledge to be gained by participating in their forums. You'll also likely find J2ME Gamer useful for keeping up with news on Java-powered devices and software releases. J2ME Gamer is located at http://www.j2megamer.com/.

J2ME.org

Similar in some ways to J2ME Gamer, J2ME.org is a discussion forum for all facets of J2ME programming, rather than those that focus strictly on gaming. There is a game programming forum, however, so you should still stop by the site and see whether there is anything there to interest you. You can visit J2ME.org at http://www.j2me.org/.

Forum Nokia's Mobile Games Community

If you want to focus on a specific device manufacturer in building on to your foundation of J2ME game programming knowledge, then look no further than Forum Nokia's Mobile Games community. This site is an incredibly deep online resource rich with articles that you absolutely shouldn't miss, even if you aren't targeting Nokia phones. One interesting and unique type of article on this site is the case study, where the development of a commercial mobile game is analyzed in detail. You can find several mobile game case studies along with lots more information at http://www.forum.nokia.com/main/0,6566,050,00.html.

Wireless Developer Network

Taking a step back from a specific manufacturer, the Wireless Developer Network is a good place to visit to check the pulse of the wireless industry as a whole. You won't find too much in the way of hardcore mobile game programming information, but you will find highly useful news and commentary related to the wireless world and where it's headed, along with general mobile programming articles. Visit the Wireless Developer Network at http://www.wirelessdevnet.com/.

GameDev.net

Moving right along, not everything about mobile game programming has to focus on the "mobile" part of the equation. I encourage you to visit some general game programming websites because there are several good ones out there. GameDev.net is one of the good ones, and it provides useful nuggets of information ranging from programming articles to book reviews to job postings.

GameDev.net is an extremely deep site in terms of how much content is there to sift through and learn from. If nothing else, check out the Game Dictionary, which breaks down every major term associated with game programming. You can find GameDev.net at http://www.gamedev.net/.

Gamasutra

Another all-purpose game developer website is Gamasutra, which is described as "the art and science of making games." Pretty good description. Similar to GameDev.net, you'll find a wide range of useful stuff on here, including news, feature articles, job postings, game programming schools, and more. Definitely don't miss Gamasutra at http://www.gamasutra.com/.

Game Developer Magazine

One last excellent source for general game programming tips and tricks is Game Developer magazine, which is really the only print magazine devoted solely to game development. Game Developer focuses primarily on the development of commercial PC and console games, but it is nonetheless very useful in keeping up with the latest game programming trends and techniques. You can pick up a copy of the magazine at your local bookstore, or check out their website at http://www.gdmag.com/.

Gamelan

Gamelan, which is part of Developer.com, is one of the original Java resource directories, and has served me well for years. As Java has grown, so has Gamelan, and it now includes a section devoted solely to J2ME. You won't find too much focus on game programming in particular, but this is a great site to brush up on your Java skills. Check out Gamelan at http://www.developer.com/java/.

JavaWorld

Continuing with another general Java resource, the JavaWorld online journal is an excellent publication by IDG Communications that always has some interesting Java programming articles. Split roughly between news and tutorials, JavaWorld is a handy resource to help you stay up to date on happenings in the world of Java...hence the name! The JavaWorld website is located at http://www.javaworld.com/.

The Official Java Website

Last but not least on this tour of mobile game development resources is Sun Microsystems' official Java website, which contains all the latest official Java information and tools produced by Sun. You should definitely keep an eye on this site because it is the central location for obtaining official Java updates such as new releases of the Java SDK and J2ME Wireless Toolkit. It also has a pretty extensive set of online documentation, including a really nice Java tutorial. The official Java website is located at http://java.sun.com/.

Creating Graphics for Mobile Games

Even though mobile games are constrained in terms of screen size and resolution, a game's graphical appearance is the first impression a user has of the game. And although I'll still argue that game play is the ultimate measure of how engaging a mobile game is, weak graphics can limit the success of an otherwise cool game. For this reason, it's important for you to take the time to carefully create graphics and animation for your games that are sure to catch someone's attention. The good news is that the size restrictions on mobile game graphics make it a little easier to create mobile game graphics than graphics for PC or console games.

Assessing Game Graphics

If you aren't fortunate enough to have a staff of artists at your disposal, you are like the rest of us and have to work graphical magic with the limited resources at hand. Even if you decide to get help from an artist on your game graphics, you still need to have a solid understanding of the role of the graphics in your game. Either way, any insight that a game developer has into the process of creating game graphics can only serve to ease the development and improve the visual appeal of the game. This appendix gives you a good dose of this insight.

Before you begin any actual graphics creation, it's important to decide exactly what you need in terms of game graphics. You already should have the game pretty well defined before progressing to this stage. The next step is to take what you know about the game and assess the graphical content required to make it a reality. This consists of making decisions regarding the game's graphical elements and itemizing the graphics needed.

Determining the Game Screen Size

The first major decision to make regarding a game's graphics is the size of the game screen, which is usually driven by the mobile phone that you're targeting. The game screen is the rectangular surface on the screen where the game is displayed, not including any standard user interface components such as a system menu. The best way to determine the game screen size for a particular phone is to run the Skeleton MIDlet from Chapter 3, "Constructing a Mobile Game Skeleton," and observe the screen size that it reports. This reported size is actually the canvas size that is available for game graphics, which is the size you need to use when designing graphics.

Unlike PC games, you don't have much say in the game screen size for a mobile game because it will be entirely dictated by the target phone. However, if you want to avoid a different version of your game for every different screen size, you might be able to generalize the graphics so that they work on a variety of different screen sizes. One way to accomplish this is to design your game to a specific screen size that is no smaller than the smallest possible screen you wish to target. Then on larger screens you can just center the game screen and leave blank space or a bitmap pattern visible around the game area.

Another approach to supporting a range of screen sizes without having multiple versions of a game is to rely on graphics that are scalable. This typically involves designing games around primitive graphics that are drawn without the aid of any bitmaps. Scaling bitmaps just doesn't work well, but there is no problem at all scaling lines, rectangles, ellipses, and so on. And don't forget that a lot of classic arcade games utilize vector graphics, which are essentially the same as primitive graphics in mobile games developed with J2ME.

Reaching the Target Audience

The target audience for your game can impact the graphics requirements a great deal. Games for children typically use graphics with bright colors to help keep their interest. If you're developing a game aimed at teenagers or an older crowd, the graphics pretty much depend on the game itself. Many teens and young adults are attracted to games with realistic violence and a lot of gory graphics. Both inside and outside the commercial game community, there is much debate about violence in video games, and the decision to include bloody graphics in your game is ultimately your own to make.

Movies are a good example of how the target audience dictates the graphic detail. Children gravitate toward cartoons; the characters are easily recognizable and contrast well with the background. Within cartoons, there are varying levels of graphic detail typically associated with the target age group for the cartoon. Older kids usually are more interested in cartoons that more closely approach realism. Similarly, most adults prefer movies with human actors instead of cartoons.

It is sometimes possible to aim primarily for a particular target audience while also including elements that appeal to other audiences. This approach is sometimes referred to as *shotgun marketing* because the appeal of a game spreads across a wide group of people. Shotgun marketing is regularly employed in movies with great success. As examples, consider the immensely popular Pixar animated movies, which clearly target children but always include plenty of humor that adults can appreciate.

Construction Cue

Establishing a Game Setting and Mood

Perhaps even more important than the target audience of your game is the setting and mood of the game. Where is your game taking place, both in time and in location? If it's a futuristic space game, your graphics might include metallic colors contrasting with dark space backgrounds. A gothic vampire game probably would have dark, gloomy graphics set mostly at night. By using dark colors, you can more effectively portray the gloomy mood of the game, with creatures emerging from the moonlit shadows.

In these two game examples, I've alluded a great deal to the colors used for the graphics. This is important because colors can really dictate the mood of a game more effectively than specific graphical images. The best way to understand the impact of the colors on the mood of a game is to think about the dimmer switch on a light. Have you ever dimmed the lights in a room and noticed the immediate change in mood reflected by the dimming? Whether the mood is interpreted as gloomy or romantic, it is dramatically altered nevertheless. This lighting technique is used frequently in movies and commercial PC and console games, and can certainly be used in mobile games as well.

You can easily apply the dimmer idea to your game graphics by altering the brightness of the graphics in a graphics editor. Most graphics editors provide image filtering features that enable you to specifically alter an image's brightness. You learn about some popular shareware graphics editors a little later in the "Exploring Graphics Tools" section of this appendix.

Adhering to a Graphics Style

The style you choose for your game graphics is the final requirement you need to address before moving on to creating them. More than likely, you already have an idea of the style, so this decision probably won't take too much time. Graphics style basically means the look of the images, such as cartoon style, lifelike, rendered, and so on. Lifelike graphics, such as scanned photographs or digitized video, usually contain a very broad range of colors. On the other hand, cartoon-type graphics usually consist of black or gray edges with solid color fills.

After you select a graphics style, you should try to keep all the graphics consistent throughout the game. It probably wouldn't be a good idea to have a scanned background with cartoon characters moving around in front of it. On the other hand, maybe your game has some Roger Rabbit–type theme to back up this mix of graphics. It's totally up to you; just remember that a more consistent style used for graphics results in a more absorbing and realistic game.

The game's graphics style is related closely to how the graphics are created. It is hard to commit to a cartoon style for the graphics if you don't have access to an artist and have no artistic abilities yourself, for example. So, while you're thinking about the style you want for the game, weigh into your decision the resources you have for carrying out the graphics development.

Exploring Graphics Tools

Whether you create your own graphics or hire an artist, you will need a graphics utility at some point in the graphics development process. Even if you don't need to change the content of the graphics, you often will need to resize or change the transparency color of the images. A nice graphics editor is the most important tool for developing and maintaining game graphics. Although you might end up wanting to invest in a professional graphics editor with a wider range of features, such as Adobe Photoshop or Adobe Illustrator, you can't go wrong by starting out with a good shareware editor.

Construction Cue

It is worth noting that Adobe Photoshop is the standard for bitmap image editing in the professional game developer community, and Adobe Illustrator is very popular for creating vector graphics. If you can afford the money to buy one or both of these applications and the time to learn them, you will certainly reap big benefits.

This section focuses on some popular shareware graphics editors you can use to create and edit bitmap images for Windows games. They all support the PNG graphics format, which is recommended for mobile games, and provide varying degrees of image processing features.

Image Alchemy

Image Alchemy, by Handmade Software, is a very extensive graphics editor and conversion utility with versions available on a wide range of platforms. Image Alchemy reads and writes more than 90 different image formats. Although it is geared more toward image conversion than editing, its strong conversion features and incredibly wide support for multiple platforms make it a very useful graphics utility to have.

Handmade Software has versions of Image Alchemy for almost every major computer platform. It even has an online demo version that enables you to convert images over the Web via a connection to its Image Alchemy server.

You can get information about Image Alchemy and download the latest version from the Image Alchemy website, which is located at http://www.handmadesw.com/.

Paint Shop Pro

Paint Shop Pro, by Jasc Software, is a graphics editor for Windows with a full suite of editing, conversion, and image processing tools. Paint Shop Pro contains a wide variety of paint tools, as well as image filters and conversion features for most of the popular image formats. Paint Shop Pro is arguably the best shareware graphics editor for Windows.

You can get information about Paint Shop Pro and download the latest version from the Jasc website, which is located at http://www.jasc.com/.

Graphic Workshop

Graphic Workshop, by Alchemy Mindworks, is another graphics editor for Windows that is comparable to Paint Shop Pro. Graphic Workshop is geared more toward image conversion rather than editing. However, you might find some useful features in it that complement Paint Shop Pro, so definitely take a look at them both.

You can get information about Graphic Workshop and download the latest version from the Alchemy Mindworks website, which is located at http://www.mind-workshop.com/.

Construction Cue

> Keep in mind that there are plenty of other packaged commercial image editing tools that you might want to also consider. Although they are usually more expensive than their shareware counterparts, you will likely find that they are packed with powerful features.

Creating and Editing Graphics

You've learned how to assess the graphical requirements for games and the different types of game graphics, but you still haven't really covered the specifics of how to create graphics. Unfortunately, there is no simple explanation of how to create graphics. As in all art forms, there is much about the subject that must be grafted out of experience. However, I want to cover the basic techniques of creating graphics for games, and then you can chart your own course.

Line-Art Graphics

The first method of creating graphics is to use *line-art graphics*. I refer to this method as "line art" because it encompasses practically all hand-drawn graphics, whether drawn and scanned from paper or drawn in a software paint program. Either way, you have total control over the colors used and the resulting image. Cartoon-type graphics fall in this category.

You usually draw line-art graphics by hand on paper and scan them, or you use a graphics editor to draw and modify the image. The freehand technique is useful if you have some traditional art experience. The graphics editor approach usually is better if you don't have any art experience because you can "cheat" to a certain extent by using software image processing tools. An in-between solution is to draw rough outlines of what you want on paper, scan them as digitized images, and color and clean them up in a graphics editor. This is a really nice way to create graphics because you get to draw freehand and still benefit from software tools, while ultimately maintaining complete control over the image.

3D Rendered Graphics

3D rendered graphics have pretty much taken over the commercial game world. There is a reason for this; rendering provides the capability to create incredibly complex and realistic 3D graphics that sometimes aren't even possible with free-hand drawing, especially when it comes to animation. Before I get into that, you should quickly learn how modeling and rendering works.

Using 3D modeling software such as Caligari's trueSpace or Discreet's 3D Studio Max, you create mathematical wireframe 3D objects. Of course, the majority of the math is hidden, so all you really have to worry about is learning how to model 3D objects with the software tools. These modeling programs provide all kinds of methods for creating and manipulating the wireframe objects into just about any 3D shape you can imagine. After you come up with a shape with which you're happy, you specify the surface of the object along with any sources of light. You even can place cameras to get different views of the object. After specifying all these attributes, you tell the application to render the object's image.

Rendering is the process of composing a graphical image of a purely mathematical object. Rendering can yield incredible results for game graphics, and I highly suggest looking into it. However, it usually takes a fair amount of practice to get good at creating and working with wireframe objects to a point where you can create complex models. On the other hand, it might come easy to you. Either way, rendering can be a lot of fun, and you can achieve results far beyond the artistic grasp of most game programmers.

In the past, rendered objects have sometimes been criticized for having a certain graphical style that is hard to shake. Remember that rendering is a computer process, so it's hard to make rendered objects show emotion as you can with hand-drawn images. Keep in mind that a delicate balance of tools usually generates the most effective results. You might find that rendering is great for producing back-grounds, whereas hand-drawn images are better for individual characters. If you do decide on a mixture of graphics-creation techniques, be sure to blend their respective styles with each other as best you can.

One final note about rendering: I mentioned that rendering can make creating animations much easier. Most modeling/rendering software packages come with tools that enable you to place and move a camera. You usually have the option of moving individual objects—as well as the camera—over time to generate animations. You can generate amazing animations with relatively little work with these types of tools.

Scanned Photography and Video-Captured Graphics

Another interesting way to create graphics for games is to use scanned photography and video-captured graphics. Scanned photography basically consists of scanned photographic images captured with a digitizing scanner. These can be useful, but because of the two-phase photographic development/image scan process, they aren't used too much in games except maybe for creating textures. A texture is an image that models a piece of a graphical surface that can be tiled without notice. On the other hand, video-captured graphics, which rely on a very similar concept, have been used a great deal; these graphics were used in the original DOOM game. Using video-captured graphics involves setting up a video camera and grabbing frames of video of an object as bitmapped images. Video-captured graphics differ from video sequences in that video-captured graphics are used to generate snapshots of different views of an object, and not a real-time animation.

One problem with video capturing is that it usually involves having to build a small video studio with lighting and a backdrop, not to mention buying the necessary video equipment to record and capture digital video. You also have to be able to somehow construct physical models of the game objects. However, if you are willing to go the extra step and do these things, the results certainly are worth the trouble.

Background Graphics and Textures

Background graphics are any graphics that appear behind the main objects in the game, such as walls, forests, clouds, and so on. Many background graphics, such as walls, benefit from textured bitmap images. Textures are very useful primarily because they take up relatively little space: They are tiled repeatedly to create a larger image at runtime. I highly recommend using textures whenever possible. Textures are used extensively throughout this book in creating tiled layers for games.

Libraries of royalty-free textures are available that can serve as a great resource for finding game textures. Of course, you are free to draw your own textures, but be warned that drawing a textured image so that it can be tiled correctly with the edges blending smoothly is a little tricky. You can find texture artwork at The Clip Art Connection website, which you learn about a little later in the "Finding Graphics" section.

Animated Graphics

The animation frames for an object in a game sometimes are referred to as *phases* of the object. The phases depict the movements that the object goes through independent of positional motion. The phase animations usually mean different things for different objects. A fire object might have four frames of animation that depict the movement of the flames, for example. On the other hand, a tank's phases in a battle game might consist of the rotations of the tank facing in different directions.

It also is possible for objects to change phase in more than one way. In this case, you will have a two-dimensional array of animation frames rather than a horizontal strip. An example would be a crawling soldier with different animations reflecting the crawling motion. You might have eight rotations for the soldier along with two different frames to show the leg and arm crawling movement.

Practically speaking, you would need more frames of animation than these examples show, especially when it comes to rotation. Four frames really isn't enough to depict smooth rotation of an object. I recommend a minimum of eight frames when you are showing an object rotating, unless the object is very small. Given that graphics in mobile games are often small, four frames will work in some situations.

Finding Graphics

If you've decided that creating game graphics isn't for you, you have a few options. The first is to try to find royalty-free art. This isn't always a very viable option because games typically require very unique graphics. However, you might be able to find interesting clip art that will work for your game graphics. The last thing I want to do is to discourage you from trying a possibly useful outlet for obtaining graphics.

A good starting point for finding existing clip art graphics is The Clipart Connection website, which is located at http://www.clipartconnection.com/. The Clipart Connection contains links to many different clip art sites, as well as sites to artists and commercial stock art collections. This site is definitely worth checking out.

Another excellent clip art site is the Clip Art and Media website for Microsoft Office, which is located at http://office.microsoft.com/clipart/. I know: You're thinking Office is boring business software that couldn't possibly have anything to offer game graphics. Not only does Microsoft's Clip Art and Media site have clip art categorized by keyword and organized by type, but it also has sound effects that are organized in a similar fashion.

One final option, and the one I suggest when you don't have the ability to create your own graphics and you can't find anything by way of clip art, is to hire an artist to draw or render the graphics for you. You might be surprised by how inexpensive it can be; some people might even be willing to draw the graphics free just to be involved in a game. (Just don't forget to give them full credit, a free copy of the end product, and probably a nice thank you card or email.)

Before you contact an artist, be sure to have a very solid idea of what you want. It's a good idea to write down all your thoughts on the game and what it should look like, including sketches or written descriptions of the graphics. The better the communication between you and the artist, the more likely it is that he or she will deliver graphics to your liking. You might want to ask for some samples of the artist's work to check out the style and see whether it matches what you have in mind. The last step is to work up a formal agreement with the artist, outlining exactly what is expected on both ends of the deal, along with a due date that is agreeable to both parties.

Java Programming Primer

Be sure to check out the bonus Java Programming Primer included on the CD-ROM. Ideally, you should have a fairly solid grasp on the Java programming language before diving into this book. But maybe it's been a while since you used Java, or maybe you're just adventurous enough to tackle mobile game programming with a passing knowledge of Java. If you're in either of these camps, this Java Programming Primer is for you. It isn't intended to teach you everything there is to know about Java—there are plenty of other good books that do that. Instead, this primer attempts to provide you with enough core Java knowledge to dive into mobile game programming.

Index

Display class for MIDlets, 51-52

Donkey Kong Junior, 221

double-buffered animation, 106-107

DOWN_PRESSED key state, 121-123

downloading

games from Handango.com website, 27

Tile Studio, 205

Dragon's Lair, game history, 325

draw( ) method

HSCanvas class, 262-263

RecordStore class, 438-439

Space Out game, game screens, 416-417

TiledLayer class, 217

drawArc( ) method (Graphics class), 75-76

drawImage( ) method (Graphics class), 80-81

drawing graphics primitives

arcs, 75-76

images, 79-81

lines, 73-74

rectangles, 74-75

text, 77-78

drawLine( ) method (Graphics class), 73-74

drawRect( ) method (Graphics class), 74-75

drawRoundRect( ) method (Graphics class), 75

drawString( ) method (Graphics class), 78-79

drifting sprites in High Seas game, creating, 250-252

DriftSprite class

barrier variables, 251-252

speed variables, 250

E

Elevator Action game, 355

emulators

J2ME game development, 32

J2ME Wireless Toolkit, generic devices, 42

energy units for pirate ships, tracking (High Seas game), 245

evading objects in roaming AI games, 275

event-based games (multiplayer), 299-300

bandwidth considerations, 299

design complexities, 299

examples, 299

exception handling, 360-361

explosion bitmap image, Space Out game, 400

explosion sprite, Space Out game, 400

explosions in Space Out game, adding, 421-422

exporting maps as CSV files, 204-205

F

fillArc( ) method (Graphics class), 76

fillRect( ) method (Graphics class), 75

fillRoundRect( ) method (Graphics class), 75

film

animated, popularity of, 94

frame rates, 92

Final Fantasy, 31

computer animation film, 94

FIRE_PRESSED key state, 121-123

first-person shooter (FPS) games, 94

flushGraphics( ) method

GameCanvas class, 107, 447

TiledLayer class, 217

I

images

graphics primitives,
drawing, 79-81

size optimization, 379

tiled layers, 198

index numbers, 199

larger than screen, 199

map creation, 200-206

map formatting,
206-208

sizes, 199

typical uses, 200

information bar (High Seas
game), 244-245

input synchronization for
multiplayer games, 301-302

insert( ) method (LayerManager
class), 224

int getHeight( ) method (Layer
class), 448

int getWidth( ) method (Layer
class), 448

int getX( ) method (Layer
class), 448

int getY( ) method (Layer
class), 448

ITU-T devices, key sets, 42

J

J2ME (Java 2 Micro Edition),
15-16, 32

audio support

MIDP 2.0 Media API,
156

Mobile Media API, 156

emulator (J2ME Wireless
Toolkit), 35-36

game development
requirements

compilers, 32

emulators, 32

MIDlet development
process, 33-34

pre-verification of
classes, 32-33

security constraints, 32

K virtual machine, 16

manufacturer support, 16

MIDlets

assembly tools, 34-35

development process,
16, 33-34

JAR file contents, 32-33

suites, 33

MIDP specification, MIDlets,
32

J2ME Gamer website, 455

J2ME Wireless Toolkit

generic devices, emulation
support, 42

KToolbar

MIDlet game
construction, 39

MIDlet game tests,
39-41

MIDlet project
management, 37-38

memory monitoring
functions, 392-394

MIDlet assembly tool, 34-35

over-the-air provisioning
(OTA), 36

profiler functions, 388-392

tool functions

bytecode verifier, 35-36

J2ME emulator, 35-36

KToolbar, 35-37

provisioning server,
35-36

versions, downloading, 35

J2ME.org website, 456

JAD files (application
descriptors)

MIDlet distribution, 60-61

MIDlet suites, 33

JAMDAT Mobile website,
wireless syndication, 366

JAR files

contents for MIDlets, 32-33

MIDI songs, playing (MIDP
2.0 Media API), 186-187

MIDlets, compressing,
59-61

How can we make this index more useful? Email us at indexes@samspublishing.com

N

National Television Standards Committee (NTSC), frame rates, 92

navigation controls, phone keys (J2ME), 21

networks

Connect 4 game

canvas programming, 336-344

client/server coding, 330-336

connection design, 329-330

data reduction and minimization, 382-383

MIDlet programming

datagram packet creation, 305-306

datagram packet receptions, 307

datagram packet sends, 306-307

Generic Connection Framework (GCF), 304-305

Mobile Information Device Profile (MIDP), connection properties, 25

sockets, 302

datagram, 303

stream, 303

synchronization

hybrid solutions for multiplayer games, 302

input method for multiplayer games, 301-302

maintaining for multiplayer games, 300

state method for multiplayer games, 301

new games

High Seas game, starting, 263-264

Space Out game, launching, 417-418

newGame( ) method

HSCanvas class, 263-264

Space Out game, 417-418

Nintendo Entertainment System (NES), 120

Donkey Kong Junior, 221

Game Boy, 9

Nokia

games development history, 11

J2ME support, 16

Mobile Games Community website, 456

Nutting Associates, Computer Space game, 9

O

obfuscators (code), optimization tool, 387

objects

2D sprite animation, collision detection, 100-102, 123-125

cleanup, memory usage reduction, 382

recycling, memory usage reduction, 381-382

transparencies, 2D sprite animation, 99

use of, memory usage reduction, 381

Olympic MIDlet

building, 81-84

program code

testing, 84

writing, 81-83

openRecordStore( ) method (RecordStore class), 428-431

operator precedence as bug cause, 358-359

optimization

coding tips, 384

code shrinking, 387

compiling without debug information, 384

elimination of common subexpressions, 385

S

U - V

W - Z

Your Guide to Computer Technology

www.informit.com